Pine-Thomas Productions

Jane Wyman, playing the title character in *Lucy Gallant*, is flanked by producers Bill Pine (left) and Bill Thomas.

Pine-Thomas Productions

A History and Filmography

David C. Tucker

McFarland & Company, Inc., Publishers
Jefferson, North Carolina

ALSO BY DAVID C. TUCKER
AND FROM MCFARLAND

Gale Storm: A Biography and Career Record (2018)
Martha Raye: Film and Television Clown (2016)
Joan Davis: America's Queen of Film, Radio and Television Comedy (2014)
Eve Arden: A Chronicle of All Film, Television, Radio and Stage Performances (2012)
Lost Laughs of '50s and '60s Television: Thirty Sitcoms That Faded Off Screen (2010)
Shirley Booth: A Biography and Career Record (2008)
The Women Who Made Television Funny: Ten Stars of 1950s Sitcoms (2007)

All photographs are from the author's collection unless otherwise indicated.

LIBRARY OF CONGRESS CATALOGUING-IN-PUBLICATION DATA

Names: Tucker, David C., 1962– author.
Title: Pine-Thomas Productions : a history and filmography / David C. Tucker.
Description: Jefferson : McFarland & Company, Inc., Publishers, 2019 |
Includes bibliographical references and index.
Identifiers: LCCN 2019029156 | ISBN 9781476677439 (paperback) ∞
Subjects: LCSH: Pine-Thomas Productions—History. | Pine-Thomas
Productions—Catalogs. | Pine, William H. | Thomas, William C.,
1903–1984. | Motion picture producers and directors—United
States—Biography.
Classification: LCC PN1999.P45 T83 2019 | DDC 384/.80979494—dc23
LC record available at https://lccn.loc.gov/2019029156

BRITISH LIBRARY CATALOGUING DATA ARE AVAILABLE

ISBN (print) 978-1-4766-7743-9
ISBN (ebook) 978-1-4766-3710-5

Front cover: Bill Thomas (left) and Bill Pine, at the helm of their own
production company, were a team to be reckoned with (author's collection).

Printed in the United States of America

*McFarland & Company, Inc., Publishers
Box 611, Jefferson, North Carolina 28640
www.mcfarlandpub.com*

To the memory of the late THELMA MAE KLING (1927–1998),
who had the idea to write about Pine-Thomas Productions
about 40 years before I did.

Acknowledgments

I was fortunate that this project enjoyed support and encouragement from members of the Pine and Thomas families, who justifiably take pride in the accomplishments of their forebears, and shared my belief that this story was worth telling. Carol Thomas Pantages, daughter of Bill Thomas, was especially helpful; her remarkable memory and generosity with her time opened a window into the heyday of her father's company. Angel Pine, Bill's granddaughter, had fewer personal memories, as she was only a little girl when he passed away, but eagerly joined me on the journey to uncovering his story as fully as possible. Her contributions to this book ultimately went beyond what either of us had originally anticipated. Through Angel, I met Dennie Marks, Bill Pine's grand-niece, who provided additional family history.

Bob Hanks graciously chatted with me about his parents, Robert Lowery and Jean Parker, two of Pine-Thomas' favorite actors of the 1940s. Others who filled in pieces of the puzzle were Bill Jeffries, grandson of Bill Thomas, Bill Berke, Nick McLean, Sr., and Shonda Holm Croly.

It was a special privilege to talk with Miss Arlene Dahl, who starred in three of Pine-Thomas' popular films of the 1950s, and readily shared her recollections. At the time we spoke, she was working on her autobiography. I'm eager to read it.

The late Thelma Kling approached Bill Thomas in the 1970s about a memoir. Although the book was never published, Kling captured Thomas' colorful memories in his own voice and committed them to paper. I hope it would please her to see that her efforts were not for naught. My thanks to Ms. Kling's daughter-in-law, Jacque Slayden, as well as Carol Thomas Pantages for permission to quote from the draft manuscript.

Archivist John R. Waggener, researcher Barbara Allen Bogart, and archives assistant Hailey Woodall provided invaluable help accessing the Maxwell Shane and Frank McDonald papers at the University of Wyoming's American Heritage Center. Ned Comstock at the University of Southern California sent pertinent information from that institution's invaluable Cinematic Arts Library. I also appreciate the contributions of author Boyd Magers, who furnished access to Bill Thomas' unpublished memoir and personal scrapbook, and Eric Monder, the "Lost Film Finder," who lived up to his billing.

As always, Ken McCullers and Louise Tucker provided moral support, while Lynn Kear and James Robert Parish continue to be both colleagues whose work I admire and valued friends.

Table of Contents

Preface

"Producers William Pine and William Thomas are a couple of former publicity men who, some years ago, placed their fingers on the pulse of the American moviegoer—and decided it was beating too slowly. The boys developed a formula for speeding up the heartbeats of 90,000,000 film fans weekly, and contrived to put their idea to the test. They began making pictures based on the newspaper headlines of the day and/or on people in unusual and dangerous occupations. It apparently was just what the public wanted because success was immediate and lasting."
—*Mr. Reckless* pressbook, 1948

In the early 1940s, the B movie was a familiar part of almost every film fan's moviegoing experience. Ticket buyers in that era typically got a package of entertainment and features for the price of one admission—along with the main attraction, the A-budgeted feature film, there was often a newsreel, a cartoon, and a second, shorter movie to boot. The B movie, a gimmick originated during the Great Depression, when the idea of "two movies for the price of one" helped lure patrons into theaters, was at the height of its popularity. Rather than combine two high-priced pictures, studios began to issue lower-budgeted films intended expressly to serve as a second feature. Some moviegoers paid these films little attention, or didn't even bother to sit through them. But those who read the opening titles of the lowly "added attraction" would frequently see the phrase "A Pine-Thomas Production."

Between 1941 and 1947, a Pine-Thomas production, issued under the auspices of Paramount Pictures, was typically an action-filled B movie, running about 65 minutes. The movie title explicitly promised the viewer excitement and suspense. *Flying Blind!* *Midnight Manhunt! Tornado!* The heroes were brave, down-to-earth guys who worked in dangerous occupations, and often lost a hapless buddy to an industrial accident along the way. Though they couldn't offer stars who were top box office favorites of the day, a Pine-Thomas picture always had actors with name recognition, ones the audience had grown to like over the years—Richard Arlen, Chester Morris, Nancy Kelly. As Bill Thomas later wrote, "We enjoyed telling a story. We loved complicated plots, realistic heroes, and villains that faced retribution if they persisted in their dastardly deeds."[1]

With America's entrance into World War II, Pine-Thomas branched out, and began making action films about various units of the U.S. military. Pictures like *The Navy Way* and *Submarine Alert* made cinematic heroes of everyday American men who did their utmost to support the war effort, selflessly putting themselves into danger while holding the enemy at bay. One columnist joked in the mid–1940s that audiences could keep up to date on military activities and projects just through regular attendance at Pine-Thomas movies.

Though the B movie was, in many ways, given little attention or respect by Hollywood bigwigs, there was nonetheless art and skill involved in making a good one. As most producers well knew, a tight budget and a fast shooting schedule often precluded efforts to please viewers with production values. Too often, B movies, especially those produced by Poverty Row studios like Monogram and Producers' Releasing Corporation (PRC), had even the briefest running times padded with dialogue scenes. Longtime B producer Robert L. Lippert was known to say, "Talk's cheap! Action's expensive!" According to film historian Don Miller, in his 1973 book *B Movies*, Pine and Thomas "specialized in action and adventure pictures with no pretense to art, only to the box office, and did fabulously well without producing much of artistic value." But, as author Bob Herzberg has pointed out, "Pine and Thomas were … showmen who almost invariably delivered the goods. Their films usually had a modicum of dialogue and a maximum of low-budget adventure … the stories moved."[2]

Pine-Thomas films stood out in the 1940s for two reasons: they were inexpensively made movies that earned a lot of money for Paramount Pictures, and they were made so quickly and efficiently that industry insiders sat up and took notice. Comedian Bob Hope joked about the sign left behind one day at the studio barber shop. His chair empty, the barber had supposedly scrawled a note, "Have part in a Pine-Thomas picture, will be back in fifteen minutes." Hope added, "I stuck around and he was back in ten!"[3]

Who were the men behind Pine-Thomas Productions? William H. Pine (1896–1955) and William C. Thomas (1903–1984) were two former press agents, both affiliated for many years with Paramount Pictures. As publicity flacks, they had often been frustrated by the effort it took to stir up public interest in films lacking obvious elements to make a moviegoer take out his wallet and buy a ticket. If they could produce their own movies, they told each other, they would be damn sure to make ones that sounded exciting.

In 1940, they took a leap of faith and formed their own production company. Because aviation was then a hot subject at the box office, they began by making thrillers about pilots and their exploits. Initially, Paramount agreed to

Longtime friends as well as business partners, William H. Pine (left) and William C. Thomas drew on their experience as press agents to produce movies that entertained audiences without pretension—or undue expense.

release Pine-Thomas films, but it was up to the producers to finance them. Tapping every available source of money, they raised $86,000 to make their first picture, a black-and-white drama called *Power Dive*, released in the spring of 1941. Made at a fraction of the cost expended on Paramount's big-budget aviation drama, *I Wanted Wings*, Pine and Thomas' film raked in money at the box office.

The success of their first films convinced Paramount executives that the two producers were canny operators, careful with a buck, who could make inexpensive B movies that looked good and would reap substantial profits. Soon it would be unnecessary for Pine and Thomas to raise money for their films. Instead, for more than ten years, lasting into the early 1950s, Pine-Thomas Productions would be under exclusive contract to make as many as six movies per year on Paramount's dime.

In order to turn out so many films quickly and affordably, Pine and Thomas developed a foolproof formula for giving moviegoers the most for their money, delivering pictures that generally looked more expensive than they really were. Scripts were completed and set in stone before production was underway, so that no time or money would be wasted shooting footage that wouldn't be used. Shooting schedules were cut as short as possible, and the director worked to plan out the filming scene by scene before any actors arrived on set. Actors would be hired for the fewest days possible, and worked a strenuous day for the modest salaries they earned. Those who showed themselves especially reliable and efficient would be called back to the company again and again.

Pine and Thomas even served cast and crew a midday meal on their movie sets, a clever way to insure that no one would be late getting back from lunch. And they insisted on shooting away from Paramount soundstages, with their own hand-picked crews, avoiding the substantial overhead costs that bulged the budget of the studio's bigger films. Experienced B-movie directors like Frank McDonald and William Berke, experts at getting solid footage into the can with minimal delay, took the helm of most of the company's pictures; occasionally, Pine or Thomas himself sat in the director's chair, yet another cost-saving measure.

As producers, they recognized the publicity value of stories that echoed the headlines Americans read in their daily newspapers. In 1942, they took note of intense public interest in a massive highway project through Alaska, constructed by the U.S. Army Corps of Engineers as a wartime supply route. Pine and Thomas promptly registered the title *Alaska Highway* with the Writers' Guild, and had a film in release several months later, incorporating genuine documentary footage of the project. A few years later, they hurried to lay claim to the title *Tokyo Rose*, their 1946 film giving an exciting if largely fictitious account of the wartime propagandist's activities and capture.

While most of the early Pine-Thomas films adhered to a proven formula, the two producers were not ones to get stuck in a rut. Even before their action dramas had worn out their welcome, the producers began branching out, demonstrating their versatility by making comedies and musicals. But after World War II, they recognized that moviegoers' tastes were changing. Rather than packing it in, or sticking stubbornly to an outdated production model, Pine and Thomas gradually moved into bigger-budget films, making three per year rather than six. Holding their breaths, they authorized their biggest budget yet for the 1948 Western drama *Albuquerque*, complete with a sizable paycheck for box-office draw Randolph Scott. The experiment paid off, and in the late 1940s they wound down their program of second features.

Still, their years of experience in rapid-fire moviemaking paid dividends even when they began making more ambitious films. By the mid–1950s, they were using actors who would never have been associated with the product they turned out earlier—Jane Wyman starred in *Lucy Gallant*, James Cagney in *Run for Cover*, and Charlton Heston in *The Far Horizons*. But they still cut corners in every way they could, doing their best to spend money only on what moviegoers would see on-screen in the finished product. Their 1952 action thriller *Hong Kong*, with multiple scenes set on the streets of that ancient city, was shot on studio soundstages. For *Tripoli* (1950), they ventured out on location—to Palm Springs.

As Pine and Thomas often said, their real bosses were the moviegoing public. They understood that they needed to know what viewers wanted, and that they wouldn't find out by sitting at home in Hollywood. They instigated "listening tours," setting out on expansive publicity outings that not only plugged their newest release, but gave them face-to-face contact with theater managers and ticket buyers. Whatever moviegoers wanted, they did their best to deliver. In the early 1950s, Technicolor was in high demand, providing a stark contrast to black-and-white television shows, so Pine and Thomas ponied up the money to pay for it. If they weren't sure whether or not a story had box office appeal, they would send wires, or make phone calls, to theater operators around the country. If those who served the public directly said John Payne was popular with their customers, then Payne would be hired to star in Pine-Thomas movies.

It was gossip columnist Louella O. Parsons who first tagged William Pine and William Thomas "the Dollar Bills," and the phrase stuck. Initially, it referred to the fact that they were showing their Hollywood peers how inexpensively movies could be made. Later, it took on another meaning, when the producers' profit participation in their Paramount pictures made both partners wealthy. Though their personalities were complementary, rather than identical—Pine was the practical one who watched the budgets, Thomas the flamboyant extrovert with a flair for showmanship—the two were of such like minds when it came to moviemaking that some people couldn't keep straight which was Mr. Pine and which was Mr. Thomas. As they were longtime friends who always considered their films a joint effort, the confusion didn't bother them in the least.

After Pine's death in 1955, Bill Thomas made only three more films before packing it in as a film producer. Aside from a brief comeback in the mid–1970s, still using the name Pine-Thomas Productions, Thomas without Pine was adrift. But by then, the company they formed had secured its place in motion picture history.

This book is an overview of Pine-Thomas Productions and its films. It begins with a company history, tracing the lives and careers of the two men who made it what it was. Following is an extensively annotated filmography of Pine-Thomas' 76 features, plus five patriotic short films released during World War II. Included are the producing partners' first three films together, made under the banner of Picture Corporation of America (for Paramount release) before they were known as Pine-Thomas Productions. Paramount continued to finance and release Pine-Thomas pictures through the release of *Lucy Gallant* in 1955. Also spotlighted in the filmography are three films for United Artists, completed after Pine's death, when his son Howard and longtime company screenwriter Maxwell Shane joined Bill Thomas in what was renamed Pine-Thomas-Shane Productions. In the 1970s, some 20 years after Bill Pine's death, Thomas made two additional films, which were treated, and credited, as "Pine-Thomas Productions." Those are covered as well. For each film, a brief synopsis is provided, as well as an account of the film's production, behind-the-scenes stories, and a critical assessment.

Hollywood gossip columnist Louella O. Parsons first tagged Thomas (left) and Pine as "the Dollar Bills."

Appendices further flesh out the Pine-Thomas story. The first offers thumbnail profiles of the actors most commonly associated with the company, such as the aforementioned Richard Arlen, who made no fewer than 13 features for Pine-Thomas (plus one wartime short film). Another highlights the frequently unsung heroes of the Pine-Thomas unit—the crew members behind the scenes whose team effort made it possible to turn out acceptable movie product in a process that sometimes seemed like an assembly line.

For many film scholars and readers, motion picture history from the golden age of Hollywood focuses primarily on studying the big names and the most prominent films. Fortunately for those of us who find value and interest in lesser films, there has been increasing attention paid in recent years to B movies. As Leonard Maltin, an early advocate for the field, noted, "For real film buffs there is a certain fascination (and sometimes even charm) about those B's that makes us want to search them out and learn more about them."[4]

As a viewer, I have attempted to strike a balance when it comes to assessing Pine-Thomas films. Most were not made with an eye to posterity. It would be fruitless to pretend that their films, for the most part, could stand alongside the genuine classics of that era. Too often, a Pine-Thomas movie, especially viewed decades later, can be picked apart for its shortcomings if a viewer is of a mind to do so. He or she can snicker at the rear projection effect used to simulate exotic scenes, or criticize dialogue that's rarely more than serviceable. On the other hand, it is useful to remember that they were intended to give moviegoers of the 1940s solid, unpretentious entertainment that would help fill out a night at the movies. In the 1950s, they were designed to lure customers away from their television sets, and give them a good reason to go out instead.

Still, if there are few out-and-out gems among the Pine-Thomas filmography, there remain many pictures that are still worth a viewer's time in the 21st century. *Fear in the Night* (1947), adapted from a story by mystery writer Cornell Woolrich, is an economically made thriller with clever plot twists; it is also the film that gave young leading man DeForest Kelley, later of *Star Trek* fame, his first important role. *Noir* fans can appreciate the previous year's *They Made Me a Killer*, and perhaps wonder why charismatic leading man Robert Lowery never reached the heights of full-fledged Hollywood stardom. And as a hungry young aspiring actor, Robert Mitchum played some of his first bit parts in Pine-Thomas pictures.

Although the producing partners never lost sight of the bottom line, once in a while they developed a project that was particularly meaningful to them. *The Lawless* (1950), made with the reluctant consent of Paramount executives, was an action drama that also offered an overt message about racial and ethnic prejudice in the post-war era. Though some previous commentators have concluded that Pine and Thomas' contribution to the film was largely of the negative variety—corrupting Daniel Mainwaring's screenplay and forcing director Joseph Losey to tart up the film with melodrama—a fresh look calls this easy assumption into question.

In preparing this book, I have been fortunate to see all but a few of Pine-Thomas' films. Much of their 1940s product has fallen into public domain, and turns up in grainy, choppy prints on YouTube or the Internet Archive. A few others proved maddeningly elusive; not every film historian would be as excited as I was when I got my hands on a copy of *Shaggy*, their 1948 boy-and-his-dog drama starring Robert Shayne and Brenda Joyce (and a mutt from the L.A. pound in the title role). Unable to screen *Follow That Woman*, *Hot Cargo*, and *Waterfront at Midnight*, I instead reviewed the screenplays, held in the Maxwell Shane papers at the University of Wyoming.

Bill Pine and Bill Thomas were colorful characters, experienced at the art of generating publicity, and their moviemaking exploits were fully covered in Hollywood trade journals of the day. They were even considered sufficiently newsworthy to be the subjects of profiles in popular magazines such as *Esquire* and the *Saturday Evening Post*. Interviews with surviving family members, as well as genealogical research, added personal details to this book.

Another valuable source of information was the unpublished memoir on which Bill Thomas worked in the mid–1970s, at the urging of family friend Thelma Kling, who transcribed his recollections and shaped them into a draft manuscript. While the book never saw publication, at least one copy of the typescript survives. Now that work on this book is complete, Thomas and Kling's manuscript will be donated to an appropriate film archive, so that future researchers can benefit from it as I have.

THE DOLLAR BILLS

The two men who jointly led Pine-Thomas Productions for a 15-year period shared not only a common first name, but a philosophy about movies borne of their days as studio publicists. Their goal was simple: they wanted to make pictures that sold tickets, and brought in healthy profits. As the partners put it, "We all want to make good pictures. And a good picture is one that does well at the boxoffice."[1] That meant making the best possible films on the least money possible. At the height of their widely-heralded success, Bill Thomas said, "Bill Pine and I operate on the principle that making motion pictures is nothing but a practical business. Yes, there are artistic elements, too—perhaps. But essentially it's just a practical business, like making shoes, or airplanes, or running a restaurant."[2]

Both partners believed that producing profitable low-budget pictures called for skill and tenacity that equaled, if not exceeded, the work of producing blockbusters. If money were no object, Thomas once explained, "then picture making would be a cinch. We could buy a best seller, hire Cary Grant and Ingrid Bergman as the co-stars, and get Alfred Hitchcock to direct it. With that setup, how could we lose? The picture's sold before a camera turns on it."[3] Instead, Pine and Thomas earned their fortunes with a flair for moviemaking economy that led syndicated columnist Erskine Johnson (September 10, 1948) to observe, "There's a couple of characters that could film a movie on their Social Security checks."

The older of the two partners, William H. Pine, was born on February 15, 1896. In later years, some sources reported Bill Pine's birthplace as New York City, and his obituary in the *Los Angeles Times* (April 30, 1955) declared him a native Angeleno. However, Pine's responses to federal census takers disclose a different background. He stated that he was a naturalized American citizen, originally from Russia, whose native tongue was Yiddish. His granddaughter, Angel, confirmed that the family ancestry was Russian Jewish.

According to Pine's great-niece, Dennie Marks, he was one of nine children, born to father Moishe Aaron and mother Fruma. Little else is known of Pine's parents, who may never have come to the U.S. However, seven of their nine children, including the future Bill Pine, emigrated from Minsk, Russia, to America in 1904, at a time when there was substantial backlash in their native country against Jewish families. Brother Jacob, later known as Jack, had come to the U.S. about a year earlier.

The trip from Russia to New York City was surely an arduous one, involving travel across land (likely by rail) to a port city, followed by the voyage across the Atlantic Ocean.

The citizenship applications of Bill's sisters Ida and Hannah reported that they traveled to America aboard the S.S. *Island*, which brought its passengers from Copenhagen, Denmark. The ship reached its destination on July 23, 1904, after a 17-day journey at sea. Moishe and Fruma were not among the passengers.

The ship's manifest submitted to immigration officials at Ellis Island showed that there were four females and three males in the group, ranging in age from four to 23. The family name, as transcribed by the ship's captain, was Pinchassik. However, in later applying for citizenship, Ida spelled it Pinchosic, while sister Esther recorded it as Pinchasic. (Varying methods of translating Russian names into English may account in part for the discrepancies.) The youngest boy, who would grow up to be Bill Pine, was an eight-year-old then known as Itzke.

Pine family lore, as passed down to his great-niece, had it that the siblings were originally scheduled to depart on an earlier voyage. When one of the children's paperwork failed to come through on time, the trip was postponed. They would have reason to be glad of that, as the ship on which they first booked passage was involved in a wreck at sea, with heavy casualties. (That may have been the S.S. *Norge*, which took the same route—Copenhagen to New York—a month earlier, resulting in hundreds of lives lost, including a number of Russian immigrants.) Was it mere coincidence that shipwrecks and other maritime disasters would figure into the stories of several Pine-Thomas films, including *I Live on Danger* and *Seven Were Saved*?

Upon arrival at Ellis Island, passengers in steerage were expected to provide the name of a friend or family member who would be responsible for them in the U.S. The Pinchassiks (if that is indeed the preferred spelling) indicated that they would be met by their father, M.M. Pinchassik, of Monroe Street in New York. Aside from that notation on the ship's manifest, no further trace of Moishe's presence in the U.S. has surfaced. Bill Pine would later tell interviewers that he had been orphaned at a young age, and grew up in the home of a brother.

With the move to America came the adoption of new names for the family. Recent scholarship has challenged the long-held assumption that officials at Ellis Island routinely and cavalierly changed the names of arriving immigrants, eliminating ones they thought too unwieldy or difficult to spell. However, it was common for new arrivals in the country to modify their own names sometime after arrival, and it appears this is what the Pinchassiks did. According to scholar Kirsten Fermaglich, who has studied the topic of name changes by Jewish immigrants in the early 20th century, "my research suggests that they changed their names in disproportionate numbers compared with other groups in response to American anti–Semitism."[4]

In April 1910, the federal census found six of the siblings living on Walker Avenue in the Bronx. Here, their family name was recorded as Pinkofsky, and 24-year-old Jacob (later Jack), a carpenter, was shown as head of the household. They had already changed their first names from those reported at Ellis Island six years earlier, or adapted them to common English spellings. Hode became Ida, Chana became Hannah, and Itzke was called Isaac. Listed as a boarder in their home was 22-year-old Max Shur, who married Hannah a few weeks later.

By the time he applied for a marriage license in 1916, the onetime Isaac Pinkofsky had renamed himself yet again, becoming William H. Pine. Various sources during his lifetime, including a 1945 profile in *Time* magazine, gave Pine's middle name as "Hoy." However, when registering for the draft in 1942, he recorded his full name as "William

Howard Pine," and that is what appears on his death certificate. Eventually, all his brothers and sisters adopted the same last name.

After achieving success in Hollywood, Pine rarely spoke publicly of his young days. But *Saturday Evening Post* reporter Richard English, profiling the Dollar Bills in 1953, elicited a few reminiscences from him. Pine stated that he attended DeWitt Clinton High School (then located in Manhattan's Hell's Kitchen neighborhood). While still in school, he held a job as a copy boy for a newspaper, the *New York American*. In his senior year, he became a full-time reporter, earning $18 per week. English wrote that the budding journalist was "assigned to the night shift at Bellevue Hospital, which, because of its famous psychopathic ward, he still regards as a great training ground for anyone going into show business."[5]

Bill Pine began his own family when he married Anna Baum (born June 14, 1888). Several years older than Bill, she was a native New Yorker whose family background, on her father Aaron's side, was German. Her mother Hannah, whose maiden name was Polak, had been born in England, to parents who came from Holland. The 1910 census found Annie, as she was then called, living at home with her parents in the Bronx, working as a milliner. She and Pine applied for a marriage license on June 12, 1916, in Manhattan, and were married two days later, on Anna's 28th birthday. The ceremony, performed by a rabbi, took place at the Hotel Bon Ray, a luxurious facility on Madison Avenue at 92nd Street.

At the age of 21, Pine became a father with the birth of his son Howard Benjamin on April 4, 1917, who would be his and Anna's only child. By the time of the 1920 census, Pine was living with his wife and son on 178th Street in the Bronx. Later biographical profiles stated that he studied journalism at Columbia University, and his census response indicated that he was by then employed as a newspaper editor. "But where I learned about show business," he said some years later, "was when I quit being a reporter and went out as an advance man for the Ringling Brothers circus."[6] Pine also served as publicity man for dancer Gilda Gray; according to Bill Thomas, Pine "found her when her name was Mary Michalski [Michalska], changed it to Gilda Gray, and overnight skyrocketed the shimmy dancer into a national sensation."[7]

In Chicago, Pine was offered a job doing publicity for the Balaban and Katz chain of theaters, where Gray had been a featured performer. At their peak, A.J. Balaban and his brother-in-law, Sam Katz, owned more than 100 theaters in the Midwest, with a particularly strong concentration in the Chicago area. In 1926, the Famous Players-Lasky Corporation, forerunner to Paramount Pictures, obtained a controlling interest in the Balaban-Katz chain. It was Sam Katz who ultimately sent Pine to California, putting him to work publicizing Paramount films.

Variety (June 7, 1932) advised, "William Pine, under Bill Hollander in the B. & K. advertising department in Chicago, has left for the [West] Coast to become attached to the Paramount studio…. Pine will create new ideas for exploitation of Par[amount] stars and new product." By the end of the year, the same publication noted that the studio's press office had been divided into two units. Tom Bailey took charge of publicity efforts, while Pine was assigned to cover advertising and exploitation, both men reporting directly to Arthur Mayer of the New York office. *Hollywood Filmograph* (December 17, 1932) noted, "These departments will operate separately but with complete cooperation and coordination of ideas."

It was early in his days at Paramount's West Coast office that Pine met the man who would become his partner in Pine-Thomas Productions. William Carroll Thomas was born August 11, 1903. He was the only son of Harry (1875–1949) and Anna Louise Fletcher Thomas (1881–1959), both natives of Missouri, who had married in September 1899. Though he was born and raised in the Los Angeles area, Thomas' family had no show business connection; his father worked as an auditor for a railroad, while his mother was a homemaker. However, as Thomas later enjoyed pointing out, he had been born the same year that *The Great Train Robbery* made history, ushering in the age of films that told a complete story.

He grew up in Alhambra, at the family home on South Sixth Street. Thomas later told his daughter that as a youngster he had a serious bout with diphtheria, a disease that then had a high fatality rate. He recovered, and attended Alhambra High School, where his complete lack of skills with his hands almost cost him a diploma, as he flunked a required shop class more than once. But his interests lay elsewhere anyway. Intrigued by movies from a young age, Thomas began working as an extra in silent films while still a teenager.

"When I was a kid I used to hang around the studio gates after school and during vacations," Thomas later explained, "and every once in a while there would be a job. "The first important job was playing the drums in a dance hall for a [1922] Dorothy Dalton picture called *The Siren Call*."[8] In his youth, Thomas supported himself working as a drummer in nightclubs; according to his daughter Carol, he formed a band known as "Billy Thomas and the Ragtime Rascals." Largely self-taught, unable to read music, Thomas had a sense of showmanship that kept him in demand at a time when there were plentiful venues for live music.

Studio portrait of Bill Thomas, 1940s.

The gigs paid well enough—at their peak, about $150 a week—for him to buy his own car. As he grew older, however, he realized that he didn't want to devote his life to playing the drums in smoky nightclubs. Though he recalled in his memoir that he was not a highly skilled drummer, his daughter Carol said he retained a lifelong interest in music, adding, "He was kind of a frustrated musician. He loved live music."[9]

After high school, Thomas enrolled at the University of Southern California, studying journalism. During his stay there, he served on the editorial staff of the school's newspaper, the *Daily Trojan*, reporting on sports. He received his degree in 1924.

His first full-time job in the motion picture industry came when he was hired as a publicity man at MGM, with a starting salary of $40 a week. While the training was valuable, his pay in those early years was so modest that he made extra money by renting out his car for use in films. Since the posh car he had bought from his earnings as a drummer—a Moon roadster—could often be rented to producers for $25 a day, Thomas joked, "My car was more successful in the business than I was."[10]

Thomas parlayed his stint at MGM into a more lucrative job as publicity director for the Pantages Theaters, one of the most successful chains on the vaudeville circuit. He learned much from working alongside Alexander Pantages (1867–1936), the flamboyant Greek immigrant who operated more than 80 vaudeville theaters at the height of his success. The two men's paths had actually crossed earlier, according to Carol Thomas Pantages, as her father Bill and Alexander Pantages' son Rodney Alexander (1905–1986) were college classmates and friends. The connections didn't end there. Many years later, after Bill Thomas and his second wife Louise had divorced, Rodney, who was Carol's godfather, would marry the former Mrs. Thomas. (They remained wed until Pantages' death in 1986; Louise Pearce Thomas Pantages passed away in 2000.)

Thomas later described Alexander Pantages as "a self-made man who parlayed a tiny Alaska gold mine into a multi-million-dollar chain of vaudeville palaces extending across the United States and into Canada."[11] Unlike other vaudeville impresarios, Pantages eagerly incorporated movies into the programs of his theaters. Pantages' entrepreneurial skills, in Thomas' estimation, drew on "a delicate balance between impetuosity and good common sense." The young publicist would remember his boss' flamboyant sense of showmanship when he began making strides in the motion picture industry.

While working for Pantages, Thomas married for the first time, wedding young socialite Genevieve Butler on June 9, 1928. Like Thomas, his new bride had attended the University of Southern California. Unfortunately for the young couple, they were married at a time when Thomas was almost constantly busy with work. Genevieve Thomas soon tired of his long and unpredictable hours working with the Pantages company, which, as Carol Thomas Pantages later noted, was seemingly "a 24-hour-a-day job. He was just very seldom home." She commented, "They split up very amicably."

Within a few years, however, the popularity of motion pictures, as well as the Great Depression, was encroaching badly on the profitability of vaudeville. Making matters worse, Alexander Pantages became involved in a personal scandal in 1929, accused of sexually assaulting a teenaged girl in his private office (a charge of which he was ultimately acquitted). Having maintained and developed his contacts with motion picture studios, Thomas returned to that industry, accepting a publicity job with Paramount Pictures.

Paramount was still a comparatively young company, having taken shape from the 1916 merger of Adolph Zukor's Famous Players Film Company and the Jesse L. Lasky Feature Play Company. Like most motion picture companies, Paramount was struggling to stay afloat as the Depression worsened, going into receivership in 1933. Thomas was assigned to work in Bill Pine's department. Together, they would help drum up some much-needed box office business for the studio, and form a lifelong friendship.

Thomas and Pine quickly demonstrated a knack for dreaming up attention-getting publicity stunts. Reading the script for *Island of Lost Souls* (1932), Thomas suggested a contest, "Search for the Panther Woman," which would award a featured role to some newly discovered beauty. The gimmick worked well enough to be done a second time in a distaff version, when Buster Crabbe was named *King of the Jungle* for a film of the same name. Their third go-round, on behalf of *Search for Beauty* (1934), was the first step toward turning beautiful Texas-born redhead Clara Lou Sheridan into Ann Sheridan.

Both Pine and Thomas pleased Paramount executives with their work, and advanced rapidly. *Daily Variety* (February 3, 1934) reported new assignments for both men: "Bill Pine will take over the post of director in charge of exploitation for Paramount in New York.... Bill Thomas has been appointed director of studio advertising." In April 1935, *Motion Picture Daily* noted that Thomas had been named executive assistant to Pine, now Paramount's advertising and publicity director. Of Pine, Thomas would later say, "He wasn't big physically, about five-feet, ten-inches in his stocking feet, but he commanded the respect and attention of others."[12] With Pine as his boss, Thomas later recalled, "our associations were always pleasant, even if somewhat argumentative at times, arguments that he usually won."[13]

During Pine and Thomas' early years at Paramount, the studio's salvation as a moneymaker was Mae West, whose films were enormously popular. They recalled a memorable promotional gimmick they dreamed up for one of Miss West's pictures. Told that the film would be titled "It Ain't No Sin," the young publicists conceived of the idea of training some 200 parrots to repeat the phrase on cue. "We lived with those parrots for weeks," Pine recalled some years later. "We were ready to ship them to the movie writers when the producer of the picture called us," reporting that the title had been dropped in favor of *She Done Him Wrong*.[14]

Both men mastered the skill of calming and comforting skittish stars. Pine said he routinely kept within reach a bundle of Mae West publicity photos. "When I saw Mae working herself up to a temperamental williwaw, I'd pull out a few pictures and say, 'Look, Miss West.... Look at this one. Isn't it a beauty!' Calmed her down every time."[15] Thomas, for his part, was remembered by Hollywood columnist Florabel Muir for "running interference for Mary Astor" at the height of the scandal concerning her notorious diary. Said Muir, "He did a good job of thwarting the reporters without making enemies of any of us."[16]

As press agents, both shared the frustration of trying to stir up public interest in pictures that probably shouldn't have been made in the first place. Bored by an expensive epic they caught one night at Grauman's Chinese Theatre, Thomas complained, "That picture is so bad that even the footprints in the concrete should have walked out." Pine concurred, saying, "We could make a better picture than that for one tenth the dough."[17] Soon they would turn their dream into a self-imposed challenge.

From early in their careers, both men learned the value of getting out of the office, and interacting with customers and theater owners in the field. When Paramount was skittish about using the title *Death Takes a Holiday*, worried that the word "death" was off-putting to ticket buyers, Pine and Thomas tried an experiment. They concocted a publicity campaign for two previews, one in Sacramento and the other in Fresno. The campaign was identical, except that in the latter city the film was retitled "Stranger's Holiday." As reported in *Variety* (February 6, 1934), the picture "did just fair business with the new title, while at Sacramento with the original title pic opened a three-day engagement to more than double its average business" and continued to exceed expectations for the days that followed.

During his time at Paramount, Bill Thomas met former "Goldwyn Girl" Louise Pearce (1913–2000), who would become his second wife. According to Carol Thomas Pantages, her parents met when Thomas attended a football game with a college friend, whose date was Louise Pearce. Later, when Thomas was single once again, he contacted his pal and asked about "that redhead you had at the football game." Louise, according to her daughter, had only a vague recollection of meeting Bill Thomas, but agreed to a date. They would be married on December 4, 1933, a union that would last more than 36 years. Their daughter Carol was born in December 1937.

While serving as Paramount's publicity head, Pine was offered the chance to work directly with the studio's highly successful producer-director Cecil B. DeMille (1881–1959). He earned Associate Producer credits for DeMille's films of the late 1930s and early 1940s, including *The Buccaneer*, *Union Pacific* and *North West Mounted Police*. His widely varied duties in that capacity included budgeting, scouting of locations, and ultimately publicity tours promoting the finished films. For *The Buccaneer*, Pine oversaw the work of a second unit shooting at Catalina Island, with DeMille back at the studio giving instructions by short-wave radio. For *Union Pacific*, Pine was "sent to San Francisco to talk to descendants of the original builders of the railroad," working to give the film an air of authenticity.[18] In late 1939, Pine traveled to Ottawa, Canada, where he submitted the script of DeMille's forthcoming picture about the Royal Canadian Mounted Police for approval by the agency's commissioner. A few weeks later, when heavy snows precluded filming of *North West Mounted Police* on location in Canada, Pine took a chartered plane "over 4000 miles of Texas and the great southwest in an aerial reconnaissance looking for a river site that can double for a locale on the real Canadian plains."[19]

The job sometimes brought with it unforeseen hazards. According to Paramount publicity, Pine was injured during production of *The Buccaneer*, when a camera toppled over on him: "The camera was splintered, and so was Pine." Another mishap took place during a location shoot in New Orleans, according to *Motion Picture Daily* (July 24, 1937), when Pine, driving a car with several passengers from the film company, was startled by a wasp that flew into his shirt, open at the neck. Pine lost control of the vehicle, which was upended, leaving one cameraman with a sprained knee, but fortunately no more serious injuries.

While being a member of DeMille's unit may not have seemed the best preparation for the world of low-budget filmmaking—his films of the late 1930s and early 1940s typically had seven-figure budgets—DeMille had nonetheless exerted a strong influence on his hardworking young protégé's career. Pine said in 1953, "He's still the greatest showman in the business, and what I didn't learn with him isn't worth knowing."[20] Only after the success of his first picture with Thomas, *Power Dive*, would Pine give up his Paramount job with DeMille.

Widely viewed as the natural choice to head Paramount's publicity department when the position opened up, Thomas was dejected when he wasn't chosen, and promptly went job hunting. Offered a publicity post at RKO, he leveraged that opportunity into a better salary to work for Harry Cohn at Columbia. But Cohn was never known as a pleasant boss, and soon Thomas began longing for his old stomping grounds at Paramount. As he would later write, "I was drawn to Paramount as Moses was to Mount [Horeb]. It was my destiny."[21]

Still, working at Cohn's studio paid some unexpected dividends. Columbia's movies tended to be less lavish than Paramount's, and being on the scene Thomas picked up a few tricks that would serve him well when he became a B movie producer. He remembered two lessons in motion picture economy that he took to heart: "shooting on paper" (i.e., preproduction planning that avoided waste when filming got underway), and hiring actors for a specified number of days.

It was during his Columbia stint that Thomas began working on motion picture stories with his friend Maxwell Shane, also a former publicity man. Thomas saw his name on a movie screen for the first time when he and his writing partner were credited with the original story for the musical comedy *This Way Please*, starring Buddy Rogers and Betty Grable, released by Paramount in 1937. Shane would go on to become one of the most important and prolific screenwriters associated with Pine-Thomas, so much that he was jokingly described as "the hyphen in Pine-Thomas."

In the early 1940s, much would be made of Pine and Thomas' seemingly effortless transition from press agents to independent producers. However, just as Pine learned about the ins and outs of production at DeMille's side, Thomas too seized a chance to develop his skills. The *Los Angeles Times*' Edwin Schallert reported in November 1937 that Bill Thomas "becomes a full-fledged producer at Paramount, under the jurisdiction of Hal Hurley," then the head of the studio's B-film unit.[22] The announcement indicated that Thomas' initial project would be "Midnight Cargo," a story about "truck piracy" he had written with Maxwell Shane, to star Leif Erickson.

However, Thomas earned his first production credit when he persuaded his Paramount bosses to make a college picture called *Campus Confessions* (1938), starring a young Betty Grable. By Thomas' account, he was left holding the bag when assigned screenwriters Lloyd Corrigan and Erwin Gelsey failed to complete a usable screenplay. Reluctant to admit that he was unable to control people in his employ, Thomas instead worked feverishly over a weekend with Maxwell Shane, and delivered a completed script on Monday. The story dealt with the students of Middleton College, an institution whose chief benefactor, wealthy Wayne Atterbury, Sr., had no use for athletics, insisting that the school be devoted solely to developing minds, rather than bodies. His stuffy young son, enrolled as a freshman at the college, finds himself caught between his father's wishes and his desire to fit in with a lively, fun-loving crowd.

What Thomas assembled was a fast-paced piece of light entertainment that included comedy, romance, and a sports angle. Noting the popularity of basketball, Thomas incorporated the sport into the story, recruiting a real-life champion, Hank Luisetti, to play a featured role. Included in the cast were a few actors who would later be part of the Pine-Thomas team, including co-stars Richard Denning and Bill Henry, as well as character actor Dick Elliott.

Even at this early stage, Thomas appreciated the importance of saving money, and delivering maximum value for minimal prices. Allowed to use a portion of the Paramount lot to represent the Middleton College campus, Thomas invited any of the studio's young secretaries to drop by anytime they had a few free moments, where they could carry a few books through the backgrounds of scenes, saving money on paid extras to populate the student body.

Daily Variety's reviewer attended the preview and reported (September 13, 1938), "Thomas has carried through his production task with results that would do justice to a veteran, not only in the matter of script supervision and the selection of his personnel, but in devising ways and means of so successfully filming the basketball sequence." *The Hollywood Reporter* (September 13, 1938) concurred, saying, "William Thomas should be credited with a good job in his initial production chore."

In the rapid succession typical of B-picture production, Thomas produced (under Hurley's supervision) nine more films in the next two years: *King of Alcatraz* and *Illegal Traffic* (both released in 1938); *Sudden Money, Some Like It Hot, Million Dollar Legs* (again with Betty Grable), *$1,000 a Touchdown* (all 1939); and *The Farmer's Daughter, Comin' Round the Mountain*, and *Golden Gloves* (all 1940). Listening to a radio broadcast announcing the transfer of prisoner Al Capone from Alcatraz to another facility, Thomas envisioned a villainous character based on the real-life mobster, and the resulting picture was ultimately issued as *King of Alcatraz*. Two of his films were comedy vehicles for actress Martha Raye, a Paramount contract player whose star was on the wane after experiencing rapid success in films only two years earlier. Again taking into account the box office appeal of athletics, Thomas placed Miss Raye in *$1,000 a Touchdown*, a comedy with a football angle.

Always a shrewd thinker and a glib talker, Thomas emerged victorious from an argument with Joseph Breen of the Hays office, who twice refused the use of the producer's preferred title, "Some Like It Hot," for a musical comedy starring Bob Hope. Though the censor found the phrase risqué, Thomas protested that not only were ballrooms and dance halls commonly referred to as "hot spots," but that his preferred title was also part of a well-known nursery rhyme. One trade paper reported that Thomas pled his case via a telegram, which read, "Some like it hot, some like it cold, some like it in the pot nine days old. Ye gods! Can't we even use nursery rhymes for titles?"[23]

Thomas quickly became a successful member of Paramount's B unit, reporting to Hurley. But when a regime change in Paramount found Hurley swept out the door, most of his loyal staff, including Thomas, soon followed. An announcement in the "Wandering around Hollywood" column of *Showmen's Trade Review* (June 1, 1940) proclaimed that Paramount "will completely abandon the production of B pictures and henceforth will devote itself exclusively to the making of A product." That edict wouldn't last long. But in the meantime, Thomas sought new opportunities.

After leaving Paramount, Thomas, always able to land on his feet, had a brief stint as a screenwriter at RKO, working with producers Gene Towne and C. Graham Baker. Columnists reported that Thomas took pride in the fact that he had received a studio paycheck every week for 16 years, since his 1924 graduation from USC. His association with Towne and Baker, however, he recalled as short-lived and more than a little odd. Towne, said Thomas, had a penchant for conducting story meetings while stretched out in his bed at home, naked, sipping a mixed drink and savoring a cigar. Although the movie scenario Thomas and his fellow screenwriter Lewis R. Foster developed met with Towne's approval, the film was never made. Towne and Baker's version of the classic *Tom Brown's School Days* (1940) lost money for the studio, and RKO pink-slipped everyone in their unit before another picture could go into production.

While they were no longer working together, Pine and Thomas remained friends, meeting frequently for lunches. By Thomas' account, the venture that would become Pine-Thomas Productions began over coffee at Lucey's, when Pine proposed a series of modestly budgeted films. "I've got this idea," Pine told his friend, "for a series based on the *Tailspin Tommy* cartoon strip about aviation. They'll be Westerns. Only we'll put the hero in a cockpit, not a saddle."[24] Public interest in aviation was strong, and both men recognized the potential box office appeal of a topical subject. (Whether or not he was aware of it at the time, Pine's idea had occurred to other filmmakers as well. Universal had obtained the rights to Hal Forrest's comic strip several years earlier, releasing two serials featuring the character. In 1939, Tailspin Tommy returned to the screen in a short-lived series based at the Poverty Row studio Monogram.)

Though Thomas preferred to avoid labeling their films as a series, feeling that it would result in flat budgets and limited returns, he sparked to the idea of producing a trio of films with pilot heroes. Knowing the importance of titles promising action and intrigue, Thomas came up with three that evening—*Power Dive, Forced Landing*, and *Flying Blind*. There were no stories yet, just titles.

With some trepidation, Thomas turned down a safer bet—a $300 a week screen-writing job at Universal—to throw in his lot with Pine. He credited his friend Sam White, a colleague from the Hurley B unit at Paramount, with persuading him to take the leap of faith. A. Mike Vogel in *Motion Picture Herald* (December 21, 1940) applauded the news of the new partnership, predicting "product that should ring the bell" and crediting Pine and Thomas with "the savvy and imagination to fashion the kind of product theatre-men will have little difficulty in selling."

Pine and Thomas rented office space for their new enterprise at the Fine Arts Studio on Sunset Boulevard, home to several independent production companies. Their accommodations were functional, but hardly glamorous—although the soundstages were in good enough shape, the facility had dirt roads leading around the lot, and rundown wooden cottages that would serve as office space. "I'll admit," Thomas later wrote, "the studio looked like a relic from the silent movie days, but it cut thousands in overhead. That's what mattered to Bill and me."[25]

As independent producers, Pine and Thomas had to secure financing for their initial film effort. Paramount's Y. Frank Freeman was hesitant to bankroll them, doubtful that the aviation adventures they described to him could be made as cheaply as they promised. He offered a distribution deal with Paramount, but not the studio's monetary backing, forcing them to raise the budget themselves. Once all other sources of income seemed to be tapped out, Thomas cashed in his life insurance policy, and tossed that money into the pot. So that at least one of them would have a steady income, Pine maintained his job with DeMille for the time being. Still, much was riding on the success of *Power Dive*.

The initial deal with Paramount called for three low-budget films, with stories relating to aviation. Pine and Thomas initially dubbed their company "Picture Corporation of America." Pine was still in DeMille's employ, and could not yet take screen credit. *Showmen's Trade Review* (January 11, 1941) commented, "Both of the boys know their way around, on the scripting and production end, and their first subject will be something to look forward for. We're rooting for you, boys." Trade paper announcements indicated that John W. Rogers would join the organization as a vice-president and chairman of the board; he served as associate producer on Pine and Thomas' first three films together.

Pine and Thomas were friendly with veteran actor Richard Arlen, who had been a stalwart at Paramount in the 1930s. Though his career was past its peak, Arlen still earned a solid living working regularly in B movies, and was a reliable draw to movie patrons who liked action films. Lured with a percentage of the action, he readily signed with the neophyte producers as their first star. Jean Parker, a former MGM contract player, was cast in the female lead. Both had a real-life interest in aviation that lent itself well to the parts they would play.

Power Dive went into production in late January 1941, with principal photography lasting only a few days. Once a rough edit of the film had been assembled, Thomas was troubled by the feeling that something was amiss. He consulted Sam White, who screened the rough cut and then asked to see the original screenplay. White told Thomas bluntly, "What you guys have done is cut out all the questions and left in only the answers. Every kind of a story development that was required before the climax is out."[26] In the interests of making a fast-paced picture, the young producers had cut to the chase, almost literally, to the film's detriment. White supervised a substantial re-edit of *Power Dive*. With little

The picture that started it all: Pine and Thomas' *Power Dive,* released in 1941 to good reviews and strong box office returns.

or no money available for extra shooting days, White said, "I shot a couple of close-ups of a double with goggles. I put in all kinds of fast cuts to help build suspense in places where they hadn't covered it properly."[27]

Finally, it was time for Paramount executives to see the results of their deal with Pine and Thomas. Too jittery to attend the screening for studio bigwigs, Thomas hovered nervously outside as the picture played. Finally, more than an hour later, his partner Pine emerged from the screening room and flashed an "okay" sign at Thomas. As Sam White later recalled it, Thomas "just collapsed on the ground. He didn't completely faint, but he was in a kind of a shock."[28]

The film was screened for trade publications just prior to its April release. *The Hollywood Reporter* (April 3, 1941) enthused, "Mr. Thomas and Mr. Pine prove at once that they are gifted with plenty of production intelligence, a valuable sense of speed in marketing their wares, and knowledge of where the audience heart is located, for *Power Dive* has everything it takes to win the fans.... This first [of the company's announced three films] will make the fans keen for the other two and ensures the success of the new Pine-Thomas company."

A review in *American Cinematographer* (May 1941) said that *Power Dive* compared favorably with Paramount's other recent aviation drama, *I Wanted Wings*, despite the fact that "the entire production of *Power Dive* probably cost less than the single item of airplane rental on the other film.... It's a quickie—but it has all the photographic quality of a major production." Particular praise was given to the cinematography of John Alton, who would go on to win an Academy Award for his work on *An American in Paris* (1951).

Of their second release, *Forced Landing*, a *Film Daily* reviewer commented (July 3, 1941), "If the boys keep up the standard used in this film, they are going to make a lot of friends who operate theaters." By the summer of 1941, Pine and Thomas' trio of aviation adventures had all played theaters to satisfying response. The third picture, *Flying Blind*, elicited a telegram from studio executive Bob Gilham to Pine and Thomas: "There's nothing shoddy about this cheapie. You got a lot for your dough!"[29] Said *Film Daily* (August 20, 1941) about the same production, "With each succeeding picture Producers Bill Thomas and Bill Pine with their Associate Producer John W. Rogers, show more reasons why Paramount should consider their releasing contract a very valuable asset."

Having demonstrated their abilities, the young producers were offered a multi-picture contract with Paramount. After stipulating that they would not be required to shoot on the studio lot (which would drive up overhead costs), they happily signed a deal, and Pine-Thomas Productions was officially underway. As *Motion Picture Herald* (October 25, 1941) reported after a visit to the Pine-Thomas offices, "On a horseshoe floor plan are laid out the offices of the men and their associates, Maxwell Shane, top scripter, Doc Merman, production manager, the director on the job, the assistant director, and in the center the clerical staff. They've got inter-office phones but don't need them ... the whole of the layout could be duplicated in at least one Hollywood executive chamber without crowding the occupant."

Writer W.E. Oliver noted, "Their first production, *Power Dive*, cost under $86,000, was completed in nine weeks after the cameras started and now is jostling Class A pictures at the boxoffice for grosses." Costs were kept down, Oliver explained, by shooting off the Paramount lot, and precise preproduction planning: "Flat contracts are let on directing, camera work, set designing and writing. A name cast is hired by piece work. The shooting time is worked out almost to the hour, with the full schedule on set and locations only

10 days."[30] In addition, miniature sets were employed before shooting began to plan camera angles and lighting.

Once filming was underway, script changes were verboten. As Bill Pine explained, "If scripts are right before the camera grinds, the producer and director will know—not guess—what they want. No picture will go into work with eight or 12 or 16 days of prepared script, allowing the rest of the schedule to hang in uncertainty while thousands of dollars per day are charged against the payroll."[31] Or, as Thomas later advised producers bent on cost-cutting, "Don't throw away 1800 feet of film. Edit your script."[32]

As both men readily acknowledged, their production manager Lewis B. Merman, known to one and all as "Doc," deserved much of the credit for keeping things moving on their sets. They explained to reporters that their much-valued employee "has a very loud whistle on a string around his neck to call attention to any momentary loss of production time, but he seldom has to use it, and generally he just opens his mouth. His language is louder and more to the point."[33] Though he rarely received an on-screen mention for his work as production manager, Merman would be credited as Associate Producer on some later Pine-Thomas films.

Producing action-oriented films meant that, despite the best pre-production planning, Pine and Thomas had to be ready to deal with the unexpected once shooting was underway. While capturing aerial footage for *Forced Landing*, crew members Fred Jackman, Jr., and Doc Merman were injured when dust storms and gale winds knocked around their small plane. "Jackman was cut on the arm," according to *Daily Variety* (April 10, 1941), "and Merman knocked unconscious when his head was slammed against the cowling."

One area in which Pine and Thomas pointedly chose not to pinch pennies was in hiring talent—they knew that it would be a mistake to cut corners too tightly where actors were concerned. According to journalist Victor Gunson, "They are willing to pay to get experience. They tell you very frankly they are not running an acting school. Experience, of course, eliminates many takes and wasted footage."[34]

In November 1941, with their first films performing well at the box office, Pine and Thomas celebrated the company's first anniversary. Congratulatory telegrams came from their stars Jean Parker ("Neath all the fun, you have my love and gratitude for this year ever") and Richard Arlen ("Am proud to be with you. All the luck in the world for continued success"), among others. Loyal to the cast and crew members who had worked well with them from the beginning, Pine and Thomas continued to rely on them. Their follow-up films would find the producing partners broadening their horizons, making murder mysteries (*No Hands on the Clock*) and action melodramas (*I Live on Danger*). With *Wildcat* (1942), they made the first of a series of action films based on risky blue-collar occupations, a formula that would prove a reliable winner.

Though Pine and Thomas regarded their films as a group effort, the company's success rested largely on its two founders, who each brought different skills to the fore. As columnist Robbin Coons (March 1, 1942) described them, "Pine is tall, dark, sharp. Thomas is chubby, fair, with a face as guileless as a kewpie's. Pine carries the firm's dignity. Thomas is the lively table-hopper type." Writer John Reddy, profiling the team in a 1945 *Esquire* magazine article, said, "Pine is forty-eight years old, given to brooding over mundane matters like budgets and production schedules. Thomas, on the other hand, is forty-one, blond and pink-cheeked, and has never outgrown his press agent's exuberance…. Thomas is the idea man of the team and Pine the businessman." According to Carol Thomas

The one-year anniversary of Pine-Thomas Productions was cause for celebration by producers and players alike. Pictured (left-right) are Bill Thomas, Mary Carlisle, Richard Arlen, Bill Pine, and Eva Gabor.

Pantages, her father typically worked a five-and-a-half day workweek, going into the office until noontime on Saturdays.

Bob Hanks, whose parents Jean Parker and Robert Lowery worked often in Pine-Thomas films, described the producing duo as "yin and yang," adding, "They fit together beautifully and became very successful."[35] Actress Arlene Dahl, who starred in three films for the unit, said of the two men's symbiotic relationship, "They were like twins. They would often finish each other's sentences."[36]

Carol Thomas Pantages agreed that the partners' skills complemented each other, saying, "My dad was probably the more creative one." However, she noted that Pine was a strong contributor behind the scenes, watching the company finances, and was particularly good at dealing with Paramount's New York office. Her father said of Pine, "He loves to work.... He is never happier than when sitting at his more or less disorderly desk, with a dozen problems to solve and no time to do it.... When any particularly puzzling production problem arises into which he can get his teeth, he positively beams."[37]

Unable to entice actors with lavish salaries, Pine and Thomas looked for other ways to reel in their stars. Knowing that Nancy Kelly had left 20th Century–Fox in 1940, bored with the films she had been assigned, Thomas took her to lunch to pitch the female lead in *Tornado*. "There's nothing a real actress likes to play better than a hellcat," he explained, describing to Miss Kelly the social-climbing, hard-edged saloon singer he wanted her to play. Eager to sink her teeth into a meaty part, the actress signed on the dotted line. For Chester Morris, who Thomas described as "an intelligent guy—he likes books," they tempted him with a script adapted from a published novel.[38]

In March 1942, they finalized a deal with Paramount for the 1942-43 season, with the studio providing 100 percent of the financing. According to *Daily Variety* (March 3, 1942), Paramount anticipated that the duo's first six films "will gross around $2 million," making a new deal a no-brainer for studio executives. The producers negotiated a fairly simple bookkeeping deal with Paramount. Once each film had grossed 170 percent of its production costs, Pine and Thomas would receive a percentage of the profits. By 1945, *Time* magazine (August 6) estimated that the partners would "collect about $700,000 (before taxes) for their work."

With the advent of World War II, they expanded their repertoire to make films that saluted servicemen in various branches of the U.S. military. Like their civilian heroes, their military heroes were regular guys dedicated to a tough job, and danger was always lurking. Over the next few years, pictures like *Minesweeper*, *Aerial Gunner*, and *The Navy Way* gave moviegoers a look at the many ways the Armed Forces were fighting the enemy.

Pine and Thomas' bread-and-butter films of the 1940s, which comprised the majority of Paramount's B releases, could be used in multiple ways by exhibitors. Theaters in bigger cities often employed them as second features for more expensive Paramount films. In Abilene, Texas, a downtown theater played P-T's *Dark Mountain* (1944) as an "added attraction" to the Claudette Colbert—Fred MacMurray comedy *Practically Yours*. Moviegoers in Jefferson City, Missouri, buying tickets to see Preston Sturges' *The Great Moment* (1944) were offered P-T's *Timber Queen* as part of the package deal.

In small town theaters, Pine-Thomas films served a different purpose. Servicing a limited audience, and trying to insure frequent repeat business, exhibitors faced the problem of, as film historian Brian Taves explained, "providing a sufficiently steady quantity of new material to alter theater programs twice a week or more, constantly tempting patrons by continuously changing offerings."[39] In those situations, a Pine-Thomas film could stand on its own, taking in as much money as it could before giving way to another picture a few days later.

After committing to celluloid such workplace action dramas as *Wrecking Crew* and *High Explosive*, Pine and Thomas told journalists that the sight of some dangerous machinery frequently prompted one to say eagerly to the other, "You could kill a man with that." As one report had it, "Once they saw workmen demolishing a Los Angeles building with a giant swinging steel ball. They promptly got permission, moved in a camera, and used the ball to demolish their own villain…. Other victims have appeared to be conked fatally by airplane propellers or drowned in crude oil…. A Los Angeles Harbor ship launching provided the free tidal wave to capsize their hero's speedboat."[40] Pine explained, "Any dope can kill off a character with a gun or a blunt instrument. We like to be more imaginative…. We usually kill, or at least maim, several people in each picture, and we hate to repeat ourselves."[41]

As the partners proudly bragged in 1944, "We've let you hitch-hike rides with the dare-devils who transport nitroglycerine, get the bends with deep sea divers attached to Uncle Sam's minesweepers, make hairbreadth escapes with the lumberjacks from toppling redwood giants, face the blazing guns of scheming Nazi spies with the F.B.I., and suffer agonizing hours in the coal mines when thousands of tons of the black diamonds came crunching downward."[42]

Always, before committing to a picture, the Dollar Bills brainstormed advertising copy, insuring that the finished product could be successfully marketed. If the story didn't lend itself to snappy promotion, it was abandoned before a single camera rolled. As producers, they were unapologetically focused on movies that would sell tickets. Discouraged by some advance reaction to *Torpedo Boat* (1942) in trade papers, Pine and Thomas were cheered when none other than Cecil B. DeMille told them, "Don't follow the critics. They'll lead you to the poorhouse!"[43] Or, as Pine himself later put it, "When public tastes change, Hollywood pictures will change…. When there's a public that pays to see Shakespeare, we'll make it for them."[44] Syndicated columnist Erskine Johnson (September 4, 1946) later remarked, "All they're after is your money, son, but with a fine sense of professional ethics they'll give you value received in the way of all the entertainment that experience and ingenuity can provide, and no silly pretensions about it."

Production typically began with shooting footage for which the stars were not needed. "In our business, backgrounds are all important," Pine explained. "We film them with a skeleton crew, and use stunt men to double for the stars, not only for risky scenes, but also for long shots." This method allowed the producers to hire name actors for as little time as possible. "By the time we're ready for the principals," Pine said, "we've figured out exactly how many days each of them will have to work. If … we can finish with the star in a week, we can afford to get a fairly big name and pay him well. But if we need the star three weeks we'll have to hire some one [*sic*] who'll work for a lower salary."[45]

Once production was underway, as Thomas explained, "the crew and stand-ins report to work at 7:30 in the morning. At 8 o'clock, the actors walk on the set and the scene is ready for them. They start the scene right away because it has all been worked out before hand. When we finish the first scene—boom—we go to the next one. The electricians are always working on the scene ahead so we won't waste any time."[46]

Always on the lookout for a more efficient workplace, Pine and Thomas eventually began serving lunch to cast and crew, usually in the latter's office. "Players, director and key technicians dine with the producers off picnic plates. It gives everybody a chance to talk about the work done in the morning and to be done in the afternoon ahead." Most importantly, as Erskine Johnson (July 8, 1943) noted, "nobody is ever late getting back from lunch."

In their first few years of operation, Pine and Thomas developed an informal stock company of cast and crew members who were able to work under hastened circumstances, and entered into the spirit of mutual cooperation. Veteran character actor Lucien Littlefield, seen in Pine-Thomas' *One Body Too Many*, commented, "I never saw anything like this place. Never. You start working for 'em, and they take the whole cast to lunch every day on the house, and pretty soon even the actors are trying to help them."[47]

Both men occasionally took the director's chair on Pine-Thomas films. Pine directed five of the company's feature films, beginning with *Aerial Gunner* (1943). Thomas followed suit a few years later, directing *Midnight Manhunt* (1945) as well as all four of the unit's "Big Town" series.

Because many of their films of the early to mid–1940s dealt with military themes, Pine and Thomas had to curry the favor of higher-ups in the armed services. Having done so, they found that, once their script had been given the OK, they could often arrange cooperation from officers at military bases, allowing them to shoot scenes that

Two candles on the cake denote two successful years of Pine-Thomas Productions for founders Bill Thomas (left) and Bill Pine.

contained more production values. Their leading male roles were so action-packed that, according to a column item in the *Hollywood Reporter* (September 24, 1942), Thomas "invariably warns actors that if they work for him the government will classify them [for military service] as 1-A. Those who can take a Pine-Thomas shooting schedule can stand anything."

As early as 1943, despite the steady success of their Paramount output, Pine and Thomas realized that they were in danger of being typed. Their skill at making low-budget action pictures was widely acknowledged, yet they felt it wise to diversify. With that in mind, they began developing ideas for comedies and musicals. Comedian Jack Haley was signed to play the lead in their first musical comedy, *Take It Big* (1944); he ultimately starred in four features for the unit.

The producers also looked to the popular medium of radio for inspiration. In 1945, Pine and Thomas paid a reported $100,000 for the screen rights to the hit newspaper drama *Big Town*, which had begun its 15-year run in 1937. Philip Reed and Hillary Brooke were signed to play Steve Wilson and Lorelei Kilbourne, the characters originated on radio by Edward G. Robinson and Claire Trevor. In rapid succession, four films made it to the silver screen before the series breathed its last with *Big Town Scandal* (1948). Another radio tie-in was the Pine-Thomas musical comedy *People Are Funny* (1946), adapted from the hit audience participation show.

After several years, Richard Arlen opted not to continue in Pine-Thomas films, harboring an ambition to break out of the B movie rut. Louella O. Parsons reported in her column (January 20, 1944) that Robert Lowery had instead signed a two-year contract to play lead roles for the outfit. In 1945, Paramount contract player Ann Savage would make two films for Pine-Thomas, shortly before she obtained her release from the studio, and played the part for which modern-day *noir* fans know her, in PRC's *Detour*. Two years later, Miss Savage returned to the fold for a third assignment, in *Jungle Flight*.

By the mid–1940s, the efficiency and speed of Pine-Thomas' filmmaking was such that they were often making films faster than Paramount could schedule them for release. A report in *Daily Variety* (October 15, 1946) indicated that the company had already completed *Danger Street*, *Fear in the Night*, *Jungle Flight*, *Seven Were Saved*, *Adventure Island*, and the first two films in the "Big Town" series. Six more scripts were said to be ready for production on short notice.

The success of Pine and Thomas' company allowed both families to live in comfort in Beverly Hills. According to Carol Thomas Pantages, their houses were some three blocks apart, with the Thomases on Alta Drive and the Pines on Hillcrest. Carol was doted on by her father; "he would just spoil me to death," she said. But while his inclination was always to say yes to anything his daughter wanted, she noted, Thomas would usually add, "Check with your mother," who was the disciplinarian of the family.

According to Thomas, his partner's leisure time activities included swimming in his own pool, adding to his collection of watches, and indulging in travel. Pine followed football and baseball as a fan, rather than a participant. "His favorite indoor sports," Thomas added, "are poker and gin rummy, at both of which he is remarkably proficient, as I can vouch for to my cost."[48] Pine and wife Anna became grandparents with the birth of Howard's daughter Wendy. After his first marriage ended in divorce, Howard wed Judith Beaumont in 1948, and they would have two daughters, Angel and Elizabeth.

At the end of World War II, the producing partners sensed that changes were underway in the motion picture business. No longer could they count on audiences wishing to see wartime melodramas. Pine and Thomas began seeking out stories that offered exotic locations, and sometimes period costumes. Budgets crept up accordingly, with *Adventure Island*, their first film in color, costing $250,000. Still, they continued to demonstrate their facility for doing a lot with relatively little. Of *Fear in the Night*, syndicated columnist Hedda Hopper (February 19, 1947) wrote, "I'm convinced that the heads of all our studios should insist that every one of their producers should study it. Featuring newcomers, it cost only $200,000 and was shot in 13 days."

With bigger-budgeted pictures on their minds, Pine and Thomas, as reported in *Daily Variety* (December 9, 1946), "have formed new producing company, Clarion Productions, to turn out minimum of one high-budget picture annually for Paramount release." *Albuquerque* would be the first film made under the auspices of Clarion Productions, and Pine and Thomas paid the most substantial star salary they'd ever offered to secure the services of Western star Randolph Scott for the lead. Pine and Thomas rolled the dice and pulled out all the stops for *Albuquerque*, released in 1948. Their gamble paid off, with an investment of approximately $790,000 expected to return $3,000,000 in grosses for Paramount.

Pine and Thomas took out trade-paper ads proclaiming that box office response to

Bill Thomas (left) and Bill Pine had a ball upon learning that their first big-ticket film, *Albuquerque*, brought in more than $2 million at the box office.

the bigger-budgeted *Albuquerque* had been "most gratifying," and added, "Henceforth, we will devote our efforts exclusively to the production of three important top-budget productions annually." Already in production at the time of the advertisement was *El Paso*, starring John Payne and Gail Russell, reportedly their first film to boast a $1 million budget. With *El Paso*'s cast headed by Payne, Russell, and Sterling Hayden, Thomas commented, "We've got people working in this one who two years ago wouldn't have been caught dead in a Pine-Thomas picture."[49]

Their only misstep during this period came with *Manhandled* (1949), a murder mystery starring Dorothy Lamour and Dan Duryea, which was their first film in nearly a decade to roll snake eyes at the box office. Thomas later surmised that there was simply too much Lamour product in release at the time—including *The Lucky Stiff*, a comic murder mystery for which comedian Jack Benny was the credited producer, but Pine and Thomas had been contracted to provide production assistance. Ultimately, they had to wait for a television sale for *Manhandled* to turn a modest profit.

For a time in the late 1940s, Pine and Thomas alternated higher-budgeted films with B pictures that hewed to their previous guidelines. But changing times in the motion picture industry had hit B producers hard, leading to the demise of Poverty Row studios like Producers' Releasing Corporation (PRC). The 1948 court decision that forced Paramount Pictures to divest its ownership of movie theaters also contributed to the dwindling interest in low-budget second features. By the early 1950s, cheaply made action dramas were increasingly becoming the province of television, and no longer held the same attraction for moviegoers. *Special Agent*, released in the summer of 1949, was Pine and Thomas' last black-and-white B.

Still, Paramount had faith in the Dollar Bills' ability to continue bringing home winners. The *Hollywood Reporter* (January 20, 1950) reported that Pine and Thomas had signed a new two-year deal with Paramount, calling for six films. First up on the agenda was to be "High Venture" (subsequently retitled *Passage West*). While the names of Pine and Thomas were well-known within the motion picture industry by the mid- to late-1940s, they were largely anonymous where moviegoers were concerned. As Thomas jokingly lamented during a publicity tour for *The Eagle and the Hawk* (1950), "All I do is choose the script, directors, actors and technicians. I put up the money for the film. I do all the worrying and take all the risks. But when one of my film[s] is premiered, and I pull up in front of the theater, every time some kid will look in the car window and shout, 'He ain't nobody!'"[50]

If movie fans didn't buy tickets to Pine-Thomas films, it wouldn't be because they hadn't heard about them. Always astute at sweet-talking their way into free publicity, the producers struck gold when they offered Houston-based columnist Paul Hochuli a bit part in *The Eagle and the Hawk*. In a letter reproduced in Hochuli's *Houston Press* column (June 7, 1949), Thomas wrote, "Now don't get hostile, Hoc, at the thought of playing a low down varmint. Your physical appearance is not your fault and it is intelligent to capitalize on what assets you possess...." The badinage between the two men, and the chance for Hochuli to make his acting debut, not surprisingly resulted in Pine-Thomas films getting substantial space in the *Houston Press*.

In the early 1950s, many in the motion picture industry were terrified by the prospect of television, and what it would do to movie ticket sales. Pine and Thomas, breezing along with an ambitious schedule of new films, claimed they were not. "There has been a stove in every house for a long time, but the restaurants are still in business," Thomas pointed out. Added his partner, "The wife may be satisfied to sit around and look at television six nights a week, but the seventh night she wants to go out."[51]

Though strong box office returns continued to be their primary goal, one project in particular so appealed to Pine and Thomas that they were willing to risk thinking outside the box. Not without difficulty, they persuaded Paramount executives to bankroll *The Lawless*, a drama about a heroic newspaper editor fighting prejudice against Mexican-Americans in a small town. As the *Los Angeles Times'* Philip K. Scheuer remarked (July 28, 1950), "This took courage ... on the part of William H. Pine and William C. Thomas, who have usually been content to produce action melodramas which were sufficient unto themselves. *The Lawless* has the action, the melodrama—and something more." Though it was made less expensively than some of their recent features, it had a budget that ultimately climbed northward of $400,000, making it a risky proposition if ticket buyers perceived it as an art film.

They faced early opposition from Paramount studio head Y. Frank Freeman, who, according to Thomas' recollection, told them, "You boys have always produced the old stalwart shows. Play it safe—stick to thrills and action. Let 'sleeping causes' lie!"[52] Ultimately, Freeman agreed to give two of his most successful producers enough rope to hang themselves, and the result was a well-made thriller with thematic weight.

Reviewing the finished product in *Time* magazine (July 3, 1950), a reviewer cracked that seeing such a socially significant film made by Pine-Thomas was "as unexpected as a slum documentary by Cecil B. DeMille." In fact, by melding the elements of action, excitement, and social commentary, Pine and Thomas had succeeded in exposing *The Lawless* to a wide audience. Said Pine, "It's the first picture of that type that's not an out-and-out preachment."[53]

Although Paramount executives had been hesitant about the box-office appeal of *The Lawless*, which was so atypical of Pine-Thomas' product, reaction from civic leaders was positive. W. Henry Cooke, chairman of the Los Angeles County Conference on Community Relations, wrote to the producers congratulating them on "a thrilling and daring introduction of a vital question to the American people. *The Lawless* was not fiction. It was a report to the people.... Your vision and your sensitivity to the powerful influence of the story of *The Lawless* opens the way for more films of this type."[54]

If movies were becoming franker, so was press coverage of their stars. With the studio system breaking down, movie fans were reading provocative stories about their favorite stars' private lives, whether it be illegitimate children, use of illicit drugs, or other controversies. Thomas told syndicated columnist Bob Thomas (June 24, 1950), "I think when a star gets in trouble with the police and is convicted of an offense that is odious to society, he should be fired from the industry. Then it would serve as an example to other stars who might think they can get out of line and get away with it." According to his partner Pine, publicized Hollywood scandals had even affected exhibitors whom they met on their publicity tours. They were sometimes asked, "Why are there so many Communists in Hollywood?" Pine noted, "Our only answer is that Thomas is a Republican and I am a Democrat."

The new decade, and their turn to more ambitious films, brought new actors into the Pine-Thomas fold. In 1951, they signed leading man Ronald Reagan for their Western *The Last Outpost*. After it was in the can, Reagan told Thomas, "I finally found some producers who like actors."[55] He would go on to make two more P-T films. Over the course of their association, the future U.S. president had ample opportunity to appreciate his bosses' relentless salesmanship, praising them as "the only producers in town who go out and keep selling their product until that last buck is in. When I think of all the rubber chicken they have eaten at luncheon clubs all over the country to help sell pictures I've been in, I almost get a guilt complex."[56]

But their most prolific leading man of the 1950s would be John Payne, who had spent much of the previous decade as a 20th Century–Fox contract player. Best-known for his starring role in the holiday classic *Miracle on 34th Street,* Payne's stint at Fox often found him cast in musicals. Once he began free-lancing, Payne longed for tougher, more action-oriented parts, and the Dollar Bills were happy to oblige him, starting with the Western *El Paso*. Redheaded leading ladies continued to be a company staple as well. After spotlighting Jean Parker in so many 1940s films, Pine and Thomas pictures of the next decade often starred either Rhonda Fleming or Arlene Dahl.

While Pine and Thomas continued to be active producers, by 1951 their earlier films began appearing on television. The producers signed a deal with ABC to screen ten of their 1940s films on the network's owned-and-operated stations in Los Angeles, New York, Chicago, Detroit, and San Francisco. Films in the package were *Caged Fury, Dangerous Passage, Fear in the Night, Follow That Woman, Shaggy, Swamp Fire, Take It Big, Tornado, Wildcat,* and *Wrecking Crew*. According to *Daily Variety* (August 17, 1951), the television network paid an estimated $175,000, earning the right to have each film played twice within the next ten months.

In 1952, the Pine-Thomas unit moved onto the Paramount lot, after 11 years of operating out of facilities offsite so as to reduce studio overhead. The unit retained its autonomy, however, as well as 12 employees who continued to staff the company's departments. An article in the studio's in-house publication, *Paramount Parade*, identified the key players in Pine and Thomas' company: production manager Howard Pine, comptroller Herman Darstein, film editor Howard Smith, and publicity head A.C. Lyles. Secretarial support was furnished by Dorothy Whitney (Thomas' assistant, who also helped with casting), Frances Steens (who worked with Pine), and Lyles' secretary Peggy Wheeler. Pine and Thomas' assistants, as well as Lyles, had been with the organization from the beginning.

The first Pine-Thomas picture to be produced at Paramount's facilities would be "Caribbean Gold," starring John Payne and Arlene Dahl (subsequently released as *Caribbean*). With the luxury of upped budgets, the producers were able not only to offer more spectacle than in their earlier films, but also to provide a bit of star treatment to their players. According to Miss Dahl, who ultimately did three films for Pine and Thomas, "They were on the set constantly, making sure we had everything we needed. They were very generous to me." Given the benefit of Edith Head's wardrobe, and striking Technicolor cinematography, the actress admitted, "I loved the costume films."

Often asked to share their expertise on picture-making, the Dollar Bills were careful to say they hadn't abandoned the need for input from exhibitors and the ticket-buying public. Pine said, "The public is Hollywood's boss.... There are very few workers who don't know their boss. We should meet as many of the bosses as possible."[57] When out on one of their listening tours, they liked to encourage customer involvement in their work; in one 1951 outing, they encouraged visitors to suggest an appropriate name for their completed but as-yet-untitled "logging and sawmill drama" (ultimately released as *The Blazing Forest*).

The producers put their money—and their shoe leather—where their mouths were. The *Screen Producers' Guild Journal* (July 1952) stated that, during the previous year, Pine and Thomas had visited more than 60 cities personally for promotional activities. They had appeared on more than 200 radio programs, and 30 television shows, as well as calling on some 125 newspapers. Bill Thomas' article in the same issue said, "It is time that the major studios not only permit, but urge, even demand," such participation by producers. "He will not only bring more money into the box-office, but he will also make better pictures as a result of his exhibitor and customer contacts."

Pine and Thomas also believed strongly that, with television growing by leaps and bounds in the late 1940s, theater owners and managers had to step up their game as well. Flinging down the gauntlet, they wrote, "With scattered exceptions, the exhibitor today contributes nothing except the theatre. He wants the production and sales end to handle everything for him. That won't work. The exhibitor has to pitch in with all of us." Otherwise, they projected, an exhibitor could "watch his fans stream to the ball park, the football game or to the television set."[58]

Thomas told the Associated Press' Dorothy Roe, "The public is more discriminating than ever before. Today a picture has to be a real smash before a man will spend his money to see it. If there's no movie they want to see, they can always go to a baseball game or stay home and watch TV."[59] Still, he didn't think that television could yet encroach upon what a Pine-Thomas picture had to offer the viewer, saying, "Television shows still can't compete with spectacles like guys riding logs, avalanches wiping out wagon trains...."[60]

They were early proponents of Technicolor, after releasing several films in the less expensive Cinecolor process. As Pine said in 1949, "Technicolor is a star, and a star that's available to us. Whoever you ask, they all want it ... so that's what we're planning to give them."[61] They did exactly that for most of their 1950s pictures, starting with *The Eagle and the Hawk,* offering a vividly hued contrast to black-and-white TV screens. Their enthusiasm for the process caused one columnist to quip that the Dollar Bills might soon be rechristened "The Technicolor Twins." They jumped into the 3-D fad with *Sangaree,* and soon began to employ Paramount's VistaVision wide-screen process as well. Even as their films grew increasingly ambitious, and the partners worked as hard as ever, Thomas admitted that he and his partner were never completely satisfied with the finished products: "Every picture had some things we liked, and some we didn't. We never produced a perfect picture."[62]

Even after leaving B movies behind, the producing partners still had to contend with the reputation that, ironically, their 1940s success had bestowed on them. Too many exhibitors still associated the names Pine and Thomas with low-budget films. *Film Daily* (August 1, 1952) pointed out that their 1952 release, *Caribbean,* had done quite well when initially released in one of Philadelphia's best theaters: "The picture opened to almost $5000 and appears headed for a $28,000 week and a holdover." The trade paper chided exhibitors who had dismissed the picture out of hand as "another routine Pine-Thomas production," saying, "The boxoffice potential of a motion picture must be judged not on the name of the producer, the stars, the cost or any other consideration but the merits of the picture itself."

Pine and Thomas were proclaiming that they had substantially revamped their approach to filmmaking, in keeping with the 1950s marketplace. With *Run for Cover,* starring James Cagney, ready to go into production, Thomas said, "We will recognize no budgetary limitations on the pictures we want to make. And, incidentally, Paramount is 100% behind us in this switchover. We still are going to make commercial pictures, not artistic ones, but it's no longer commercial to make the kind of pictures we've been making."[63] Bigger pictures generally required star names, and the Dollar Bills soon had contracts in force for upcoming projects with James Cagney, Jane Wyman, and Fred MacMurray. Whereas Pine and Thomas had paid Richard Arlen $5,000 to star in a movie 15 years earlier, by 1955 Cagney received a $200,000 paycheck for *Run for Cover.* Still, Pine claimed that they "won't take a big actor for a part if he's hard to get along with.... Instead we'll take a smaller guy and enjoy life."[64]

In late 1954, Pine and Thomas announced that the forthcoming *Lucy Gallant,* starring Miss Wyman, would be the final release under their contract with Paramount. With the studio releasing fewer films than in years past, Pine and Thomas increasingly found themselves pressured to avail themselves of Paramount facilities and staff, which inflated their overhead costs. Emphasizing that the severing of their ties with Paramount was "a most friendly one," they explained to *Daily Variety* (December 17, 1954) that they would follow the industry trend toward independent production: "Only after we have acquired a story property, developed a screenplay and set the stars and director will we seek further financing or the release for a picture."

The producers told the *Los Angeles Times'* Edwin Schallert that they read around 30 scripts a week between them (counting both finished screenplays and potential source material in book or short story form). For ones they found promising, synopses and story ideas were sent to theater operators around the country: "If the theater men say

Friends and colleagues gather to wish Bill Pine a happy birthday, ca. 1954. Looking over his shoulders are son Howard Pine (left) and Bill Thomas (right). Longtime Pine-Thomas publicist A.C. Lyles is pictured at upper right.

they think their patrons would like to see the story filmed, we purchase it. If not, we reject it."[65]

Long before cineastes had begun to enshrine film directors as "auteurs," Pine and Thomas bristled when Rouben Mamoulian complained in a speech at a Screen Directors Guild of America function that he and his peers deserved more credit. Mamoulian asserted that directors typically brought creativity to a project, often having to battle with producers who tried to rein them in. Those were fighting words to veteran producer and screenwriter Thomas, who told *Daily Variety* (June 17, 1953), "By a large percentage most of the work on a picture stems from the producer. It is the producer who sees picture possibilities in a book or play; it is a producer who charts the course of the project; it is a producer who employs a writer, and after he and the writer are quite a ways along, then employs a director.... No one man makes a motion picture—it is, instead, the result of combined talents."

Their stint as freelancers lasted only a few weeks. In February 1955, Pine and Thomas signed a contract with United Artists' Arthur Krims to make three pictures. With *Lucy Gallant* in theaters, Pine and Thomas took out a trade ad announcing other forthcoming projects: "Lincoln McKeever," based on a novel by Eleazar Lipsky, "The Mountains Have

No Shadow," from Owen Cameron's book, an adaptation of Lionel White's "The Big Caper," and another version of Cornell Woolrich's "Nightmare." But the duo's time together was running much shorter than either of them realized.

Bill Pine died on April 29, 1955, at Los Angeles' Cedars of Lebanon Hospital, where he had been a patient for the past several days. Although a heart episode had landed him there, he was said to be holding steady under his doctor's care. As Louella Parsons told the story in her syndicated column the following day, "Death came very suddenly, so suddenly that Bill was eating his luncheon … with his wife sitting by his side. He told her that the soup was delicious. He had no more than said the words than he clutched his side and was dead before the nurses reached him." Arriving at the hospital shortly afterwards, Bill Thomas saw Pine's son sadly shaking his head in the corridor, and knew the other half of Pine-Thomas Productions was gone. Named as Pine's survivors, aside from wife Anna and son Howard, were six of his nine siblings and three granddaughters.

Paramount vice-president Y. Frank Freeman was chosen to deliver the eulogy at Pine's memorial services on May 2, 1955. Rabbi Bernard Harrison conducted the funeral in the chapel of the Hollywood Cemetery. Active pallbearers included several men associated with Pine-Thomas Productions, including screenwriter/producer Maxwell Shane, actors Richard Arlen and William Demarest, and comptroller Herman Darstein. Among the honorary pallbearers was Cecil B. DeMille, for whom Pine had worked as an associate producer. In a statement, DeMille said, "He was one of the best associates and best friends I have ever had. His wisdom, unlimited ability and rare personal gift made Bill a truly exceptional person." Bill Thomas noted, "For 23 years Bill Pine was my dearest and closest friend. I will always be proud that he was my partner."[66] Louella Parsons added (April 30, 1955), "Few men had the love of life and the capacity for enjoyment that he did."

According to the *Los Angeles Times* (May 27, 1955), Pine's will, as submitted for probate, primarily benefited his widow, who would be the beneficiary of a trust set up to support her for the remainder of her life. Films on which Pine had served as co-producer continued to be released in the months after his death, including *Lucy Gallant* and *The Far Horizons*.

Bill Thomas and his remaining colleagues would make only three more films in the 1950s—*Nightmare, The Big Caper,* and *Bailout at 43,000.* The company was renamed Pine-Thomas-Shane Productions to acknowledge the continuing contributions of screenwriter and producer Maxwell Shane. Thomas served as president, with Shane as vice-president. William Pine's son, Howard Pine, rejoined the unit as a partner, leaving his position as a producer at Universal-International to do so. (According to the *Los Angeles Times*' Edwin Schallert [May 13, 1955], UI executives had "very reluctantly" let him out of his contract, as they foresaw strong returns for the picture he'd recently completed, *The Private War of Major Benson.*) Though Thomas, facing an uncertain future, was unsure his late partner's son should give up a steady job at Universal, the younger Pine made the move nonetheless.

The *Independent Film Journal* (May 14, 1955) reported that the company's deal with United Artists specified "a maximum of three top-budget Pine-Thomas Productions to be made this year under a flexible production program." Bill Thomas insisted that his longtime partner's widow, Anna, receive what would have been his share of the profits from the films, and she continued to do so until her death in November 1963. After leaving Paramount, Pine and Thomas had relocated their setup to the Pathe Studios in

Culver City. But after only a short time, finding that space too full of memories, Thomas and his new partners moved to the Samuel Goldwyn Studios on North Formosa Avenue. There, the last P-T releases of the 1950s would be made, with United Artists providing the financing and retaining 50 percent of the proceeds. First up came *Nightmare*, a bigger-budgeted remake of their 1947 success *Fear in the Night*, with Edward G. Robinson and Kevin McCarthy (fresh from *Invasion of the Body Snatchers*) as box office bait.

As early as 1954, the Dollar Bills had been urged to apply their expertise to developing modestly budgeted shows for television. Bill Thomas told *Daily Variety* columnist Dave Kaufman (November 26, 1954), "We listen, but we like pictures. Some day we may do it, but not now." That day came in the fall of 1956. The company ventured into the lucrative television market, developing three potential series, *Outpost*, *Johnny Pilgrim*, and *Court-Martial*.

The former, starring Lex Barker, was to be an independent project, while *Pilgrim*, toplining William Bishop as a private investigator, was a co-production with ABC-TV. *Outpost* (given as *Outpost!* in some column items) was a drama centering on the U.S. Cavalry, while *Court-Martial* would draw on case histories from various branches of the military. Signed to appear in the *Johnny Pilgrim* pilot, aside from star Bishop, were Stanley Clements, Wally Vernon, Joyce Meadows, and Richard Bakalyan. Ted Post was assigned to direct the pilot, from a Paul Monash script. Monash also co-authored the *Outpost* pilot script, with Martin Berkeley; Byron Haskin was chosen to direct that pilot presentation. Supporting Barker in the *Outpost* pilot were Charles Bronson, Douglas Fowley, and Rita Lynn.

Variety's Jack Hellman reported (November 8, 1956) that the company was taking an unconventional approach to selling their prospective series. Thomas told him, "Our pilot[s] … won't be half-hour episodes to start off the series, but more a visual presentation to ad agencies with all the human touches illustrated by the star himself." Barker, for example, hosting the *Outpost* presentation, "will personally address the client, telling him about the story line with illustrative footage, and assuring him that he'll personally handle the commercials." This "intimate touch," Thomas believed, would go a long way to clinch the deal with the potential sponsor. However, it soon became apparent that a sample episode was indeed what was needed to sell the product.

Another planned show was known as "Beverly Hillbillies"—five years before that became the title of Paul Henning's hit CBS sitcom. According to *Daily Variety* (May 3, 1957), Thomas' project was a "musical [that will] offer country music both instrumental and vocal." Martin Berkeley was attached to the project as screenwriter.

Ultimately, none of the projected series made it to the prime-time schedule. When the *Outpost* pilot aired as an episode of the syndicated anthology series *Studio 57*, *Daily Variety* (January 3, 1957) was unimpressed. While crediting the half-hour drama with "lots of action and ambitious production values," the trade paper's reviewer complained about "slapdash scripting" and said that the show's reliance on dated Western clichés would "relegate it mainly to the moppet trade."

Thomas also hoped to make a biographical film based on the life of circus impresario P.T. Barnum. Trade paper announcements indicated that Bob Hope, whom Thomas had known since their days at Paramount in the 1930s, would take the lead role in "There's One Born Every Minute," with Frank Tashlin to write and direct. The project never went before the cameras, with Bob Hope signing instead to do *Alias Jesse James*, also under Tashlin's direction.

Released in the spring of 1957, *Bailout at 43,000* would ring down the curtain on the company's production activities, after a 17-year run. It was, fittingly, an aviation story, with their longtime leading man John Payne as the star. *Variety* announced (April 10, 1957), "Pine-Thomas production unit has finally been dissolved after almost 17 years, following Howard Pine's return to a producer berth at Universal." Thomas told the trade paper that he would continue to produce films, and had secured rights to two scenarios, Jane Kubeck's "The Calendar Epic" (about a merchant ship in World War II) and Frank Kane's juvenile mob story "Key Witness."

After the dissolution of the partnership, Bill Thomas would not make another motion picture for nearly 20 years. He was disenchanted by the growing control that name stars insisted on having over their own motion picture roles, in his view usurping the function of the producer as he had always known it. Thomas later wrote, "An icy air stabbed my innermost being when I considered disbanding the company. Still, there was something overwhelmingly lonely about being a Single Bill, when I had been a Double Bill so long people didn't bother to distinguish who was Pine and who was Thomas."[67]

Thomas remained largely out of public view throughout the 1960s, investing with limited success in real estate, and enjoying the good life. In 1961, *Boxoffice* magazine (May 8, 1961) reported that Thomas had entered into a partnership "with producer-distributor Tom J. Corradine in plans for production and distribution in association with Jules Weill of Colorama Features." Anticipated projects included pictures to be called "The Unholy One" and "The Frozen Jungle." However, the films never came to pass.

He and second wife Louise were divorced by the late 1960s, but within a few years the renewal of an old acquaintance would lead to Thomas' third marriage. In the mid–1940s, Thomas had been introduced by Chicago-based columnist Irv Kupcinet to a young woman named Louise Lambert. More than a quarter-century later, she and Thomas crossed paths again. Lillian Louisa Purcell, who went by her middle name, was a divorcee with two children, working at the upscale boutique Giorgio's on Rodeo Drive in Beverly Hills. Louisa became the third Mrs. Thomas in January 1972. After five years of marriage, Thomas reported, "She is a perfect wife for me, and I'm hard to please."[68] The couple initially lived in Corona del Mar, then later took up residence in Palm Springs. The last residence they shared would be an apartment in Beverly Hills.

With his professional activities at a low ebb, Thomas also enjoyed spending time with his daughter and grandchildren. Grandson Bill Jeffries said, "I have fond memories of attending Dodger games with him and driving to [the] beach all the way on side streets. He did not like the freeway."[69] By then, Carol Thomas was married to her second husband, Alexander Pantages, a union that would last until she was widowed in 2016.

Pine-Thomas Productions had been dormant for nearly 20 years when Thomas reactivated it in the mid–1970s. In part, it was a remark by actress Helen Hayes, decrying the lack of talented producers in the industry at that time, that inspired his comeback. The projects he did in that area would continue to carry the name of his late partner, in tribute. However, the passage of time meant that he could no longer surround himself with the capable crew that had worked with Pine-Thomas in the company's heyday. He would also be entering a motion picture marketplace that had undergone substantial change since his last film.

Thomas' major comeback project was *Cat Murkil and the Silks*, a low-budget melodrama about teenage gangs, featuring a cast of mostly unknown actors. Production began on the film in the summer of 1975. In addition, as the *Independent Film Journal* (February

18, 1976) reported, "Pine-Thomas Productions has formed Cine Producers Alliance, a subsidiary handling foreign production and co-production activity. CPA has made a co-production deal with Toho Films of Japan on *High Seas Hijack*, and has purchased five Italian features, all filmed in English." Thomas hired American actors Peter Graves and Gigi Perreau to shoot some additional footage for the Toho film *Tôkyô-wan enjô*, a maritime thriller, and titled it *High Seas Hijack* for the American marketplace.

Daily Variety (June 7, 1976) reported that "Pine-Thomas plans to supply exhibitors with not less than eight attractions." With *Cat Murkil and the Silks* newly released, and *High Seas Hijack* in production, the next film in the works was to be "Horrible Little Howie," from a screenplay by Larry Hilbrand; John Bushelman was set to direct. A casting notice in *Drama-Logue* (May 29, 1976) called for "an 'angelic faced' 10 year old boy villain who can play a 'Bad Seed' male version of Patty McCormick [*sic*]." A trade paper ad listed as in preparation two other titles, "Hell Born" and "Swamp Ape." However, *Cat Murkil*, though designed to have appeal in the contemporary film market, was not a box office success, either under that title or in its second go-round as *Cruisin' High*, and *High Seas Hijack* never made it beyond a few playdates at drive-ins.

He also considered a television venture, a special program to be called "Entertainment on Skis," which was to present "novelty and comedy and musical acts with all performers on skis." Announced in trade papers in 1977, the project never came to fruition.

If his days as an active producer were winding down, Thomas was known and respected in Hollywood circles nonetheless, and he was flattered when a freelance writer and family friend, Thelma Kling, suggested that his exploits be chronicled in a book. He spent a number of hours reminiscing about his career, and Kling drafted a manuscript that took the form of an as-told-to autobiography.

On April 2, 1984, Bill Thomas passed away at his Beverly Hills residence, the cause of death given as cancer. According to daughter Carol Thomas Pantages, he had remained relatively active and in good health until about a year before his death. Listed as survivors were his wife Louisa, three daughters (including two that were Louisa's by her previous marriage), and five grandchildren. A memorial service was held a few days later at All Saints Episcopal Church in Beverly Hills, at which Thomas' grandson Bill read a letter of tribute from then–U.S. President Ronald Reagan, who still looked back fondly on his association as an actor with the Pine-Thomas unit some 30 years earlier. Bill Jeffries said of his grandfather, "He was an incredibly kind, humble, and generous man. He had a sharp wit and I don't recall him letting little stuff get him down. He was also an avid storyteller and would always reminisce about his times working in the movie industry with passion and fond regard."[70]

Even after Pine-Thomas Productions had slipped into Hollywood history, Bill Pine and Bill Thomas' legacy continued to influence moviemaking. The modestly budgeted Westerns produced in the 1960s by former Pine-Thomas publicity man A.C. Lyles showed that he had absorbed many of the techniques of his former bosses. Pine's descendants not only continued to be active in the motion picture industry, but also maintained an affiliation with Paramount Pictures.

Bill's son Howard Pine (1917–1999) enjoyed a successful career that lasted for more than 40 years, into the late 1980s. He learned the business from the ground up on his father's sets. As Howard later recalled of his first assignment, "Dad gave me a broom and told me to sweep down the stage 'and see how you do.'"[71] He did well enough to advance over the next several years to the position of production manager, and became a producer

A PINE-THOMAS PRODUCTION "CRUISIN HIGH" Starring DAVID KYLE
Co-starring STEVE BOND • KELLY YAEGERMANN • RHODES REASON • Directed by John Bushelman
Written and Produced by William C. Thomas • Released by ELLMAN FILM ENTERPRISES, INC.

Coldly received by audiences under its original title, *Cat Murkil and the Silks* had a second shot at box office success as *Cruisin' High*.

at Universal in 1954. Four of his own films saw release the following year, ranging across genres from Westerns to comedies. Resigning from Universal after his father's death, Howard rejoined Pine-Thomas Productions, where he co-produced (with Bill Thomas) *The Big Caper* and *Bailout at 43,000*. From there, Pine went on to amass dozens of credits as a production manager, and later a production executive. He was credited as Executive Producer on films such as *The Competition* (1980) and *The Survivors* (1983).

The third generation of Pines in the film industry included two of Howard's daughters. Elizabeth Pine worked as a costumer, both in motion pictures (*Annie, Jagged Edge*) and in the television series *Blue Thunder*. Although her sister Angel initially aspired to be an actress—she has a small role as Jason Robards' daughter in *Divorce American Style* (1967)—she too went on to a substantial career behind the scenes. "It was just the family business," she said of her entrée into the film industry. "I didn't think twice about it."

Her first studio job found her in film shipping at Paramount, which delighted her father. "He was so happy I was starting at Paramount, because it meant so much to him." Her grandfather's longtime associate, A.C. Lyles, worked in the next building, and when she retrieved film canisters from the vault, she spotted Pine-Thomas films on the shelves there. Admitted to the film editors' union, Angel began to learn the art of film cutting. She was mentored by the late Garry Marshall, with whom she apprenticed on *Nothing in Common* (1986). As a post-production supervisor, her credits included *Pretty Woman* (1990) and *We Were Soldiers* (2002). She also toiled on the corporate side, as a post-production executive, and was credited as associate producer on Marshall's 1996 comedy *Dear God*.

Angel Pine had only a short time to know her grandfather, who died before her fifth birthday. However, she retained a few memories of visiting him in his office, and as a child stayed in the Palm Springs vacation home of Bill and his wife Anna. She remembered him as having "a tremendous presence.... He had a certain air about him."[72] Fifty years after her grandfather's passing, she continued to represent the Pine family on prominent motion picture projects.

No doubt it would please Bill Pine and Bill Thomas to know that, of the major movie studios active during the Golden Age of Hollywood, it is Paramount Pictures that still survives as of this writing. It seems a safe bet that they might be taken aback by film budgets in the 21st century, and one can easily imagine them saying of using CGI

Bill Thomas, pictured circa 1982, never lost his love for movies.

effects to create scenes, "Well, what fun is *that*?" But, as studio executives and stockholders watch the always-unpredictable audience response to movies, a statement made by the Dollar Bills decades ago still holds true.

"If there are any rules, you can bet we don't make them in Hollywood. They're made by the guy who walks up to the boxoffice and buys a ticket. And as far as we can figure out, the only rule he sticks by is that he must get his money's worth."[73]

Feature Films

Power Dive (1941)

Cast: Richard Arlen (*Brad Farrell*), Jean Parker (*Carol Blake*), Helen Mack (*Betty Coles*), Roger Pryor (*Daniel McMasters*), Don Castle (*Doug Farrell*), Cliff Edwards (*Squid Watkins*), Billy Lee (*Brad Coles*), Thomas Ross (*Professor Blake*), Louis Jean Heydt (*Johnny Coles*), Ralph Byrd (*Jackson*), Helen Lynd (*Mabel*), Tom Dugan (*Waiter*), Alan Baldwin (*Young Reporter*), Pat West (*Bob*), Edward Earle (*Col. Ryan*), James Seay (*Radio Operator*), Wheeler Oakman (*Sam*), William Hall (*Army Sergeant*)

Crew: James Hogan (*Director*), Maxwell Shane, Edward Churchill (*Screenplay*), Paul Franklin (*Story*), John W. Rogers (*Associate Producer*), John Alton (*Director of Photography*), J.R. Cosgrove (*Special Photographic Effects*), F. Paul Sylos (*Art Director*), Robert Crandall (*Editor*), C. Bakaleinikoff (*Musical Score*), Farrell Redd, W.M. Dalgleish (*Sound Recording*)

Released May 1941. 68 minutes.

Experienced test pilot Brad Farrell, who suffered a broken leg on his most recent flight for McMasters Aviation, is determined that his younger brother, Doug, will not follow in his footsteps. When Doug shows up in Los Angeles with his newly received aeronautical engineering degree in hand, Brad gets him a job as a draftsman at McMasters, but the younger sibling is still set on flying.

The brothers meet beautiful Carol Blake, who wants their help getting McMasters to review her father's plans for an experimental plastic plane. Both are attracted to her (though Brad has been known to say, "Women and planes shouldn't mix"), but her priority is her father, blinded in an accident three years earlier, who is counting on the chance to have his plane put into production.

The rivalry between the brothers intensifies as they both vie to win Carol's love. Impressed by Professor Blake's designs, Brad persuades his employer to put the plane into production. An opportunity to test the plane for Army officials puts both brothers in peril, with Brad forced to think fast if he hopes to survive.

"There's a gold mine in the sky!" declared a Pine-Thomas ad promoting this, the first of its airplane adventure trilogy. Made at a reported cost of $86,000, *Power Dive*'s low budget doesn't intrude badly here, though a key crash scene is a bit too obviously

How many people does it take to make a Pine-Thomas programmer? The crew of their first film, *Power Dive*, poses with leading lady Jean Parker (seated, third from right).

spliced in from stock footage. Making their company's first feature provided with the young producers with some stressful moments. They arranged to shoot exteriors at the Metropolitan Airport in Van Nuys, giving those scenes a more authentic, polished look than they could have achieved on studio soundstages. But filming at a working airport had its downside, as Pine and Thomas' crew soon discovered. "There was so much civilian training, testing and military work going on," Thomas explained, "that the sound mixer couldn't hear what the players were saying."[1] Weather, too, threatened to interfere with the proceedings, leading Thomas to say ruefully, "If we don't get four days of sunshine soon, folks will wonder what ever became of Bill Thomas."[2]

Best-known for starring in *Wings* (1927), leading man Arlen is well-cast here as a handsome, heroic type slightly past his prime. It's a role he will repeat, with minor variations, in several future Pine-Thomas productions. Perhaps Pine-Thomas' Most Valuable Player (onscreen, at least), Jean Parker plays the first of her 12 characters for the company. For the most part, she's called upon to do what the leading lady usually does in a picture of this genre: stand on the airfield gazing anxiously upward to the sky.

From the moment we see that Brad keeps framed photographs on the wall of three colleagues who died in plane accidents, we know that a fourth man will join the display before the end titles appear. When that happens, Helen Mack (1913–1986) is given the opportunity to play a dramatic scene, which she does quite capably. Don Castle (1917–1966), as Doug, is almost constantly grinning in his early scenes, to the point of distraction, although later plot developments will wipe the smile off his face. He and Arlen are believably cast as brothers.

Providing the comedy relief is character actor Cliff Edwards (1895–1971), only a year after his famous role in Walt Disney's *Pinocchio*, playing Brad's goofy mechanic Squid. Squid, who has a way with malapropisms, also relies on a variety of good-luck charms, telling Brad, "Airplanes ain't safe. You're defying the law of gratitude." Simple-minded Squid, seeing Brad off on a cross-country flight, asks his buddy to slow down over Nebraska and drop off a letter, so as to save him some postage.

According to *Daily Variety* (January 8, 1941), actress Marsha Hunt was signed for a featured role in the film, but she did not appear in the finished product. The *Los Angeles Times* (January 24, 1941) reported that Pine and Thomas released Miss Hunt from her obligation when she was offered a long-term contract at MGM. According to syndicated columnist Jimmie Fidler (January 11, 1941), actor Neil Hamilton was sought for the supporting character of Daniel McMasters; Pine and Thomas balked at his agent's demand for $750 a week, selecting $500-a-week Roger Pryor instead. Pryor would go on to appear in six more P-T films over the next few years.

In the story, Brad breaks a world record by flying from Los Angeles to New York in seven hours and 18 minutes. In real life, such a feat would have cut about ten minutes from a transcontinental speed record set by Howard Hughes in 1937.

REVIEWS: "Mr. Thomas and Mr. Pine prove at once that they are gifted with plenty of production intelligence, a valuable sense of speed in marketing their wares, and knowledge of where the audience heart is located, for *Power Dive* has everything it takes to win the fans…. They've come up with a show that looks as if much more money went into it than actually did." *Hollywood Reporter*, April 3, 1941

"Everything runs according to the accepted formula … but the programmer is well-cast, moves fast, and contains several aerial thrills for action-minded fans…. Jean Parker gives a routine performance as the wide-eyed heroine." *Film Bulletin*, June 14, 1941

Forced Landing (1941)

CAST: Richard Arlen (*Lt. Dan Kendall*), Eva Gabor (*Johanna Van Deuren*), J. Carrol Naish (*Andros Banshek*), Nils Asther (*Col. Jan Golas*), Evelyn Brent (*Dr. Vidalek's Housekeeper*), Mikhail Rasumny (*Christmas*), Victor Varconi (*Hendrick Van Deuren*), John Miljan (*Gen. Valdane*), Frank Yaconelli (*Zomar*), Harold Goodwin (*Petchnikoff*), Thornton Edwards (*Felig*), Bobby Dillon (*Nando Banshek*), John Gallaudet (*Maj. Xanders*), Harry Worth (*Vidalek*)

CREW: Gordon Wiles (*Director*), Maxwell Shane, Edward Churchill (*Screenplay*), John W. Rogers (*Associate Producer*), John Alton (*Director of Photography*), Fred Jackman, Jr. (*Special Photographic Effects*), F. Paul Sylos (*Art Director*), Robert Crandall (*Editor*), Ben Berk (*Set Decorator*), James Wade (*Wardrobe*), Farrell Redd, W.M. Dalgleish (*Sound Recording*), Dimitri Tiomkin (*Musical Supervisor*)

RELEASED July 1941. 67 minutes.

Grounded in the U.S., pilot Dan Kendall accepts a job in the Air Corps of the country of Mosaque ("an island in the middle of the Pacific"). Awaiting his first assignment, Dan comes to the rescue of beautiful young Johanna Van Deuren, who's almost run down in the street. Attracted to Johanna, Dan puts the moves on her, unaware she's the fiancée of commanding officer Col. Golas. A brawl between the two men results in Dan being jailed. He's offered an early release if he'll resign from his Air Corps commission, and go to work for the Mosaque civil airline. Since two of the airline's planes have crashed recently, it is not a desirable assignment, but Dan accepts.

His first task is to fly supplies to a fort being constructed under the supervision of Johanna's father, a Dutch engineer. After Johanna receives word that her father has taken ill, Golas asks Dan to take her along on the trip. Arriving at the fort, Dan and Johanna see that work has come to a stop, and learn from her father that the workers have not been paid for two months. Dan persuades them to resume work, promising to return with a payroll within three days.

On the trip back, Dan lands when he sees the wreckage of another plane, which was flown by his buddy Petchnikoff. Hoping to find his friend still alive, Dan is instead captured by bandit Andros Banshek, who has been hijacking planes carrying military payroll. Banshek explains that he was formerly a general in the Mosaque government ("a fine, free government"), but went underground when the current regime took over. As Dan and Johanna are trying to escape Banshek's compound, the bandit's young son Nando is shot. Dan persuades Banshek that the only alternative is to fly with his son back to the city, where a qualified doctor can treat him. Just as Banshek is developing trust in Dan and Johanna, the doctor's housekeeper blows the whistle so as to collect the reward posted for Banshek's capture.

After Banshek is shot and killed, Dan and Johanna, now in love, are free to return to the city. General Golas accepts the loss of his fiancée to Dan, seemingly in good grace, and says he will escort Dan back to the fort to insure successful delivery of the payroll. Once underway, however, Dan finds that Johanna has stowed away on his plane, and that Golas has murderous intentions for the man who replaced him in her affections.

Offering customers action from the first minute (a stock footage plane crash that leads into the opening titles), this is a tidy little thriller that tells its story compactly and entertainingly. According to the program given to press members at an early preview, *Forced Landing* was intentionally set in no identifiable country. "Expected to be welcome entertainment for Latin-American audiences, too, *Forced Landing* steers clear of an actaul [*sic*] location ... the 'heavy' language spoken is nobody's talk. Such lines as 'Hoste fierta du lunda vendanzu' are merely 'double-talk.'"[3]

Aerial scenes were shot in the Palm Springs area. Susan Hayward was among the young actresses reported to have tested for the female lead. According to the *Los Angeles Times'* Edwin Schallert, writers Hugh Wedlock and Howard Snyder made an uncredited contribution to the *Forced Landing* screenplay, adding some comedic sequences.[4]

Arlen, again the two-fisted hero, shows Dan's bravado as a pilot ("I can fly that crate with my two arms around a blonde.") An experienced pilot in real life, Arlen was flying his own vehicle in several key scenes.

This was the film debut of 23-year-old Eva Gabor (1919–1995), cast as "a girl with danger in her sultry eyes," nearly a quarter-century before Lisa Douglas landed in Hooterville on TV's *Green Acres*. Plopped down amidst a sea of varying accents (of varying authenticity), it doesn't much matter that she's playing a young Dutchwoman with a Hungarian accent. The screenwriters have some fun with her shaky understanding of Dan's English. He's trying to find out why she came to Mosaque, and asks her, "How come?"

She replies, "On a boat." This film represents what's most likely a moviegoer's only opportunity to see one of the Gabor sisters at the helm of a military plane under attack.

J. Carrol Naish (1896–1973), considered by Hollywood in the 1940s a specialist in "ethnic" roles, contributes a little comedy with his portrayal of Banshek. Passing by a "Wanted" poster with a reward for his capture, he glares at the $5,000 amount and mutters, "Cheap-a-skates!" Naish had previously played a villain in *King of Alcatraz* (1938), produced by Bill Thomas at Paramount before the formation of Pine-Thomas Productions. Also trolling for laughs, with limited success, is Mikhail Rasumny (1890–1956), playing Dan's less-than-reliable mechanic Christmas ("He was a Christmas present to his mother, but she couldn't exchange him," Dan says).

Anyone who bought a ticket looking forward to seeing fifth-billed Evelyn Brent (1899–1975) was in for a letdown, as her part is extremely small. After being AWOL for the first 45 minutes of the film, she gets a great entrance, when the camera unexpectedly pans to reveal her sinister-looking face observing Banshek from the shadows. Unfortunately, she is given only one line to speak ("When do I get the reward?"), and is in and out of the movie in less than a minute.

Theaters that played *Forced Landing* reported solid business, letting Pine, Thomas, and their Paramount bosses know that the young producers were on the right track.

REVIEWS: "This is the second Bill Pine—Bill Thomas effort for Paramount release, and if the boys keep up the standard used in this film, they are going to make a lot of friends who operate theaters.... Miss Gabor is lovely and possesses that continental charm that has clicked before." *Film Daily*, July 3, 1941

"Plenty of action, thrills, suspense and romance for youngsters and oldsters alike ... an interesting story as timely as your daily newspaper." *Showmen's Trade Review*, July 19, 1941

Flying Blind (1941)

CAST: Richard Arlen (*Jim Clark*), Jean Parker (*Shirley Brooks*), Nils Asther (*Eric Karolek*), Marie Wilson (*Veronica Gimble*), Roger Pryor (*Rocky Drake*), Eddie Quillan (*Riley*), Grady Sutton (*Chester Gimble*), Dick Purcell (*Bob Fuller*), Kay Sutton (*Miss Danila*), Charlotte Henry (*Corenson's Secretary*), Joseph Crehan (*Nunnally*), William Hall (*Lew West*), Dwight Frye (*Leo Qualen*), James Seay (*Dispatcher*), George McKay (*Police Lieutenant*), Scott Groves (*Messenger Boy*), Mildred Shay (*Saleswoman*)

CREW: Frank McDonald (*Director*), Maxwell Shane, Richard Murphy (*Screenplay*), John W. Rogers (*Associate Producer*), Fred Jackman, Jr. (*Director of Photography*), F. Paul Sylos (*Art Director*), Robert Crandall (*Editor*), Ben Berk (*Set Decorator*), James Wade (*Wardrobe*), Farrell Redd, W.M. Dalgleish (*Sound Recording*), Dimitri Tiomkin (*Musical Score*)

RELEASED August 1941. 69 minutes.

An unusually bumpy flight on General Air Lines causes boss Mr. Nunnally to chew out pilots Jim Clark and Rocky Drake, though the fault was really the latter's. Frustrated, Jim quits his job and takes stewardess Shirley Brooks with him to form "Honeymoon Air Service," a single-plane company that takes couples from Los Angeles to Las Vegas to get married.

Flying Blind was the third of Pine and Thomas' trio of aviation thrillers that established them as successful B-movie producers.

Despite all the accouterments of love and marriage surrounding him in his business, Jim is too busy with the new venture to pay proper romantic attention to Shirley, who loves him. When she accepts the proposal of another man, Jim plots to get his rival out of the way, by arranging a phony job for him in New Jersey.

Jim, along with Shirley and mechanic Riley, transports a lively group of passengers for an overnight stay in Las Vegas. Among them are slow-witted Scoutmaster Chester Divine and his bride-to-be, chatterbox Veronica. Also aboard, posing as another bridegroom, is enemy agent Eric Karolek, who has stolen the plans for a transformer that is a vital component of the Army's new bomber. When Rocky Drake shows up for the return flight, asking to be flown back to Los Angeles, Jim reluctantly agrees, not knowing his former co-pilot is in cahoots with Karolek. When word comes over the radio of a murder that took place at the Las Vegas airport, Karolek's identity is revealed. He disables the plane's transmitter, and demands at gunpoint to be taken to Mexico.

En route, a storm and an engine block that shakes loose conspire to disable the plane's controls, forcing Jim to make an emergency landing. The passengers and crew are stranded in a remote area, with matters made much worse when Chester tries to light a signal fire and sets the dry brush around them ablaze. Finding the missing transformer aboard the plane, Jim realizes only a few hours remain to warn officials before the new Army bomber will take off, and be headed for disaster without the stolen part.

Although a consistently entertaining film, *Flying Blind* may have left action fans a bit disappointed in its first half, which literally never gets off the ground. For half an hour or so, the main story element concerns Jim and Shirley's stalled romance, and the schemes and misunderstandings keeping them apart. Those action fans who stuck it out, however, or wandered back into the auditorium from the concession stand, were rewarded with an exciting second half that provides gunplay, a brush fire, and plenty of aerial thrills. According to Pine-Thomas publicity, the concept of a "Honeymoon Air Service" was taken from a similar company operated by Richard Arlen in real life.

Arlen is well-suited to his lead role, playing a decent man who lacks the instinct for romance; as his former boss Nunnally tells him, perhaps overstating his case, "You've got an adding machine for a brain, and a checkbook for a heart." Vivacious Jean Parker has one of her better early roles for Pine-Thomas here, as the script gives her varied emotions and reactions to play. She even makes convincing the scene in which her character nonchalantly hands the bad guy his gun during an onboard fight, convinced the whole incident is phony, just her man's attempt to put on a heroic front for her.

Lending interest in the supporting cast are Marie Wilson (1916–1972), playing a character not unlike the one she will later make famous on radio and TV's *My Friend Irma*, and Grady Sutton (1906–1995) as her slightly befuddled spouse. Eddie Quillan (1907–1990) supplies comedic support as well, as a nervous mechanic who's awaiting the birth of his child. Nils Asther (1897–1981) exudes pure villainy as the enemy agent. Dwight Frye (1899–1943), only a few years from his early demise, shows up briefly as well.

This is the first of two Pine-Thomas films to offer a supporting part to former child actress Charlotte Henry (1914–1980), who had been given a star buildup several years earlier by none other than Pine and Thomas, when they were Paramount publicity men promoting *Alice in Wonderland* (1933). Seen as Miss Davila is actress Kay Sutton (1915–1988), whose real-life elopement with "Honolulu millionaire" Clifton Stokes Weaver threatened to disrupt the production schedule.

Richard Murphy (1912–1993), who would contribute to the screenplays of three early P-T films, went on to create TV's *The Felony Squad*.

REVIEWS: "It's a fast moving, timely drama with some excellent comedy interwoven into the script and the result will please theatergoers in any walk of life. Performances are well night perfect … on the directorial side, Frank McDonald rates a big hand for his top-flight job." *Showmen's Trade Review*, August 23, 1941

"Paced at high speed and peppered with humor which builds up to a lethally melodramatic high point, the film includes not a dull moment in its running time." *Motion Picture Daily*, August 19, 1941

No Hands on the Clock (1941)

CAST: Chester Morris (*Humphrey Campbell*), Jean Parker (*Louise Campbell*), Rose Hobart (*Marion West*), Dick Purcell (*Red Harris*), Astrid Allwyn (*Gypsy Toland*), Rod Cameron (*Tom Reed*), George Watts (*Oscar Flack*), James Kirkwood (*Warren Benedict*), Billie Seward (*Rose Madden*), Robert Middlemass (*Chief Bates*), Grant Withers (*Harry Belding*), Lorin Raker (*Clyde Copley*), George Lewis (*Dave Paulson*), Ralph Sanford (*Officer Gamble*), John Gallaudet (*Alex*), Keye Luke (*Severino*), Jack Norton (*Bartender*), Milburn Stone (*FBI Man*)

CREW: Frank McDonald (*Director*), Maxwell Shane (*Screenplay*), Geoffrey Homes (*Novel*), Fred Jackman, Jr. (*Director of Photography*), F. Paul Sylos (*Art Director*), William Ziegler (*Editor*), Karl Zint (*Sound Recording*), Irvin Talbot (*Musical Director*), Paul Sawtelle (*Music Score*)

RELEASED December 1941. 76 minutes.

Investigator Humphrey Campbell of the Flack Missing Persons Bureau makes a collect call to tell his boss Oscar Flack that he found the young woman they were hired to locate—and married her. Moments later, the Campbells are witnesses to a bank robbery. Insisting nothing will stop their Reno honeymoon, Humphrey leaves the scene, and is annoyed when Oscar turns up at their hotel seeking his help with a case. With the encouragement of new wife Louise, who's been promised a mink coat by Oscar if she goes along, Humphrey reluctantly agrees to investigate the disappearance of Hal Benedict, son of a local rancher.

Among the missing Benedict's associates, who hang out at the Truckee River Hotel nearby, are a beautiful blonde who seems suspiciously eager to make Humphrey's acquaintance, a piano player, and a redhead named Irene Donovan who may have been Hal's girlfriend. Paying a visit to Irene's house, Humphrey finds her dead, a silver dollar in her hand, and Warren Benedict's pretty young ward Rose at the scene of the crime.

Humphrey soon realizes that he's been roped into an assignment that's far more complex than he was promised by his boss, and one that results in him being suspected of murder by the local police. His involvement with, in rapid succession, a blonde, a redhead, and a brunette do little to ease Louise's second thoughts.

With bank robber Red Harris and his gang as well as two FBI men on his trail, Humphrey learns that he bears a striking resemblance to a former Harris gang member. Letting himself be taken into custody by the revenge-seeking Harris, Humphrey must persuade the gang leader to join forces with him to identify the real murderer.

Maxwell Shane's screenplay adapted a 1939 novel of the same title by Daniel Main-waring, who published it under his "Geoffrey Homes" pseudonym. It was the second to feature the author's Humphrey Campbell character, who was introduced in *Then There Were Three* (1938). Shane's somewhat loose adaptation of the book used a number of its plot elements, as well as names for some of the key characters. However, Humphrey's wife Louise is an invention of the screenwriter; in the novel, he's a bachelor. Some aspects of Humphrey's character, notably his fondness for milk, come from Homes' novel. In the book, Humphrey's boss is Oscar Morgan, of the Morgan Missing Persons Bureau. The title *No Hands on the Clock* refers to a large timepiece at the Darwin Mortuary, seen by Louise from the window of the Campbells' hotel room. It makes an intriguing film title, but has little to do with the story at hand. Still, paying customers get a bank robbery, two murders, blackmail, car chases, and assorted gunplay.

By what will soon become Pine-Thomas' standards, this is a relatively long film at 75 minutes. Even so, screenwriter Shane had enough difficulty fitting in all the plot elements that more than one reviewer found the end result hard to follow. The final scene finds Campbell using everything but a chalkboard and a pointer to explain the plot.

One slightly odd scene finds Humphrey Campbell stripping to his underwear to take a shower, and then recoiling in embarrassment when his new wife opens the bathroom door. Since he's seemed anything but the bashful type up to that point, the scene tells us either something about the state of motion picture censorship in 1941, or something about the state of the newlyweds' relationship.

Though we're told Warren Benedict is a prosperous rancher, the budget doesn't allow for a look at his property. Instead, we see a brief scene shot in close-up at the entrance to the ranch, and then scenes set in the more modest nearby home of his lady friend, Marion West.

Chester Morris (1901–1970) makes his Pine-Thomas debut with an assured performance. He will ultimately star in eight pictures for the company, all within a three-year period. A few months after the release of *No Hands on the Clock*, he will begin his popular series of "Boston Blackie" programmers, which will keep him occupied for nearly a decade.

Jean Parker has some comic moments as the detective's wife who watches in dismay as her honeymoon turns

Marriage to detective Humphrey Campbell (Chester Morris) will never be dull, as new wife Louise (Jean Parker) learns in *No Hands on the Clock*.

into a business trip. Along the way, she's locked into the bathroom, subjected to an unexpected shower while fully clothed, and forced to drink milk (which gives her hives) to cover for her new husband.

Keye Luke (1904–1991) is unbilled for his single scene as a former manservant at the Benedict ranch. Perennial movie drunk Jack Norton (1889–1958) plays the bartender in the Nugget Room, who looks askance at Humphrey, and his refreshment of preference—milk. This is a relatively early role for Rod Cameron (1910–1983), who within a few years would establish himself as a reliable star of B Westerns and serials. Early casting notices indicated that actress Florence Rice had been cast in the film, though she didn't turn up in the finished product.

Though Pine and Thomas had taken an option on multiple novels featuring the Humphrey Campbell character, this was the only film to result from the pact. However, author Mainwaring would become an important contributor to the outfit's future films.

REVIEWS: "So numerous are the clues introduced to lead the audience away from the culprit ... that even after the murder or murders have been solved and the goings-on explained, many in the audience are likely to remain as mystified as ever." *Motion Picture Daily*, December 8, 1941

"Although the characters of the private detective ... and his meddling bride ... suggest a series, the succeeding films will have to be better than this.... The film is fast-moving even if a swift succession of murders, gun battles, and wild chases do not always make for sustained interest." *Film Bulletin*, December 15, 1941

Torpedo Boat (1942)

CAST: Richard Arlen (*Skimmer Barnes*), Jean Parker (*Grace Holman*), Mary Carlisle (*Jane Townsend*), Phillip Terry (*Tommy Whelan*), Dick Purcell (*Ralph Andrews*), Ralph Sanford (*Hector Bobry*), Oscar O'Shea (*Captain Mike*), Warren Hymer (*Marine*), William Haade (*Big Sweeney*), Virginia Sale (*Mrs. Sweeney*), Ella Boros (*Secretary*)

CREW: John Rawlins (*Director*), Maxwell Shane (*Screenplay*), Paul Franklin, Aaron Gottlieb (*Story*), Fred Jackman, Jr. (*Director of Photography*), F. Paul Sylos (*Art Director*), Freddie Rich (*Music Score*), William Ziegler (*Editor*), L.J. Myers (*Sound Recording*)

RELEASED January 1942. 70 minutes.

Buddies Skimmer Barnes and Tommy Whelan have developed an idea for a new model of torpedo boat. Their entry into a race goes awry when their boat collides with one entered by well-to-do Jane Townsend. But their prospects improve when their friend Ralph Andrews, manager of a shipbuilding factory, gives them jobs there. The friendship of Skimmer and Tommy is tested when the latter falls in love with and marries nightclub singer Grace Holman, who is his pal's ex-girlfriend. Skimmer, however, finds that he is growing fond of Jane Townsend.

Skimmer and Tommy finally succeed in getting a test for their prototype boat, but the experiment turns tragic when the boat crashes, and Tommy is killed. Skimmer tries to set things right by constructing a new model, while Jane works to perfect his earlier design. Both boats are put to the test by the Navy, in a competition that could turn deadly for Skimmer and his friends.

According to *Daily Variety* (September 3, 1941), screenwriter Maxwell Shane's basic idea for *Torpedo Boat* might actually have practical application in U.S. naval operations: "Shane centered his yarn about a fleet of tiny, swift boats carried by a big mother ship, much as airplane carriers transport war planes. In his story Shane has the sides of the vessel opening up and the small boats dashing to the fray." The concept was sufficiently intriguing that boat designer Ralph Shelley created models and plans that were to be shared with Navy leaders; Shane said the Navy would be given free rein to use his idea in any way officers saw fit.

Early trade announcements indicated that a Paramount contract player named Frances would take the female lead; they disagreed on whether that would be Frances Farmer or Frances Gifford. Mary Carlisle (1914–2018) worked only once with Pine-Thomas; the onetime MGM contract player was a WAMPAS Baby Star of 1932. Ella Boros, employed as a secretary in Paramount's publicity department, made her screen debut as an actress in *Torpedo Boat*—cast as a secretary.

This was the only P-T directorial assignment for John Rawlins (1902–1997), who was at the helm of numerous B films in the 1940s, including two entries in the "Dick Tracy" series.

Though some industry naysayers were telling Pine and Thomas that movie audiences were tired of wartime stories, *Torpedo Boat* gained an unexpected timeliness with the attack on Pearl Harbor in December 1941. Said the *Los Angeles Times*' Philip K. Scheuer (January 4, 1942), "*Torpedo Boat* is one of those modest Pine and Thomas affairs which might have slipped by without a ripple a month ago, but which today sounds like prophecy." Paramount hurried the film into release, also sending a print to the Naval Affairs Committee of the U.S. House of Representatives.

REVIEWS: "Production seems to be a series of process shots which offers no support to the weak story idea. It has been done many times before and in a more credible manner.... Considering material, Arlen and Terry turn in acceptable performances." *Film Daily*, January 19, 1942

"This action picture is not up to the standard previously set by Producers Pine and Thomas. The story is much too involved and complicated for this type of picture.... No sympathy is aroused for Arlen at all until the very end." *Showmen's Trade Review*, January 17, 1942

I Live on Danger (1942)

CAST: Chester Morris (*Jeff Morrell*), Jean Parker (*Susan Richards*), Elisabeth Risdon (*Mrs. Morrell*), Edward Norris (*Eddie Nelson*), Dick Purcell (*Norm Thompson*), Roger Pryor (*Bert Jannings*), Douglas Fowley (*Joey Farr*), Ralph Sanford (*Angie Moss*), Edwin Maxwell (*Wingy Keefe*), Patsy Nash (*Dilly*), Joe Cunningham (*Inspector Conlon*), Bernadene Hayes (*Jonesy*), Billy Nelson (*George "Longshot" Harrison*), Vicki Lester (*Keefe's Secretary*), William Bakewell (*Mac*), Charlotte Henry (*Nurse*), Anna Q. Nilsson (*Mrs. Sherman*), Eddie Kane (*Doctor*), Herbert Rawlinson (*Chief of Police*), Edward Keane (*Chief Inspector E.G. Lambert*), Bill Cartledge (*Newsboy*)

CREW: Sam White (*Director*), Maxwell Shane, Richard Murphy, Lewis R. Foster (*Screenplay*), Lewis R. Foster, Alex Gottlieb (*Original Story*), Fred Jackman, Jr. (*Director of Photography*), F. Paul Sylos (*Art Director*), William Ziegler (*Editor*), Charles S. Althouse (*Sound Recording*), Freddie Rich (*Music Score*)

RELEASED June 1942. 73 minutes.

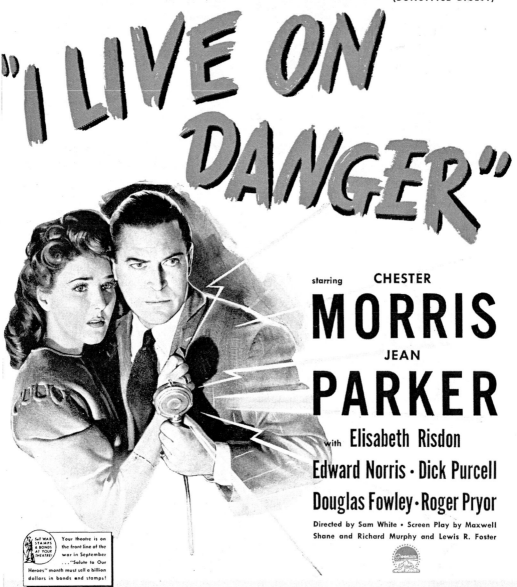

Trade-paper ad for *I Live on Danger*, emphasizing the positive reviews it received, and the hoped-for star power of Jean Parker and Chester Morris.

Jeff Morrell, "Special Events Reporter" for the Allied Broadcasting radio network, is competing with his rival Norm Thompson to be chosen for a business trip to London. Thompson brings in a big scoop when he's first on the scene at the murder of a gambling racketeer, and sees young Eddie Nelson, recently released from prison, running away. While Thompson covers the story of a manhunt for Nelson, Jeff's partying with a couple of showgirls, causing him to miss his assignment to broadcast a boxing match live.

Jeff's blunder results in him being fired, but boss Bert Jannings changes his tune when Jeff is the only reporter on hand a passenger ship, the S.S. *Lorna Queen*, explodes and burns just a short distance offshore. Jeff recognizes one of the survivors as Susan Richards, pictured with the fugitive Nelson in a newspaper photo. Taking charge of Susan while she's dazed, Jeff installs her at his mother's house, where she recuperates, not disclosing her true identity.

Newspapers report that Nelson has been killed, but Jeff deduces that he is alive, and that Susan has arranged a rendezvous with him. Tipping off the police, Jeff is responsible for getting Nelson captured, and the young man is soon sentenced to death.

Having fallen in love with Susan, Jeff is taken aback to learn that Nelson is her brother, not her boyfriend. But given his part in convicting Nelson, Susan wants nothing more to do with him. With only days left until Nelson is executed, Jeff continues pursuing the case that the police consider closed, determined to prove his innocence.

I Live on Danger was originally announced as "I'll Be Back in a Flash." According to director Sam White, it was the early career of Walter Winchell that inspired the lead character—"Winchell was the guy who broke the ice on that type of reporting."[5]

This is a very entertaining film, with Morris well-cast as a hotshot reporter who only belatedly begins to understand that the tragedies he reports affect people's lives. Morris is seen in a brief action sequence immediately preceding the opening titles, jumping out of the frame at a roaring fire he's covering after saying to his radio audience (and moviegoers), "Don't go away! I'll be back!" He makes amusing the scene in which Jeff, unable to reach the scene of a prizefight on time, tries to improvise his broadcast from a hotel ballroom, using whatever's at hand to generate sound effects to support his totally imaginary blow-by-blow coverage.

Jean Parker appears at about the 20-minute mark to play Susan, a young woman with a not completely lily-white past. As Jeff tells her, "When I picked you up on the beach, you were a story," but Parker's performance shows how her predicament humanizes the fast-talking newsman. Though it comes as a bit of a surprise to see that freewheeling, cynical Jeff still lives at home with Mom, Elisabeth Risdon (1887–1958) and Morris have a nice mother-son rapport in their scenes together.

Pine-Thomas stalwart Ralph Sanford (1899–1963) can't do much with the weak comedy scripted for Jeff's sidekick Angie, a chubby man who's a glutton for food. He's more effective in the scene where he chides his friend for his callousness about human lives, warning him that one day he will understand when a story affects him personally. Dick Purcell is seen as Jeff's smoother, more professional rival, of whom Morrell complains, "His delivery's about as exciting as a pause for station identification!" Roger Pryor (1901–1974) plays yet another reasonable boss whose patience is tried by an impulsive Pine-Thomas hero, at one point declaiming to Jeff, "Have pity on my blood pressure and cover that fire!" Former silent-screen star Anna Q. Nilsson (1888–1974) has a nice bit as one of the shell-shocked survivors of the *Lorna Queen* disaster, being pressed by Jeff for news as she is still struggling to process the horrific situation.

White, who enjoyed working with leading man Chester Morris, thought the final product "a dandy little picture."[6] Moviegoers' opinions, as reported by exhibitors in *Motion Picture Herald*'s "What the Picture Did for Me" column, varied. In the December 19, 1942, issue, one theater owner complained, "Very weak—both on entertainment and business. One of those we'd have been happier not to have played." But in a small Oklahoma town, another exhibitor reported (October 17, 1942), "Good action picture and good business."

REVIEWS: "Chester Morris plays one of those fast chattering radio commentators that are allegedly always on the spot with blow-by-blow reports of prizefight or disaster for the networks…. [The film] has an experienced cast and sufficient production values to permit a wide range of scene." *Motion Picture Herald*, June 13, 1942

"…fairly entertaining program fare. It is a rehash of an old theme … but since the action is steady, and there is some excitement and suspense, one's interest is held fairly well." *Harrison's Reports*, June 20, 1942

Wildcat (1942)

CAST: Richard Arlen (*Johnny Maverick*), Arline Judge (*Nan Deering*), William Frawley (*Oliver Westbrook*), Larry "Buster" Crabbe (*Mike Rawlins*), Arthur Hunnicutt (*"Watch-fob" Jones*), Elisha Cook, Jr. (*Harold "Chicopee" Nevins*), Ralph Sanford (*"Grits" O'Malley*), Alec Craig (*Joseph Campbell*), John Dilson (*Gus Sloane*), Will Wright (*John Smithers*), Jessica Newcombe (*Martha Smithers*), Billy Benedict (*Bud Smithers*), Dick Elliott (*Harris*), Sam Flint (*Giles*), Tom Kennedy (*Fred*), Fred Sherman (*Culley*)

CREW: Frank McDonald (*Director*), Maxwell Shane, Richard Murphy (*Screenplay*), North Bigbee (*Original Story*), Fred Jackman, Jr. (*Director of Photography*), F. Paul Sylos (*Art Director*), William Ziegler (*Editor*), Charles S. Althouse (*Sound Recording*), Freddie Rich (*Music Score*)

RELEASED September 1942. 70 minutes.

Wildcatter Johnny Maverick is on his way to the town of Antrim Bend, where a sizable reward is being offered to the first man who strikes oil. En route, he picks up a hitchhiker, young Harold Nevins, who wants to break into the oil business himself.

Despite putting his best foot forward with a flashy car and wardrobe, Maverick is nearly broke. After he and Nevins, whom he nicknames "Chicopee" after his hometown, find signs of oil seepage on one piece of property, Maverick bluffs his way into obtaining a lease and equipment despite his lack of funds. He's unhappy to see that his former boss, Mike Rawlins, is setting up his own rig nearby; Maverick still blames Rawlins for shorting his pay when he worked for him, and the men race to see who can get their operations up and running sooner.

Time pressures, competition from Rawlins, and the use of aging equipment take their toll on Maverick's crew when Chicopee is killed in a fall. Con artists Oliver Westbrook and Nan Deering, arriving in Antrim Bend to fleece the local poker players, read about Chicopee's death in the newspaper, and hatch an idea. Nan appears at Maverick's camp and claims to be Nevins' sister, leading a guilt-ridden Johnny to promise her his ex-partner's share of the proceeds. Staying on to act as camp cook while awaiting her reward, Nan finds her sympathies drawn to Johnny and his men, and begins to regret her plan to rook him.

As time, money, and options run out, Mike Rawlins is on the verge of successfully sabotaging Maverick's operation. An angry Maverick says he'll blow up his own rig before letting Rawlins take over, not anticipating that there will be a surprising result. Meanwhile, after Rawlins takes pleasure in telling his rival that his lady friend Nan is in no way related to the late Chicopee Nevins (something she herself was about to confess), Maverick's whole world seems to be collapsing.

Described by Paramount publicists as "literally bristling with spectacular action and exciting adventure," *Wildcat* launched what would become a familiar pattern in Pine and Thomas' pictures, following the heroics of a bold crew of blue-collar men as they work in a dangerous industry. In the first couple of reels, Johnny Maverick, with his fast-talking, slightly dishonest ways, seems a role better suited to Pine-Thomas' other favorite leading man, Chester Morris. Still, Richard Arlen is his usual professional self, handling the characterization well.

Sporting the mustache that seemed to be part-and-parcel of his villainous roles, Buster Crabbe (1908–1993) makes his first appearance for Pine-Thomas Productions as bad guy Mike. Some ten years earlier, Crabbe had been given his earliest Hollywood break when he won the "King of the Jungle" promotional contest organized by then-press agents Pine and Thomas, and subsequently appeared in *Illegal Traffic* (1938), one of Thomas' earlier Paramount Bs. It's a bit surprising to see character actor William Frawley (TV's "Fred Mertz") billed above Crabbe in the opening titles. However, Frawley does in fact have more screen time here, with Crabbe's role as Mike Rawlins being distinctly subordinate.

According to the *Los Angeles Times*' Edwin Schallert (December 13, 1941), Pine and Thomas encountered "considerable difficulty" selecting a leading lady for *Wildcat*, envisioning "a girl of the Jean Harlow type." The assignment finally went to actress Arline Judge (1912–1974). Cast as a shadier lady than the typical female lead of a Pine-Thomas film, Judge skillfully manages to convey both the character's hard-boiled edges, as well as the softer side that emerges as she falls in love with Johnny Maverick.

Off-camera, Judge had clearly mastered the skill of roping a man, as she was married eight times. According to columnist May Mann, Miss Judge's divorce from millionaire Dan Topping (later co-owner of the New York Yankees) had left her in fine financial shape in the early 1940s, but she was bored in retirement, and convinced Pine and Thomas that "she'd work her inch-long fingernails to the bone for a chance [at a comeback]. And they plumped her into a picture."[7] *Daily Variety* (January 13, 1942) reported that Pine-Thomas had "signed Arline Judge to a three-picture optional contract," but her only other released film for the company after *Wildcat* was *Take It Big* two years later.

Elisha Cook, Jr. (1903–1995), coming to *Wildcat* not long after filming his well-remembered role in *The Maltese Falcon*, plays a relatively normal, if slightly intense, young man here. Arthur Hunnicutt (1910–1979), as one of Maverick's loyal crew members, has fun with his character, a man who calmly tells anyone who'll listen that he's been dead for years. Busy character actor Dick Elliott (1886–1961), whose working relationship with Bill Thomas dated back to *Campus Confessions*, makes the first of several appearances for Pine-Thomas here.

Visiting the set during production, columnist Robbin Coons (March 1, 1942) watched as Richard Arlen and Buster Crabbe prepared for a fight scene. With his eye, as always, on the money, Bill Pine was heard to complain, "Holy smoke! Rehearsing 20 minutes and no scene yet!" An early scene shows Maverick nearly out of gas while driving to the drilling site. Extracting 80 cents from his passenger Chicopee, Johnny is able to gas up enough to finish the trip. That price would have fetched about five gallons at the time.

REVIEWS: "…moderately entertaining program fare [with] some fast action, comedy, and romance … the direction and the performances are nothing to brag about." *Harrison's Reports*, August 29, 1942

"Despite the familiar basic texture of the yarn, writers and director Frank McDonald have tossed in plenty of lusty action around the oil fields and maintain good pace throughout…. Oil-well fire is expertly staged and neatly cut for brief but effective presentation." *Variety*, September 2, 1942

Wrecking Crew (1942)

CAST: Richard Arlen (*Matt Carney*), Chester Morris (*Duke Mason*), Jean Parker (*Peggy Starr*), Joe Sawyer (*Fred Bunce*), Esther Dale (*Mike O'Glendy*), Alexander Granach (*Joe Poska*), Evelyn Brent (*Martha Poska*), Billy Nelson (*Tom Kemp*), William Hall (*Red*), Frank Melton (*Pete*), Fred Sherman (*Emil*), Alec Craig (*Charlie*), Nigel DeBrulier (*Father Zachary*), Byron Foulger (*Mission Worker*), Ralph Dunn (*Bartender*), Dick Elliott (*Salesman*), Jody Gilbert (*Woman in Bar*)

CREW: Frank McDonald (*Director*), Maxwell Shane, Richard Murphy (*Screenplay*), Robert T. Shannon, Mauri Grashin (*Original Story*), Fred Jackman, Jr. (*Director of Photography*), F. Paul Sylos (*Art Director*), Alex Widlicska (*Special Effects*), William Ziegler (*Editor*), Charles S. Althouse (*Sound Recording*), Freddy Rich (*Music Score*)

RELEASED November 1942. 72 minutes.

The O'Glendy Wrecking Company has won a contract to demolish a 12-story hotel. With the company in financial straits, owner "Mike" O'Grady (widow of the founder) has guaranteed rapid completion of the work with a $10,000 bond, putting extra pressure on the men in her crew.

As work gets underway, Duke Mason shows up needing a job. He and foreman Matt Carney are old friends, but Carney is reluctant to hire him; several of his crew members say that Duke is a jinx, and that accidents happen on worksites when he's around. Mike, who has a soft spot for Duke, gives him a job anyway. But when crew member Joe Poska is killed in an accident, Duke is blamed by some of his coworkers.

Duke hears a mission worker on the street proclaim that the key to success in life is helping others. That night, when he sees a beautiful young lady being tossed out of a bar, he steps in to assist her. Admitting that she's been reduced to stealing to survive, Peggy intends to throw herself into the river and end it all. Duke doesn't believe she's serious, but when she tries, he fishes her out of the water and installs her temporarily at his apartment, telling people she's his cousin. Matt, immediately attracted to Peggy, begins romancing her, unaware that she's no relation to his buddy Duke, who also takes a liking to her.

The guys convince Mike to hire Peggy as a stenographer at the demolition company, and from then on things seem to look up. Matt persuades Mike that a night crew is needed to finish the work by the deadline, and Duke is given the job of foreman. When Duke finds a cigar box containing cash in the wreckage of the building, he uses it to help one of his men have an operation on his injured arm, and to help support Joe Poska's widow. He concludes that Peggy is his good-luck charm, and has broken his jinx.

The climactic action scene between Chester Morris (left) and Richard Arlen is depicted in this lobby card for *Wrecking Crew.*

A disgruntled ex-employee, Kemp, who's taken to drink, tries to get his job back, but Duke turns him down. In retaliation, Kemp lets loose the cannonball used for demolition. The resulting damage slows down work on the demolition, and Duke is blamed for the incident.

Having finished his engineering degree and ready to begin a new life, Matt proposes marriage to Peggy. After a falling-out between the two men over the cannonball incident, Duke quits in a huff, asking Peggy to accompany him. Learning that Matt wants to marry Peggy, Duke maliciously informs his buddy that she's not in fact his cousin, and that she was a thief when he first met her.

With Duke on his way out of town (alone), Matt and Mike receive word that the remains of the crumbling building are beginning to collapse, with high winds threatening to send wreckage flying into the busy street below. Matt, working high above the street, is trapped by a falling beam, leaving last-minute arrival Duke to decide whether or not to help his longtime friend.

Perhaps it was inevitable that, having made money with pictures starring Richard Arlen and Chester Morris individually, Pine and Thomas decided to team them up. The result works well, with Arlen predictably cast as the sensible good guy and Morris taking the role of the irresponsible charmer. According to Bill Thomas, both actors graciously insisted the other should take top billing. Ultimately, the matter was settled by a coin flip, done by none other than columnist Louella Parsons, giving the picture some welcome publicity. Having previously co-starred nearly ten years earlier in Paramount's *Golden Harvest* (1933), Arlen and Morris would do so again for Pine-Thomas in *Aerial Gunner*.

Reminiscent of bigger-budgeted films like *Manpower* (1941), this tells a not wholly original story of two men working together at a dangerous job who both develop an interest in the same woman. Jean Parker is a relative latecomer, making her entrance nearly 20 minutes into the film, but does well with her scenes.

For the modern viewer, the early scenes are perhaps a bit too setbound to fully convey the sense of danger the filmmakers wanted. But the climax, which finds Matt and Duke stranded atop the rapidly crumbling remains of the building, still generates a sense of excitement and urgency.

The great character actress Esther Dale (1885–1961) has one of her bigger and more interesting roles here as the seemingly tough, but kindly, woman trying to run a company staffed by men. It's undeniably fun to see her pick up an office chair and smash through a wooden door, ready to break up a fight between Arlen and Morris. Several years earlier, Miss Dale and Jean Parker had played mother and daughter in RKO's *The Farmer in the Dell* (1936).

Evelyn Brent, a long way from her starring roles, is seen briefly as Mrs. Poska, widow of the worker killed in a fall. This is the first of five P-T films for character actor Joe Sawyer (1906–1982), who was known to Baby Boomers as Sergeant Biff O'Hara on TV's *The Adventures of Rin Tin Tin*. The ubiquitous Dick Elliott gets the movie started with his appearance as a traveling salesman who arrives for a stay at the hotel, only to learn it's about to be demolished.

"Built around the men who risk their necks daily for bread-and-butter, the men who clear the tracks for metropolitan growth," said trade ads for *Wrecking Crew*, promising it maintained the Pine-Thomas tradition of "solid, saleable thrill films with a punch and pace to keep any audience happy!" Responses submitted by exhibitors to *Motion Picture Herald*'s "What the Picture Did for Me" column (August 14, 1943) varied. In Kentucky: "Good ordinary action picture. Please[d] action fans and no complaints. Good business." But in small-town North Carolina, another theater owner reported, "Very slow moving, acting very poor and story nothing to write about. Crowd not pleased; were expecting something different."

The *Hollywood Reporter*'s Irving Hoffman, in his "Tales of Hoffman" column, reported a good-natured exchange between Pine-Thomas Productions and the owners of a demolition and salvage company based in Mississippi. Claiming that the film had encouraged friends and associates to make "disparaging remarks" about their work, the real-life wreckers offered a job as superintendent to Chester Morris, who seemingly knew more about the techniques of demolition than their own workers did. In their light-hearted response, the Dollar Bills said they would send out Morris "if you can come here and write our next script." They added, "If you are amazed at the manner in which Chester Morris made the sixteen-story building in *Wrecking Crew* disappear, please be advised that on the side Chester is also an amateur magician."[8]

REVIEWS: "For good action screenfare [*sic*] this holds a lot of entertainment. The story is interesting and exciting … suspense is built up to such a degree that most audiences will find themselves hanging onto the edge of their seats." *Showmen's Trade Review*, November 7, 1942

"Thrills, excitement and suspense run high…. There are some good comedy situations, human interest, and a love triangle … should more than satisfy the action fans." *Harrison's Reports*, November 7, 1942

Aerial Gunner (1943)

CAST: Chester Morris (*Sgt. Foxy Pattis*), Richard Arlen (*Lt. Jonathan Davis*), Jimmy Lydon (*Pvt. Sandy Lunt*), Lita [Amelita] Ward (*Peggy Lunt*), Dick Purcell (*Pvt. Lancelot "Gadget" Blaine*), Keith Richards (*Sgt. Henry Jones*), William Benedict (*Pvt. Jackson "Sleepy" Laswell*), Olive Blakeney (*Mrs. Sanford Lunt*), Robert Mitchum (*Sgt. Benson*), Barbara Pepper (*Blonde at Shooting Gallery*), John James (*Johnson*), Gil Frye (*Lt. Brandt*), Edward Earle (*Squadron Commanding Officer*), Frank Fenton (*Colonel*), Kirk Alyn (*Officer in Canteen*), Charles J. Jordan (*Trainer*)

CREW: William H. Pine (*Director*), Maxwell Shane (*Screenplay*), Jack F. Dailey (*Story Idea*), Fred Jackman, Jr. (*Director of Photography*), William Ziegler (*Editor*), F. Paul Sylos (*Art Director*), Charles S. Althouse (*Sound Recording*), Ben Berk (*Set Decorator*), Daniele Amfitheatrof (*Music Score*)

RELEASED March 1943. 78 minutes.

Jon Davis and Foxy Pattis have known each other since they were kids on the streets of New York. But while Jon grew up to build a career in the District Attorney's Office, Foxy (son of an ex-con) lives a more checkered life, just avoiding criminal prosecution. Foxy is enraged when his father commits suicide, believing that Jon and his colleagues hounded the old man into taking his own life. Jon narrowly evades a violent confrontation with Foxy.

Enlisting in the military, Jon is selected to attend gunnery school in Texas, where he's none too happy to find he'll be trained by none other than Sgt. Foxy Pattis. Fellow members of the crew under Foxy's watch include the always-drowsy "Sleepy" Laswell, who's having difficulty adjusting to daytime hours after holding a night job, "Gadget" Blaine, proud of his self-proclaimed ability to fix anything, and young Private Sandy Lunt. Lunt seems an unlikely choice to make a good gunner, but he's determined to honor the memory of his father, who died in service.

From the outset, Jon struggles with Foxy's efforts to undermine his training. Not helping matters is a rivalry that develops when both are attracted to Sandy's pretty sister Peggy. Even after Jon saves Foxy from injury during a training maneuver, the relationship between the two men is strained.

When the time comes to demonstrate their flying and shooting prowess, Jon does well, but Sandy chokes on his first try. Foxy allows him a second try, although everyone is dubious that the young recruit can handle the work. On his second flight, Sandy crashes and is killed. His sister, Peggy, blames Foxy, and refuses to see him again.

After going their separate ways, Jon does well in the service, and is promoted to lieutenant. Assigned to carry out his own bomber mission, he is surprised to find Foxy among his crew, along with Sleepy and Gadget. The bomber piloted by Jon is the last of three to return from a mission, and he comes back alone, injured. Confined to a hospital bed, Jon is urged by officers to tell the story of what happened on his perilous mission, and what became of the crew.

At first glance, *Aerial Gunner* looks like the typical Pine-Thomas product of the early to mid–40s, but in fact it represented an effort by the producers to step up their game, and make a product that could successfully compete with A pictures. With a 78-minute running time, it's longer than their typical B film, and enjoyed a longer shooting schedule. The company traveled to Harlingen, Texas, where the Harlingen Aerial Gunnery School had opened in 1941. Exterior scenes were filmed on the site, utilizing many of its enlisted men as extras and in bit parts. Robert MacArthur Crawford's song "Army Air Force" (with that "wild blue yonder") is the economical choice for music under the opening titles.

In trying to differentiate this film from their typical output, Pine and Thomas may have made a mistake in casting two lead actors so closely associated with their B product, though both deliver satisfying performances. Their characters have the type of relationship that was familiar to fans, as when they first cross paths at flight school:

DAVIS: Small war, isn't it?

PATTIS: Yeah, and not very exclusive.

Paramount contract player Jimmy Lydon (born 1923) was cast in the role of Sandy. Though Lydon was eager to move beyond his well-known characterization as teenage nitwit Henry Aldrich in a profitable B series, his casting here represents an uphill battle against that established persona, which had been all over movie screens in 1941 and 1942. The notion of Henry Aldrich joining a military bomber unit is almost inherently funny— imagine the citizens of Centerville scurrying for cover the first time he picks up a gun!— and the presence of the Bowery Boys' Billy Benedict as a fellow recruit doesn't help. Olive Blakeney (1899–1959), who played Lydon's mother in the Aldrich pictures, does so here as well. Still, Lydon is a solid actor, and he delivers a creditable performance.

Leading lady Amelita Ward (1923–1987), making her film debut, was reportedly discovered by Pine and Thomas during their location shoot in Texas. She would subsequently become the third wife of Dead End Kid Leo Gorcey. Column items planted prior to production indicated that Bill Thomas hoped to sign Janet Gaynor, who hadn't made a movie in about five years, to the female lead in *Aerial Gunner*.

The original story idea for *Aerial Gunner* came from Jack F. Dailey, a former Paramount publicity man who had worked for Pine. Enlisting in the Army in 1942, Dailey was appointed to oversee public relations for the Harlingen Aerial Gunnery School. He succeeded in interesting Pine and Thomas in making a film about the school and its men, with Maxwell Shane incorporating Dailey's ideas into a screenplay. After the completion of location shooting in Texas, Captain Dailey spent two weeks in Hollywood serving as technical advisor on the picture.[9]

Shane's screenplay uses a framing device, beginning with Jon's return from the deadly mission, and unfolding in flashback as he relates the saga in lavish detail to officers from his hospital bed. Jon has such a good memory he can even remember scenes he wasn't in, and his superiors show no signs of impatience as he offers years' worth of anecdotes in recalling how he and Foxy ended up on the same crew.

A lavish premiere event was hosted by the Harlingen Gunnery School in early May 1943, featuring a military parade, appearances by actors including Chester Morris and Gil Lamb, and a war bond rally.

REVIEWS: "With its timeliness and its subject matter, this is a picture that is bound to do exceptionally well at the box-offices of the nation … the picture holds a terrific amount of interest and education." *Showmen's Trade Review*, March 27, 1943

"The picture is William Pine's first undertaking as director and an achievement in two departments for a man who came from exhibition via exploitation to production." *Motion Picture Herald*, March 27, 1943

High Explosive (1943)

CAST: Chester Morris (*Buzz Mitchell*), Jean Parker (*Connie Baker*), Barry Sullivan (*Mike Douglas*), Ralph Sanford (*Squinchy Andrews*), Rand Brooks (*Jimmy Baker*), Dick Purcell (*Dave*), Barbara Lynn (*Doris Lynch*), Allan Byron [Jack Randall] (*Joe*), Vince Barnett (*Driver*)

CREW: Frank McDonald (*Director*), Maxwell Shane, Howard J. Green (*Screenplay*), Joseph Hoffman (*Original Story*), Fred Jackman, Jr. (*Director of Photography*), F. Paul Sylos (*Art Director*), Ben Berk (*Set Decorator*), William Ziegler (*Editor*), Charles S. Althouse (*Sound Recording*)

RELEASED March 1943. 63 minutes.

The Douglas Nitroglycerine Company is busier than ever, with a new contract just signed, but proprietor Mike Douglas is short on drivers. He tries to persuade ex-driver Buzz Mitchell, who's now racing midget cars, to sign on, but Buzz declines. But when Buzz is barred from racing after punching another race driver who almost caused an accident, he reconsiders and reports for work with Douglas.

Mike's secretary Connie, well aware of the dangers involved in hauling nitroglycerin, is dead set against her 21-year-old brother Jimmy taking a job as a driver. But wanting to support himself, and make enough money to marry his girlfriend Doris, Jimmy insists on trying, promising Connie he'll drive for only three months. Buzz flirts with Connie from his first day on the job, but she is carrying a torch for Mike, who's seemingly too busy with business concerns to return her interest.

Under Buzz's tutelage, Jimmy develops into a skilled nitro driver, while Connie begins to respond to the more sensitive side Buzz typically keeps hidden. But when Jimmy is killed in an accident while driving, Connie rejects Buzz outright. Desperately needing a load of nitroglycerin delivered by airplane to a raging fire, Mike enlists Buzz as pilot, promising him a $2,000 bonus. With Mike as his passenger, Buzz flies the plane, laden with explosives, on a night that unexpectedly turns foggy, leaving the two men up in the air with no visibility for a safe landing, and a gas gauge dangerously near empty.

High Explosive is a quintessential example of the Pine-Thomas B thriller of the 1940s, though it's a bit surprising that Richard Arlen is AWOL. The film's pace is brisk, the acting is highly competent, and several scenes (notably Jimmy's doomed effort to stop a runaway truck loaded with nitro) are exciting. While some of the plot developments are easy to foresee, the story keeps moving, and the aviation element, introduced relatively late in the film, adds an element of adventure. A Paramount ad in *Variety* (April 8, 1942) announced that the producers had bought the rights to an original story, "You Can't Live Forever," which ultimately found its way to the screen as *High Explosive*.

Chester Morris is happily cast as Buzz, who breezily dismisses the dangers of his work ("Only saps get hurt"), and has a brash exterior, but redeems himself when push comes to shove. He strikes a careful balance with his performance, making Buzz likable even when he's feeling his oats, and believably playing his developing maturity and responsibility. Jean Parker does well as Connie, her fear and tension surrounding the perils of Douglas' workplace both credible and moving. Still a newcomer to film work, Barry Sullivan (1912–1994) projects sincerity and strength as Mike Douglas (long before there was a television host by that name), and is well-matched with Parker. He had previously worked with Pine and Thomas on the patriotic short film *We Refuse to Die*. Rand Brooks (1918–2003), known for his featured performance in *Gone with the Wind*, has one of his better, more sizable film parts here as Connie's kid brother. Barbara Lynn (born 1922) was borrowed from 20th Century–Fox for her supporting role, one of only a handful on her brief filmography.

The film takes place in the recent past, as America is not yet at war in the early scenes, with the screenplay raising the stakes when Mike and his friends hear the news that Pearl Harbor has been attacked. It gets off to an awkward start, with Buzz's driving in an auto race depicted by unconvincing rear projection work, but is otherwise capably shot, performed, and edited. As in the upcoming *Alaska Highway*, the script of *High Explosive* makes the case that men who provide needed supplies for the war effort are as valuable in their own way as the men who enlist.

REVIEWS: "Although the story is ordinary, it holds one's attention ... because of the fast action and the numerous thrills. One is held in tense suspense during the closing situations...." *Harrison's Reports*, March 27, 1943

"Picture unfolds at a speedy pace, and contains sufficient excitement and meller [melodrama] ingredients to satisfy the action-minded customers.... Frank McDonald neatly paces direction from compact script...." *Variety*, March 24, 1943

Alaska Highway (1943)

CAST: Richard Arlen (*Woody Ormsby*), Jean Parker (*Ann Caswell*), Ralph Sanford (*Frosty Gimble*), Bill Henry (*Steve Ormsby*), Joe Sawyer (*Roughhouse*), Eddie Quillan ("*Shorty*" *Jones*), Harry Shannon (*John "Pop" Ormsby*), Edward Earle (*Blair Caswell*), Keith Richards (*Hank Lincoln*), Jack Wegman (*Sgt. Swithers*), Gary Gray (*Boy*), Kit Guard, Charles Sullivan (*Workers*)

CREW: Frank McDonald (*Director*), Maxwell Shane, Lewis R. Foster (*Screenplay*), Fred Jackman (*Director of Photography*), William Ziegler (*Film Editor*), F. Paul Sylos (*Art Director*), Charles S. Althouse (*Sound Recording*), Ben Berk (*Set Decorator*), Freddie Rich (*Music Score*)

RELEASED June 1943. 67 minutes.

After the Japanese attack on Pearl Harbor, the U.S. government makes it a top priority to complete a highway running between Alaska and Canada, which can be used to transport supplies for military operations. Working with engineer Blair Caswell to accomplish the project within a few months is "Pop" Ormsby, owner of the Ormsby Road Building Company. When the project is announced, Pop is counting on both his adult sons to join the crew. But while Steve, who aspires to be an engineer, readily signs on, his older brother Woody wants to play a more active role in the war, and plans to join the Marines.

Meeting up with their childhood friend Ann Caswell (Blair's daughter), who's now a beautiful young woman, makes Woody reconsider his plans. Ormsby and his men fight the elements, and undertake risky blasting operations, to clear the path for the new road, expected to meet at the halfway point with a second crew starting out from the opposite end.

But tensions arise between the Ormsby brothers when both find themselves pursuing Ann romantically. A competition between the brothers results in a co-worker being injured, and Steve, realizing he is losing Ann to Woody, insists on a transfer. Seeing progress on the road threatened, Ann's father pressures her to prevent Steve from leaving, so she breaks things off with Woody. As the lovers quarrel, a dangerous fire breaks out, and Woody must guide Ann to safety. But when a co-worker dies as the men fight the fire, Woody now decides he should bail out of the construction project. Before he can do that, a landslide puts the lives of Steve and a co-worker in jeopardy, and Woody is needed to step in for the rescue.

The main attraction of *Alaska Highway* in 1943 was its topicality. The U.S. Army Engineering Corps did construct a road such as the one depicted, completing the job in November 1942, with much public interest accompanying the project. Pine and Thomas were able to incorporate some footage of the actual work into this film, which begins with an acknowledgment thanking Canadian authorities "for authentic scenes filmed on the Alcan Highway." A narrator is used for some of these segments, which are inserted rather awkwardly into the fictional story of the film. Though the real-life construction of the highway was praised for being completed in a short time, *Daily Variety* columnist George E. Phair cracked (November 4, 1942), "Wait until Bill Pine and Bill Thomas get busy on the picture…. Those boys can build a cinematic highway at 35 miles an hour."

Still, production was not without challenges. As Bill Pine later recalled, "We found a road under construction about 30 miles in the mountains back of Reno." The location offered a suitably snowy look—for a time. "But by the time we got ready, the snow had melted and it looked like trouble for us and the budget, which are the same thing." The company enlisted the aid of a special effects man, who told them calmly, "We'll add the snow by process and no one will ever know the difference."[10] Once *Alaska Highway* was in the can, Pine and Thomas donated to the U.S. government much of the road-building equipment they had purchased to use in the film. Some of it they had already had to duplicate, with wooden models taking the place of real bulldozers, as the equipment was too heavy to rest comfortably on the floor of a soundstage.

Alaska Highway spends too much time back at camp with the men building the road, with setbound scenes that won't captivate an action-craving audience, and largely one-note characterizations. Trite comedy relief includes a subplot about possession of an electric blanket for the cold nights, and crew member Frosty's efforts to find love through a matchmaking firm.

Audience reactions at the time varied. An exhibitor in rural Iowa, reporting to the *Motion Picture Herald*'s "What the Picture Did for Me" column reported (March 11, 1944), "We had the biggest crowd in two years…. This picture is good and the farmers ate it up." But in Colorado, another theater owner complained, "The title drew a crowd but sent them home very disappointed. There is nothing in this picture."

Richard Arlen is competent as the hero who initially balks at working on a highway during wartime, saying, "I want to sling lead at the Japs, not mud." Arlen would have reason to remember the *Alaska Highway* shoot; during production, Bill Thomas introduced him to a smitten young fan, Maggie, who would become the actor's third wife. Jean Parker handles her assignment capably as the young lady both male leads knew in her childhood as "Sticky Face." For a time, in the middle of the picture, it seems as if the scriptwriters have simply forgotten Miss Parker and her character, but she does resurface eventually.

Given one of his bigger roles for Pine-Thomas here, Ralph Sanford provides much of the comedy relief as "Frosty," a crew member so dubbed because he is always feeling cold. No, the front man of the Rolling Stones is not to be found among the cast of this picture; he was born a few months after its release. This Keith Richards (1915–1987) is a character actor who has a smallish part as one of Ormsby's crewmen. Edward Earle, as Ann's father, has more to do here than he will in most of his other Pine-Thomas appearances.

Early trade paper blurbs indicated that director Frank McDonald, who had a background as a stage actor, would play a featured comic character in the film. Said one source, "He came into [Pine and Thomas'] office to give a demonstration of the kind of actor he'd want for the part, and the producers so highly approved his impersonation that they prevailed upon him to do the role."[11] However, this didn't come to pass.

REVIEWS: "Little imagination has been put into the treatment, and much of the action is slowed down by too much dialogue ... some interesting stock shots [are] not enough ... to overcome the triteness of the plot." *Harrison's Reports*, June 26, 1943

"With a title like *Alaska Highway* it should be easy to sell this picture ... those who definitely look for an epic, however, are in for disappointment." *Showmen's Trade Review*, June 26, 1943

Submarine Alert (1943)

CAST: Richard Arlen (*Lewis Deerhold*), Wendy Barrie (*Ann Patterson*), Nils Asther (*Dr. Arthur Huneker*), Roger Pryor (*G.B. Fleming*), Abner Biberman (*Commander Toyo*), Marc Lawrence (*Vincent Bela*), John Miljan (*Bambridge*), Patsy Nash (*Tina Deerhold*), Ralph Sanford (*Agent Freddie Grayson*), William Bakewell (*Pomeroy*), Dwight Frye (*Haldine*), Edward Earle (*Dr. Barclay*), Milburn Stone (*Lt. Winston*), Jack Carr (*Old Mill Gate Guard*), Edward Van Sloan (*Dr. Johann Bergstrom*), Will Wright (*Sheriff*), Harry Hayden (*Larson*), Robert Middlemass (*Johnny's Father*)

CREW: Frank McDonald (*Director*), Maxwell Shane (*Screenplay*), Fred Jackman, Jr. (*Director of Photography*), F. Paul Sylos (*Art Director*), Ben Berk (*Set Decorator*), William Ziegler (*Editor*), Charles S. Althouse (*Sound Recording*), Freddy Rich (*Music Score*)

RELEASED June 1943. 64 minutes.

American tankers transporting oil needed for the war effort are being torpedoed by a Japanese U-boat that targets them using leaked information about their routes and departure times. FBI agents determine that messages are being sent using a small but powerful radio transmitter, but are unable to pin down its location, as it is portable and moved frequently. Fleming, of the FBI, suggests that the Bureau arrange for some of the city's top radio engineers to be fired, in the hopes that one or more of them will be hired to share their technical expertise with the enemy.

Among those sacked is Lewis Deerhold of the Inter-American Broadcasting Company, who thinks he was targeted because he spent time overseas. The timing of his dismissal is particularly difficult for Lew, who is the guardian of his young niece, and was saving money for an operation she needs. Lew meets a woman, Ann Patterson, when he helps her stave off a purse snatcher, and the two begin a romance.

After applying for work at a radio repair shop, Lew is unexpectedly offered a job by

Stars Wendy Barrie and Richard Arlen get a bad reception from the enemy in *Submarine Alert*.

Dr. Arthur Huneker, who operates a health farm called the Old Mill Hot Springs. Lew is told the work he's doing is supporting a initiative involving radio therapy for the doctor's patients, but he's actually repairing the transmitter stolen from an inventor by the enemy. Ann, who works for Fleming, finds a clue in Lew's apartment that leads her to believe he may be disloyal to the U.S., and working in cahoots with the Nazis. When he is summoned to the FBI offices, Lew sees Ann's purse in Fleming's office, and in turn believes she has betrayed him.

While Lew is being questioned by the FBI, both the Nazis and an FBI agent search his apartment, and in the ensuing confrontation Agent Grayson is shot and killed. The police arrive at the scene only moments after Lew finds Grayson's body; he escapes from their clutches, leaving them to assume he committed the murder. Returning to the health farm, Lew persuades Dr. Huneker that he is happy to join their cause, for the right financial rewards. His ruse almost works, but his efforts to save the life of a shipping company executive being held prisoner there reveal his true loyalties. On the lam from the Nazis, Lew is picked up on the road by Ann. Both now suspicious of each other, they must join forces if they are to prevent the destruction of three more American tankers within the next few hours.

Submarine Alert began life as "Interceptor Command," a drama about fighter planes. When a high-ranking Air Force official asked Pine and Thomas to reconsider making the film (because the script called for enemy aircraft to penetrate American airspace), the producers regrouped and turned it into an underwater story. The result was an entertaining spy melodrama given a brisk pace by director Frank McDonald. Action fans get their money's worth, with extensive stock footage of maritime disasters, an exciting car chase, gunplay, and a slam-bang finale. McDonald frames some interesting shots, including a rather grisly one (for the period) of a terrified man about to be caught under the grinding teeth of a tractor.

Overall, there's a real boys' adventure feel to the story, making it appropriate that one of the good guys in the final reel is a youngster receiving and translating code on his ham radio set. In that spirit of innocence, the hero and heroine, trapped in a blisteringly hot steam room where the temperature has surpassed 140 degrees, don't yield to the temptation to remove, or even unbutton, any clothes as they near death from the stifling heat.

Arlen, sporting a mustache he hasn't worn in previous Pine-Thomas appearances, gets a real workout physically, if not dramatically. Wendy Barrie (1912–1978), who certainly knew her way around a B movie by 1943, gives a solid performance in her only Pine-Thomas outing. Child actress Patsy Nash, in her second feature for the company, is, to be perfectly frank, dreadful as Arlen's niece Tina. Mercifully she has little screen time. (Incredibly, Bill Thomas later claimed that, in casting Tina, he auditioned and rejected Margaret O'Brien, who would become a major child star with the release of *Journey for Margaret*).

Marc Lawrence's sinister countenance is used to good effect in his characterization of strong-arming bad guy Bela (dubbed "Laughing Boy" by Arlen in one scene). *Dracula* fans will enjoy seeing both Edward Van Sloan and Dwight Frye in supporting roles.

Reviews: "Few of the recent crop of mellers [melodramas] contain as much action as this Japanazi [*sic*] spy-ring yarn.... Target is to get the onlookers upon the edges of their theater chairs and keep 'em there. It succeeds." *Film Daily*, June 28, 1943

"A fast, suspenseful action melodrama, enacted with spirit by able performers and directed with care and skill from a timely, topical story." *Daily Variety*, June 22, 1943

Tornado (1943)

Cast: Chester Morris (*Pete Ramsey*), Nancy Kelly (*Victory Kane Ramsey*), Bill Henry (*Bob Ramsey*), Gwen Kenyon (*Sally Vlochek*), Joe Sawyer (*Charlie Boswell*), Marie McDonald (*Diana Linden*), Morgan Conway (*Gary Linden*), Nestor Paiva (*Big Joe Vlochek*), Frank Reicher (*Mr. Linden*), Edward Earle (*Banker*), Clyde Dilson (*Nugent*), Vince Barnett (*Alvin*)

Crew: William Berke (*Director*), Maxwell Shane (*Screenplay*), John Guedel (*Novel*), Fred Jackman, Jr. (*Director of Photography*), William Ziegler (*Editor*), F. Paul Sylos (*Art Director*), William Lynch (*Sound Recording*), Ben Berk (*Set Decorator*), Freddie Rich (*Music*), Ralph Freed, Frederick Hollander, Frank Loesser (*Songs*)

Released July 1943. 82 minutes.

After a prologue showing the destruction that a tornado wreaked on the town of Linden in 1939, we meet Pete Ramsey, a miner employed at the Linden family's mine. Pete, a good-hearted blue-collar guy, is instantly attracted to Victory Kane, a singer who walks into the local tavern and promptly faints from hunger.

Pete's younger brother Bob yields to the cajoling of pretty young Sally Vlochek, daughter of a miner, who wants to be taken on a tour of the mine where her father works. While Sally is onsite, an accident occurs, and the resulting explosion and cave-in leaves workers injured, and Sally blinded. Pete rescues Sally from the cave-in, and her father, known as Big Joe, vows revenge if he ever learns who took her into the mine.

Told of his heroic actions, the snooty Linden family invites Pete, with Victory in tow, to a party they're throwing. At first, Pete is flattered to be invited, but he feels patronized by the rich guests, and leaves angrily. Nonetheless, old Mr. Linden rewards Pete's bravery with a promotion to superintendent.

Victory accepts Pete's marriage proposal after a short acquaintance. Brought up in poverty and surviving on the lower rungs of show business, the new Mrs. Ramsey readily admits that she wants a luxurious life, with a large house, servants, and furs. Pete's growing ambition wins him another promotion, to mine manager, but in the process he is alienating his old friends, the miners who work under his increasingly heavy-handed command.

Surveying a piece of property that Victory inherited from a miner who had a crush on her, Pete realizes that there is valuable ore on the land. He arranges financing to open his own company, putting him in competition with the Lindens. Several of Pete's former friends refuse to work at his new company, but Sally, back from a sanitarium with her sight restored, is hired as his secretary.

Gary Linden, less scrupulous than his father, senses that Pete's mining operation will cut into his family's profits, and devises a scheme. Gary convinces Sally's father that it was actually Pete who was responsible for her injury at the mine, and Big Joe gets himself a job at the Ramsey mine so that he can sabotage the operation. When an explosion instigated by Big Joe stops work for several weeks, Pete's finances take a hit, and Victory is none too happy to have her income curtailed. With the town of Linden in the path of the oncoming storm, Gary puts the moves on Victory, Pete struggles to save his business, and the two men are set for a deadly confrontation.

The Dollar Bills paid a modest $500 to radio writer/producer John Guedel for the rights to his (apparently unpublished) novel, *Cyclone*, on which *Tornado* was based. Pine and Thomas will write a much larger check a couple of years later, to acquire film rights to Guedel's hit radio show *People Are Funny*. Before settling on the final title, the film was known as "Cyclone," and as "Black Tornado." A July 1942 item in Louella O. Parsons' syndicated column reported that Pine and Thomas originally sought Sylvia Sidney to play Victory, with Thomas telling Parsons that he immediately visualized her when reading Guedel's novel.

In the finished film, the storm footage is limited, seen only for a few minutes at the beginning, and a few more near the end. Pine and Thomas employed a combination of newsreel footage and some special effects using miniatures to accomplish the scenes. For the 70 or so minutes between, this is primarily a melodrama about the interlocking lives of rich and poor folks in a small town, and a woman's ambition to live like the "real ladies and gentlemen" she meets at the Linden estate. The film is pointedly set prior to America's entry into World War II, which doesn't figure at all into the plot.

This is the first of several pictures Nancy Kelly (1921–1995) will make for Pine-Thomas in 1943–44. After being under contract at Fox in the early 1940s, her film career seemed to be firmly tied to B movies; a Broadway play, *Flare Path*, in which she co-starred, opened in December 1942, but ran for only 14 performances. Kelly's *Tornado* character, Victory, is avaricious and duplicitous (she acknowledges to Pete that she feigned the faint in order to get a free meal), but Kelly retains some audience sympathy for the flawed woman who can't overcome her hunger for soft living. She's the recipient of Chester Morris' admiring compliment, "Baby, I don't know what you've got, but in that dress, you got it!" She will play another saloon singer in *Gambler's Choice,* again opposite Morris.

Behind the scenes, romance blossomed when Miss Kelly took a shine to one of Pine-Thomas' most valuable crew members. According to Bill Thomas, the actress, recently divorced from actor Edmond O'Brien, was an enthusiastic poker player: "Before long Nancy and cameraman Fred Jackman, Jr. were splitting a deck of cards. They married. It didn't last, but they were fine people."[12]

Up-and-coming Marie McDonald (1923–1965) is stunningly beautiful, but has little to do as Gary's snobbish sister. Gwen Kenyon (1916–1999), stuck with the good-girl role of Sally, nearly fades into the wallpaper. Morgan Conway (1903–1981) is well-cast as the spoiled rich boy with superficial charm and a cold heart. He will go on to play *Dick Tracy* at RKO the following year, again under Berke's direction.

From time to time, Pine-Thomas films will invoke the name of longtime company employee L.B. Merman, who worked as production manager or associate producer on most of the firm's output. Here, Merman is the name of the street listed on the invitation to Pete and Victory's wedding reception.

REVIEWS: "[Director] William Berke keeps the pace rolling neatly, and script deftly builds suspense. Morris capably handles the lead spot, with Miss Kelly neatly delivering as the unsympathetic showgirl." *Daily Variety,* August 10, 1943

"Bill Thomas and Bill Pine have done it again. They've packed plenty of action, drama, a dash of comedy and two song numbers into an item of good entertainment turned out with a low budget…. Nancy Kelly does her best job of acting in some time…." *Motion Picture Herald,* August 14, 1943

Minesweeper (1943)

CAST: Richard Arlen (*Richard Houston a/k/a Jim Smith*), Jean Parker (*Mary Smith*), Russell Hayden (*Seaman Elliot Nash*), Guinn "Big Boy" Williams (*Ichabod Ferdinand "Fixit" Smith*), Chick Chandler (*Seaman "Corny" Welch*), Douglas Fowley (*Lt. Wells*), Frank Fenton (*Lt. Ralph Gilpin*), Emma Dunn (*Mrs. Smith*), Charles D. Brown (*Commander Lane*), Grant Withers (*Madigan*), Ralph Sanford (*Cox*), Billy Nelson (*Boatswain Heims*), Robert Mitchum (*Ryan*), Will Wright (*Naval Officer*), William Haade (*Bosun*), Dub Taylor (*Stubby Gordon*)

CREW: William Berke (*Director*), Edward T. Lowe, Maxwell Shane (*Screenplay*), Fred Jackman, Jr. (*Director of Photography*), Howard A. Smith (*Film Editor*), F. Paul Sylos (*Art Director*), Frank Webster (*Sound Recording*), Ben Berk (*Set Decorator*), Mort Glickman (*Music*)

RELEASED November 1943. 67 minutes.

When amiable "Fixit" Smith finds a man lying along the side of the road, knocked out, he helps him up and offers him a ride. The man identifies himself as Jim Smith, and explains that he was in a fight with a hobo while riding in a train boxcar toward Los Angeles. Fixit takes a liking to Jim and invites him to the Smith home, letting him borrow some clothes. There, Jim is attracted to Fixit's pretty niece Mary, who's been dating seaman Elliot Nash.

With the Japanese having recently bombed Pearl Harbor, Fixit plans to reenlist in the Navy, and suggests that Jim do likewise. Unbeknownst to his new pal, Jim is actually the missing Lt. Richard Houston, a Navy deserter who is an experienced deep sea diver. Both are quickly accepted for active service (Jim using a phony birth certificate), and Jim undergoes training as a gunnery mate. With his prior Navy experience, which he keeps a secret, he shows himself able to handle the work in a way that impresses his superiors. Jim and Fixit are assigned to serve aboard a minesweeper, helping keep waterways clear of Japanese mines. Jim attracts attention when he recognizes one of the mines they find as a new type of weapon. While it is being disentangled from a net they are repairing, the mine detonates, killing two of the outfit's men. Jim and Elliot Nash are chosen to undergo additional training in mine disposal under the supervision of Lt. Gilpin, who thinks Jim looks vaguely familiar but can't place him.

When Jim narrowly escapes injury on a mission, Lt. Gilpin finds an engraved pocket watch among the seaman's belongings that leads him to suspect he is actually Richard Houston. While Gilpin investigates, Jim goes on leave. When Fixit advises him that Elliot seems to be on the verge of proposing to Mary, Jim embarks on a gambling spree, hoping to raise the money he needs to buy her a ring. Jim is late returning from his leave, and Fixit tries to cover for him. When Fixit, filling in for Jim, is killed on duty, Jim holds himself accountable. He ashamedly confesses his past to Mary, and the ways in which gambling ruined his Navy career, no longer feeling worthy of her love.

Hearing an announcement that all Navy men are needed for urgent duty, Jim reports. Lt. Gilpin, who has discovered his real identity, is ready to send Richard Houston to the brig. But Jim persuades his commanding officer to let him take part in a dangerous diving mission, knowing he is needed.

Production on *Minesweeper* began in April 1943. The film offers Richard Arlen a few more opportunities for dramatic acting than he has had in previous Pine-Thomas films, and he rises to the occasion. Jean Parker, on the other hand, has relatively little to do, and scant footage is devoted to explaining how and why their two characters fall in love. Guinn "Big Boy" Williams (1899–1962) offers one of the stronger supporting performances as the quirky, likable Fixit. Others seen as seamen here are the always-distinctive Dub Taylor, Chick Chandler (as a sailor with a propensity for corny jokes), and a young Robert Mitchum, who appears only briefly.

Underwater photography was still enough of a novelty in 1943 that several reviewers commented favorably on its use here.

REVIEWS: "An improbable story with mediocre dialogue and music.... The chief asset of the picture are underwater scenes, which are accurate, exciting and unusually well done." *Motion Picture Reviews*, January–February 1944

"Mildly entertaining ... there is no novelty either in the plot or presentation, and the outcome is obvious ... except for one or two situations, the film is sorely lacking in excitement." *Harrison's Reports*, November 13, 1943

Timber Queen (1944)

CAST: Richard Arlen (*Russ Evans*), Mary Beth Hughes (*Elaine Graham*), June Havoc (*Lil Boggs*), Sheldon Leonard (*Smacksie Golden*), George E. Stone (*Squirrel*), Dick Purcell (*Milt Holmes*), Edmund MacDonald (*Joe Birsdell*), Horace MacMahon [McMahon] (*Rodney*),

Tony Hughes (*Harold Talbot*), William Haade (*Rawson*), Clancy Cooper (*Barney*), Jimmy Ames (*Strudel*), Al Murphy (*Cueball*), Dewey Robinson (*Wenzel*), Garry Owen (*Taxi Driver*)

CREW: Frank McDonald (*Director*), Maxwell Shane, Edward T. Lowe (*Screenplay*), Fred Jackman, Jr. (*Director of Photography*), Victor C. Lewis, Jr. (*Editor*), Howard Smith (*Supervising Editor*), F. Paul Sylos (*Art Director*), Frank Webster (*Sound Recording*), Ben Berk (*Set Decorator*), Willy Stahl (*Music Score*)

RELEASED January 1944. 65 minutes.

Given a medical discharge from the Air Force, pilot Russ Evans drops by a nightclub, the Golden Goose, to see his buddy Ken's widow, Elaine. Elaine, a singer at the club, and Russ are mutually suspicious at first; he believes she married Ken on short acquaintance for the inheritance she received, some valuable timber land. Elaine, on the other hand, knows that Russ is partner with Harold Talbot in a business firm that's soon to foreclose on a loan against that land and make a tidy profit.

Unaware that his business partner committed him to a deal exploiting Ken's need for ready cash, Russ resolves to help Elaine raise the $30,000 she needs to keep the land. Borrowing $10,000 from nightclub proprietor Smacksie Golden, Russ assembles a crew to harvest as much timber as possible before Elaine's mortgage payment is due. Accompanying them to the site are Elaine, who's now convinced that Russ is sincere about helping her, and her brassy pal Lil, who's not so sure, pointing out that, as a partner in Talbot and Evans, Inc., he stands to win either way.

Added unexpectedly to the logging crew are Smacksie, along with his diminutive "bodyguard," Squirrel, who go on the lam once the Golden Goose's other owners find out Smacksie skimmed the cash from the office safe. Seeing that Russ and his men are making a go of the logging, Talbot arranges a few acts of sabotage to slow down the work. When a crew member is killed in an accident, most of the other lumberjacks quit. Trying to protect his investment, Smacksie calls upon his vengeful partners from the nightclub to do likewise by rounding up all the "4-Fs with muscles" they can to staff the project.

Talbot counteracts by arranging to having the nearby river dammed, cutting off the only route Russ and his men have to transport the logs they cut. When Russ abruptly leaves the site without explanation, Elaine, who's fallen in love with him, hesitates to believe, as Lil does, that he's bailing out on them. Meanwhile, Russ is carrying out a daring plan that involves his airplane, and a load of dynamite in tow.

Timber Queen is a typically action-packed, lively Pine-Thomas B picture, enhanced by more outdoor shooting than some previous ones have offered. The comedy relief here is stronger and more prominent than in some earlier efforts as well, aided by some sharp dialogue, and good performances from the supporting cast.

Arlen once again plays the sensible good guy who rolls up his sleeves and gets things accomplished. Though he's top-billed, Arlen is presumably not playing the title character. That honor goes to Mary Beth Hughes (1919–1995), a former Fox contract player who busied herself with quite a few B movies in the mid- to late-1940s. Here, she's cast as what advertisements called "a blonde baby who made those timber wolves howl!" She gives the character of Elaine beauty, glamour, and just a bit of grit, befitting a woman who's worked hard to make her way in the world. The pairing of Arlen and Hughes' characters is believable and refreshingly unsentimental. In the nightclub scenes that open the film, Hughes' character is seen singing Mercer and McHugh's "You're the One."

Turning in colorful supporting performances are June Havoc (1912–2010), as Elaine's smart-mouthed pal Lil, and Sheldon Leonard (1907–1997) as a guy who believes he's running "a class joint" in the Golden Goose, but whose speech and background belie his pretensions. He and Havoc team well for the romance that develops between them as the film progresses, and play effectively off George E. Stone (1903–1967) as "Squirrel," his unlikely, none-too-brave bodyguard. This was the final Pine-Thomas release for Dick Purcell, who died unexpectedly of a heart attack in April 1944.

Timber Queen would mark Richard Arlen's last appearance in a Pine-Thomas film for some four years to come. According to Bill Thomas, Arlen was determined to advance in his career, and made an ultimatum, saying, "From now on, it'll be Arlen in 'A's' or Arlen in nothing."[13] Unfortunately, this proved to be a goal beyond his reach, and before the year was out, he was toiling in modestly budgeted films like Republic's *The Big Bonanza*. Arlen returned to the Pine-Thomas fold in 1948, when he accepted the lead in *Speed to Spare*.

The similarly-titled *The Timber Queen*, released by Pathe in 1922, was a serial starring Ruth Roland in "a brilliant, breath-catching, stunt-filled story of the big timberlands of the Pacific coast."

REVIEWS: "Plenty of villainy and a fair quota of exciting moments are offered the patrons…. Sheldon Leonard … makes the most vivid impression [and] steals the play whenever he's around." *Independent Film Journal*, January 8, 1944

"An undistinguished program comedy-melodrama, hampered by a story that creaks with age, and by obvious melodramatic situations…. There is some excitement towards the finish." *Harrison's Reports*, January 8, 1944

The Navy Way (1944)

CAST: Robert Lowery (*Johnny Zumano*), Jean Parker (*Ellen Sayre*), Bill Henry (*Malcolm Randall, Jr.*), Roscoe Karns (*Frankie Gimble*), Sharon Douglas (*Trudy*), Robert Armstrong (*Harper*), Richard Powers [Tom Keene] (*Steve Appleby*), Larry Nunn (*Billy Jamison*), Mary Treen (*Agnes*), Wally Pindell (*Joslin*), John "Skins" Miller (*"Pop" Lacy*), Joseph Crehan (*Chaplain Benson*), Olive Blakeney (*Mrs. Jamison*), Barbara Brown (*Mrs. Randall*), Roy Gordon (*Malcolm Randall, Sr.*), Rosina Galli (*Mrs. Zumano*), George Humbert (*Mr. Zumano*), Sarah Padden (*Mrs. Gimble*), Ralph Peters (*Hammy Jerome*), Tom Tyler (*Ranch Hand*), Will Wright (*Baldy*), Lyle Latell (*Agnes' Cousin*), Edward Earle (*Commandant*)

Crew: William Berke (*Director*), Maxwell Shane (*Screenplay*), L.B. Merman (*Associate Producer*), Fred Jackman, Jr. (*Director of Photography*), Howard Smith (*Editor*), F. Paul Sylos (*Art Director*), Frank Webster (*Sound Recording*), Ben Berk (*Set Decorator*), Willy Stahl (*Music Score*)

RELEASED February 1944. 74 minutes.

A new batch of recruits arrives for training at the U.S. Navy's facility in Illinois. Among them are Johnny Zumano, a scrappy guy who grew up in "a dirty, stinking tenement," and is angry that he was called up to military service just as his career as prizefighter "Johnny Jersey" was beginning to take off. Well-heeled Malcolm Randall, Jr., however, scion of a wealthy family, is actively seeking the chance to accomplish something on his own, rather than rest on his family's laurels. Steve Appleby, several years older than the other men, joins the Navy after his son was killed in the Service, and becomes a fatherly influence on young, wet-behind-the-ears Billy Jamison, away from home for the first time. Also on deck is goofy Frankie Gimble, who impulsively enlisted at the age of 38 after having a falling-out with his girlfriend Agnes.

As the men undergo intensive training on land in preparation for their duties as seamen, Johnny has difficulty adjusting to military discipline. His fists help him win a boxing match for Company 101, but his fellow recruits don't approve of the rough way he knocks out his opponent, unaware that Johnny's compensating for an injured hand. Johnny's impulsive whistle at lovely Pharmacist's Mate Ellen Sayre gets him into trouble as well, but she takes a liking to him nonetheless. The tension between poor boy Johnny and rich boy Malcolm eases considerably after the former saves the latter from drowning during a training exercise.

When Johnny and the others successfully graduate from their training, Johnny proposes to Ellen, but she puts him off, saying it isn't the right time for them to think about marriage when he's due to ship out anytime. However, while Johnny takes advantage of some leave time to visit his family back home, Ellen finds herself falling in love with Malcolm. Feeling betrayed, Johnny gets drunk and threatens to desert the Navy. Malcolm steps in to help, but it appears that Johnny may have ruined his chance to make good.

The Navy Way, according to studio publicity, was "the thrilling action story of how the Navy's fighting men prepare for their share in the big invasion." Though it was comparatively unusual for a B-movie company to incur the expense of a location shoot, Pine and Thomas will do so on several occasions for their 1940s films, when there is a significant advantage to be gained in terms of authentic locations and production values that can't be easily replicated on a soundstage. In this case, company members went to the U.S. Naval Training Center in Great Lakes, Illinois, where many of the film's exterior scenes were shot, and where real recruits appeared alongside the actors in some scenes. The officers and men of the Training Center receive an acknowledgment from the producers in the opening titles. While the film title can't be called a cheat, exactly, anyone who bought a ticket looking for intense maritime drama went home disappointed. There's plenty of Navy lore here, and some interesting scenes, but the story is strictly a landlubber. Our heroes haven't even shipped out for the first time when the curtain falls.

Two of Pine-Thomas' favorite actors of the 1940s, Robert Lowery and Jean Parker, are here teamed for the first time, though by this point Parker must have felt as if she were cheating on Richard Arlen or Chester Morris. Lowery and Parker have strong chemistry as a couple, not surprising since they would later marry in real life. That didn't happen, though, until seven years after *The Navy Way* was made, and around the time of its release Miss Parker married someone else. Lowery's character is clearly taken with hers from his first glimpse; when a fellow recruit points out that she's a WAVE, he retorts, "Yeah, I like the way she ripples!"

Lowery definitely has the male lead here, with Bill Henry a fairly distant second, although the latter gets more to do as the film goes on. Lowery's character was a familiar movie type even in 1944, the hothead who has trouble buckling down to military discipline, but the actor does well in the role. He capably delivers a tear-jerking speech depicting his character's come-to-Jesus moment (rather literally) in the final reel.

Roscoe Karns (1891–1970) doesn't go overboard with the characterization of Frankie, the chief comic relief part, supported by Mary Treen, in the first of her Pine-Thomas appearances, as his plain-Jane fiancée. She will enjoy a more substantial role in *High Powered*. Johnny's parents are written as ethnic stereotypes, and played the same way, with Dad in particular seeming to have wandered in from an episode of *Life with Luigi*. Shane's screenplay gives us not one but two clinging mothers to their sailor sons, with Frankie's surely taking the prize when she has to be restrained from climbing into the taxi departing for his honeymoon.

According to *Showmen's Trade Review* (April 1, 1944), *The Navy Way* was screened in late March at the U.S. Naval Training Station, with live coverage on the Navy's radio broadcast, "Meet Your Navy." After the screening on the base, a premiere for the public was held in nearby Waukegan. Star Robert Lowery led the group of actors in attendance at the premiere functions. Co-star Richard Powers (1896–1963) was better known as Tom Keene, the name under which he played numerous Western heroes. Powers told *Daily Variety* (October 18, 1943) that he was startled to receive a personal thank-you note from Bill Thomas after production, which praised his "very serious and intelligent performance" and added, "We all enjoyed working with you and hope to have the pleasure again soon." The actor, whose motion picture career dated back to the silent era, couldn't remember the last time a producer had extended such a gesture.

REVIEWS: "*The Navy Way* is a swell money title for a service picture, and Pine and Thomas do justice to it with a swell entertainment.... The film will really rate as a supporting attraction, and is good for top billing on many playdates.... Robert Lowery emerges as a grade A bet for stardom.... He has never looked better in any Hollywood appearance." *Hollywood Reporter*, February 25, 1944

"Robert Lowery 'comes off' splendidly as the hero of The Navy Way. He has a compelling personality and the role he plays affords plenty of clash in the plot.... The spirit of the picture, and its Great Lakes realities are excellent." *Los Angeles Times*, June 2, 1944

Gambler's Choice (1944)

CAST: Chester Morris (*Ross Hadley*), Nancy Kelly (*Mary Hayes/Vi Parker*), Russell Hayden (*Michael McGlennon*), Lee Patrick (*Fay Lawrence*), Lloyd Corrigan (*Ulysses Rogers*), Sheldon Leonard (*Chappie Wilson*), Lyle Talbot (*Yellow Gloves Weldon*), Maxine Lewis (*Bonnie D'Arcy*), Tom Dugan (*Benny*), Charles Arnt (*John McGrady*), Billy Nelson (*Danny May*), Clancy Cooper (*Tim Riley*), Dick Elliott (*Barber*), Byron Foulger (*Man from Akron*), Thomas E. Jackson (*Police Sergeant*), Milton Parsons (*John Anderson*), Bert Roach (*Bob*), Cosmo Sardo (*Croupier*), Virginia Sale (*Mary's Aunt*), Jack Mulhall (*Harry*)

CREW: Frank McDonald (*Director*), Maxwell Shane, Irving Reis (*Screenplay*), Howard Emmett Rogers, James Edward Grant (*Original Story*), Fred Jackman, Jr. (*Director of Photography*), Howard A. Smith (*Editor*), F. Paul Sylos (*Art Director*), James Cochran (*Sound Recording*), Ben Berk (*Set Decorator*), Mort Glickman (*Musical Director*)

RELEASED April 1944. 65 minutes.

In late 19th century New York, Ross, Mary, and Mike are kids growing up in a blue-collar neighborhood. When Ross steals a wallet, and is sentenced to reform school, they are separated. Nearly 15 years later, Ross is employed in a gambling joint run by Chappie Wilson, but has plans to open his own place. Financed by hard-boiled widow Fay Lawrence, who wants him as her man, Ross prepares to become Chappie's competitor. When Chappie is talked into hiring a singer for his place, Vi Parker, known as "The Garter Girl," proves to be a grown-up Mary Hayes. Ross recognizes her, and takes her to see their old pal Mike, who's now a policeman.

After a fight with Chappie, Ross' club opens, with Vi joining him to provide entertainment. Fay, jealous of Vi, tries to fire her, but Ross dismisses his investor, paying her off with a post-dated check. Mike proposes marriage to Vi, though his earnings as a cop are modest. Vi finds herself torn between the two men, charming Ross, whose scruples are flexible, and good-guy Mike, who can't relate to the tough life Vi has lived in order to survive.

Used to having influence with local politicians, Ross arranges for his buddy Mike to get a promotion he didn't really earn. Mike is hesitant, but accepts the job with the understanding that there are no strings attached. Meanwhile, Fay is in cahoots with Chappie to settle a few scores. They arrange for Ross to be beaten by hired thugs, but he manages to turn the tables. In the ensuing fracas, Mike's policeman buddy is shot and killed. Mike, knowing the criminal activity pertains to the local gambling establishments, decides they must all be shut down, knowing this will put him at odds with Ross.

With the help of a crooked alderman, Ross arranges for Mike to be busted down to patrolman, and the gambling continues unabated. Mike is recruited by the governor's special prosecutor to continue his crackdown with the state's help, setting up an inevitable confrontation involving Chappie Wilson, Ross, and Mike, with Vi caught in the crossfire.

A snappy script, Frank McDonald's efficient direction, and a capable cast make *Gambler's Choice* pleasing entertainment, even if the plot is overly familiar. Production values rise to the occasion, believably recreating a period atmosphere and setting. Though Nancy Kelly seems a bit sedate for the role of a hardened nightclub singer, she gives a strong performance nonetheless, and Morris is once again the charming rogue, a role he'd practically patented by this point. Russell Hayden (1912–1981) is well-cast as the straight-arrow hero who doesn't look like quite as much as fun as Morris' free-wheeling character. Hayden even garners a laugh when he's busted to a patrolman gig in the sticks, where, as he grumbles, "A gopher just died of loneliness."

Pine and Thomas bolster the cast with fine actors in support, notably the gifted Lee Patrick (1901–1982) as tough Fay Lawrence, who knows what she wants and pays for it, in more ways than one. Her confrontation with "guttersnipe" Vi makes a viewer sit up and take notice. The always-watchable Dick Elliott gets the film off to a happy start in the opening scene, and Sheldon Leonard competently plays exactly the type of character moviegoers expected him to play in the 1940s. Other familiar faces turn up in minor roles.

According to the *Motion Picture Herald* (December 25, 1943), Hayden was inducted into the Army the day following the completion of shooting.

REVIEWS: "*Gambler's Choice* … has many moments of fast action, but it is handicapped by an oft-told story that weaves a too familiar pattern.… Director Frank McDonald managed to extract a fair share of excitement.…" *Motion Picture Daily*, April 28, 1944

"The formula of the good man, the bad man, and the girl beloved by both gets an entertaining refreshment by the Pine-Thomas unit.… Frank McDonald's direction whips up considerable suspense and weaves in the atmosphere and behavior of the era very well." *Daily Variety*, April 25, 1944

Take It Big (1944)

CAST: Jack Haley (*Jack Noel*), Harriet Hilliard (*Geraldine Clinton*), Mary Beth Hughes (*Gaye Livingstone*), Frank Forest (*Harvey Phillips*), Arline Judge (*Pert Martin*), Richard Lane (*Eddie Hampton*), NTG [Niles T. Granlund] (*Himself*), Fritz Feld (*Dr. Dorian D. Dittenhoffer*), Fuzzy Knight (*Cowboy Joe*), Lucile Gleason (*Sophie*), George Meeker (*John Hankinson*), Monty Montana, Pansy the Horse, Rochelle and Beebe (*Specialties*), Ozzie Nelson and His Orchestra (*Themselves*), Johnny Arthur (*Desk Clerk*), Byron Foulger (*Mr. Jones*), Will Wright (*Rodeo Judge*), Evelyn Finley (*Violet Thompson*), Hal K. Dawson (*Al Baxter*), Clyde Dilson (*Angry Diner*), Ralph Peters (*House Detective*)

CREW: Frank McDonald (*Director*), Howard J. Green (*Screenplay*), Joe Bigelow (*Additional Dialogue*), Lester Lee, Jerry Seelen (*Songs*), Carlos Romero (*Song Staging*), Maxwell Shane (*Associate Producer*), Fred Jackman, Jr. (*Director of Photography*), Howard Smith (*Supervising Editor*), Henry Adams (*Editor*), Jack Noyes (*Sound Recording*), F. Paul Sylos (*Art Director*), Ben Berk (*Set Decorator*), Rudy Schrager (*Musical Director*), David Chudnow (*Musical Supervision*)

RELEASED August 1944. 75 minutes.

After three years, entertainer Jack Noel is sick of his demeaning, poorly paid job as half of a horse act. He receives a happy surprise when a letter advises him that he has inherited a Nevada ranch from his uncle. Jack invites his friends Eddie Hampton (the other half of his horse) and Gerry Clinton (the showgirl who plays the horse's "trainer") to accompany him out West.

On arrival, a mix-up results in Jack and his friends going to the B-Bar-A ranch, rather than the A-Bar-B, which is the one he actually owns. The B-Bar-A is a swanky hotel and dude ranch; wanting to assess the place for himself, Jack registers as "Walter Raleigh," and proceeds to make a nuisance of himself, interfering in its operations. He's instantly attracted to lovely Gaye Livingstone, despite the slow-building romance that's been developing between him and Gerry. Unbeknownst to Jack, Gaye is only using him to make another man jealous.

Jack is disconsolate to learn that he has been staying at the wrong place, and even more so when he sees what a dilapidated hovel his ranch is. He realizes his mistake only after inviting most of his Chicago nightclub friends, as well as his therapist, Dr. Dittenhoffer, to come for a visit. Jack's friends join forces to renovate the A-Bar-B, and convert it into a spiffy dude ranch, where they will provide the entertainment.

Although the plan is initially successful, Jack hits a serious snag when Harvey Phillips, owner of the B-Bar-A, informs him that there's a lien on the property, payable in a few days, which he just purchased from the bank. Determined to stop Phillips from taking over, Jack invests most of the money they earn from paying customers in an entry fee for skilled rider Cowboy Joe to enter the local rodeo. But when Joe falls ill with the mumps just before the event, Jack, Gerry, and their friends must call on their own skills to compete in the rodeo, in hopes of saving their ranch.

Take It Big, the Dollar Bills' first musical, gets off to an inauspicious start, with comedy that isn't particularly amusing, and a hero who fails to arouse our sympathy. But once the action moves out West, things begin to pick up, and the entertainment value, especially the music, takes a turn for the better. Co-producer Bill Pine, a longtime friend

Ozzie Nelson (left) and Harriet Hilliard (Nelson) have a hands-on approach to Jack Haley in *Take It Big.*

of Clara Bow, arranged to shoot exteriors at the retired actress' ranch in Nevada. During preproduction, the film was known as "Rhythm Ranch."

Leading lady Harriet Hilliard (1909–1994) is cast as Gerry, the woman who isn't fully appreciated by Haley's character, while Mary Beth Hughes, in her second Pine-Thomas film of the year, plays a glamorous gold-digger who uses Jack only to make a better prospect jealous. It's a bit disconcerting to see Harriet, in real life Mrs. Ozzie Nelson since 1935, explain to him in a scene that she's just not attracted to him, the way she is to Jack. Ozzie and Harriet's song together, "Sunday, Monday, and Always" (by Johnny Burke, James Van Heusen, with special lyrics by Ozzie) is a strong specialty number. Though his role is smaller than his wife's, Ozzie gets a good line or two, as when he observes of Jack's rundown ranch, "This isn't a hotel, it's a bear trap with wallpaper!" Hughes, playing a distinctly secondary character despite her prominent billing, gives us pause when she remarks, of would-be suitor Jack's fervent smooch, "I haven't been kissed like that since I fell and caught my lip in the vacuum cleaner!"

Among the featured players, Arline Judge is a standout as Gerry's smart-mouthed pal, who dubs Jack "the familiar face with the jokes to match," and Johnny Arthur (1883–1951) steals a scene in his minor role as a hotel clerk. Lucile Gleason (1888–1947) doesn't have much to do as Jack's ranch manager, while Fritz Feld (1900–1993), as his therapist, gets more screen time, but not the best material. Dewey Robinson (1898–1950), seen briefly as a workman, gets a line that will sail over the heads of most modern viewers when he asks, as therapist Dr. Dittenhoffer tries to give Jack advice, "Wouldn't he do better with Mr. Anthony?"

REVIEWS: "While the story behind this comedy with music is a mere thread, the picture provides a smattering of good variety entertainment. Jack Haley, Harriet Hilliard and Ozzie Nelson offer their best in view of the material with which they have been supplied." *Showmen's Trade Review*, June 10, 1944

"Pine-Thomas' initial venture into the production of musicals results in good entertainment. Howard J. Green's screenplay has several fun-provoking situations and many gags. Frank McDonald provided excellent direction and the laugh score is high." *Film Daily*, June 9, 1944

Dark Mountain (1944)

CAST: Robert Lowery (*Don Bradley*), Ellen Drew (*Kay Downey*), Regis Toomey (*Steve Downey*), Eddie Quillan (*Willie Dinsmire*), Elisha Cook, Jr. (*Whitey*), Ralph Dunn (*Chief Sanford*), Walter Baldwin (*Sam Bates*), Rose Plumer (*Pattie Bates*), Virginia Sale (*Aletha Bates*), Byron Foulger (*Harvey Bates*), Johnny Fisher (*Hunk*), Alex Callam (*Det. Dave Lewis*), Eddie Kane (*Waiter*), Angelo Desfis (*Bookkeeper*)

CREW: William Berke (*Director*), Maxwell Shane (*Screenplay*), Paul Franklin, Charles Royal (*Original Story*), Fred Jackman, Jr. (*Director of Photography*), Howard Smith (*Supervising Editor*), Henry Adams (*Editor*), F. Paul Sylos (*Art Director*), Ferol Redd (*Sound Recording*), Ben Berk (*Set Decorator*), Willy Stahl (*Music Score*)

RELEASED September 1944. 56 minutes.

Young forest ranger Don Bradley, newly promoted to head of the Dark Mountain district, takes advantage of a furlough to go into town and propose marriage to his childhood friend Kay. Upon arrival, he's dismayed to learn that Kay recently married another man. Kay's new husband Steve supposedly earns his living at "wholesale merchandising," but she soon realizes he's a dealer in stolen goods. Ruthless, Steve has an inspector getting wise to his racket murdered, and himself kills two of his gang members when they are picked up by the police. Kay wants to leave him, but he says she's an accessory to his crimes, and that they will go on the lam. Telling her they'll go their separate ways until the heat dies down, Steve instead waits for Kay to seek help, as he expected, from good guy Don. Don, not knowing the full story, installs Kay in a vacant cabin on Dark Mountain. For days, Steve fumes at being cooped up in the cabin, while Kay refrains from further implicating Don, not letting him know of her husband's presence. Eventually, Don deduces that Kay is not living there alone, and responds to a summons arranged by Steve, who intends to kill him.

From the film's opening moments, we know that Don is goodhearted, as we see him brave the flames of a forest fire to save two horses trapped in a barn. Fortunately, his understanding boss forgives him, even after getting decked when he tries to prevent Don from going after the horses. Once Don is drawn into the danger surrounding Kay, Steve congratulates his wife, assuming she intended to "use that ranger for a chump."

The script makes then-timely allusions to wartime shortages of consumer goods, as when Kay's uncle, who runs a general store, complains he can't obtain the radio tubes his customers want. "Our customers ain't the same when they can't listen to Bob Hope!" his wife exclaims. Sleazy Steve, on the other hand, says, "If you have the right connections, you can get anything."

Clocking in under an hour, *Dark Mountain* moves briskly, with Robert Lowery and his gorgeous leading lady Ellen Drew (1915–2003) making a handsome couple. Production values are modest; although the script implies that Steve lures Kay, in part, with the promise of a luxurious life, the one room of their house we see looks pretty ordinary. In the film, Don tells the story of an Indian legend concerning storms that take place on the mountain, and the film's original title, *Thunderbolt*, referred to this.

Eddie Quillan adds some humor as Don's assistant and best buddy, Willie, as does his dog Luther, who even joins in on the chase at the finale. Once again, as in *Flying Blind*, Quillan's character has a wife who's frequently discussed but never seen, in this case a WAC who's apparently substantial enough that he uses Don as a model for the sweater he's knitting her.

Guerdon Ellis, supervisor of the Tahoe National Forest, was recruited to serve as the film's technical advisor. According to the *Independent Film Journal* (April 15, 1944), Dick Purcell was "signed for an important role in *Dark Mountain*," but by the time the column item appeared in print, he had already suffered his fatal heart attack.

REVIEWS: "Pine-Thomas productions have earned a reputation for pace and action which their latest release does not quite sustain. *Dark Mountain* opens with a forest fire and closes after a mad automobile chase, but sags rather badly in the middle…. William Berke, who directed, has done little to enliven the long wait between the early excitement and the chase in the end."—*Motion Picture Herald*, September 9, 1944

"It is a high speed, exciting action melodrama with a good plot and plenty of wallop, just the kind of fare present-day customers like. Its production quality is all that could be desired, William Berke's direction is excellent and the performances are above par, all of which adds up to another P-T success."—*Hollywood Reporter*, September 5, 1944

One Body Too Many (1944)

CAST: Jack Haley (*Albert Tuttle*), Jean Parker (*Carol Dunlap*), Bela Lugosi (*Merkil*), Blanche Yurka (*Matthews*), Lyle Talbot (*Jim Davis*), Douglas Fowley (*Henry Rutherford*), Fay Helm (*Estelle Hopkins*), Bernard Nedell (*Morton Gellman*), Lucien Littlefield (*Kenneth Hopkins*), Dorothy Granger (*Mona Rutherford*), Maxine Fife (*Margaret Hopkins*), William Edmonds (*Professor Hilton*), Lyle Latell (*Detective Agency Manager*), Ralph Peters (*Insurance Agent*)

CREW: Frank McDonald (*Director*), Winston Miller, Maxwell Shane (*Screenplay*), Fred Jackman (*Director of Photography*), Howard Smith (*Supervising Editor*), Henry Adams (*Film Editor*), F. Paul Sylos (*Art Director*), Paul Schmutz (*Sound Recording*), Ben Berk (*Set Decorator*), Alexander Laszlo (*Musical Score*)

RELEASED November 1944. 75 minutes.

Mild-mannered insurance salesman Albert Tuttle shows up for an evening appointment with eccentric millionaire Cyrus Rutherford, hoping to sell him a $200,000 life insurance policy. Unbeknownst to Tuttle, he's too late; Rutherford is dead, and his relatives have gathered for the reading of the will. An "ardent student of the stars," Rutherford has left instructions that he is to be buried in a glass-topped vault with a view of the sky. Until this has taken place, all his heirs, including his butler and house-keeper, must remain in his house. Should his burial wishes be disregarded, the terms of his will are to be reversed, with the largest beneficiary receiving the least money, and vice versa.

When Albert presents himself at Rutherford's door, he's mistaken for the private detective hired to guard the millionaire's corpse until burial can take place. Left in a locked room with the coffin, Albert is knocked out cold with a fireplace poker, and awakens to find the body missing. Although it soon turns up again, it's apparent that one of Rutherford's heirs means to bury him underground, so as to gain a greater inheritance. When a falling stone almost kills Rutherford's pretty niece, Carol Dunlap, she entreats Albert to stay for the night and keep her safe. Unable to resist her plea, Albert agrees to the plans of Gellman, Rutherford's lawyer, to hide in the coffin and await a second attempt to steal the body. For his trouble, Albert nearly winds up in a watery grave himself, before Carol comes to his rescue, and one of the inmates of the house kills Gellman.

While changing clothes, Albert stumbles onto a secret passageway that may help solve the mystery. He stumbles out of the bedroom of Mona, the wife of Rutherford's nephew, just moments before she's found murdered. Locked up by the other family members, who believe he killed Gellman and Mona, Albert struggles to come to Carol's rescue when she's taken hostage by the real killer.

One Body Too Many, though played primarily for comedy, is yet another of those stories about potential heirs spending time in a spooky old mansion. It draws on familiar tropes of the genre, including a portrait with eyes that follow someone across a room, trap doors, and secret passageways. The latter comes into play for a lengthy, and mildly risqué (for 1944) sequence in which Jack Haley, clad only in a towel wrapped around his waist, fumbles his way into the bedrooms of other guests. Losing the towel, he takes cover in a laundry hamper, where he's later found nervously sharing the space with a feisty mother cat and her kittens.

The box office successes of *The Ghost Breakers* (1940), starring Bob Hope, and *Hold That Ghost* (1941), with Abbott and Costello, had demonstrated the financial viability of films mixing thrills and scares with comedy. Although the comic situations take precedence over the murder mystery, and some of the plot details wouldn't bear close examination, should anyone take the trouble, the movie does offer a few genuinely eerie moments.

Production began in January 1944, under the working title *Too Many Bodies*. Syndicated columnist Harrison Carroll (January 27, 1944), making a set visit, was given a look at the mansion's library, of which Bill Thomas told him, "In this set we have real production value. Do you see that goldfish bowl? Did you know they sell goldfish by the inch? Three dollars an inch. It may put us over the budget."

In his second film for Pine-Thomas, Haley gives an energetic performance, though there were comedians of the day who could probably have made the film funnier. He has no better than lukewarm chemistry with Jean Parker, who seems to be drawn to him mostly because it's in the script that she should do so.

Fans of third-billed Bela Lugosi (1882–1956) may be disappointed by his supporting role as vaguely sinister butler Merkil, who spends much of the film's running time trying to serve coffee that may be laced with rat poison. *Daily Variety* (July 20, 1943) reported that Pine and Thomas had negotiated with Boris Karloff to appear in the film. Former Broadway leading lady Blanche Yurka (1887–1974), as Merkil's cohort, the equally forbidding housekeeper, has even less to do.

REVIEWS: "Cast troupes solidly for comedy results in portraying the screwball characters peopling the excellent script.... Jack Haley bangs out a slick comedy performance." *Daily Variety*, October 18, 1944

"Fast and furious entertainment ... a comedy thriller that will please persons still able to be excited by a display of all the standard props of the old school of melodrama." *Independent Film Journal*, October 28, 1944.

Dangerous Passage (1944)

CAST: Robert Lowery (*Joe Beck*), Phyllis Brooks (*Nita Paxton*), Charles Arnt (*Daniel Bergstrom*), Jack La Rue (*Mike Zomano*), John Eldredge (*Vaughn*), Victor Kilian (*Buck*), Alec Craig (*Dawson*), William Edmunds (*Captain Saul*), Will Wright (*Postal Clerk*)

CREW: William Berke (*Director*), Geoffrey Homes (*Screenplay*), Fred Jackman, Jr. (*Director of Photography*), Howard Smith (*Supervising Editor*), Henry Adams (*Editor*), F. Paul Sylos (*Art Director*), Frank McWhorter (*Sound Recording*), Ben Berk (*Set Decorator*), Alexander Laszlo (*Music Score*)

RELEASED December 1944. 60 minutes.

After six years' hard work in the oil fields of British Honduras, young Joe Beck is summoned to the office of lawyer Daniel Bergstrom in the port town of St. Angel, where he's told he will inherit $200,000 from his late grandfather if he can verify his identity. After showing his birth certificate and other identification, Joe is given the necessary paperwork to claim his money in Galveston, Texas. Bergstrom advises him to take a ship called *The Southern Queen* a few days later, remarking that, with the papers Joe now has in hand, almost anyone could collect the inheritance. Just outside Bergstrom's office, Joe is jumped by a thug, who's knocked into the ocean in the resulting fight. A passerby, ship's steward Dawson, comes to Joe's aid. Joe decides it would be prudent to get out of St. Angel, and, against Dawson's advice, books passage on the ship where he's employed, the rather ratty *Merman*.

On board the *Merman*, Joe gets acquainted with beautiful Nita Paxton, who's fleeing a low-paid singing gig at "a dirty little cabaret." Joe and Nita are attracted to each other, but he's uncertain whom he can trust after someone aboard tries to kill him. Dawson, who warns him the ship is dangerous but won't tell him why, abruptly turns up dead in Joe's cabin. After disposing of the body, Joe urges Nita to leave the dangerous ship at the next stop, but she refuses. Re-boarding so as not to be separated from Nita, Joe encounters two new passengers—lawyer Bergstrom, and a man who now claims he's Joe Beck, and entitled to the money. Joe fights them off successfully, not telling them that he mailed the valuable papers to himself in Galveston, rather than bringing them aboard ship.

Joe learns that Captain Saul is practicing insurance fraud, intentionally causing costly wrecks. Nita tells him that Dawson, who was her friend, was an undercover investigator. With Dawson dead, Nita feels compelled to carry on his work, but the captain purposely rams the ship into a pile of rocks. With Saul and his crew having jumped ship,

Joe and Nita are stranded on the slowly sinking vessel with Bergstrom and the impostor Joe, who may or may not be willing to cooperate in hopes of saving themselves.

This compact thriller is the first screenplay written to order for Pine-Thomas by Geoffrey Homes. Syndicated columnist Robbin Coons (July 9, 1944), paying a visit to the company offices while plans for *Dangerous Passage* were underway, found Homes (a/k/a Daniel Mainwaring) at his typewriter, pondering the next plot twist in his screenplay. "The boat with my people," he told Coons, "is on the reef. Now I've got to get 'em off. I will not call in the Coast Guard. Perhaps I'll slide it off—no, even I wouldn't believe a ship could still float after being battered on such rocks."

Lowery plays a more cynical, forceful character here than in *Dark Mountain*. He's up to the job's physical demands, including several fistfights, and has strong chemistry with Brooks. Beautiful Brooks, with a slightly husky voice, discontinued her film career in 1945, after getting married. Charles Arnt (1906–1990) gives a colorful performance as the morally ambiguous lawyer, Bergstrom, who smiles even amidst the most open villainy.

Once again, production manager L.B. Merman's name is the subject of an in-joke. Here, it's given to the rickety, rundown ship where much of the story takes place.

REVIEWS: "*Dangerous Passage* is a sea story of no mean proportions. In one wide sweep it takes in an insurance racket, a legacy intrigue and an appealing love story, all in the familiar Pine-Thomas fashion ... it is not unsafe to assume that [it], with all of its action and excitement ... will be a box office success." *Motion Picture Daily*, December 21, 1944

"...the action fans will probably find it to their liking, for it offers some exciting moments. Since the hero's life is constantly in danger, it has considerable suspense." *Harrison's Reports*, December 23, 1944

Double Exposure (1944)

CAST: Chester Morris (*Larry Berke*), Nancy Kelly (*Pat Marvin*), Jane Farrar (*Dolores Tucker*), Phillip Terry (*Ben Scribner*), Richard Gaines (*J.B. Turlock*), Charles Arnt (*Sonny Tucker*), Claire Rochelle (*Smitty*), Roma Aldrich (*Mavis*), Charles Delaney (*Joe Jackson*), Cyril Delevanti (*Henry*), Edward Earle (*District Atty. Merkle*), Kit Guard (*Butch*), Spec O'Donnell (*Messenger*), Dewey Robinson (*Mac*)

CREW: William Berke (*Director*), Winston Miller, Maxwell Shane (*Screenplay*), Ralph Graves, Winston Miller (*Original Story*), Fred Jackman, Jr. (*Director of Photography*), Howard Smith (*Supervising Editor*), Henry Adams (*Film Editor*). F. Paul Sylos (*Art Director*), Frank McWhorter (*Sound Recording*), Alex Laszlo (*Musical Score*)

RELEASED December 1944. 63 minutes.

Larry Berke, editor of *Flick* ("the picture magazine that's always there when it happens") is dissatisfied with the dull photos his staff has been bringing him. At the suggestion of magazine owner J.B. Turlock, a health and fitness nut, Larry sends a wire offering a job to photographer Pat Marvin, whose shot of a plane crash for an Iowa newspaper impressed them both. Neither of them knows that Pat is a young woman, rather than a man, but she's delighted by the opportunity to "have a crack at New York!" Less thrilled is Pat's strait-laced boyfriend, Ben, who hasn't been able to get her to commit to a future together.

Nancy Kelly has double the guys in *Double Exposure,* with boss Chester Morris (left) and boyfriend Phillip Terry.

Larry is surprised when Pat turns up at his office, but quickly offers to show his beautiful new employee the ropes. Sensing that he needs to be kept at arm's length, Pat spontaneously invents a brother who's staying with her, and tags him with the first name that comes to mind—Ben. Pat is dismayed when the real Ben turns up in New York, and talks his way into a job at *Flick*, with Larry unaware he has a rival.

Pat proves her worth as a photographer when she captures exclusive photos documenting the stormy marriage of millionaire Sonny Tucker to his sixth wife, ex–chorus girl Dolores. Dolores' seventh phony suicide attempt doesn't impress Sonny, who takes a liking to Pat, and announces he's going to Reno for a divorce. When Larry assigns Pat to take some posed photos for the magazine's "Mystery of the Week" feature, she and Ben make use of Sonny's vacant apartment, and his wife's slinky wardrobe, to stage a murder scene for which Pat plays the victim.

Before the pictures are published, Pat steels herself to admit to Larry that Ben is not her brother, but when he finds out on his own before she can do so, he's angry. Larry plots to send Ben on a mission overseas to get him out of the way. A mix-up at *Flick* results in Pat's murder scene photo being published on the front page, and when Dolores Tucker turns up dead, in a pose remarkably similar to the staged one, Pat finds herself indicted for murder.

This is an amusing and engaging comic mystery that tells a good story in just over an hour. Nancy Kelly, who would achieve her biggest success in the 1950s as the star of *The Bad Seed,* brings charm and energy to the characterization of Pat, who amply demonstrates that she possesses what Larry describes as GLUB, the quality that news photographers need—a go-getter, lucky, up-and-at 'em, "and a bunco artist at heart."

No stranger to tight shooting schedules, even star Chester Morris felt the pressure on *Double Exposure.* According to columnist Harold Heffernan (May 7, 1945), "Morris announced to the cast in an awed voice that he had changed costume 14 times that day, a record in his 13 years as a movie star." The name of Morris' character, Larry Berke, may be a tribute to director William Berke.

Paramount contract player Phillip Terry (1909–1993), previously seen in *Torpedo Boat,* was disqualified from service in World War II due to his poor vision, an affliction that his character here shares. He was at this time the husband of actress Joan Crawford. His performance as a milquetoast is quite competent, though he's handsome enough to make it doubtful that women would dismiss him so easily. At one point, after Pat gives him a less-than-passionate response to his attentions, he turns and makes an aside to the audience, complaining, "I get kissed more on the cheek!"

Pine-Thomas had two films released in mid–December 1944, this and *Dangerous Passage*; in both, Charles Arnt plays a colorful character role. The filmmakers would return to the offices of *Flick* magazine three years later, in *Danger Street.*

REVIEWS: "An entertaining program murder-mystery melodrama with amusing comedy situations.... Nancy Kelly ... is particularly good. As a matter of fact, the direction and the performances are superior to the story values." *Harrison's Reports,* December 23, 1944

"Morris is excellent in the lead spot, breezily handling his assignment with Nancy Kelly spotted nicely in the femme lead.... William Berke hits a fast and lively pace in the direction." *Daily Variety,* December 18, 1944.

High Powered (1945)

CAST: Robert Lowery (*Tim Scott*), Phyllis Brooks (*Marian Blair*), Mary Treen (*Cassie McQuade*), Joe Sawyer (*Spike Kenny*), Roger Pryor (*Rod Farrell*), Ralph Sanford (*Sheriff*), Billy Nelson (*Bill Madden*), Ed Gargan (*Cal Williams*), Vince Barnett (*Worker at Dance*), Will Wright (*Jeff Hines*), Forrest Taylor (*Dance Host*), George Lynn (*Joe Jackson*), Clancy Cooper (*Plant Boss*)

CREW: William Berke (*Director*), Milton Raison, Maxwell Shane (*Screenplay*), Milton Raison (*Original Story*), Fred Jackman, Jr. (*Director of Photography*), Howard Smith (*Supervising Editor*), Henry Adams (*Editor*), F. Paul Sylos (*Art Director*), Don S. McKay (*Sound Recording*), Ray Berk (*Set Decorator*), Alexander Laszlo (*Music Score*)

RELEASED February 1945. 62 minutes.

Best friends Marian and Cassie are on the way to a construction site, hauling a trailer they have fitted up as a lunch wagon. At Cassie's urging, they offer a ride to hitchhiker Tim Scott, who's on his way to take a job as a grape picker nearby. When Tim takes a turn at the wheel, the trailer comes uncoupled from the car, and the three are involved in an accident in which the other motorist is the local sheriff.

Our heroes run afoul of local law enforcement in this scene from *High Powered.* **Pictured (left to right) are Robert Lowery, Phyllis Brooks, Mary Treen, and Ralph Sanford.**

Tossed into jail by the angry lawman, the three are unable to raise the $100 fine they've been assessed. Stopping by to bail out one of his workers is Rod Farrell, an old friend of Tim's who's now the boss of the construction site where the ladies were headed. He bails out all three, and puts them to work.

The plant being built under Rod's supervision is to manufacture "100-octane gas for airplanes" needed in the war effort. Although trained as a "high man" (able to work atop cranes and other construction equipment), Tim hasn't worked in the field since an accident in which he fell six stories, was injured, and a co-worker was killed. With a deadline for finishing the job only a few weeks away, Rod badly needs workers, and Tim agrees to work long enough to pay him back.

The ladies set up their lunch counter at the construction site, where Marian attracts the interest of Rod, though she's secretly interested in Tim. Cassie, meanwhile, is romanced by goofy Spike, who keeps telling her she reminds him of his ex-wife.

An act of sabotage slows work at the site, and suspicion falls on Tim. Rod tries without success to cure his old friend's fear of heights. But when a brawl breaks out at the Boilermakers' Ball, landing several of his crew in jail, Rod tries to handle a potential accident himself, winding up trapped high above the ground and knocked unconscious. Tim must overcome his fears if he is to save his friend, and regain his self-worth.

Somewhat reminiscent of Pine-Thomas' earlier effort, *Wrecking Crew*, this too centers on a crew of men doing dangerous construction work, and on one worker who must prove himself after he is blamed for an industrial accident. Like some other of the company's films, *High Powered* leans heavily on stock footage and rear projection to create the ambience of a busy construction site, and the dizzying heights the crew workers must climb. In the script, Tim's condition is described as "hypsophobia" rather than "acrophobia."

Lovely Phyllis Brooks is effective as the leading lady, a character who wants to start her own business because she was tired of "being chased around counters by café owners." Will Wright (1894–1962), seen as comedic characters in other Pine-Thomas films, has more dramatic opportunities here, playing an older crew member who wants the plant to succeed because his own son is serving in the military.

Mary Treen (1907–1989) and Joe Sawyer provide the comic relief as plain-spoken Cassie and her would-be beau. Though she's looking forward to a job where she can serve "Hot Meals for Hungry Bachelors," Sawyer's Spike isn't exactly what she had in mind. "You can't help being ugly, but you could stay indoors," she snaps at him on one occasion. Later, after the umpteenth mention of his ex-wife, she says in frustration to her clumsy beau, "She didn't divorce you. She's just hiding." Treen, who began her show business career as a dancer, demonstrates a flair for physical comedy in a scene that anticipates one done by Lucille Ball nearly ten years later in *The Long, Long Trailer*. It shows Cassie being tossed around the runaway trailer, food flying everywhere as she loses her balance and winds up a wet, floury mess.

In the *Motion Picture Herald*'s "What the Picture Did for Me" column (July 28, 1945), an Oklahoma exhibitor deemed the film "Satisfactory for double bill. It will please." In Dewey, Oklahoma, the manager of the Paramount Theatre warned that it "wouldn't stand alone," saying he was unable to recoup the cost of the film rental.

REVIEWS: "One of the better Pine-Thomas programmers.… The exciting moments, including a climactic rescue of an unconscious man high atop a swaying boom, will provide thrills aplenty.… Robert Lowery is handsome and capable as the hero." *Independent Exhibitors' Film Bulletin*, March 5, 1945

"Film has been well paced by Director William Berke, numerous fight scenes handled for punch, and the Lowery top scene when he mounts the high boom to rescue Pryor, is a swell topper for the capably produced meller." *Box Office Digest*, February 28, 1945

Scared Stiff (1945)

CAST: Jack Haley (*Larry Elliot*), Ann Savage (*Sally Warren*), Barton MacLane (*George "Deacon" Markham*), Veda Ann Borg (*Flo Rosson*), Roger Pryor (*Richardson*), George E. Stone (*Mink*), Robert Emmett Keane (*Professor Wisner*), Lucien Littlefield (*Charles/Preston Waldeck*), Paul Hurst (*Sheriff*), Arthur Aylesworth (*Emerson Cooke*), Eily Malyon (*Mrs. Cooke*), Buddy Swan (*Oliver Waldeck*), Walter Baldwin (*Deputy*), Dick Curtis (*Bus Driver*), Charles Williams (*Reporter*)

CREW: Frank McDonald (*Director*), Geoffrey Homes, Maxwell Shane (*Screenplay*), Maxwell Shane (*Associate Producer*), Fred Jackman, Jr. (*Director of Photography*), Howard Smith (*Supervising Editor*), Henry Adams (*Editor*), F. Paul Sylos (*Art Director*), William R. Fox (*Sound Recording*), Ray Berk (*Set Decorator*), Alexander Laszlo (*Music*)

RELEASED June 1945. 65 minutes.

From heroes to half-wits, Pine-Thomas takes a turn toward the comedic in *Scared Stiff*.

Bungling reporter Larry Elliot's incompetence is about to get him fired, but he's given one last chance by his editor, who assigns him to cover a festival being held at a winery in Grape City. Distracted by his interest in Sally Warren, a pretty antiques dealer, Larry unwittingly buys a ticket to Grape Center instead. On the bus to Grape Center, along with Sally, Larry is oblivious when the passenger next to him is stabbed while the bus goes through a dark tunnel.

With the phone wires cut, the corpse missing, and the bus drained of gas, Larry and his fellow passengers are ordered by the tavern manager to stay put until the sheriff arrives. Since he was the victim's seatmate, the other bus passengers look with suspicion at Larry who, as is his wont, didn't notice a thing. Oliver Waldeck, a child prodigy chess player, amuses himself by spreading a story that the body was beheaded, and then planting a toupee-topped head of lettuce in Larry's luggage to unnerve him.

Sally tells Larry that she's there to purchase a rare, valuable set of chessmen, which are jointly owned by feuding twin brothers Charles and Preston Waldeck, and asks for his help. While visiting the vault where Charles keeps his half of the set, he and Larry are assaulted and knocked out, and the chess pieces stolen.

The sheriff arrives, unaware of the murder, but on a manhunt for escaped criminal "Deacon" Markham. Knowing he will lose his job if he fails to cover the Grape City event 40 miles away, Larry tries to escape, but is locked into his room by a sheriff's deputy. Markham and his sidekick Mink, hiding in Larry's room, take him captive. They're soon joined by Sally and fellow passenger Flo Rosson, who reveals herself to be an insurance investigator. The all-out chase that ensues finally results in recovery of the stolen chessmen, the revelation of the guilty party behind the murder of the bus passenger, and the realization that Larry's nose for news is no better than it ever was.

After the previous year's comedy thriller *One Body Too Many,* the Dollar Bills returned to the genre, again with Jack Haley as the star, with this less successful effort. *Scared Stiff* has too much plot and too many characters for its own good. Haley has a couple of good comic moments, but doesn't get the material here to support more frequent laughs.

Ann Savage (1921–2008), who will attract considerable attention later in the year with *Detour,* is fine in an ingénue assignment that doesn't demand much of her beyond charm, which she conveys in ample supply. Some viewers may quite sensibly refuse to believe that both Savage's character, and another glamorous passenger played by Veda Ann Borg, are seemingly so taken with the bumbling nitwit Haley portrays, who remarks at one point, "I ought to win a Pulitzer Prize for stupidity!" Character actress Eily Malyon (1879–1961), who could have given the film some genuine menace, never gets the opportunity to do so, and is largely wasted as the tavern manager's wife.

Prior to production, the film was known by the title "You'll Be the Death of Me." Several years later, it would be released to television with the meaningless title *Treasure of Fear,* probably because Paramount wanted to reuse the original title for a Dean Martin–Jerry Lewis comedy that came out in 1953.

REVIEWS: "A poor program murder-mystery melodrama, with the accent on comedy, most of which is so silly that the spectator finds it difficult to refrain from yawning.... No fault can be found with the performances, for there is not much that the players could do with the material." *Harrison's Reports,* April 14, 1945

"In these days of film shortages, it is truly surprising to find to what poor use precious celluloid is put, not to mention talent and expense ... some minor laughs and thrills, but

[this] hardly compensates for the general inanity and incoherence prevalent throughout." *Independent Exhibitors' Film Bulletin*, April 16, 1945

Midnight Manhunt (1945)

CAST: William Gargan (*Pete Willis*), Ann Savage (*Sue Gallagher*), Leo Gorcey (*Clutch Tracy*), George Zucco (*Jelke*), Paul Hurst (*Murphy*), Don Beddoe (*Lt. Max Hurley*), Charles Halton (*Henry Miggs*), George E. Stone (*Joe Wells*), Paul Harvey (*McAndrews*), Ben Welden (*Hotel Manager*), Edgar Dearing (*Desk Sergeant*), Pat Gleason (*Dispatcher*), Robert Barron (*Policeman*)
CREW: William C. Thomas (*Director*), David Lang (*Screenplay*), Maxwell Shane (*Associate Producer*), Fred Jackman, Jr. (*Director of Photography*), Howard Smith (*Supervising Editor*), Henry Adams (*Editor*), F. Paul Sylos (*Art Director*), John Carter (*Sound Recording*), Ray Berk (*Set Decorator*), Alexander Laszlo (*Music Score*)
RELEASED July 1945. 63 minutes.

At the fleabag Empress Hotel, a mysterious man sneaks into Room 114 and shoots the occupant, relieving him of a packet of diamonds. The victim staggers to his feet after his assailant leaves, though he's badly wounded.

Across the street, at the Last Chance Gangster Wax Museum, policeman Murphy claims he saw the body of gangster Joe Wells in a nearby alley, but his superior, Lt. Hurley, isn't impressed, reminding him that Wells was reported dead years ago. Newspaper reporter Sue Gallagher, who lives in an apartment above the museum, isn't inclined to believe it either, until she stumbles on Wells' body in the stairwell. Needing a story to ingratiate herself with her bosses at the *Chronicle*, Sue moves the corpse into the wax museum, replacing one of the figures in a tableau. Clutch Tracy, assistant to Mr. Miggs, the nervous proprietor of the wax museum, phones his friend, reporter Pete Willis, to tip him off to the story. Pete, who is Sue's ex-boyfriend, tries to pump her for the story, but she resists. Meanwhile, Mr. Miggs finds Wells' body, and is persuaded by Clutch that they should take it away by car and dispose of it elsewhere.

Jelke, the man who shot Wells, follows the trail of blood drops from the hotel room and confronts Sue. At gunpoint, she admits where she hid the body, but it's already gone when Jelke searches there. He's caught in the act by Pete, who claims to have the body and makes an appointment to meet Jelke in one hour. Lt. Hurley arrests Sue for stealing the corpse, but Jelke bails her out of jail. By this time, Miggs and Clutch have dumped the body in a freight car at the railroad yard, but when Sue accompanies Jelke there, it's been moved again. He takes her along to Pete's apartment, where Jelke shows Pete and Sue the diamonds he retrieved from Wells' body. Jelke, who tells them the gems were stolen by Wells in South America, promises to split the $5,000 reward with Pete and Sue if they help him retrieve the body.

Pete plays along with Jelke, still on the trail of the story, and all three wind up at the ferry, where Jelke double-crosses them. Planning to make his escape with $250,000 worth of diamonds, and stash Wells' body where it will never be found, Jelke has Pete and Sue over a barrel, but Pete too has a few surprises up his sleeve.

Bill Thomas made his directorial debut with *Midnight Manhunt*, a lively thriller spiced with a liberal dose of comedy. As the limited budgets of the Pine-Thomas films didn't allow for many directorial flourishes anyway, he proves himself able to take charge with satisfactory results. A more experienced director—or one given more time and money—might have made more of the potentially eerie environment of a wax museum shrouded in darkness.

The film's title changed more than once before it finally hit theaters. Early announcements called it "Cheezit, the Corpse." Once someone thought better of that, it became "Hard to Handle," which in turn gave way to "One Exciting Night." The latter title was still attached to the picture when it was previewed for trade papers.

Leading man William Gargan (1905–1979) would make five Pine-Thomas quickies in the second half of the 1940s. In his autobiography, the actor described many of his films from the period as "schlemiel pictures ... the kind you see today on the late late show."[14] Ann Savage, just a few months before her iconic part in *Detour*, gives Sue a tough exterior. Roughly conked over the head by Zucco's character, she doesn't let it slow her down for long, and at the film's climax more than holds her own in a vigorous waterfront fight.

Though most of the characters are types of various kinds, the capable character actors entrusted with playing them make the most of the lines and situations they're given. Leo Gorcey (1917–1969), taking a breather from his East Side Kids series, plays fast-talking, not overly bright Clutch, who, like other of the actor's characters, has a way with a malapropism. Busy character actor Charles Halton (1876–1959) is cast as the Nervous Nellie proprietor of the wax museum, whose recurring complaint amidst the goings-on is, "I'm very tired." George Zucco (1886–1960) offers, as always, a smoothly professional performance, his character Jelke showing genuine menace even in the film's comic moments. George E. Stone, who has enjoyed more sizable roles with Pine-Thomas, has little to do as Wells but be insulted; another character describes the gangster as a "little rat-faced guy with a pinhead like a carp."

REVIEWS: "The combination sought is that of balance between laughs and chills, and by accelerating pace both in dialogue delivery and scene succession the picture gets through its sixty-odd minutes without any too many opportunities to be taken seriously." *Box Office Digest*, June 9, 1945 (as "One Exciting Night")

"With almost the entire action taking place either in a shadowy waxworks museum or in dark streets, the production budget was an extremely modest one.... Although the film contains a few laughs ... there is no mystery or suspense." *Film Bulletin*, June 11, 1945

Follow That Woman (1945)

CAST: William Gargan (*Sam Boone*), Nancy Kelly (*Nancy Boone*), Regis Toomey (*Barney Manners*), Byron Barr (*John Evans*), Edward Gargan (*Butch*), Don Costello (*Nick*), Pierre Watkin (*J.B. Henderson*), Nella Walker (*Mrs. Henderson*), Audrey Young (*Marge Andrews*), Ben Welden (*Joe*)

CREW: Lew Landers (*Director*), Maxwell Shane, Winston Miller (*Screenplay*), Ben Perry (*Story*), Maxwell Shane (*Associate Producer*), Fred Jackman, Jr. (*Director of Photography*), Howard Smith (*Supervising Editor*), Henry Adams (*Editor*), F. Paul Sylos (*Art Director*), Glenn P. Thompson (*Set Decorator*), Joseph I. Kane (*Sound Recording*)

RELEASED December 1945. 69 minutes.

Bored with attending society parties, a young lady named Nancy persuades her reluctant date Bill to escort her to a less-than-high-class nightclub called The Downtown Club, owned by an ex-con named Nick. Also on the scene is policeman Sam Boone, who's there to apprehend a gangster. Seeing Sam draw his gun and approach his suspect's table, Nancy jumps to the wrong conclusion, mistaking the officer of the law for a holdup man. She knocks him out cold with a bottle.

Two years later, with Sam and Nancy Boone happily married, the couple pays a return visit to the Downtown Club, as they do every year on their anniversary. Sam, now proprietor of his own private detective agency, is handed a note from singer Marge Andrews, who was a witness in one of his earlier cases, asking him to meet her in her dressing room. With Nancy in tow, Sam answers Marge's summons only to find the singer dead on the dressing room floor, and a window open from which the killer escaped.

Due to report for Army duty, Sam resists becoming involved in the case, leaving the scene before the police arrive. Nancy, wishing she could help with her husband's business while he's in the military, is in the office when a wealthy client, J.B. Henderson, calls wanting to hire the agency to locate Marge Andrews. Sam's partner, another ex-policeman named Butch, doesn't feel competent to take on the assignment, but Nancy accepts it eagerly.

Nancy, whose knowledge of detection comes from her reading of mystery novels, decides to play amateur detective in his absence. She is surprised when she calls on Nick at the Downtown Club, who denies that Marge was killed there. A search of the late Miss Andrews' apartment throws suspicion on Barney Manners, who operates an illicit gambling club. Sam's former partner, Butch, unable to keep Nancy from investigating, sends an urgent letter to Sam at his army camp, saying, "You better make Nancy stop trying to be Dick Tracy.... She won't listen to me so you better talk to her." Sam obtains a seven-day leave, and goes home to check on his wife.

Shortly after Sam's return, he finds Nancy has gone undercover at Barney Manners' club, going incognito as a hard-boiled cigarette girl named Maisie LaRue. Once her cover there is blown, Nancy turns up next at the lavish home of client J.B. Henderson, posing as his French-accented maid, Yvonne (according to the screenplay, "all made up like a maid in a Lubitsch movie, very trim and pert.")[15] With only a few days before Sam must return to his military post, he must solve the mystery of Marge's murder—unless Nancy beats him to it.

Ben Perry's original story was titled "Crime on My Hands," also one of the working titles for the film. The screenplay for *Follow That Woman* was completed under the title "Crime on Her Hands." Production began in early February 1945, and concluded about three weeks later. According to *Daily Variety* (January 29, 1945), Pine and Thomas encountered some difficulty casting the feminine lead: "First Helen Walker obtained her release from Paramount because she wouldn't take the role. Now it looks as if Marjorie Reynolds might elect to take a penalty rather than accept the part." Miss Reynolds supposedly liked the story, which the Dollar Bills thought "one of the best scripts on their production sked this year," but thought the allotted shooting schedule inadequate to do it properly. Finally, in late January, Nancy Kelly signed for the role.

If not likely to be mistaken for anything but a modest B film, *Follow That Woman* offers a fun outing for the leading lady, who gets into a variety of scrapes and jams—and costumes—in a story running just over an hour. Leading man William Gargan also gets

All dolled up for their starring roles in *Follow That Woman*: William Gargan and Nancy Kelly.

a few funny lines, as when he casually insults his wife to the Hendersons (who are unaware that she, undercover as their maid, is listening intently):

> SAM: As a matter of fact, I only married her because I was sorry for her. Poor girl ... legs like pipe lines ... so knock-kneed that every time she takes a step it sounds like a 3-cushion billiard shot ... and [indicating front teeth] a very bad set of uppers. All phony.

The film also features Gargan's brother Ed, a character actor; both had worked for the company previously, though not together. This was the first of two Pine-Thomas pictures to feature actress Audrey Young (1922–2012). A few years later, Miss Young would become the second wife of writer-director Billy Wilder, whom she met when she played a minor role in his film *The Lost Weekend* (1945). Here, Miss Young plays nightclub singer Marge, described in the screenplay as "a very ripe looking dame indeed, with a throaty voice and a very sexy way about her."

In the *Motion Picture Herald*'s "What the Picture Did for Me" column (March 30, 1946), a small-town Oklahoma exhibitor wrote, "This is a little program picture which just got by on Bargain Night. If you never play it, you will not miss anything."

REVIEWS: "A fast-paced murder mystery with the emphasis on comedy.... Although the film is episodic, suspense is maintained fairly well and the identity of the killer will come as a surprise to the average who-dun-it fan.... One of the better Pine-Thomas programmers." *Film Bulletin*, September 3, 1945

"*Follow That Woman* stands up as tongue-in-cheek murder mystery made for escapist entertainment and not for critical discernment. Slowly-paced at start, momentum gradually picks up, and if you don't take it seriously, film is entirely acceptable for secondary billing … [William] Gargan's smoothness balances frantic comicking of [Nancy] Kelly." *Daily Variety*, August 20, 1945

They Made Me a Killer (1946)

CAST: Robert Lowery (*Tom Durling*), Barbara Britton (*June Reynolds*), Lola Lane (*Betty Farrington*), Frank Albertson (*Al Wilson*), Elisabeth Risdon (*Ma Conley*), Byron Barr (*Steve Reynolds*), Edmund MacDonald (*Jack Conley*), Ralph Sanford (*Patrolman Roach*), James Bush (*Frank Conley*), Paul Harvey (*District Attorney Booth*), John Harmon (*Joe Lafferty*), Edward Earle (*Dr. Reeves*), Will Wright (*Henry, the Blacksmith*), Dorothy Vaughan (*Nancy*), Victor Potel (*Willoughby*), Gil Frye (*Hospital Intern*)

CREW: William C. Thomas (*Director*), Geoffrey Homes, Winston Miller, Kae Salkow (*Screenplay*), Owen Francis (*Original Story*), Fred Jackman, Jr. (*Director of Photography*), Howard Smith (*Supervising Editor*), Henry Adams (*Editor*), F. Paul Sylos (*Art Director*), Frank Webster (*Sound Recording*), Glenn Thompson (*Set Decorator*), Alexander Laszlo (*Music Score*)

RELEASED May 1946. 64 minutes.

After his kid brother is killed in an auto wreck, young mechanic Tom Durling decides to leave Chicago and start over in a new location. Traveling to California, he stops in the town of Santa Marta, looking to raise money by selling his used car. At the car lot, he meets Betty, an attractive young woman who says her boyfriend might be interested in buying the car for her. When the Conley brothers show up, they pull a gun on Tom and force him to drive to the local bank, where they commit a robbery. Betty's acquaintance Steve Reynolds, a bank clerk, stops by the car to speak to her, and is shot in the ensuing gunfire.

During the high-speed getaway, the car is wrecked and Tom left behind to face the music. Since a policeman was shot and killed during the holdup, he finds himself charged with murder. Shortly afterwards, Steve Reynolds, the only one who could explain that both he and Tom were innocent bystanders, dies in the hospital.

Tom escapes from the hospital and begins following Steve Reynolds' sister June, an attractive young schoolteacher. Tom approaches June surreptitiously and tells her they must work together to clear his name, and Steve's. Although wary of Tom's motives, June goes along with him. When Tom is almost captured again, while trying to have his locked handcuffs removed, June helps him escape, and is now complicit with him.

Obtaining the suitcase Betty left behind at the boardinghouse where she and Tom stayed, he finds restaurant doilies that she used to patch the worn case. Recalling some of her conversation as "hash house talk," Tom concludes that this is a clue to where she may have worked in the past, and to tracking her down. After trying several places, June gets a job at the roadhouse of Ma Conley, after two policemen who are regular customers mention the girl, Betty, who used to work there.

Deducing that Betty and her gang are hiding in the basement of the restaurant, Tom breaks in. Tempted to shoot them and run with the $100,000 they stole, he is stymied when June intercedes. Taken captive by the gang, Tom must devise a plan to not only escape, but bring the criminals to justice.

Shot in the summer of 1945, *They Made Me a Killer* is a highly entertaining picture in the *film noir* mode, with the script providing intriguing twists and turns in the plot at regular intervals. This is a good role for Robert Lowery, who skillfully plays a basically decent man led by circumstance into a situation that may corrupt him. He's convincing as the man with whom June can fall in love, and also in the moments where he's sincerely tempted to go astray, and fend for himself in a suddenly hostile world.

Barbara Britton (1919–1980), in the first of three Pine-Thomas appearances, gives a fine performance as June, who is initially sympathetic to Tom, then develops feelings for him, yet is unable to be certain of his motives. A proper young woman (previously employed as a schoolteacher) who finds herself being drawn into a world of criminals, she is eminently respectable. (Obliged to share a motel room with Tom, she assigns him to sleep on an ironing board placed in a alcove, leaving him to crack, "I can go to sleep and get my pants pressed at the same time.") Britton may be best-known for co-starring with Richard Denning in the 1950s TV series *Mr. and Mrs. North*.

Byron Barr (1917–1966), seen as June's ill-fated baby brother, is not the actor who later changed his name to Gig Young. This Barr had only a handful of real opportunities on the silver screen, but does fine here. Elisabeth Risdon and Lola Lane (1906–1981) give color to the supporting female parts; this was Miss Lane's last film released before she retired.

Syndicated columnist Harrison Carroll (July 7, 1945) reported that a fight scene between leading man Lowery and bad guy James Bush accidentally resulted in the star getting a punch in the nose for real. "That did it," cracked Doc Merman. "Now you'll play the last five reels in profile." Lowery retorted, "Yeah, and I suppose you'll shoot the love scenes over the back of my head."

This is one of several Pine-Thomas films to take place in a fictitious California town, Santa Marta. Judging from this film, as well as *Special Agent* and *The Lawless*, it isn't the most desirable of communities, as it's plagued with bank robberies, train holdups, and racial tensions.

Trades reported that *They Made Me a Killer* was Pine-Thomas' 30th feature for Paramount. Said a North Dakota theater owner, reporting to *Motion Picture Herald*'s "What the Picture Did for Me" column (November 23, 1946), "A very good midweek picture. Robert Lowery is well liked by our patrons…. Keep these coming."

REVIEWS: "This film reaffirms the fact that good, entertaining pictures can be made on a reasonable production budget…. Robert Lowery, in the lead role, handles his part well and Barbara Britton is very beautiful and very capable as the girl who helps him clear his name." *Showmen's Trade Review,* January 26, 1946

"Here is a tight little melodrama that holds interest to the end. Co-producer William Thomas was also the director on this offering and deserves credit on both counts." *Film Daily,* January 28, 1946

People Are Funny (1946)

CAST: Jack Haley (*Pinky Wilson*), Helen Walker (*Corey Sullivan*), Rudy Vallee (*Ormsby Jamison*), Ozzie Nelson (*Leroy Brinker*), Philip Reed (*Johnny Guedel*), The Vagabonds (*Themselves*), Bob Graham (*Luke*), Roy Atwell (*Mr. Pippensiegal*), Clara Blandick (*Grandma Wilson*), Barbara Roche (*Aimee*), Art Linkletter (*Himself*), Frances Langford (*Guest Artist*),

Billy Benedict (*Usher*), Ann Jenkins (*Boogie-Woogie Pianist*), Byron Foulger (*Mr. Button*), Joe DeRita (*Mr. Hinkley*), Casey Johnson (*Jerry*), Wheaton Chambers (*Reverend Allen*)

CREW: Sam White (*Producer/Director*), Maxwell Shane, David Lang (*Screenplay*), Dorcas Cochran (*Additional Dialogue*), David Lang (*Original Story*), Fred Jackman, Jr. (*Director of Photography*), Howard Smith (*Supervising Editor*), Glenn P. Thompson (*Set Decorator*), Odette Myrtil (*Miss Walker's Gowns*), Irving Burns (*Makeup Artist*), Jack Crosby (*Dance Director*), David Chudnow (*Musical Supervisor*), Rudy Schrager (*Musical Director*)

RELEASED January 1946. 93 minutes.

Radio producer Johnny Guedel's show has just been canceled by his sponsor, Mr. Jamison, who gives him one week to create a replacement. Johnny's best writer, and long-time girlfriend, Corey Sullivan, is on a much-needed Las Vegas vacation, and reluctant to give it up. Also in Vegas is saxophonist Leroy Brinker, who suggests that she put together a new show for him.

Corey and Leroy, riding back to Hollywood together, have car trouble outside the town of Clearwater, Nevada. The nearest mechanic, Pinky Wilson, also produces a local audience-participation radio show, *People Are Funny*, in which everyday people perform wacky stunts. Seeing how well the show is received locally, Corey feigns a sprained ankle so that she can stay temporarily in Clearwater, while Leroy continues on their trip, carrying a record of the show. Bargaining with Pinky for the rights to *People Are Funny*, Corey tells Johnny to steal the record from his rival Leroy's office, convinced this will be their next hit show. Johnny unwittingly steals the wrong record, and his sponsor is not impressed with his tryout of Leroy's show *Dixie Shindig*.

When Corey arrives in Hollywood to find Johnny trying to sell Jamison the wrong show, she quickly intercedes. Johnny sets up an audition recording of *People Are Funny*, but Leroy, who also wants to produce the show, makes Jamison late for the program. When Jamison does arrive, he's mistaken for a contestant, and subjected to a messy stunt that finds him on the receiving end of a seltzer bottle. Sure all hopes of getting Pinky's show on the network are dashed, a discouraged Corey allows him to go back to Clearwater, worried that he has let his friends and neighbors down, while she and Johnny are on the outs after the disastrous audition.

According to Bill Thomas, the company paid $20,000 for the rights to make a feature film version of *People Are Funny,* a popular success on NBC radio since 1942. Maxwell Shane and David Lang's script presents a highly fictionalized account of how the show found its way to radio, with leading actor Philip Reed cast as the show's real-life producer, John Guedel (1913–2001). Guedel would go on to have another hit in 1947, when he developed the comedy-quiz show *You Bet Your Life* for Groucho Marx. As for Reed, he would become one of Pine-Thomas' most frequently employed actors, notching eight P-T appearances, including the starring role in the "Big Town" series. Leading lady Helen Walker (1920–1968) was the same actress who, about a year earlier, had severed her ties with Paramount when she balked at playing the female lead in Pine-Thomas' *Follow That Woman*. Her life and career took a tragic turn at around the time of *People Are Funny's* release, when she was blamed for a traffic accident that resulted in the death of a young serviceman (though she was subsequently acquitted).

Art Linkletter (1912–2010), who became the host of the radio program in 1943, appears here as the emcee who hosts the show-within-a-show once it's transported to Hollywood.

Philip Reed (center) enlists the help of (left to right) Jack Haley, Helen Walker and Ozzie Nelson to show that *People Are Funny*.

Jack Haley, in his fourth and final Pine-Thomas outing, is cast as the small town naïf who originates the show. He's given less to do here than in *One Body Too Many* or *Scared Stiff*, which mostly works to his advantage. Ozzie Nelson and Rudy Vallee both play less-than-admirable characters, and do so quite acceptably. So many of the cast members had regular jobs on radio shows that, according to syndicated columnist Harold Heffernan (May 7, 1945), "working out a shooting schedule turned out to be one of [Pine and Thomas'] toughest tests," accommodating rehearsal times of eight different broadcasts.

Although the real-life *People Are Funny* counted on the spontaneous reactions of contestants, placed in outlandish stunts, to provoke laughs, the film hedges its bets by casting character actors like Byron Foulger and Joe DeRita as the hapless victims. One sequence manages to stereotype two groups at the same time, when the Vagabonds don blackface to sing a song about Angelina, the waitress at the Pizzeria. (In fairness, it should be pointed out that it is part of Johnny's failed *Dixie Shindig* audition, and is meant to be seen as a lousy act.) Much better entertainment comes next on the lineup, from talented pianist Ann Jenkins.

In trade-paper ads, Paramount emphasized *People Are Funny*'s radio listening audience of 11 million, claiming that the appearances of popular stars from other shows provided "a total fan following of 50,000,000." Producer/director Sam White recalled

Paramount's Y. Frank Freeman saying, "This is a real audience picture, and Paramount's going to make a lot of money with it."[16] However, response from the viewing public and the trade was tepid at best. In *Motion Picture Herald*'s "What the Picture Did for Me" column (June 29, 1946), a disgruntled Texas theater owner reported, "A screwball comedy with a few laughs and lots of headaches. Don't depend on doing any business with this." In New Paltz, New York, an exhibitor reported (March 16, 1946), "poor business" and "many walkouts."

REVIEWS: "A curious hodge-podge of slapstick and corny comedy which will convulse most neighborhood audiences but leave the more discriminating patrons cold … it gives such personalities as Rudy Vallee and Ozzie Nelson the opportunity to kid themselves in a good-humored fashion." *Independent Exhibitors' Film Bulletin*, October 15, 1945

"A passable, but over-long, program entertainment…. The story material … is pretty weak, the action is slow in spots, and the comedy is not of the uproarious type." *Harrison's Reports*, October 13, 1945

Tokyo Rose (1946)

CAST: Byron Barr (*Pete Sherman*), Osa Massen (*Greta Nordstrom*), Don Douglas (*Timothy O'Brien*), Richard Loo (*Col. Suzuki*), Lotus Long (*Tokyo Rose*), Keye Luke (*Charlie Otani*), Larry Young (*Jack Martin*), H.T. Tsiang (*Chung Yu*), James Millican (*Al Wilson*), Grace Lem (*Soon He*), Leslie Fong (*Wong*), William Challee (*Mike Kovak*), Chris Drake (*Frank*), Blake Edwards (*Joe*), Al Ruiz (*Mel*)

CREW: Lew Landers (*Director*), Geoffrey Homes, Maxwell Shane (*Screenplay*), Whitman Chambers (*Original Story*), Fred Jackman, Jr. (*Director of Photography*), Howard Smith (*Supervising Editor*), Henry Adams (*Editor*), F. Paul Sylos (*Art Director*), Frank Webster (*Sound Recording*), Glenn P. Thompson (*Set Decorator*), Alice Barlow (*Technical Adviser*), Rudy Schrager (*Music Score*)

RELEASED February 1946. 68 minutes.

In a Japanese prisoner of war camp, American soldiers are listening to the latest broadcast of "Tokyo Rose," whose broadcast from Radio Tokyo combines popular music with propaganda aimed at undermining the morale of U.S. fighting men. One of the listeners, Pete Sherman, angrily insists the program be shut off. Pete explains that Tokyo Rose was responsible for the death of one of his fellow fighting men, Joe, who was killed by a sniper after being influenced by her words.

The prisoners' captors abruptly select 12 of them to be loaded onto a transport truck and taken on an undisclosed mission. Pete and his comrades notice that the healthiest men among them were chosen. During the journey, an American bomber attacks the truck, leaving one of the prisoners dead and another injured.

At their destination, another prison camp, the prisoners are welcomed by a smiling Colonel Suzuki, who introduces himself as Chief of Propaganda for Radio Tokyo. As long as they are cooperative, the American men are given good meals, reading material, and proper care. But Pete realizes they are being used—Suzuki and his cohorts want the soldiers to appear on Tokyo Rose's broadcast, and assure Americans back home that Japan does not mistreat its war prisoners.

A group of journalists representing neutral nations is invited to listen to the broadcast, but it is interrupted when Radio Tokyo's headquarters are bombed. In the confusion after the attack, Pete takes the clothes and the credentials of one of the reporters who was killed, Eric Nordstrom from Stockholm. He is allowed to leave the camp, and delivered to the house in Tokyo where journalists are being hosted by the Japanese.

Another journalist, Timothy O'Brien, recognizes immediately that Pete is not Eric Nordstrom, but vouches for him nonetheless. O'Brien and his wife, sister of the late Mr. Nordstrom, are willing to help Pete escape Tokyo, but he has another goal—he wants to find and kill Tokyo Rose.

The escape planned for Pete puts him into contact with a group of underground rebels fighting the Japanese regime. Among them is Japanese-American Charlie Otani. After Pete repairs the radio used by the rebels to track military movements, Charlie agrees to help Pete with his daring plan to infiltrate the Radio Tokyo studio an hour or so before he boards a ship for America, and confront the radio broadcaster he despises. But some of the people Pete has met along the way may or may not be loyal to the side they appear to take.

In trade-paper ads for *Tokyo Rose,* the studio proclaimed, "Paramount brings you the most exploitable picture to spring from the headlines!" As a publicity blurb described Tokyo Rose's campaign to hurt the morale of American fighting men, "With sly innuendo, she attempted to break their ties with those near and dear to them back home, [and] make them feel they were being deserted by their loved ones."[17] Like *Alaska Highway, Tokyo Rose* was a topical title that Pine and Thomas had registered with the Writers' Guild nearly a year prior to making the film. Although the war was still underway while it was being shot, peace was declared prior to its release. A tacked-on ending referenced the dropping of the atomic bomb on Japan.

Much of what everyday Americans knew or believed about Tokyo Rose in the mid–1940s has been discredited in the years following. The story of her apprehension, as told here, is complete fiction. However, an item in *Daily Variety* (November 28, 1945) claimed that Paramount sound men who worked on the film in post-production thought Lotus Long's voice "almost identical" to the Tokyo Rose they remembered from the war, and that their fellow servicemen who saw the finished picture would be "in for a surprise."

Top-billed Byron Barr, seen previously in a featured role in *They Made Me a Killer,* gets the star buildup from Pine-Thomas as the hero of *Tokyo Rose.* A native of St. Louis, Missouri, Barr made his film debut with a featured part in *Double Indemnity* (1944). Although he will turn up again in *Seven Were Saved* and *Big Town,* his film career was relatively short-lived.

Given special "and" billing at the bottom of the opening credits, American-born Lotus Long (1909–1990) plays Tokyo Rose. For the film's first hour, her performance is heard, but not seen, allowing for what's intended to be a surprise twist when her facial features are revealed. Pine-Thomas had originally announced a nationwide talent search to cast the role, stipulating that they needed an actress who was "a good Oriental impersonator, if not an Oriental." According to syndicated columnist Harrison Carroll (June 12, 1945) they received more than 200 applications from actresses who "say they are willing to swallow personal disgust for a film chance in a good cause."

As it turned out, the performer they were seeking was found much closer to home. Miss Long was the wife of the film's assistant cameraman, James Knott, who worked on

Richard Loo (left) menaces Osa Massen in a staged shot promoting *Tokyo Rose*.

several P-T films of the period. She reportedly won the job in *Tokyo Rose* after meeting Bill Pine when she arrived at the studio to give her husband a ride home from work. "I don't know how careful Jimmy was of my camera angles," she said lightly of her film assignment, "but the director kept telling the other actors that if they wanted their faces to show, they'd better stick close to me."[18]

Perhaps best-remembered for supporting Joan Crawford in *A Woman's Face* (MGM, 1941), Danish-born actress Osa Massen (1914–2006) is seen to good effect as the wife of Irish journalist O'Brien. Keye Luke gives a relaxed, confident performance as Charlie.

Daily Variety (October 25, 1945) noted that Bill Thomas was en route to New York "for conferences with Paramount tops, taking a print of *Tokyo Rose* with him." Meanwhile, partner Bill Pine was at the helm as filming began on *Swamp Fire*. When *Tokyo Rose* did make it to theater screens, it frequently did so as the bottom half of a double bill with the Hope-Crosby comedy *The Road to Utopia* (1945).

REVIEWS: "Here is an exploitation offering that is marked by good acting, direction and production.... Lotus Long enacts the title role ... her intriguing voice is used to good advantage." *Film Daily*, December 11, 1945

"Outlandish though the plot is, there is enough action to surfeit the most avid cops-and-robbers fan, making this better than average fare for the action houses.... Performances generally are good and Byron Barr, a newcomer, scores in the principal role." *Independent Exhibitors' Film Bulletin*, December 10, 1945

Hot Cargo (1946)

CAST: William Gargan (*Joe Harkness*), Jean Rogers (*Jerry Walters*), Philip Reed (*Chris Bigelow*), Larry Young (*Warren Porter*), Harry Cording (*Matt Wayne*), Will Wright (*Tim Chapman*), Virginia Brissac (*Mrs. Chapman*), David Holt (*Peter Chapman*), Elaine Riley (*Porter's Secretary*), Dick Elliott (*Frankie*)

CREW: Lew Landers (*Director*), Maxwell Shane (*Screenplay*), Geoffrey Homes (*Story*), Fred Jackman, Jr. (*Director of Photography*), F. Paul Sylos (*Art Director*), Howard Smith (*Supervising Editor*), Henry Adams (*Editor*), Glenn P. Thompson (*Set Decorator*), William Fox (*Sound Recording*)

RELEASED June 1946. 57 minutes.

After completing their World War II military service, buddies Joe Harkness and Chris Bigelow pay a visit to California, home of their late pal Paul Chapman, who was killed in combat. Joe and Chris have vowed to do all the things Paul's untimely death prevented him from doing. On Paul's bucket list were a tomato to be tossed at a small-time cop, the repayment of a minor debt to a friend, and a kiss bestowed on his childhood pal, Jerry Walters, a young woman who operates a successful lumber mill. Joe, expecting Miss Walters to be smart but not attractive, is only too happy to leave the latter assignment to Chris, who earns a slap in the face for planting a kiss on the quite attractive Jerry.

Paying a visit to Paul's parents, Joe and Chris learn that the successful family-run trucking business about which their friend bragged has gone badly downhill in his absence. Joe and Chris find their friend's parents and his teenage brother Pete struggling to maintain operations with only two unreliable vehicles. After Paul's father, Tim, is injured in an accident caused by ruthless rival Matt Wayne's sabotage of his truck, Joe and Chris decide to stay on for a while and help the Chapman family. In doing so, Chris puts aside the completion of his education, while Joe delays making a comeback as a baseball player. Though Chris is reluctant to admit it, his attraction to Jerry Walters is another incentive for extending their stay.

Joe and Chris quickly realize that, to compete with Matt Wayne, they need a well-paid local hauling contract. Jerry sympathizes with their problem, but is already committed to Wayne's company, more so because her boyfriend Warren Porter, who helped finance her mill, is in cahoots with Wayne. Chris mingles his romantic pursuit of Jerry with an appeal to get a trucking contract with her company, making her suspicious of his motives. Joe is more successful making a case for winning Jerry's business, but Chris is jealous, thinking Joe has personal designs on her.

Things look up when Jerry awards the Chapmans' company a hauling contract, but this only intensifies the rivalry with Wayne. Another trucking accident befalls the Chapman family, but this time there is a fatality. Blaming himself for improperly repairing the truck's brakes, Joe packs up to leave, but he and his buddy soon realize that the vehicle was sabotaged, leading to a potentially deadly confrontation with Wayne and Porter.

Hot Cargo was set for production in the summer of 1945, with trade papers announcing that Robert Lowery would play the second male lead. However, as reported in *Daily Variety* (June 5, 1945), the shoot was postponed until fall due to "adverse weather," with the mostly-indoors *They Made Me a Killer* (starring Lowery) taking its place on the production roster. Cameras finally rolled in mid–August.

Another Pine-Thomas love triangle: (left to right) William Gargan, Jean Rogers, and Philip Reed star in *Hot Cargo*.

Leading lady Jean Rogers (1916–1991) returned to films after a two-year absence to star in *Hot Cargo*; she had walked off the lot at MGM in 1943 after a fight with studio boss Louis B. Mayer. David Holt (1927–2003), seen as teenager Pete, had a fairly successful career as a child actor, but as an adult found his calling as a songwriter and music publisher. Character actress Virginia Brissac (1883–1979), enjoying one of her more sizable roles here as Mrs. Chapman, may be most recognizable as James Dean's grandmother in *Rebel without a Cause* (1955).

Hot Cargo benefits from a snappy, action-laden script that moves briskly. Although several contemporary sources attribute the script to Daniel Mainwaring (using his Geoffrey Homes pseudonym), Maxwell Shane donated a signed copy of the July 23, 1945, screenplay to the University of Wyoming with his personal papers, indicating that it was his own work. According to the American Film Institute Catalog, Homes' contribution was a story treatment called "Redwood Highway." Busy B director Lew Landers (1901–1962) cranked out eight other low-budget films in 1945; he would return to the Pine-Thomas fold with *Danger Street* (1947).

An unidentified clipping in Thomas' scrapbook told of the ribbing given to star Philip Reed about his return from real-life military service. Noting that Reed was cast in *Hot Cargo* as an ex-serviceman, Thomas cracked, "Only this time, he has decorations." Once shooting was completed, *Daily Variety* (December 20, 1945) reported, "Pine Thomas cutters are working at top speed," simultaneously editing *Hot Cargo* and *Swamp Fire*, while receiving daily rushes from the filming of *Big Town*.

REVIEWS: "P-T get most out of their budget ... action often packs a wallop. Lew Landers in his direction hops up a script which sometimes goes off the beam in dialog, and manages to maintain semblance of suspense which has satisfactory fade-out.... Exteriors in Big Trees country of Northern California [are] particularly interesting." *Daily Variety*, March 12, 1946

"*Hot Cargo*, for all the value of its basic plot idea, is simply a hodge-podge thriller which is hard pressed to maintain the spectator's interest even in the face of its brief running time. The fault lies in an inadequate script, redundant in clichés and about as pat and stereotyped in its dialogue as the lowest of the B's. With only Bill Gargan as mild box-office bait, this will find its level as a dualler in the lesser action spots." *Independent Exhibitors' Film Bulletin*, March 13, 1946

Swamp Fire (1946)

CAST: Johnny Weissmuller (*Johnny Duval*), Virginia Grey (*Janet Hilton*), Buster Crabbe (*Mike Kalavich*), Carol Thurston (*Toni Rousseau*), Pedro de Cordoba (*Tim Rousseau*), Marcelle Corday (*Grandmere Rousseau*), William Edmunds (*Emile Ledoux*), Edwin Maxwell (*Pierre Moise*), Pierre Watkin (*P.T. Hilton*), Charles Gordon (*Capt. Hal Peyton*), Frank Fenton (*Capt. Pete Dailey*), Joseph Crehan (*Capt. Sorenson*), Libby Taylor (*Hilton's Maid*), Emmett Vogan (*Engstead*), Edward Earle (*Baxter*), I. Stanford Jolley, Crane Whitley (*Coast Guard Skippers*), Carol Thomas (*Felicité*)

CREW: William H. Pine (*Director*), Geoffrey Homes (*Screenplay*). L.B. Merman (*Associate Producer*), Fred Jackman, Jr. (*Director of Photography*), Howard Smith (*Supervising Editor*), Henry Adams (*Editor*), F. Paul Sylos (*Art Director*), Louis Diege (*Set Decorator*), Harold Knox (*Assistant Director*), Rudy Schrager (*Music Score*)

RELEASED September 1946. 69 minutes.

Returning to Cypress Point, his home in the Louisiana bayou, after wartime service in the Coast Guard, Johnny Duval meets spoiled rich girl Janet Hilton when her reckless piloting of a speedboat capsizes his smaller craft. Janet likes the cut of Johnny's jib, but soon sees that his heart belongs to a local woman, Toni Rousseau. However, during Johnny's absence, a rival, Mike Kalavich, has been trying to take his place in Toni's affections.

Traumatized by his wartime experiences, in which a ship he commanded was lost, with casualties, Johnny no longer wants to serve in the Coast Guard Reserve. But his former captain wants him back on the job, and his friends conspire to convince him. Persuaded to fill in for a pilot feigning illness, Johnny begins to regain his confidence, and agrees to serve again. On duty, he encounters Janet, aboard her father's ship, and she tenaciously pursues her interest in him. Unable to get Johnny to ask her to a local dance, Janet finds another escort, and intrudes on Johnny's evening with Toni, causing a fight between the two ladies.

Seeing his pugnacious girlfriend home, Johnny tells Toni he wants to marry her in a few days, when he has time off. Before that can happen, Johnny is pressured into piloting a wealthy man's ship on a fog-shrouded night. Johnny goes ahead against his better judgment, and the result is a crackup that leaves Toni's brother dead.

Swamp Fire: Hasn't Mike (Buster Crabbe, left) heard that three's a crowd? Johnny (Johnny Weissmuller) and Toni (Carol Thurston) are too busy to explain.

With his family and friends unsure of his whereabouts, a guilt-ridden Johnny drinks himself into a stupor in New Orleans, and is injured in a traffic accident. Coming to his rescue is none other than Janet Hilton, who installs him at her father's mansion and nurses him back to health, all the while refusing to let Toni see him, and destroying her letters. Thinking he has no future with Toni, Johnny accepts a job with Janet's father, a wealthy businessman who has bought much of the land where the residents of Cypress Point have made their living hunting, fishing, and trapping. Already spoiling for a fight with Johnny, Mike Kalavich is enraged by the Hiltons' takeover of the delta, and makes sure Toni knows his rival now works for the family. When a local resident is threatened with arrest for trespassing on the Hiltons' land, Mike decides the best way to deal with the powerful newcomers is to burn them out.

Swamp Fire gets underway with a story element that was fast wearing out its welcome at Pine-Thomas—the blue-collar man who steps away from his life's work because he feels responsible for an accident in which one or more coworkers were killed. However, after some earlier films that spent too much time indoors, this film introduces viewers to a new environment, the bayous of Louisiana, and adds some fresh plot elements. The producers indulged in some on-location filming, which is not to say that the rear projection screen has been abandoned entirely. Production values are mostly good, though the footage of an alligator that threatens Toni, bringing Johnny to her rescue, is obviously spliced in from stock footage.

Leading man Johnny Weissmuller (1904–1984), a former Olympic athlete turned movie star who'd been playing Tarzan onscreen for nearly 15 years, was delighted to accept the role in *Swamp Fire*. According to Bill Thomas, Weissmuller had it stipulated contractually that he would appear fully clothed in the film, with not a loincloth in sight. Unfortunately, he was still at best a limited actor. According to Weissmuller's son, the star's recollection of the film was, "Buster Crabbe and I wrestled underwater for a few scenes, and both came out wet but richer."[19] Weissmuller also scored a gig for his kid brother Pete, who served as his stand-in, and would play minor roles in a couple of later P-T films.

Crabbe, who'd also taken a stab at playing the King of the Apes, gives a better performance than his costar, but most of the acting honors here go to the ladies. Virginia Grey (1917–2004), as snobbish Janet, and Carol Thurston (1920–1969), as passionate but goodhearted Toni, give colorful performances that considerably enliven the film. Inverting the usual stereotype of the period, dark-haired Miss Thurston is the one to root for, while Miss Grey has fun making her rich blonde character both sexy and distinctly unlikable. Their dance hall fight, occasioned by Grey's character saying to Thurston, "Why, you swamp rat!" is lively and entertaining, coming to a close with both ladies getting a dunking in the water. Marcelle Corday (1890–1971) has a few good moments as Toni's "Grand-Mere," whose blunt assessment of Mike is, "He just sit around like dead catfish on sand bar."

Making her film debut (and swan song) in *Swamp Fire* is Bill Thomas' eight-year-old daughter Carol, seen in a brief appearance as Felicité, one of Emile Ledoux's many children. Actor William Edmunds, in his first scene, scoops her up in his arms, and tells Felicité to find Mike. In her only line, Carol responds, "We'll get him, Papa!" Laughing as she looked back on it years later, Carol Thomas Pantages said, "I don't think I was very good. They never asked me again!"

REVIEWS: "Humble as it is, the story makes too heavy demands on Weissmuller's acting ability, though he will satisfy his followers with some thrills in the water.... William Pine's direction achieves his purpose of wrapping up the showmanship ingredients." *Box Office Digest*, May 25, 1946

"An unimpressive plot, stilted dialogue, and uninspired direction make this program melodrama mediocre entertainment ... on the whole the action is slow-moving and dull." *Harrison's Reports*, May 18, 1946

Seven Were Saved (1947)

CAST: Richard Denning (*Capt. Allen Danton*), Catherine Craig (*Lt. Susan Briscoe*), Russell Hayden (*Capt. Jim Willis*), Ann Doran (*Alice Hartley*), Byron Barr (*Lt. Martin Pinkert*), Richard Loo (*Col. Yamura*), Don Castle (*Lt. Pete Sturdevant*), George Tyne (*Sgt. Blair*), Keith Richards (*Mr. Smith*), John Eldredge (*Rollin Hartley*), Bill Kennedy (*Colonel*), Richard Benedict (*Sergeant*), Lorin Raker (*Hotel Desk Clerk*)

CREW: William H. Pine (*Director*), Maxwell Shane (*Screenplay*), Maxwell Shane, Julian Harmon (*Original Story*), L.B. Merman (*Associate Producer*), Jack Greenhalgh (*Director of Photography*), Howard Smith (*Editor*), F. Paul Sylos (*Art Director*), Earl Sitar (*Sound Recording*), Al Greenwood (*Set Decorator*), Capt. Kenneth H. Brettman (*Technical Advisor*), Darrell Calker (*Music Score*)

RELEASED March 1947. 72 minutes.

An American military flight to Manila, piloted by Captain Allen Danton, contains a varied lot of passengers: a newlywed couple, the Hartleys, who were previously held as war prisoners by the Japanese, an amnesiac patient known as Mr. Smith, his nurse, Lt. Susan Briscoe, and Colonel Yamura, a Japanese military officer awaiting trial for military crimes. Waiting behind at the airport is Captain Jim Willis of the Army Air Forces Air-Sea Rescue Service, who has a quarrel with his girlfriend, Susan, after telling her he agreed to serve for another year. Alice Hartley faints when she sees the face of the amnesiac patient, but lets the others believe she was just overcome by the high altitude.

Colonel Yamura overpowers his military guard, stealing his weapon, and takes the passengers and crew as his hostages. He demands to be flown to an island where he can avoid the military execution he's sure awaits him in Manila. During a melee between Yamura and Captain Danton, the copilot is shot, and the plane plunges into the ocean.

An inflatable raft keeps the passengers and crew from drowning, but they are hundreds of miles from the nearest land, and will be difficult to trace as they were far off their charted course. Several of the group argues that Yamura should be left to die, but Lt. Pinkert insists on taking him into Manila to face justice. Though Alice still maintains that she does not know "Mr. Smith," she works without success to revive his memory.

While a distraught Jim Willis and his coworkers search for the group lost at sea, Allen and Susie ration the group's emergency supplies, and try to keep morale from giving way. As bits and pieces of his past come back to the amnesiac patient, Alice ultimately confesses that he is her first husband, Philip Thompson, whom she thought was dead after both were held in a prison camp. During Hartley's turn on watch duty, Thompson disappears, and the others believe Alice's new husband killed him. When Col. Yamura suggests that Hartley is just as ruthless as he, a fight breaks out, and the raft is capsized. The men are able to set the raft afloat again, but all the group's food rations, as well as the raft's sail and oars, have been lost. Finding a message scrawled by Thompson before he went overboard, Alice and the others realize that Hartley did not kill him.

Allen continues to insist that the group has not lost the battle for survival, though things look grim. Back at the base, Jim is finally grounded from further searching for his fiancée after he contracts malaria. As days go by without rescue, the survivors of the crash contend with sharks, storms, leaks in the raft, and Allen's loss of sight. Finally, against orders, Jim rises from his hospital bed, determined to make one final search for his fiancée and her fellow passengers.

Seven Were Saved is a moderately entertaining programmer, though no threat to the greatness of Hitchcock's *Lifeboat*, released three years earlier. Publicists were guilty of more than a little hyperbole when they promised moviegoers "a brilliant combination of a tense, taut screenplay and a spectacular display of the work of the Army Air Force's Air-Sea Rescue Service." The characters spend too much time talking about what has happened to them in the past, with little of it shown. (One exception is a brief sequence showing how Jim and Susie met, when they were inadvertently assigned to share a hotel room while on leave.) Not to be counted among the film's high points is the scene in which the raft springs a leak, a problem tackled by Allen and his cohorts with a wad of bubble gum that one of them conveniently happens to have.

Catherine Craig (1915–2004) makes the character of Susan strong, attractive, and capable; Pine and Thomas would put her to work again in *Albuquerque* (1949). Ann Doran (1911–2000) mostly averts the danger of making her beleaguered character whiny, though it's an uphill battle given the script. Richard Loo (1903–1983), although Chinese by heritage and a native of Hawaii, was Hollywood's favorite portrayer of cold-hearted Japanese soldiers during the 1940s; his assignment here demands less of him than his previous turn in *Tokyo Rose*. Richard Denning, who previously worked for Bill Thomas in the collegiate comedy *Campus Confessions* (1938), filmed *Seven Were Saved* shortly after his 1946 release from the U.S. Navy. Featured actor Don Castle, returning to motion pictures after serving in World War II, was a veteran of Pine-Thomas' first film, *Power Dive*.

This is the first of several Pine-Thomas films from the period not shot by their long-favored cinematographer Fred Jackman, Jr. Jack Greenhalgh (1904–1971) will be credited as director of photography on most of the company's 1947 releases.

REVIEWS: "The fact that almost all of the sequences take place in mid-ocean, aboard a small rubber raft, stultifies whatever action the picture might have contained. The players are good, however, although they are required to take part in far-fetched sequences...." *Showmen's Trade Review*, February 22, 1947

"Picture, because of its subject matter, is assured reception at turnstiles, but lacks the excitement which should attend presentation of such a topic.... There are static pauses which have no place here, due to having to follow too many persons in too restricted an area. On other hand, [the] characterizations are well managed." *Daily Variety*, February 17, 1947

Fear in the Night (1947)

CAST: Paul Kelly (*Cliff Harlan*), DeForest Kelley (*Vince Grayson*), Ann Doran (*Lil Harlan*), Kay Scott (*Betty Winters*), Charles Victor (*Captain Warner*), Robert Emmett Keane (*Lewis Belknap*), Jeff Yorke (*Deputy Torrence*)

CREW: Maxwell Shane (*Director/Screenplay*), William Irish (*Story*), Jack Greenhalgh (*Director of Photography*), Howard Smith (*Film Editor*), F. Paul Sylos (*Art Director*), Frank Webster (*Sound Recording*), Elias H. Reif (*Set Decorator*), Rudy Schrager (*Music Score*)

RELEASED April 1947. 71 minutes.

Young bank teller Vince Grayson wakes from a vivid and disturbing dream in which he kills a man in an odd, octagonal-shaped room with mirrors all around, after which a beautiful blonde flees. In his room at the hotel where he lives, Vince begins preparing for work, only to find that some of the elements of his dream seem to have followed him into the real world. He has thumbprints on his neck, as if he'd actually struggled with the man in the dream, and there's a key in his pocket that he's never seen before—except in his nightmare.

Calling in sick at work, Vince consults his brother-in-law, Cliff, a police detective. Skeptical, Cliff says, "Either you dream a thing, or it really happened." Bewildered, Vince places a classified ad seeking a mirrored room like the one from his dream, but the responses he gets aren't helpful.

Cliff buys a new car and plans an outing to the country for himself, his pregnant wife Lil, Vince, and Vince's co-worker and girlfriend, Betty. When a sudden rainstorm cuts short the picnic they'd planned, Cliff seeks a place to get out of the downpour, and Vince directs him to a house nearby. Though the owners aren't home, Vince knows where they keep a spare key, something he can't explain. Upstairs, Vince finds the mirrored room from his dream. Furious, Cliff accuses his brother-in-law of concocting an elaborate story to cover up a murder he committed, and demands the truth.

Just then, a local sheriff's deputy walks in, and explains to Cliff and Vince (while the ladies are asleep in another room) that the house belongs to a wealthy couple, Mr. and Mrs. Belknap, and was recently the scene of a murder. Lovely young Mrs. Belknap's body was found a short distance away, run down by a car. The chief suspect was her friend—until his body was found in the closet of the mirrored room. Vince reluctantly accompanies Cliff and the deputy to the local sheriff's station, where a look at photos of the murder victims causes him to pass out cold.

Without telling his wife that her brother may be a murderer, Cliff takes Vince home, telling him he'll be back tomorrow to take him to the police station. Wracked with despair, Vince climbs out on the ledge outside his hotel room, ready to end it all. Cliff saves his brother-in-law's life, and for the first time believes there may be something to Vince's seemingly wild story.

After having a hand in writing, or co-writing, most of the previous Pine-Thomas films, Maxwell Shane hits a home run with this nifty thriller that he directed, as well as authoring the screenplay. Adapted from a short story by Cornell Woolrich, *Fear in the Night* may be Pine-Thomas' finest film of the 1940s. It offers an engaging plot that hooks the attention from the opening scene, and holds up throughout the film's running time. The film is still low-budget (reportedly in the range of $180,000), but doesn't suffer much for this. Not everything about it works perfectly—Vince's voice-over narration in the early scenes is a little overdone, trying too hard to explain his thoughts and actions instead of letting us observe for ourselves. However, the plot was an unusual one for the period, and without this it's possible audiences might have been confused.

The *Los Angeles Times'* Edwin Schallert (April 28, 1945) reported that Pine and Thomas originally acquired Woolrich's short story intending to cast Byron Barr in the lead. Instead, 27-year-old DeForest Kelley (1920–1999) won the assignment, and delivers a compelling lead performance. Nearly 20 years before he gained widespread recognition as Dr. McCoy on TV's *Star Trek*, Kelley's face was a *tabula rasa* for 40s moviegoers, which works in the film's favor. He's playing a somewhat jittery, uncertain young man (whose sister, for reasons unspecified, has been worried about him for some time). Kelley walks a narrow line playing a man who may or may not be a reliable narrator, and who we're not certain deserves our sympathy.

Other solid performances come from Paul Kelly (1899–1956), as Vince's no-nonsense brother, whose outwardly hardboiled nature is softened mostly by his love for his wife, and Ann Doran, matching Kelly well as his spirited wife, who keeps him in line with great fondness. Newcomer Kay Scott (1927–1971) does fine as the pretty, kind young woman who loves Vince throughout it all.

REVIEWS: "Tiptop job of projecting suspense makes *Fear in the Night* a nifty entry for dual bookings. It's a good psychological melodrama, unfolded at fast clip, and will please the whodunit-and-how fans…. Suspense mood is furthered by Jack Greenhalgh's lensing and the score by Rudy Schrager." *Variety*, February 19, 1947

"A spine-tingling melodrama of murder … clever use of camera angles, montage shots, musical backgrounds which dovetail neatly with the macabre situations, and convincing acting of DeForest Kelley as the man haunted by his dream." *Motion Picture Herald*, February 22, 1947

Big Town (1947)

CAST: Philip Reed (*Steve Wilson*), Hillary Brooke (*Lorelei Kilbourne*), Robert Lowery (*Pete Ryan*), Veda Ann Borg (*Vivian LeRoy*), Byron Barr (*Vance Crane*), Charles Arnt (*Amos Peabody*), Nana Bryant (*Mrs. Crane*), Frank Fenton (*Fletcher*), Roy Gordon (*Post*), Eddie Parks (*Gerald Meeker*), Nella Walker (*Mrs. Johanssen*), Thomas E. Jackson (*Chief Berkley*), Harry Cheshire (*Chief Masters*), John Dehner (*Willard Erskine*), Blake Edwards (*Nixon*), Nolan Leary (*Train Conductor*), Emmett Vogan (*Joe*), Sol Gorss (*Roustabout*), Richard Lydon (*Boy*), Frank J. Scannell (*Carnival Barker*), Rose Plumer (*Nurse*)

CREW: William C. Thomas (*Director*), Geoffrey Homes (*Screenplay*), Geoffrey Homes, Maxwell Shane (*Original Story*), Maxwell Shane (*Associate Producer*), Fred Jackman (*Director of Photography*), Howard Smith (*Supervising Editor*), Henry Adams (*Editor*), F. Paul Sylos (*Art Director*), Earl Sitar (*Sound Recording*), Glenn P. Thompson (*Set Decorator*), Darrell Calker (*Music Score*)

RELEASED May 1947. 60 minutes.

Steve Wilson is traveling by railroad to take up his new job as managing editor of an urban newspaper, the *Illustrated Press*. When a train accident occurs en route, Wilson captures photographs, and sends them in to the city desk of his new employer. On his first day of work, however, he learns that the photos were deemed too grisly, and not published. Steve realizes that the *Press* is in a slump, a lethargic operation that puts out a tame product and has low circulation.

Despite the skepticism of the staff he inherited, including cynical reporter Pete Ryan, Steve insists on shaking things up, creating a paper that can successfully compete with its more popular rival, the *Chronicle*. When reporter Lorelei Kilbourne, who's been working for the *Press* since graduating college, returns from a short vacation, she hits it off with Steve, and respects his desire for a new approach.

Steve's aggressive reporting of dramatic stories (such as a college dean accused of making passes at a student) quickly boosts circulation, but Lorelei's resolve is tested when a story surfaces that involves friends of hers. Getting the details from the victim's grieving mother, a family friend, of a young woman's death, Lorelei is relieved when Steve excuses her from covering the story, but infuriated when he then assigns Pete to do so.

Threatening to quit, Lorelei postpones her decision when dispatched to cover a movie theater holdup, with the fleeing robber having a shootout with police. Picking up a dropped lipstick at the crime scene, Lorelei and Pete are convinced that the getaway thief was a woman, leading to Steve's lurid headline, "Pistol Packin' Mama Routs Police Force." The editor of the *Chronicle* accuses Steve's staff of concocting the story, and issues him a public challenge to prove it, or retract it. With some smart detective work, Lorelei and Pete track down the thief, a female sharpshooter named Vivian LeRoy, and coax her into confessing at the front entrance of the *Chronicle* building.

Steve's bravery has limits, as Lorelei discovers when he reluctantly kills a series of exposes of unsafe amusement parks, because the owner is an *Illustrated Press* advertiser. Quitting in a huff, Lorelei goes to work for the *Chronicle*, and Pete soon follows. Needing a substitute for the nixed expose articles, Steve makes a connection between two recent murders, and dubs the suspect the "Vampire Murderer." Police arrest nervous mama's boy Vance Crane for the crime, but Lorelei and Pete believe he is innocent. Doubling down, Steve publishes dirt about Crane's history in a mental hospital, bringing about another death that finally gives him pause to think about the course he's taken as an editor, and the fallout that results.

Based on a popular radio series that debuted in 1937, originally starring Edward G. Robinson and Claire Trevor, *Big Town* is the first of four entries in what will be the only film series to be produced under the Pine-Thomas banner. *Box Office Digest* (August 11, 1945) reported that Pine and Thomas had signed Maxwell Shane, who had worked on the *Big Town* radio show, to oversee the film series as writer-producer, planning to release two installments per year. Although it relies on some slightly worn tropes about the newspaper business, and the cynicism of reporters, this is a very entertaining melodrama that is little hampered by its tight budget. "You're in for a big time in Big Town when fighting Steve Wilson and lovely Lorelei Kilbourne solve the riddle of the Vampire Murders!" trumpeted studio ads. The story sets up the basic premise that will inform the series, as Steve Wilson and his colleagues acknowledge that they can do both good and evil in their posts as journalists, and ultimately conclude that they want to use their power to right wrongs.

All four of P-T's *Big Town* series will star the team of Philip Reed and Hillary Brooke. No stranger to series films, Miss Brooke (1914–1999) also graced entries in the *Maisie*, *Crime Doctor*, and *Sherlock Holmes* series. Veda Ann Borg (1915–1973) is colorful in her minor role as a gun-toting robber. Robert Lowery's secondary part as Pete doesn't make the most of his ability, and at least one reviewer suggested that he, rather than Reed, should have played the starring role.

Although early trade reviews were tepid, by the time they were published the next installment of the series was completed and awaiting release.

REVIEWS: "Philip Reed is not convincing as a dynamic managing editor who jumps the circulation of his newspaper…. Hillary Brooke … looks pretty but is given lines to read that would cause any real-life managing editor to toss her out … suitable for supporting fare on double-bill programs." *Showmen's Trade Review*, February 22, 1947

"It lacks punch and a set of convincing characters…. Somewhere after first reel or so, feeling of hard-hitting newspaper practice is supplanted by artificial set of circumstances which do not ring true…. Pine-Thomas made most of their budget in production activities…." *Daily Variety*, February 17, 1947

Danger Street (1947)

CAST: Jane Withers (*Pat Marvin*), Robert Lowery (*Larry Berke*), Bill Edwards (*Sandy Evans*), Elaine Riley (*Cynthia Van Loan*), Audrey Young (*Dolores Thompson*), Lyle Talbot (*Charles Johnson*), Charles Quigley (*Carl Pauling*), Lucia Carroll (*Smitty*), Nina Mae McKinney (*Veronica*), Vera Marshe (*Amanda Matthews*), Roy Gordon (*John Matthews*), Paul Harvey (*J.B. Turlock*), John Harmon (*Riley*), Charles Coleman (*Plumley*), Eddie Parks (*Joe*), Pierre Watkin (*Publisher*), Will Wright (*Chief Bullward*), Lorin Raker (*Henry*), Frank Ferguson (*Chief Boward*), Harry Cheshire (*Commissioner*), Hal K. Dawson (*Stevens*), Guy Wilkerson (*Jake*), Harlan Briggs (*Darstein*)

CREW: Lew Landers (*Director*), Maxwell Shane, Winston Miller, Kae Salkow (*Screenplay*), Winston Miller, Kae Salkow (*Original Story*), Benjamin H. Kline (*Director of Photography*), Howard Smith (*Editor*), F. Paul Sylos (*Art Director*), Earl C. Sitar (*Sound Recording*), Al Greenwood (*Set Decorator*), Darrell Calker (*Music Score*)

RELEASED June 1947. 65 minutes.

Pat Marvin and her boyfriend Larry Berke are on the staff of *Flick*, "the magazine that's there when it happens." Pat scores a scoop when she infiltrates an illegal gambling club and comes away with incriminating photos, but publisher J.B. Turlock balks, saying he doesn't want to put out a sordid publication. Instead, he plans to sell the magazine, which thanks to his editorial timidity is losing money.

Larry, Pat, and their staff pool their resources to buy the magazine themselves, raising the $27,000 purchase price. But when bookkeeper Riley confesses that he took some of his contribution from *Flick*'s cash fund, Larry realizes the money must be replaced before Turlock's auditors examine the books.

Having only a day or so to raise nearly $3,000, Larry promises rival editor Jack Withers of *Newsview* exclusive photos of the engagement party of wealthy Cynthia Van Loan, "the heiress who's never been photographed." To get the pictures, Larry and Pat take jobs as servants at the Van Loan mansion. Among the photos Larry captures is one of Cynthia's fiancé, Carl Pauling, kissing another woman. Pauling finds the camera Larry dropped at the scene, and tracks him to the *Flick* offices, where the editor informs him he sold the photos to Jack Withers. But before Withers can pay for the photos, Larry and Pat find him murdered. Feeling responsible for Withers' death, Larry returns to the Van Loan estate, where he and Pat set a trap. Sure that Pauling is the murderer, since Larry learned that he's broke and marrying Cynthia for her money, the editor and reporter are in for a surprise. Before he can unravel the case, Pauling has been killed, Larry is charged, and Pat begs the police chief for 30 minutes to solve the mystery before her boyfriend is incarcerated.

This is a fun, fast-paced comic mystery that, while tabbed with a meaningless title, makes more-than-adequate light entertainment. It was the final lead role for former child star Jane Withers (born 1926), just short of 20 years old when it was filmed. She's endearing as the plucky Nancy Drew–wannabe heroine, who brings her dog along on investigations, and intrepidly barges in wherever her camera can capture a story. A set visitor reported that Miss Withers was disappointed when a script rewrite toned down the romantic scene she'd looked forward to playing opposite Lowery. "After we romp all around town solving murders and putting out the magazine on the side," she said, "we were supposed to get together in the last scene for that big smooch session.... And then they tell me they've changed the whole ending. No kiss."[20]

After the release of *Danger Street*, Withers will be absent from movie screens for nine years, concentrating on her marriage and children, before making her comeback with a featured appearance in *Giant* (1956). She and Lowery work well together, and create engaging characters that enlist the audience's sympathy and interest.

Whether or not audiences of the time noticed, *Danger Street* recycles several character names and details from the earlier Pine-Thomas film *Double Exposure*. Both concern a magazine named *Flick*, with staffers named Larry, Pat, and Smitty, and a health nut owner named Turlock. Both feature scenes in which Larry's secretary uses a buzzer under her desk to signal him when Turlock arrives at the office, so that he can toss out his cigarette, and be found busy with the kind of vigorous exercise that the boss espouses. But while both films are comic murder mysteries, the basic plots are different, and none of the same actors are used. In pre-production, *Danger Street* was known by the title "Picture Snatchers," and was announced as a sequel to *Double Exposure*.

Pine-Thomas favorite Will Wright has some amusing moments as the police chief who gets in a huff every time someone tries to boss him around (saying, "Don't tell me

Former child star Jane Withers was ready for a leading lady role, complete with handsome love interest (Robert Lowery) in *Danger Street*.

what to do!"), but then proceeds to do exactly what's been suggested to him. Lucia Carroll (1916–1988) is seen as Flick's tough-talking receptionist; told by a caller that, contrary to the magazine's slogan, its staff was absent when something newsworthy took place, she snaps, "Well, if we weren't there, it didn't happen!" and hangs up. Lyle Talbot (1902–1996), as one of the suspects at the Van Loan house party, has little to do. Beautiful African American actress Nina Mae McKinney (1912–1967) is mostly wasted in a small comic characterization as the Van Loans' cook, Veronica, who doesn't intend to let a murder investigation spoil her dinner date.

REVIEWS: "The plot is too contrived to be convincing, and the behavior of the leading characters such as to be irritating to an adult audience ... 66 minutes of somewhat uninspired sleuthing." *Motion Picture Daily*, February 27, 1947

"Although everyone in the cast tries to make something of his or her role, they are helpless, hampered by ... proceedings that are so contrived and bewildering that one loses interest in the solution. The comedy, on the whole, is too forced to be amusing." *Harrison's Reports*, March 1, 1947

I Cover Big Town (1947)

CAST: Philip Reed (*Steve Wilson*), Hillary Brooke (*Lorelei Kilbourne*), Robert Lowery (*Pete Ryan*), Robert Shayne (*Chief Tom Blake*), Mona Barrie (*Dora Hilton*), Vince Barnett (*Louis Murkil*), Louis Jean Heydt (*John Moulton*), Frank Wilcox (*Harry Hilton*), Leonard Penn (*Norden Royal*), Pete Weissmuller (*Reporter*)

CREW: William C. Thomas (*Director*), Maxwell Shane (*Associate Producer*), Whitman Chambers (*Screenplay*), Jack Greenhalgh (*Director of Photography*), Howard Smith (*Editor*), F. Paul Sylos (*Art Director*), L.J. Myers (*Sound Recording*), Elias H. Reif (*Set Decorator*)

RELEASED June 1947. 63 minutes.

Illustrated Press editor Steve Wilson is dubious that a woman can handle covering the newspaper's police beat, but Lorelei insists on being given an opportunity. The initial skepticism of her male colleagues seems to be borne out when she is scooped on stories by her rival Pete Ryan, who is not above eavesdropping on Lorelei to win the upper hand.

The discovery of a dead body in the garage of married couple Harry and Dora Hilton leads to their arrests, but Lorelei, unconvinced that they are guilty, continues to investigate. The revelation that the murdered man, B.C. Squires, was Dora Hilton's first husband strengthens the case against her, while her current husband is accused of embezzling money from his business partner, Norden Royal. When Harry Hilton and his cellmate John Moulton escape from prison, the result is a deadly shootout that leaves one man dead. Lorelei's abilities as a journalist, as well as her bravery, are proven, and the *Illustrated Press* has another headline story.

I Cover Big Town was filmed in May 1946. The scenes set in the Hiltons' garage called for the use of a canine cast member; a column item in *Daily Variety* (May 27, 1946) noted that "plenty of confusion" was created on the film set "with the wardrobe man named Henry West and the dog trainer's name being Henry East." The picture's release followed so closely on the heels of *Big Town* that they played simultaneously in some cities.

REVIEWS: "A solid entry for deuce spot on any double bill. Cleverly concocted, it'll get green light from scribes for McCoy pressroom sequences, plus approval of payees for a tight plot larded with giggles." *Daily Variety*, February 24, 1947

"Here is a neat little offering which gives Hillary Brooke her best screen role to date and she takes full advantage of her opportunity.... Co-producer William C. Thomas effectively handled the direction." *Film Daily*, March 3, 1947

Adventure Island (1947)

CAST: Rory Calhoun (*Mr. Herrick*), Rhonda Fleming (*Faith Wishart*), Paul Kelly (*Capt. Donald Lochlin*), John Abbott (*Huish*), Alan Napier (*Attwater*), Val Carlo (*Joseph*), Julian Rivero (*Uncle Ned*), Iris Bynam (*Bathsheba*), Lilo Yarson (*David*), Delmar Costello (*Sally Day*)

CREW: Peter Stewart [Sam Newfield] (*Director*), Maxwell Shane (*Screenplay*, based on *Ebb Tide* by Robert Louis Stevenson and Lloyd Osbourne), Jack Greenhalgh (*Director of Photography*), Howard Smith (*Film Editor*), F. Paul Sylos (*Art Director*), L. John Myers (*Sound Recording*), Elias H. Reif (*Set Decorator*), Arthur Phelps (*Color Supervisor*), Darrell Calker (*Music Score*)

RELEASED August 1947. 66 minutes.

On a remote island, young Mr. Herrick befriends Captain Donald Lochlin and his British pal Huish, after they rescue him from drowning in quicksand. Short of food, the three plot to steal a pig from the livestock of the island's governor, and wind up in jail for their troubles. Lochlin, a disgraced sea captain whose last ship sank, is offered a release from prison if he assumes the command of a vessel carrying a cargo of champagne, which the governor wants delivered to Sydney, Australia. Lochlin insists on having his buddies as crew members, and the three set off.

Thinking his career is doomed anyway, Lochlin proposes that they take the ship to Peru, where they can sell it along with the cargo. But they are surprised to learn they have a stowaway, Faith Wishart, daughter of the previous captain. Faith pulls a gun on the trio, and insists they resume the scheduled course to Australia.

Huish breaks into the ship's cargo and gets both himself and Lochlin drunk. Under the influence, Huish tries to assault Faith, and Herrick comes to her rescue. In the ensuing fight, a fire breaks out, and most of the ship's provisions are burned. Faith is heartbroken that most of the cargo of champagne bottles consists of nothing but water, making her realize her late father was dishonest.

Off course after the melee, Herrick and his fellow passengers spot a remote island up ahead. Faith stays behind on the ship while Herrick, Lochlin, and Huish investigate. Though the island initially seems to be deserted, they discover evidence that it has been inhabited previously. They are startled by the arrival of Attwater, a well-spoken, seemingly courtly Englishman who has made the island his kingdom. After most of the native inhabitants died in a smallpox epidemic, Attwater convinced the survivors that he was a god, and has been ruling the island unchecked ever since.

Attwater displays his megalomania, having a native man thrown into a snake pit when he is caught perpetrating a small theft. Desperate for the food stores Attwater can provide, and greedy for the pearls he has accumulated on the island, Lochlin wants to kill him, but Herrick intercedes. When Faith leaves the ship and disembarks on the island,

Attwater takes a liking to the pretty young woman, and decides the other men can leave, with their larder replenished—as long as they leave her behind.

Ten years after Paramount made a much higher-budgeted version of Stevenson and Osbourne's novel *Ebb Tide* under its original name, the Dollar Bills recycled the plot, and most of the character names, in this modestly budgeted programmer. Any thematic significance or subtext in the book has been pretty thoroughly leached out of this adaptation, in favor of concentrating on fires, fistfights, and gunplay.

Adventure Island marks the P-T debut of leading lady Rhonda Fleming (born 1923), who will become one of their favorite female stars of the 1950s. Black-haired Rory Calhoun (1922–1999), in one of his first important roles, teams with Miss Fleming to make a sexy, vibrant couple. Both were borrowed from impresario David O. Selznick, who had them under personal contract; their combined paycheck came to $8,000. Paul Kelly, fresh from his strong featured assignment in in *Fear in the Night*, is just as solid here, though with less effective material to play.

Making his entrance at the 40-minute mark, Alan Napier (1903–1988) nearly steals the show as the crazed, self-satisfied Attwater. Thoroughly pleased with his small kingdom and eager servants ("I've given them all Biblical names!"), Attwater claims to be a do-gooder who takes charge of the "groveling heathens" for their own good. On their first meeting, we may wonder exactly what Attwater has in mind for Calhoun's Herrick, whom he invites to take a bath, cheerfully explaining that his mission on the island is "fishing for men." Napier's florid performance clearly pleased his bosses, who would use him again in the higher-budgeted *Manhandled*. For his part, the actor would praise Pine-Thomas in his memoir as "a splendidly efficient production company ... which paid well [and] shot fast."[21]

Shot in the "Cinecolor" process (a less impressive but far less expensive alternative to Technicolor), this was Pine-Thomas' first color film, and the Dollar Bills gave substantial publicity coverage to its sexy stars, Calhoun ("The Screen's New Swoon Sensation") and Fleming ("Hollywood's Gorgeous New Sarong Girl.") According to *Showmen's Trade Review* (April 19, 1947), at a sneak preview of the film, "Every time Calhoun appeared in close-up, the bobby-soxers drowned out the dialogue with screams and shrieks." In response, the producers cut three additional close-ups of the actor into the final print.

Also aimed at stirring enthusiasm for the picture was a contest for theater managers, offering a two-week tropical vacation as first prize. As *Motion Picture Herald* (September 6, 1947) explained, "Award will be based on the most original and complete campaign submitted, including publicity, advertising ideas, tieups, direct mail and other activities." *Daily Variety* (June 6, 1947) reported that ship owner Charles A. Williams filed a lawsuit against Paramount and Pine-Thomas Productions after completion of *Adventure Island* for "asserted damage done to vessel during filming," asking $8,701.38 for "repairs and loss of service."

REVIEWS: "The picture is compounded of dependable formula ingredients. Its occasional reliance on plot improbabilities will not bother those who like action and excitement in their outdoor dramas." *Motion Picture Daily*, August 11, 1947

"First tinter from Pine-Thomas is a home run. It's strictly escapist fare ... tricked out in Cinecolor's prettiest color job.... Calhoun and Miss Fleming aren't called upon for any heavy histrionics but they register effectively. Heroine photographs beautifully in color and will rouse the wolf calls." *Daily Variety*, August 11, 1947

Jungle Flight (1947)

CAST: Robert Lowery (*Kelly Jordan*), Ann Savage (*Laurey Roberts*), Bart [Barton] MacLane (*Case Hagin*), Douglas Fowley (*Tom Hammond*), Douglas Blackley [Robert Kent] (*Andy Melton*), Curt Bois (*Pepe*), Duncan Renaldo (*Captain Costa*), Lorin Raker (*Briggs*), Juan Torena (*Costa's Pilot*)

CREW: Peter Stewart [Sam Newfield] (*Director*), Whitman Chambers (*Screenplay*), David Lang (*Original Story*), Jack Greenhalgh (*Director of Photography*), Fred Jackman, Jr. (*Aerial Photography*), Hal Gordon, (*Editor*), F. Paul Sylos (*Art Director*), Don McKay (*Sound Recording*), Elias H. Reif (*Set Decorator*), Darrell Calker (*Music Score*)

RELEASED August 1947. 67 minutes.

Americans Kelly Jordan and Andy Melton are proprietors of J.M. Freight, flying cargo from a South American city, La Cuenta, to a mine in the mountain a few hundred miles away. They are working to pay off two planes, so that they can relocate to the U.S. The two friends find themselves quarreling over their work for mine boss Case Hagin, who pushes them to fly under conditions that are sometimes risky.

Though Jordan dubs himself "Careful Kelly," and isn't as inclined to take chances as his buddy, he's also eager to earn back some of the partnership's money he lost gambling, as he knows Andy wants to get home and see his wife and new baby. On a layover in La Cuenta, Kelly is indulging himself with wine, women and song when Andy decides to push ahead on a mission after Hagin dangles some extra money in front of him.

At Kelly's hotel, he's instantly attracted to fellow guest Laurey Roberts, a beautiful American singer, but she's too distraught to pay him any notice. On the run from her murderous ex-husband, Tom Hammond, she receives a radiogram warning her that he's due to arrive shortly. Unable to book a commercial flight for several days to come, Laurey tries to get Andy to take her as a passenger, but he's already carrying too much freight. When Andy is killed in a crash, Laurey finds herself breaking the news to Kelly, and they begin to grow closer.

With Hammond in pursuit of her, Laurey persuades Kelly to fly her out to the mining camp, without telling him the full story. On her arrival, Hagin grudgingly agrees to employ her as a cook, and over the next two weeks Laurey begins to relax. She and Kelly are well on their way to falling in love when Hammond staggers into camp, having been lost in the jungle. Using a phony name, he doesn't tell anyone of his connection to Laurey, and she is afraid to do so. When a police captain from town arrives by plane to arrest Hammond, who's being extradited, Hagin and Kelly believe she has duped them, and she's forced to head back to town with her ex-husband and his police escort. On board the plane, Hammond manages to overpower the police captain, pulls a gun on the pilot, and demands that he and Laurey be flown out of the country, despite the pilot's warnings that the trip is risky. Learning that the flight headed away from camp in distinctly the wrong direction for returning to town, Kelly takes off in pursuit of the first plane.

Though there's plenty of "flight" in *Jungle Flight*, the "jungle" is talked about more than seen, as most of the film takes place in the town of La Cuenta, or at Hagin's mining camp. Nevertheless, this is a suspenseful and well-paced film that gives moviegoers the action, romance, and excitement they were craving. The finished film was previewed for trade publications in February 1947, but not released until late summer.

Viewers who saw *Detour* may be expecting Savage's character to dispose of her worthless ex-husband tidily, but she's playing a milder character here. Robert Lowery and Ann Savage make a sexy couple, and she invests the character of Laurey with a bit of complexity that goes beyond what's in the script. Though her sexuality is relatively subtle here—Lowery, who goes shirtless in an early scene, bares more skin than his leading lady does—her allure is still more than evident.

Barton MacLane (1902–1969), going jauntily by "Bart" in the opening credits, barks most of his lines as the tough mining camp boss. He earns himself a punch from Lowery when he refers to Savage's character, on their first meeting, as "Sadie Thompson." Duncan Renaldo (1904–1980), who'd begun playing the Cisco Kid in films just a couple of years earlier, represents law enforcement in the city of La Cuenta.

Whitman Chambers' screenplay tosses in a few nice bits of dialogue. In the tradition of earlier Pine-Thomas films like *Wildcat*, the mining camp employs a distinctly lousy cook before the female lead arrives. Sniffing one bowl set before him, Lowery cracks, "I liked that billy goat better as a pet. He even smelled better." When Kelly's partner Andy declines Laurey's request to take her as a passenger, explaining that his plane is already weighted down with cargo, he explains, "Sorry, I'm overloaded now, and another ... [looking her up and down appraisingly] 125 pounds and I'd be in trouble." "A hundred and fourteen!" she retorts indignantly, and viewers won't quibble.

REVIEWS: "The plot ... is quite obvious and one is able to foresee the outcome, but, because of the dangers encountered by the hero, one is held in fair suspense. The aerial photography is particularly interesting." *Harrison's Reports*, March 1, 1947

"Peter Stewart keeps the ... script on the move with his direction although pace would have been helped by trimming another five minutes from footage.... Lowery and Miss Savage carry off the leads okay." *Variety*, February 26, 1947

Big Town After Dark (1947)

CAST: Philip Reed (*Steve Wilson*), Hillary Brooke (*Lorelei Kilbourne*), Richard Travis (*Chuck LaRue*), Anne [Ann] Gillis (*Susan Peabody*), Vince Barnett (*Louie Snead*), Joe Sawyer (*Monk*), Douglas Blackley [Robert Kent] (*Jake Sebastian*), Charles Arnt (*Amos Peabody*), Joe Allen, Jr. (*Wally Blake*), William Haade (*Marcus*), Sumner Getchell (*Harvey Cushman*), Marin Sais (*Mrs. O'Hara*), Arthur Space (*Fletcher*), Dorothy Vaughan (*Cleaning Woman*), John Holland (*D.A. Harding*), Mary Newton (*Nurse*), Guy Wilkerson (*Custodian*), Fred Aldrich (*Police Car Driver*)

CREW: William C. Thomas (*Director*), Whitman Chambers (*Screenplay*), Ellis W. Carter (*Director of Photography*), F. Paul Sylos (*Art Director*), Howard Smith (*Film Editor*), Max Hutchinson (*Sound Recording*), Glenn Thompson, Alfred Kegerris (*Set Decorators*), Darrell Calker (*Music Score*)

RELEASED December 1947. 69 minutes.

Lorelei Kilbourne of the *Illustrated Press* is annoyed when her boss, managing editor Steve Wilson, fails to congratulate her on selling a novel to a publisher. Her pride hurt, Lorelei gives her two weeks' notice. When the *Press'* owner, Amos Peabody, tells Steve his 20-year-old niece, Susan, a journalism student, is looking for a job, Steve hires her as a cub reporter, telling Lorelei she'll take over the police beat.

Susan tells Steve that the students at her school have been patronizing a private

Big Town's Crusading Newshawk Meets Mr. Murder Himself

in "the best of the Big Town series"(M.P. Herald) ..."another Big Town winner" (Hollywood Reporter) from . . . .

PINE-THOMAS

A glamour gun-moll posing as a crime-reporter by day and supplying her own victims by night, is trapped by radio's ace racket-buster when he covers his biggest story—*his own murder!*

BIG TOWN AFTER DARK

Starring

Philip Reed

and Hillary Brooke

with RICHARD TRAVIS · ANNE GILLIS · VINCE BARNETT
JOE SAWYER · DOUGLAS BLACKLEY · CHARLES ARNT
Directed by WILLIAM C. THOMAS
Original Screenplay by Whitman Chambers · Based on the radio program "Big Town"
A Paramount Picture

3rd In the "Big Town" Series based on the famous CBS radio program heard by millions every week on 143 stations —

Now playing: "Big Town"
          "I Cover Big Town"
Just released: "Big Town After Dark"
Coming soon: "Big Town Scandal"

Trade-paper ad for *Big Town After Dark,* which *Showmen's Trade Review* suggested "be paired with a western on the weekend to attract the thrill fans."

"poker joint" called the Winners' Club, and encourages him to check the place out, with an eye to writing a story. During Steve and Susan's visit, Steve is hauled into the office of owner Chuck LaRue, where he's given a beating by the boss' henchmen, and dumped unconscious a few miles away. When he wakes up, Steve learns that Susan is missing.

Using Lorelei's favorite informer, Louie, as a go-between, Amos Peabody enters into negotiations with LaRue and his men for his niece's safe return. Rather than charging him ransom, LaRue sells Peabody $50,000 worth of stock in the Winners' Club. Just as Peabody and Steve are telling the story to the district attorney, Susan turns up unharmed, and they are unable to press charges against LaRue, who points out that he never claimed to be holding her hostage.

Steve suggests that "a good old-fashioned muckraking expose" is what's needed to put a stop to LaRue's activities, but Lorelei is growing increasingly curious about Susan's part in the story. Though Lorelei soon learns that Susan lied about her background, and her whereabouts on the night of her supposed kidnapping, Steve shows no signs of heeding his colleague's warnings. Instead, after cozying up to Susan at her apartment, Steve is asked to meet with LaRue, who wants to discuss killing the expose of the Winners' Club the editor is planning. Arriving for the meeting, LaRue introduces Steve to his wife—Susan—and maneuvers him into a position where he will be charged with a double murder, committed with his own gun.

Pine and Thomas returned to the offices of the *Illustrated Press* for the third time in this disappointingly lackluster entry in the "Big Town" series. While competently made, the film lacks any sense of urgency, and director Thomas allows the pace to lag. According to *Daily Variety* (May 23, 1947), this film and the fourth in the series, *Big Town Scandal,* were made in quick succession, with the latter going into production only one day after the first feature wrapped.

Duplicitous Pete Ryan, played in the first two entries by Robert Lowery, has been dropped from the series. The role of Susan, who goes from girlish college student to hard-boiled gangster's wife, calls for a more bravura performance than former child actress Ann Gillis (1927–2018) can muster. This was her last film before appearing in *2001: A Space Odyssey* more than 20 years later. Stars Reed and Brooke, in their third go-round as Steve and Lorelei, are competent but not much more. At this point in the series, their characters are supposed to have "an understanding," romantically speaking, but the sparks aren't really there.

REVIEWS: "A weak, empty little action melodrama … limited to a few sporadic flashes of action, handicapped by a ridiculous story and poor performances…." *Independent Exhibitors' Film Bulletin*, November 24, 1947

"Plenty of action enters narrative and all the elements required for this type of film are there … pretty fair entertainment." *Daily Variety*, November 17, 1947

Albuquerque (1948)

CAST: Randolph Scott (*Cole Armin*), Barbara Britton (*Letty Tyler*), George "Gabby" Hayes (*Juke*), Lon Chaney (*Steve Murkill*), Russell Hayden (*Ted Wallace*), Catherine Craig (*Celia Wallace*), George Cleveland (*John Armin*), Irving Bacon (*Dave Walton*), Bernard J. Nedell (*Sheriff Ed Linton*), Karolyn Grimes (*Myrtle Walton*), Russell Simpson (*Abner Huggins*), Jody Gilbert (*Pearl Eager*), Dan White (*Jackson*), Walter Baldwin (*Judge Fred*

Martin), Lane Chandler (*Mr. Clark*), Dick Elliott (*Harvey*), Ray Hyke (*Stagecoach Driver*), Sam Flint (*Doctor*)

CREW: Ray Enright (*Director*), Gene Lewis, Clarence Upson Young (*Screenplay*), Luke Short (*Novel*), Fred Jackman, Jr. (*Director of Photography*), F. Paul Sylos (*Art Director*), Gar K. Gilbert (*Cinecolor Director*), Earl Sitar (*Sound Recording*), Elias H. Reif, Vincent Taylor (*Set Decorators*), Howard Smith (*Film Editor*), Mona Barry (*Costumes for Miss Britton and Miss Craig*), Jack Masters (*Wardrobe*), David Chudnow (*Music Supervisor*), Darrell Calker (*Music Score*)

RELEASED February 1948. 90 minutes.

Ex–Texas Ranger Cole Armin heads to Albuquerque to take a job offered by his wealthy uncle, who operates a freight company. Along the way, the stagecoach in which he's riding is robbed; in the resulting mayhem, one passenger is killed, and another, pretty Celia Wallace, has $10,000 stolen.

Upon arrival in town, Cole quickly learns that the name of Armin is anathema to most of the population, but stagecoach driver Juke becomes his friend, as does Dave Walton, whose little girl Myrtle Cole rescued from the runaway coach. Cole's uncle, who uses a wheelchair, is a ruthless businessman who has few scruples in maintaining his empire, and expects the same of Cole. While Cole and Juke are having a drink in the local saloon, they recognize the voice of one of the stagecoach robbers, and take him into custody. Cole realizes that his uncle was responsible for the robbery, and has the crooked sheriff in his pocket. Cole returns the $10,000 to Celia and her brother Ted, and asks for a job with their start-up freighting company, which is struggling to compete with the stranglehold John Armin has on the town and its businessmen. Cole, Juke, and the Wallaces are counting on the testimony of hired gunman Jackson, who robbed the stagecoach, to help bring their opponents to justice, but Jackson is allowed by the sheriff to escape from prison, and then promptly shot as a fugitive.

Wallace and Armin Freighting goes after contracts long held by John Armin, setting them squarely in his sights. A new young lady in town, Letty Tyler, shows up at the Wallace-Armin office just in time to interrupt a burglary in process, and is given a stenographer's job by the grateful Wallaces. Miss Tyler is, in fact, an industrial spy planted by John Armin, and gives her crooked employer inside information that helps him disrupt the work of the fledgling company.

John Armin's chief thug, Steve Murkill, fails at disrupting Ted's first hauling job, and having Ted shot in the leg by one of his uncle's hired men makes Cole that much more determined to proceed. Armin tries another tack—having a fire set in his own offices, and then pinning the arson job on his nephew. Cole has an alibi that he refuses to disclose, but his young fan Myrtle discloses that he was visiting Letty at the time the fire broke out. The news gets Cole cleared of the arson charge, but throws a wrench into his growing romantic relationship with Celia, who doesn't know that Cole just caught on to Letty's double-crossing. The judge orders that Cole and his uncle each put up a "peace bond" of $5,000, to be forfeited if there is any more violence involving the business rivals.

Discouraged by the constant brushes with the law, and being cold-shouldered by a jealous Celia, Cole decides it would be better for him to return to Texas. But with Juke's help, he's persuaded to stay, and finds himself unexpectedly taking the reins on a dangerous run when one of Ted's drivers falls out. Against the odds, Juke, Cole, and their men are successful bringing a load of ore down from the remote mine—but what awaits them back in Albuquerque forces them into a violent confrontation, as Cole's uncle takes desperate measures to keep control of his empire. With Letty having put things right between Cold and Celia, he has an even better reason to take a stand, and make a lasting place for himself in the town.

By Pine-Thomas' standards of the 1940s, *Albuquerque* was a major production, and the Dollar Bills pulled out all the stops they could afford to keep it from languishing at the bottom of a double bill. Their names, and the usual "A Pine-Thomas Production," were nowhere to be found in the opening titles of *Albuquerque*, made under the auspices of Clarion Productions. Paramount executives, according to an item in *Variety* (July 16, 1947), "have issued orders that their names are not to be used in any way in connection with bally[hoo] for *Albuquerque*." The screenplay was adapted from a 1940 Luke Short novel, "Dead Freight from Piute," after Thomas picked up a tattered paperback copy at a used-book store.

A big picture called for a big star, and the producing partners ponied up $75,000, plus a sizable percentage deal, to sign Randolph Scott as their leading man. At that time, his name on the marquee was enough to send thousands of Western fans moseying up to the window to buy tickets, and this film shows why. Much as it stretched the budget to sign Scott, it was a smart move. If he's in no danger of copping an Oscar here, his star quality is nonetheless clearly on display.

He's confident in his fighting and riding scenes, and his charisma elevates the role beyond what the script provides. Western fans don't generally regard *Albuquerque* as one of Scott's better films in the genre, but his presence goes a long way to make it work. His scenes with young Karolyn Grimes (previously seen in *It's a Wonderful Life*) as a little girl who adopts Cole as her best friend are charming. For anyone who ever yearned to see Scott entertaining a little girl with hand puppets—or, for that matter, Gabby Hayes doing a bathtub scene—here's your chance. As an adult, Karolyn Grimes remembered, "This was my first western picture…. I got to ride in stagecoaches and on horses. I even had my own pet burro."[22]

Albuquerque employs some of the same actors who had done yeoman's work in Pine and Thomas' smaller films. Second-billed Barbara Britton plays glamorous but untrustworthy Letty Tyler, whose loyalties are put to the test. Britton's subtle performance works well in portraying a woman who says, when push comes to shove, "Any scruples I might have had went on the bargain counter when I took this job. But you can count me out of any more murder plans." Not so prominently billed, though she logs more screen time, is Catherine Craig as Celia Wallace, who holds our interest and sympathy with a less flashy character. Other familiar faces like Dick Elliott turn up in smaller roles.

Hayes, playing the type of character he all but patented, has some amusing scenes, many of them centering on his romantic interest in the proprietress of Pearl's Tonsorial Parlor. For most of the film, we see Pearl through his eyes while she remains off-screen, depicted via his dialogue as a no-nonsense lady who yearns to take her clippers to his beard and give him a good makeover. Only in the film's closing moments does character actress Jody Gilbert (1916–1979) bring her to life.

Scott's star contract came with an option to choose his own director, and he made a solid selection in Ray Enright, who delivers a well-crafted film here. Unfortunately, Enright failed to hit it off with Pine and Thomas, who saw red when the director came down hard on featured player Russell Hayden. Ultimately, the director and his employers called a truce, and Enright reined in his criticism of Hayden, who's quite competent in the secondary role of Ted.

Another clause in Scott's contract caused some difficulties, as he had been guaranteed sole star billing above the film's title. Unfortunately, Barbara Britton had also been promised star billing, and when she saw the finished film, she filed a lawsuit against Paramount and the Pine-Thomas organization. She asked for $200,000 in damages, stating that not billing her alongside Scott (as she had been in Columbia's *Gunfighters* just a year earlier) would damage her career. According to Bill Thomas, the legal action was ultimately settled out of court by Paramount, with a modest payout to the actress. The contretemps apparently didn't affect Britton's long-lasting friendship with her leading man. "Randolph Scott was a kind man and we were good friends for years," she told interviewer Colin Briggs. She credited Scott with giving her the choice of whether she'd rather play Letty or Celia. "I chose to be on the wrong side of the law," she recalled, "as the character was against my usual type."[23]

In early 1949, Pine and Thomas took out an ad in *Variety* (January 5) to announce that, following the success of *Albuquerque*, "Henceforth, we will devote our efforts exclusively to the production of three important top-budget attractions annually." The ad stated that *El Paso* was already completed, *Manhandled* was in production, and preparations were underway for *Captain China*. However, there were still several more Pine-Thomas B films awaiting release.

REVIEWS: "The acting is splendid, with Barbara Britton being seen in a new type of role, and Randolph Scott giving his usual stalwart performance…. One of the most exciting sequences is that of the thrilling ride down a treacherous mountain road by Scott and Hayes, riding heavily-laden freight wagons." *Film Daily*, January 20, 1948

"*Albuquerque* has all the ingredients needed for a first-rate big-time western—except a good script … while the plot simmers, it never boils over into the sort of rousing action and excitement one has a right to expect of this kind of picture…. Ray Enright's direction gets the most out of the material at hand." *Independent Exhibitors' Film Bulletin*, February 2, 1948

Caged Fury (1948)

CAST: Richard Denning (*Blaney Lewis*), Sheila Ryan (*Kit Warren*), Buster Crabbe (*Smiley*), Mary Beth Hughes (*Lola Tremaine*), Frank Wilcox (*Dan Corey*), Sam Flint (*Dr. Branson*), Hugh Prosser (*Ringmaster*), Lane Chandler (*Policeman*)

CREW: William Berke (*Director*), David Lang (*Screenplay*), Ellis W. Carter (*Director of Photography*), Lewis H. Creber (*Art Director*), Howard Smith (*Film Editor*), Frank McWhorter (*Sound Recording*), Alfred Kegerris (*Set Decorator*), Harry Lubin (*Music Score*)

RELEASED March 1948. 61 minutes.

It's the end of the season for the Corey and Murray Circus, and tensions are running high. Trainer Blaney Lewis notices that Sultan, the lion featured in the finale, is jittery, and suggests to the act's stars, clown Smiley and lion tamer Lola, that they cut the routine short. Lola refuses, and has a narrow escape from being injured when the escape door from the cage jams at a critical moment.

Lola senses that she has competition for her job from Kit Warren, a horsewoman who wants a more important part in the show. Kit's fiancé, Blaney, thinks the gig is too dangerous, and wants Kit to settle down with him and get married. Smiley, with two beautiful women vying to be featured in his act, strings both of them along, but decides he's ready for a new leading lady.

Before the season's final performance, Smiley once again sabotages the escape route from the lion cage, and when Sultan erupts in anger, a trapped Lola is mauled and killed. The death is ruled accidental, and Smiley promptly offers Lola's job to Kit. Kit's insistence on furthering her career puts a strain on her relationship with Blaney, and she breaks up with him. Though he doesn't think she is ready for the lion-taming job, Blaney begins training her during the circus' hiatus at its winter quarters. Smiley tries to put the moves on Kit, but she is hesitant, even though she is on the outs with Blaney.

His vendetta picking up steam, Smiley does his best to rile Sultan, in hopes of getting Blaney injured, but it's the clown himself who suffers a broken arm in the ensuing attack. Blaney realizes Smiley's murderous intent, but he and Kit grow close once again while Smiley is sidelined from the act. When boss Corey catches Smiley in another act of sabotage, the resulting melee, which includes a car chase, leaves both men apparently dead. With Smiley out of the way, Blaney and Kit marry, take over the starring roles in the lion-taming act, and a few months later she is expecting a baby. Just as everything seems to be going right for Blaney and Kit, a familiar face resurfaces to exact his revenge.

Crabbe, in his second villainous part for Pine-Thomas, provides suitable menace as the performer whose billing as "The Craziest Clown in the World" is all too apt. Early in the film, he establishes himself as unscrupulous, trying to curry favor with ambitious Kit by leering, "No telling what might happen if you're nice to a guy like me." Mary Beth Hughes gives the character of Lola a nasty edge, making it a pity that her scenes are relatively few. With a fairly small number of speaking roles, the film lacks the opportunities for character players that Pine-Thomas' output normally offers.

No, that's not Leo the MGM lion in the film's opening titles, it's Sultan. *Daily Variety* columnist Florabel Muir reported (September 23, 1947) that cast members, who'd been teased by production manager Doc Merman for being hesitant to go too near the lions' cage, "got back at him by putting all his birthday presents the other day in the cage where he had to retrieve them, and from under the roaring beasts' noses."

The finished film incorporates a fair amount of stock footage to convey the color of circus life. Editor Howard Smith does a more-than-capable job of integrating it into scenes. Upon its release, *Caged Fury* frequently filled the bottom half of a double bill headed by Pine and Thomas' more ambitious *Albuquerque*.

REVIEWS: "A rip-roaring action-crammed circus yarn that is aimed at the youngsters and avid action fans and hits the bulls-eye. One of the best in the P-T series of programmers for.... Paramount.... Director William Berke uses his considerable knowhow to maintain the accelerated pace...." *Independent Exhibitors' Film Bulletin*, March 1, 1948

"An exciting circus story, complete with snarling lions, hand-to-hand combat, a fire and an auto chase. It will be a mighty pleaser in the market for which it is aimed.... Production values are excellent and careful use has been made of circus montage and other action clips that give a gloss beyond budget expenditure." *Variety*, February 18, 1948

Mr. Reckless (1948)

CAST: William Eythe (*Jeff Lundy*), Barbara Britton (*Betty Denton*), Walter Catlett (*Joe Hawkins*), Minna Gombel [Gombell] (*Ma Hawkins*), Lloyd Corrigan (*Hugo Denton*), Nestor Paiva (*Gus*), Frank Jenks (*Cab Driver*), Ian MacDonald (*Jim Halsey*), James Millican (*Pete*), Francis Pierlot (*the Rev. Stanislaus*), Sam Flint (*Guard at Oil Field*), Russ Conway (*Al*), Frank Marlowe (*Cab Driver*)

CREW: Frank McDonald (*Director*), Maxwell Shane, Milton Raison (*Screenplay*), Ellis W. Carter (*Director of Photography*), Lewis H. Creber (*Art Director*), Howard Smith (*Film Editor*), Earl Sitar (*Sound Recording*), Alfred Kegerris (*Set Decorator*), Harry Lubin (*Music Score*)

RELEASED March 1948. 66 minutes.

Itinerant oil man Jeff Lundy, back in California after two years drilling in Louisiana, pays a visit to his buddy Gus, a middle-aged restaurant owner. Jeff is surprised to learn that not only is Gus closing his restaurant, having lost his lease, but he's also marrying his longtime waitress Betty. Gus and Betty plan to relocate to the area where Jeff and his buddy Pete will be doing their next job, and make a living serving meals to the crew workers. Jeff angrily accuses Betty, whom he dated before going to Louisiana, of marrying an older man just to earn a "meal ticket," but Betty points out that he had made no commitment to her. Betty appreciates that Gus, though plain-featured and a bit uncouth, has been kind to her and her ne'er-do-well father, Hugo, who keeps backsliding into drinking and gambling.

Arriving at the new drill site in Ponca City, Jeff and his friends take up residence at the boarding house of Ma and Pa Hawkins. Jeff tries to steer clear of Betty, but Gus keeps bringing them together, and elicits a promise from the younger man that he will serve as best man at the wedding. Jeff pressures Betty to call it off, arguing that she does not love Gus, but she says she has made a commitment and will stick to it.

On the eve of the ceremony, Betty's irresponsible father is being pressed by coworker Jim Halsey to pay an overdue gambling debt he owes. When Hugo is unable to secure the money, an angry Halsey locks him in an unused oil tank, causing him to be late for his daughter's wedding. Tracking down Hugo's whereabouts, Gus takes a beating in a fight with Halsey, resulting in a postponement of the wedding ceremony. Hugo narrowly escapes injury after the well where he's trapped begins to fill with oil, and Halsey is fired from the rig. Halsey gets his revenge by causing an accident in which Jeff is badly injured. Jeff, who'd planned to leave the area so as to give Betty and Gus a chance to make their marriage work, is temporarily bedridden at Ma Hawkins' place, as is Gus.

By the time Gus is well enough to reschedule the nuptials, Betty has reconsidered, and realized she cannot marry him. Learning that both his fiancée and his friend Jeff are preparing to leave town (though not together), Gus finally realizes whom Betty truly loves, and heads off to a violent confrontation with Jeff, high atop the oil rig.

At times, *Mr. Reckless* seems like an amalgam of previous Pine-Thomas efforts. Once again, we find men drilling for oil (*Wildcat*), small business owners setting up a lunch wagon at a worksite (*High Powered*), and two men in love with the same woman (too many to name). Like several previous Shane screenplays, this script draws suspense from scenes taking place high atop a dangerous worksite. Still, the film works fine on its own terms, helped by some good performances. The script carries out its romantic triangle

William Eythe (left) and Nestor Paiva fight for the hand of Barbara Britton in this pressbook ad for *Mr. Reckless*. Most moviegoers could probably guess the outcome of that rivalry.

well, without making anyone the villain in the troublesome situation. Perhaps its biggest flaw is the hasty wrap-up that makes two key characters seem a bit callous.

This is the first of William Eythe's two starring assignments for Pine-Thomas. Previously on the rise as a young leading man at 20th Century–Fox, Eythe (1918–1957) found himself offered little but B movies after that studio cut him loose in 1947. Here he's cast as what studio publicity described as "a derrick daredevil who is easy to love and hard to kill." ("Hard to Kill" was the film's working title.) He will work again with the Dollar

Bills in *Special Agent.* Eythe's leading lady Barbara Britton doesn't fare quite as well as she did in *They Made Me a Killer,* but keeps audience sympathy and interest as she juggles her relationships with two men.

The two attractive young stars, while more than competent, are nearly upstaged by the cast of veteran character actors surrounding them. Nestor Paiva (1905–1966) breathes life into the somewhat stereotypical character of Gus, making him believable both as a good-hearted, basically decent man, as well as one who struggles to control a temper that flares easily. Minna Gombell (1892–1973), whose name is misspelled in the opening titles, also registers effectively as boardinghouse keeper Ma Hawkins. Plain-spoken in the great tradition of movie landladies, she clearly has a soft spot for young Jeff Lundy, remarking at one point, "There's a chunk o' man for you. If I was just a few years younger...."

The film's pressbook urged local theater managers to arrange publicity gimmicks in various venues around town. Suggestions included a tie-in with banks ("Be Mr. Cautious with your money and see Mr. Reckless at the ... Theatre") and the employment of a pretty young lady seated on a park bench with a sign reading, "I'm waiting for Mr. Reckless." Another idea: "paging Mr. Reckless in hotel lobbies, restaurants, cafes, etc."

REVIEWS: "Producers Pine and Thomas went back to their first pattern for this melodrama but brightened its business prospects by supplying William Eythe and Barbara Britton for billing strength.... Failure to build much sympathy for the hero detracts from the story's impact, but several actionful incidents carry interest adequately." *Motion Picture Herald,* February 14, 1948

"A moderately paced picture which builds to an exciting climax.... Considerable waste footage is devoted to comedy relief, but all in all feature stacks up as acceptable entertainment.... William Pine and William Thomas as producers ... have given picture highly atmospheric mounting, with an eye aimed always at popular acceptance." *Daily Variety,* February 13, 1948

Speed to Spare (1948)

CAST: Richard Arlen (*Cliff Jordan*), Jean Rogers (*Mary McGee*), Richard Travis (*Jerry McGee*), Roscoe Karns (*Kangaroo*), Nanette Parks (*Jane Chandler*), Pat Phelan (*Pete Simmons*), Ian MacDonald (*Pusher Wilkes*), Paul Harvey (*Al Simmons*), Eddy Waller (*Charlie Blane*), Gloria Marlen (*Molly*), Roy Gordon (*Mr. Maxton*), George Eldredge (*Driving Instructor*), Guy Wilkerson (*Pop*), Lee Phelps (*Waiter*), Brick Sullivan (*Truck Driver*)

CREW: William Berke (*Director*), Milton Raison (*Screenplay*), Ellis W. Carter (*Director of Photography*), Lewis H. Creber (*Art Director*), Monty Pearce (*Film Editor*), Earl Sitar (*Sound Recording*), Alfred Kegerris (*Set Decorator*), Darrell Calker (*Music Score*)

RELEASED May 1948. 57 minutes.

Stunt-car driver Cliff Jordan loses his job after an argument with his boss about back pay he's owed. Reunited with his old buddy Jerry McGee, branch manager of the National Express Company, Cliff accepts a job working alongside Jerry. His ability to stick with a regular job, and settle down, is doubted by Jerry's wife Mary, who once dated Cliff. Hauling freight seems a little tame to Cliff after his previous career, and he has to be cautioned more than once about driving too fast, and following procedures. Coworker "Kangaroo," sidelined from driving after an accident that impaired his reflexes, cautions

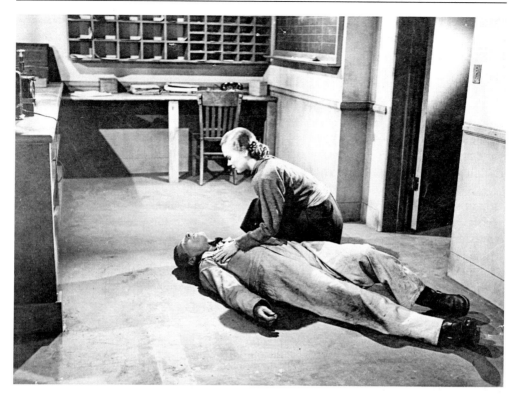

Cliff (Richard Arlen) has fallen for Jane (Nanette Parks) in *Speed to Spare*.

Cliff that tracking devices in the company's trucks are recording his driving patterns at all times, and breaking rules will get him fired.

After completing his training to drive a big rig, Cliff is added to the rotation of regular drivers for the company, taking the place of Pusher Wilkes, a troublemaking driver with a propensity for coming to work with a hangover. Pusher is demoted to working as a mechanic, and vows revenge against Cliff. On his first assignment, Cliff courts trouble when he picks up a passenger, a young woman wanting to rush her baby to the hospital; Jerry gives him another chance, mindful of his wife's warning about Cliff's reliability.

Soon Pusher's sabotage leads to accidents happening on Cliff's watch, endangering his employment with the company. Cliff, serious about wanting to settle down after too many years living for the moment, romances Jane Chandler, who works in National Express' office. Jane is the steady of younger driver Pete, but Cliff tries to encroach on his coworker's territory behind his back. When Jerry refuses a $500 offer to deliver some explosive chemicals—a type of work National Express lacks a license to do—Cliff arranges privately to do the job surreptitiously, adding the cargo to a rig he's driving. Cliff is unaware that, once again, Pusher has tampered with the vehicle, and he's horrified to learn, after being delayed by a fistfight with Pete, that Kangaroo took the dangerously loaded rig in his place.

Though it could easily have been the company slogan of Pine-Thomas Productions, *Speed to Spare* was instead the title of this short-and-sweet programmer about the trucking industry. According to Bill Thomas, he found the title on a newspaper's sports page; it was the name of a racehorse. Columbia had used the same title for a thriller about race drivers about ten years earlier. Trade advertisements for the P-T film promised "Danger-drivers ... crashing through the night with a cargo of death! 40 tons of disaster on the loose in a runaway trailer ... while life and love hang in the balance!"

The film is a semi-remake of Pine-Thomas' *High Explosive,* released five years earlier, though no credit is given to original screenwriters Maxwell Shane and Howard J. Green. As Chester Morris' character did in that film, Arlen's Cliff Jordan loses his job after settling an argument with his fists, goes to work for a freight-hauling company, romances the young lady who works in its office, and can't resist a substantial cash offer to make a perilous delivery. Roscoe Karns plays a character whose function in the story is similar to Ralph Sanford's "Squinchy" in *High Explosive.*

Richard Arlen returns to the Pine-Thomas fold in a leading part after a four-year absence. Jean Rogers (1916–1991), best-known for playing Dale Arden in two *Flash Gordon* serials of the 1930s, is second-billed for what is basically a supporting character, Jerry's wife. Pat Phelan (1915–2003), as clean-cut Pete, gives a stiff performance in one of his few substantial film roles.

At Bill Thomas' suggestion, screenwriter Milton Raison actually took a ride on a tractor-trailer from Los Angeles to Denver in wintertime to give authenticity to his script. "I remember riding downhill into a sudden patch of fog," Raison wrote, "and emerging on a curve which was not only icy, but happened to be fully occupied by a stalled passenger car. How we got around that one I'll never know, for I closed my eyes. But we skidded only a few hundred yards—in the right direction, luckily."[24]

REVIEWS: "*Speed to Spare* is an intelligently done drama of the trucking business.... Pine and Thomas have endowed the film with their customary shrewd supervision and, as a consequence, they may look forward to the customary boxoffice payoff." *Hollywood Reporter,* February 16, 1948

"Director William Berke has endowed the interesting and thrill-packed screenplay by Milton Raison with everything the action fan can ask in 57 minutes, eliciting convincing performances by an expert cast, headed by the indestructible Richard Arlen." *Independent Exhibitors' Film Bulletin,* March 1, 1948

Big Town Scandal (1948)

CAST: Philip Reed (*Steve Wilson*), Hillary Brooke (*Lorelei Kilbourne*), Stanley Clements (*Tommy Malone*), Darryl Hickman (*Harold "Skinny" Peters*), Carl "Alfalfa" Switzer (*Frankie Snead*), Roland Dupree (*John "Pinky" Jones*), Tommy Bond (*Waldo "Dum Dum" Riggs*), Vince Barnett (*Louie Snead*), Charles Arnt (*Amos Peabody*), Joe Allen, Jr. (*Wally Blake*), Donna DeMario [Martell] (*Marion Harrison*), John Phillips (*Joe Moreley*), Reginald Bilado (*Cato*), Lane Chandler (*Store Owner*), Edward Earle (*Court Clerk*), Sam Balter (*Basketball Game Announcer*), Don C. Harvey (*Lt. Peterson*), Thomas E. Jackson (*Police Chief*), Richard Keene (*Jimmy O'Brien*), Grandon Rhodes (*Judge Hogan*), Harry Shannon (*Captain Henry*), Charles C. Wilson (*"Chronicle" Editor*), Archie Twitchell (*Newspaper Man*)

CREW: William C. Thomas (*Director*), Milton Raison (*Screenplay*), Ellis W. Carter (*Director of Photography*), F. Paul Sylos (*Art Director*), Howard Smith (*Film Editor*), Frank McWhorter (*Sound Recording*), Glenn Thompson, Alfred Kegerris (*Set Decorators*), Darrell Calker (*Music Score*)

RELEASED May 1948. 60 minutes.

Bail bondsman Louie Snead implores reporter Lorelei Kilbourne to help after his young nephew, Frankie, is one of five juveniles caught robbing a sporting goods store. Since the boys are first offenders, Lorelei asks the judge to give them probation, rather than sentencing them to reform school. "Boys sent to reform school often to return to prison, as hardened criminals," she argues, although the store owner wants the thieves prosecuted to the fullest extent. Since the boys come mostly from broken homes, the judge agrees to do so only if a responsible local citizen will assume responsibility for them. Before he knows it, Lorelei's boss and boyfriend, *Illustrated Press* managing editor Steve Wilson, is appointed to the task.

Lorelei persuades Steve that it would be a good deed, as well as good publicity for the *Press*, if they were able to rehabilitate the young men. Steve agrees to give them jobs at the newspaper and, because they were caught stealing basketball equipment, to turn the paper's former building into the "Illustrated Press Recreation Center." The newspaper announces its campaign to fight juvenile delinquency with the slogan, "The *Illustrated Press* Builds Better Boys."

Steve enjoys coaching the boys' basketball team, the Big Town Big Shots. But while the other boys have seemingly gone straight, Tommy Malone is taken with the fancy car driven by two-bit hoodlum Joe Moreley. Joe allows him to take the wheel for a drive, but when they hear police sirens, Joe admits the car is hot, and ducks for cover. Thinking quickly, Tommy hides the car in the basement of the recreation center. But when he discovers stolen furs in the trunk, Tommy demands to be cut in on Joe's fencing racket.

Tommy, newly flush with cash, is satisfied with the arrangement, which allows him to impress his girlfriend, Marion. He raises more money by betting on the basketball games in which the Big Shots play, until Steve finds out and forbids him to do it again. Joe and his cohort, Cato, aren't willing to let their young helper off so easily. They pressure him into throwing one of the Big Shots' games, so they can collect on a large wager. Wishing he could walk away, Tommy, who will be sent to reform school if he's caught doing anything illegal, finds himself more deeply imbedded in Joe's operation than ever.

When Tommy's friends find the stolen furs stored in the basement, he confesses his involvement. The boys try to return the furs to the store, but the police respond to an alarm while Tommy and Pinky are on the scene; Pinky, trying to escape, is shot by a policeman and killed, while Tommy gets away. Learning that two of their protégés were involved in the break-in, Steve and Lorelei worry that their efforts to reform the boys have failed. Going into a high-stakes game for the basketball game, Tommy is trapped between his desire to do the right thing, and the knowledge that an armed Joe is in the audience, demanding that he throw another game.

Big Town Scandal once again uses basketball as a key story element, as co-producer Bill Thomas had done ten years earlier in *Campus Confessions* (1938). The fourth and final of the "Big Town" series is serviceable, though the story takes little advantage of the newspaper environment. Modern audiences are apt to find distasteful the characterization of Waldo. He's described in dialogue as "a deaf-and-dumb boy," which was accepted usage for the day, but the screenplay takes it a step further, tagging him with the nickname of "Dum-Dum," which even nice-guy Steve calls him. Waldo does get to perform one heroic act near the end of the film. The film was retitled *Underworld Scandal* for television release.

At times, *Big Town Scandal* could easily be mistaken for a Bowery Boys film; actor Stanley Clements (1926–1981), who plays Tommy, took a leading role in the last films of

IT'S BULLETS
VS.
BASKETBALL...
as Steve Wilson
Fights a Juvenile
Crime Wave!

A mobster's bullet strikes
BIG TOWN'S star basket-
shooter down...as the fighting newspaper editor and
his glamor gal reporter
smash the grip of a
crooked gambling czar
on a gang of thrill-
hungry kids!

LATEST in the
thrilling BIG
TOWN screen
series—Based On
The Famous Ra-
dio Program!

Paramount
presents

"BIG TOWN" SCANDAL

starring

PHILIP REED · HILLARY BROOKE

with

STANLEY CLEMENTS · DARRYL HICKMAN
CARL "ALFALFA" SWITZER
ROLAND DUPREE · TOMMY BOND
Directed by WILLIAM C. THOMAS
A PINE-THOMAS PRODUCTION

2 COLS. x { 100 LINES ... 200 LINES
          { 7 inches ... 14 inches

MAT 205

"It's bullets vs. basketball" in *Big Town Scandal*, which brought P-T's newspaper series to a close.

that long-running series, in the mid–1950s. Pretty Donna DeMario (born 1927), seen briefly as his girlfriend, would soon change her professional name to Donna Martell, and work steadily on television in the 1950s. Character actor Grandon Rhodes (1904–1987), cast here as a municipal judge, will play minor parts as figures of authority in future Pine-Thomas films, becoming the governor of Texas in *The Eagle and the Hawk*, and a naval commodore in *Tripoli*.

REVIEWS: "Has all the elements to satisfy as program fare, with good performances and suspense added to hold the interest.... Stanley Clements adds another good bad-boy role to his impressive list of such characterizations ... will appeal to the general public." *Showmen's Trade Review*, May 29, 1948

"Delivers up fair melodramatic material which is exploitable and substantial. It is produced in the manner of other Pine-Thomas numbers which means it is pat, smartly paced and complemented with a supply of action." *Film Daily*, May 27, 1948

Shaggy (1948)

CAST: George Nokes (*Robbie Calvin*), Brenda Joyce (*Laura Calvin*), Robert Shayne (*Bob Calvin*), Jody Gilbert (*Tessie*), Ralph Sanford (*Fuzzy*), Alex Frazer (*Max*), William Haade (*Gonnell*), Dan White (*Joe Simms*), Shaggy the Dog

CREW: Robert Emmett Tansey (*Director*), Maxwell Shane (*Original Screenplay*), Ellis W. Carter (*Director of Photography*), F. Paul Sylos (*Art Director*), Howard Smith (*Film Editor*), Wilton Holm (*Cinecolor Director*), Frank McWhorter (*Sound Recording*), John MacNeil, William Magginetti (*Set Decorators*), Ralph Stanley (*Music Score*)

RELEASED June 1948. 72 minutes.

Young Robbie Calvin, growing up on his widowed father's ranch, is caught by surprise when Bob Calvin returns from a trip to San Francisco with a new bride, Laura. A former schoolteacher, Robbie's stepmother, not accustomed to rural life, has difficulty adjusting to her change in lifestyle, admitting, "Ever since I was a little girl, I've been deathly afraid of animals." She objects to the presence of Robbie's raccoon, Squeaky, in the house, causing the pet to be banished to a cage in the barn. Along with Squeaky, Robbie also has a dog, Shaggy, who helps the Calvins and their hired hands with raising and protecting their sheep.

When a neighboring rancher, Gonnell, finds a few of his sheep killed, he accuses Shaggy, which Robbie's dad initially refuses to believe. Bob tells his son to keep Shaggy in his room at night, but the dog sneaks out to visit his lady friend and the puppies she's just given him. Meanwhile, Laura's best efforts to win the love and acceptance of her new stepson are met with difficulties. She plans a surprise eighth birthday party for Robbie, but the evening ends in disaster when the boy finds that his raccoon has been poisoned. Laura, regarded with suspicion by Robbie and his father, confesses to Bob that she may have made a mistake in coming to live on the ranch, while Robbie professes his hatred for her.

Shaggy defends his canine family against a wild predator that has been preying on the sheep. With the mountain lion operating under the cover of night, the humans are unaware of his existence. But when Shaggy, who fought with the cat, comes home bloody, and more dead sheep are found, Bob decides that his son's dog is indeed a killer, and must be destroyed. Taking off into the hills after Robbie, who's run away after letting Shaggy go free, Laura is unprepared to cope with the dangers she finds, and must depend for her safety on her stepson and his dog.

Top-billed George Nokes (1936–1986), a child actor often billed as "Georgie," meets capably the demands of his starring assignment, which includes some action sequences as well the ability to shed tears in dramatic scenes. Young Master Nokes had some genuine film classics on his resume, albeit not always in sizable roles. He appeared in *Song of the South*, *The Best Years of our Lives*, and *It's a Wonderful Life*.

Brenda Joyce (1917–2009) was at the time best-known for replacing Maureen O'Sullivan in the still-popular "Tarzan" series, beginning with *Tarzan and the Leopard Woman* (1946). The actress isn't to blame if her character's chief motivation, a fear of animals, doesn't really ring true. Her terrified reaction to a raccoon comes across as overdone since she seems to have no fear of dogs, is shown to be a competent horse-woman, and reacts with little more than stunned silence when the mountain lion finally appears.

Robert Shayne (1900–1992), probably best known for his 1950s performances as Inspector Henderson on TV's *The Adventures of Superman*, is competent if uninspired as Robbie's less-than-sensitive dad, who introduces the boy to a woman he's never before met, and tells him to regard her as his new mother. The screenplay doesn't give Shayne and Miss Joyce much opportunity to present a loving couple, and the actors have no particular chemistry. Frequent Pine-Thomas player Ralph Sanford, in his final release for the company, is cast as genial, harmonica-playing farmhand Fuzzy. Fuzzy's wife, Tessie, serves as the Calvins' housekeeper. Jody Gilbert, in her third Pine-Thomas appearance, neatly handles the character of down-to-earth Tessie, even though the role is underdeveloped.

Director Robert Emmett Tansey (1897–1951) had a long list of film credits, leaning heavily toward Westerns. Maxwell Shane's somewhat contrived screenplay, not one of his better efforts for Pine-Thomas, asks us to accept that a woman afraid of wild animals apparently consented to go live on a working ranch without hesitation.

Boy-and-his-dog movies were considered solid box office in the mid- to late-1940s; MGM had cleaned up with a series of Lassie films, while Columbia had a profitable low-budget series featuring a dog named Rusty. According to the *Los Angeles Times*' Edwin Schallert (April 23, 1947), the starring part in the film, that of Shaggy himself, was assigned to "a mutt secured from the city pound," winning out over dozens of thoroughbreds who'd been auditioned. The newly anointed star received his own title card in the opening credits, with an "introducing" credit.

On its original release in 1948, syndicated columnist Frank Morriss (August 12, 1945) remarked, "Mother, if she takes Junior to see it, can doze off secure in the knowledge that he will not see anything to influence his tender susceptibilities." Modern viewers might see it differently, as the film contains story elements that would likely upset today's children, as well as a level of violence that would be problematic in a 21st century children's film. They may be more apt to agree with Laura, who at one point exclaims, "Guns! Blood! Killings! I just can't take any more!"

A visitor to the Pine-Thomas offices while the film was in preproduction found the Dollar Bills wrestling with a problematic scene involving a fight between the title character and a lion. "We've got to get the sequence by the SPCA and still wring every bit of drama from it," Thomas explained. "In England, where we do 30% of our business, exhibitors

Top dog *Shaggy* (not pictured) is supported by two-legged actors (left to right) Brenda Joyce, George Nokes, and Robert Shayne.

won't take a picture in which an animal is slain. Our problem is to make a heel of the lion and a hero of the dog without either getting hurt."[25] The action footage was realistic enough to inspire the producers to announce in the opening titles that the film was made under the supervision of the American Humane Association.

On the set, according to Carol Thomas Pantages, her father and his colleagues ran into difficulty staging the scenes in which the mountain lion menaces the farmers' sheep. Upon seeing the lion approaching, she said, "Half the herd dropped dead from heart attacks! The mountain lion literally scared them to death." Once the finished film was in the can, *Daily Variety* (May 15, 1947) reported that Pine and Thomas "now have a flock of movie conditioned sheep for sale," described by the latter as "hams in sheep's clothing."

REVIEWS: "This is good product for the neighborhood and subsequent-run houses, and will also make a satisfactory lower-half offering in the metropolitan areas. It is an appealing, entertaining, homespun tale … that will please the average moviegoer." *Showmen's Trade Review*, April 17, 1948

"The principals seem a little embarrassed by the banality of the lines they have to read and the pace lags a bit in spots, but by quickie standards it is a very neat job. Superior camera work by Ellis Carter helps put it over." *Independent Exhibitors' Film Bulletin*, April 26, 1948

Waterfront at Midnight (1948)

Cast: William Gargan (*Mike Hanrahan*), Mary Beth Hughes (*Ethel Novack*), Richard Travis (*Socks Barstow*), Richard Crane (*Dennie Hanrahan*), Cheryl Walker (*Helen Hanrahan*), Horace McMahon (*Hank Bremmer*), John Hilton (*Woody*), Douglas Fowley (*Joe Sargis*), Paul Harvey (*Commissioner Ryan*), Keye Luke (*Loy*)

Crew: William Berke (*Director*), Bernard Girard (*Screenplay*), Ellis W. Carter (*Director of Photography*), Lewis H. Creber (*Art Director*), Alfred Kegerris (*Set Decorator*), Howard Smith (*Film Editor*), Harry Lubin (*Music Score*), Ben Winkler (*Sound Recording*)

Released June 1948. 63 minutes.

Police Lieutenant Mike Hanrahan has been assigned to clean up criminal activity centered in the city harbor. The ringleader is Socks Barstow, with whom Mike has previously clashed, costing him a demotion. Now the police commissioner tells him his expertise is badly needed to get crime at the waterfront under control.

Mike's cocky, egotistical younger brother, Dennie, is a former Army pilot having trouble adjusting to civilian life. After narrowly escaping serious injury while piloting a plane for his current employer, Dennie is grounded, told he's suffering from nerves. Uninterested in joining his brother in the police force, Dennie hoists a few at the Diamond Pier Café, flirting aggressively with hostess Ethel Novack. Hearing his complaints, she suggests he ask Socks Barstow for a job. At his recommendation, Dennie accepts a job at a car rental agency, not realizing that Barstow, the agency's co-owner, intends to use Mike Hanrahan's younger brother to take the heat off his criminal activities. When Dennie is told by his boss to give a ride to Hank Bremmer, one of Barstow's men, he is implicated in Bremmer's shooting of a boat owner who refuses to continue renting his vessels to criminals. Investigating the shooting, Mike is shocked to realize that Dennie is involved with Barstow.

When the police boat tracking the criminals is bombed, Mike arranges for newspapers to report that he died in the explosion. Allowing even his wife to believe he was killed, Mike continues to work the case undercover. After an argument in which he demands a better share of the proceeds from Barstow's enterprise, Dennie is shot and killed by Barstow. Seeing an opportunity to dispense of his lawman rival, Barstow stashes Dennie's corpse in a boathouse, and then lures Mike into a confrontation there where he fires his gun in darkness. Discovering his brother's body, a heartsick Mike believes that his shots killed his brother, and resigns from the police force. Just as his life hits rock bottom, Mike gets help from an unexpected source in clearing his name and bringing the bad guys to justice.

Pine and Thomas acquired the rights to Bernard Girard's original screenplay in April 1947, and had the film in production by fall. Ads proclaimed, "A wayward kid turns stool pigeon for a double-crossing wharf-moll and sets his own brother up for a hi-jack mob's blazing guns!"

Gargan, once again, is cast as a "regular Joe" who lives (per the screenplay) in "a small white stucco house on an average middle-class street" with his wife Helen. A modest guy, he says of his work as a policeman, "I make enough for a nice life. And it's no grind. I can always knock off a little time to go fishing…. There's a good feeling about the job—because you're doing something for people…."[26]

Reviewers didn't rave about *Waterfront at Midnight*, but predicted that the audience would find it solid entertainment.

This was the first Pine-Thomas appearance for young Richard Crane (1918–1969), who'd been playing minor roles in films since 1940s *Susan and God*. Later the star of TV's *Rocky Jones, Space Ranger*, Crane would be cast once again by the Dollar Bills in *Dynamite*. Mary Beth Hughes enacts the bad girl (albeit one not without her principles), as she had done earlier in the year for *Caged Fury*. Richard Travis (1913–1989) is the villain, one similar to his character in the previous year's *Big Town after Dark*. His character, "Socks" Barstow, gained his nickname from his fondness for knitted footwear, commenting at one point, "I've got such tender feet. Just like my old man." Cheryl Walker (1918–1971), in her final film role, plays Mike's sensible wife Helen, while Keye Luke appears briefly as the proprietor of Loy's Chop Suey Café.

For director William Berke, *Waterfront at Midnight* was his final Pine-Thomas release, though he would continue to stay busy, directing low-budget movies as well as several early television shows, until his death in 1958. Girard, author of the screenplay, went on to a modestly successful career as a director and screenwriter; his better-known films include *Dead Heat on a Merry-Go-Round* (1966) and *The Mad Room* (1969).

Boxoffice magazine, in its "Exploitips" column (May 8, 1948) recommended that theater managers drum up interest in the film by filling their lobbies with "ship's lanterns, lifebelts, ropes, nautical flags," and the like. Even better to annoy the local populace was a suggestion to "install a fog horn atop the marquee and arrange to have it blown at intervals."

REVIEWS: "Pine-Thomas deliver a very good action-drama that moves at a swift pace. William Berke does a nice job of directing and scenarist Bernard Girard deserves a hand for his better-than-average screenplay. William Gargan, a solid action bet, scores with his police officer heroics." *Showmen's Trade Review*, May 8, 1948

"A capable filler for dual bills. Neat action, good suspense and fast pace answer all demands of the market. Production has been given good mounting for budget, and William Berke's direction makes the most of actionful screenplay.... Cast is uniformly good." *Variety*, May 5, 1948

Disaster (1948)

CAST: Richard Denning (*James Reid/Bill Wyatt*), Trudy Marshall (*Jerry Hansford*), Damian O'Flynn (*Lt. Dearborn*), Will Wright (*Pop Hansford*), James Millican (*Sam Payne*), Jack Lambert (*Frosty Davenport*), Jonathan Hale (*Police Commissioner Jerome*), Emory Parnell (*Father Mulvaney*), Glenn Strange (*Davis*)

CREW: William H. Pine (*Director*), Thomas Ahearn (*Screenplay*), Ellis W. Carter (*Director of Photography*), Lewis H. Creber (*Art Director*), Howard Smith (*Film Editor*), Tom Lambert (*Sound Recording*), Alfred Kegerris (*Set Decorator*), Harry Lubin (*Music Score*)

RELEASED December 1948. 59 minutes.

At the Los Angeles airport, Police Lieutenant Dearborn is watching new arrivals in hopes of locating a murder suspect, 28-year-old James Reid. When Reid disembarks, he and Dearborn get into a scuffle, during which the suspect escapes.

Pursuing his fugitive by car, Dearborn tracks him to a church, where there's no sign of him. Reid comes out atop the church, where Pop Hansford of the Hansford Construction Company is painting the exterior, high above the street. Posing as another workman, James evades the policeman, and talks his way into a job with Pop's company. At first just trying to bluff until Dearborn leaves the scene, James decides to take the job, after Pop's pretty daughter Jerry offers him a cot on which to sleep.

Adopting the alias Bill Wyatt, Reid learns the skills of being a "steeplejack" for the company that specializes in doing repair work at great heights. Coworker Sam Payne, assigned to train Bill, takes a dislike to him, noting his interest in Jerry. Sam tells Bill that he and Jerry are engaged, which comes as news to Pop.

The Hansfords' small company is bidding for a big contract with the Board of Education. A letter from the Board of Education advises that the Hansford Company's bid will be evaluated after the background of the firm and its employees have been checked. With Sam acting territorial about Jerry, Pop and Bill crash the couple's date at a nightclub, where coincidentally Lieutenant Dearborn is entertaining a lady friend. When Bill's interest in the lieutenant's table attracts notice, Bill claims the woman is an old flame he'd rather avoid, and hastily leaves the club.

With some gentle prodding from Pop, "Bill" confesses that he's James Reid, and tells his story. While employed as a steelworker, he got into a fight with the foreman over a crooked card game, and was fired. Coming back to the worksite for his pay, Reid discovered the body of his ex-boss, killed with Reid's hammer. The only possible witness who can clear him is a coworker, Frosty Davenport. Reid has been unable to locate Davenport since, but believes he is in Los Angeles, and is "the key to a mighty important lock."

Pop suggests placing an ad in the newspaper seeking a workman with Frosty's credentials as a welder. Before Frosty surfaces for a job interview, Sam is injured in an accident for which he blames Bill. The accident receives newspaper coverage featuring Bill's picture; Pop fires him for his own protection, knowing Lt. Dearborn will recognize him as James Reid and seek him out. When Reid does confront his former colleague, the police arrive on the scene just as Frosty implicates him, forcing another hasty escape for the wanted man.

Planning to leave town and start over, Bill is visited by Pop just as they hear a radio announcement of a plane crashing into a nearby building, and an urgent call for steeplejacks to assist at the scene. When Pop, working at the scene, is trapped beneath a falling girder, Bill must decide whether to come to his rescue, fully aware that to do so will allow Dearborn to capture him.

Some familiar P-T themes resurface in *Disaster*, though this is writer Thomas Ahearn's only screenplay for the company. Pine and Thomas acquired the rights to Ahearn's story in 1946. Elements that have worked well in pictures like *Wrecking Crew* are trotted out once again. The result is basically a no-frills action film, serviceable but hardly memorable. Given the budget, it's not surprising that the plane crash into a city building is not seen, but described by a radio newscaster.

Richard Denning's open, friendly countenance is used to good advantage, signaling the audience that he will prove to be a sympathetic character despite early scenes in which he evades the police, and is revealed to be a wanted man. Pine-Thomas stalwart Will Wright has a particularly sizable role here, one that's right up his alley as a character man. Leading lady Trudy Marshall (1920–2004) makes her only P-T appearance, part of a career that consisted mostly of playing minor parts in A films, and ingénues in B pictures. She was the mother of actress Deborah Raffin. Glenn Strange (1899–1973), best-known for playing Frankenstein's monster in two Universal films of the 1940s, and for

A rare break from action scenes in *Disaster*: Richard Denning (left) plays games with favorite P-T character actor Will Wright, as leading lady Trudy Marshall looks on.

his recurring role as a bartender on TV's *Gunsmoke*, is seen briefly as the ace-palming foreman who pays a high price for his dishonesty.

REVIEWS: "Action in *Disaster* builds satisfactorily, climaxing with a perilous climb and fight atop a partly destroyed building, but the picture fails to generate sustained interest, partly due to the poorly constructed screenplay, most of which can be anticipated in advance." *Showmen's Trade Review*, October 23, 1948

"This is a run-of-the-mill action melodrama, undistinguished in every department … the story is so thin that the producer had to resort to considerable padding on trivial and uninteresting incidents and dialogue to give the film its one-hour running time." *Harrison's Reports*, October 23, 1948

Dynamite (1949)

CAST: William Gargan (*"Gunner" Peterson*), Virginia Welles (*Mary*), Richard Crane (*Johnny Brown*), Irving Bacon (*Jake*), Mary Newton (*Nellie Brown*), Frank Ferguson (*"Hard Rock" Mason*), Douglass Dumbrille (*Hank Gibbons*), Phil Arnold (*Photographer*),

Keith Richards (*Danbury*), Almira Sessions (*Jennie*), Lane Chandler (*Motorist*), Dan White (*Skipper Brown*), Jason Robards, Sr. (*Hook*)

CREW: William H. Pine (*Director*), Milton Raison (*Screenplay*), Ellis W. Carter (*Director of Photography*), Lewis H. Creber (*Art Director*), Howard Smith (*Film Editor*), Tom Lambert (*Sound Recording*), Alfred Kegerris (*Set Decorator*), Darrell Calker (*Music Score*)

RELEASED January 1949. 68 minutes.

The demolition company owned by Jake is dismissed from a job after an accident in which one of his workers is killed. Jake, who's dependent on the company to support his daughter, Mary, cajoles old friend Hank Gibbons into hiring him for a big job with a tight deadline, despite the fact that his equipment is second-rate.

Jake, Mary, and his crew are attending a Christmas party at the Los Angeles boardinghouse owned by Nellie Brown when she receives a visit from her son Johnny, a veteran who's been studying engineering in college via the GI Bill. Nellie is firmly opposed to her son working as "a powder man," as his late father did, but Johnny needs a break from school and persuades Jake to hire him for his crew.

Almost immediately, Jake's crew encounters problems and setbacks, with the failing brakes on an old truck causing an accident that costs the company quite a bit of money, and nearly kills one of his men. With Jake pressed by his creditors, his friend and employee Hard Rock borrows some needed funds from an unexpected source, Nellie Brown. Nellie is still unhappy that Johnny is working as a dynamiter, and blames his attraction to Mary for the decision, but lends the money to her old friend Jake nonetheless.

On the job, Johnny butts heads with longtime crew member Gunner Peterson, who like him has an eye for Mary. Their antagonism leads to a fistfight when Gunner senses that he is losing ground in their romantic rivalry, with Mary putting off his marriage proposal. Gunner is confident that his practical work experience trumps Johnny's classroom education, and he refuses to heed the younger man's warning about an error he's making. When that mistake costs a crew member his life, a guilt-ridden Gunner decides to pack it in. Going it on his own as a "powder man," Johnny is unexpectedly injured, trapped in a cave-in. With no time to wait for excavation, as Johnny's air runs low, Mary calls upon the one person she knows can save the day.

Of all the trouble-plagued work crews seen in Pine-Thomas Bs of the 1940s, the *Dynamite* gang may be the most accident-prone. Although the script hews to the norms established in earlier films, the body count is upped, with the first fatal accident taking place only moments after the opening titles have faded. The screenplay reprises, with minor variations, a scene from *High Explosive*, with dynamite substituting for nitroglycerine. In both versions, trucks transporting the hazardous material are nearly run off the road by a careless driver, who then gets a lesson in road safety courtesy of the hero's fists. Trade ads proclaimed, "Thrills will rock your screen as a sputtering, burning fuse inches reckless powder monkeys closer and closer to Kingdom Come—while they fight for a woman's kiss."

Pretty Virginia Welles (1925–2002) had a relatively brief run as a film actress, with *Dynamite* providing one of her most substantial roles. Young leading man Richard Crane is a veteran of the previous Pine-Thomas film *Waterfront at Midnight*. This is William Gargan's final Pine-Thomas appearance; he will soon dive into the world of live TV, with his weekly series *Martin Kane, Private Eye*.

Character actress Mary Newton gives gravitas to the featured character of Nellie, Johnny's fiercely protective mother, making it a pity that her screen time is limited. In her best scene, she bitterly excoriates members of a blasting crew as "a bunch of tramps who never have a dime, never have families, never have homes. Why? So they can gamble with their lives every time they go out on a job." Other veteran character players round out the cast, some of them enjoying larger roles than they customarily did in A pictures; Frank Ferguson (1906–1978) is a particular standout as "Hard Rock," making his character colorful and convincing.

Daily Variety (April 13, 1948) reported that producer-director Pine, warned of weather not conducive to the four days of outdoor shooting scheduled for that week, tried a new tack, night-for-day shooting. He and cinematographer Ellis Carter staged scenes during the evening hours, artificially lit in such a way to simulate clear daytime weather. "Results were so satisfactory that spectator cannot tell that scenes actually weren't filmed in broad daylight. It's first time that exterior day sequences have been filmed at night, as far as is known." Pine's clever solution was estimated to save the production company some $40,000. The same publication also noted (December 8, 1947) that actor William Eythe, who had signed to star in two Pine-Thomas films, was permitted to observe the Dollar Bills in action during production of *Dynamite*: "Actor is interested in learning how to be a producer and will sit in on various production functions connected with the picture."

REVIEWS: "A routine, low-budget melodrama.... An unimportant romantic angle is dragged in by the ear.... Not much can be said for either the direction or the performances, but they are acceptable considering the weak story material." *Harrison's Reports*, November 20, 1948

"When two members of a blasting crew start disagreeing over a girl, you can expect fireworks. Literally.... There is one especially suspenseful episode when a dynamite truck goes careening brakeless down a mountain road...." *Motion Picture Herald*, November 20, 1948

El Paso (1949)

CAST: John Payne (*Clay Fletcher*), Gail Russell (*Susan Jeffers*), Sterling Hayden (*Bert Donner*), George "Gabby" Hayes (*Pesky Tees*), Dick Foran (*Sheriff La Farge*), Eduardo Noriega (*Don Nacho Vazquez*), Henry Hull (*Judge Henry Jeffers*), Mary Beth Hughes (*Stagecoach Nellie*), H.B. Warner (*Judge Fletcher*), Bobby Ellis (*Jack Elkins*), Catherine Craig (*Mrs. Elkins*), Arthur Space (*Johnny Elkins*), Steven Geray (*Mexican Joe*), Peggy McIntyre (*Mary Elizabeth Fletcher*), Joe Devlin (*Bartender*), Dewey Robinson (*Sam*), Gloria Winters (*Francine Maylon*), Irving Bacon, Eddie Parks (*Stagecoach Passengers*), Don Haggerty (*Deputy*), Renata Vanni (*Lupita Montez*), Lawrence Tibbett, Jr. (*Denton*), Pierre Watkin (*Mr. Seton*), Keith Richards (*Confederate Prisoner*), Lorin Raker (*Harvey*)

CREW: Lewis R. Foster (*Director/Screenplay*), J. Robert Bren, Gladys Atwater (*Story*), J. Robert Bren (*Associate Producer*), Ellis W. Carter (*Director of Photography*), Lewis H. Creber (*Art Director*), Howard Smith (*Editor*), Gar K. Gilbert (*Cinecolor Consultant*), Frank Webster (*Sound Recording*), Alfred Kegerris (*Set Decorator*), Mary Bowen (*Costume Supervisor*), Charles Keehne (*Wardrobe*), Paul Stanhope, Harry Ray (*Makeup Artists*), David Chudnow (*Music Supervisor*), Darnell Calker (*Music Score*)

RELEASED April 1949. 103 minutes.

With the Civil War over, Confederate Captain Clay Fletcher returns home to Charleston, intending to resume the practice of law. He's interested in knowing the whereabouts of Susan Jeffers, a young woman he was courting before the war. When he learns that she and her father relocated to El Paso, he offers to deliver some legal papers the latter must sign to settle an estate.

In El Paso, Clay quickly learns that lawlessness runs rampant. Flirtatious Stagecoach Nellie relieves him of the contents of his wallet. He steps into the local saloon just in time to witness Texas-style justice in action, as a jury convicts a local man of murder, and schedules him for an immediate hanging. Clay is shocked to realize that the tosspot judge presiding over the proceedings is Susan Jeffers' father. The judge, like the local sheriff, is under the thumb of crooked Bert Donner, head of the local El Paso Land Development Association. Clay's efforts to speak up on the prisoner's behalf get him into a fight, from which he is rescued by Don Nacho Vazquez, a Mexican citizen who owns property just over the nearby border. Vazquez explains that Donner's reign of terror has allowed him to possess most of the property for miles around.

Clay finds Susan running a local shop for ladies' hats, but she refuses to say why she didn't write to him during the war as she had promised. At first claiming she likes living in El Paso, she admits the truth after her father staggers home in a drunken stupor, saying she must stay to look after him.

Clay's original intent was to stay in El Paso only long enough to obtain the signed documents, but he senses that the local residents badly need legal help. He prevents Donner and the sheriff from grabbing the land of former Army Sergeant Johnny Elkins, who fell behind on his property taxes while serving his country. Elkins kills a deputy while protecting his ranch, and with Clay's help escapes over the border to Mexico. Clay insists that a trial date be set, and convinces Elkins to return to El Paso. Clay's buddy Pesky is charged with keeping Judge Jeffers sober until the trial, at which he acquits Elkins, and offers his own resignation. Though the people of the town, seeing a chance to get their own property back, urge the judge to keep his job, Donner and his cohorts react with a burst of violence. After the judge, Johnny Elkins, and Elkins' wife are murdered, Clay realizes that peaceable solutions will no longer suffice. "The scales of justice are tripped too far out of balance in here in El Paso," he says. "There's only one way to even them up—with a gun and a rope!" Soon, Clay, with the help of other townsmen, is meting out his own form of frontier justice—and earning a $500 reward on his head.

Daily Variety (September 23, 1948) reported that casting had been done by Pine and Thomas with an eye toward bringing in a varied audience: "John Payne and Sterling Hayden are boxoffice attractions for women, Gail Russell … is popular fare for teenagers. Eduardo Noriega who is called the Tyrone Power of Mexico … will serve dual purpose as a romantic and as a draw for the Spanish-speaking countries."

John Payne, in what may be his best part for Pine-Thomas, is well-cast in the lead. Beautiful Gail Russell (1924–1961), in the first of her three films for the Dollar Bills, has little to stretch her dramatically, and sits out many scenes. Her wardrobe consists largely of long, flowing gowns, which look rather out of place (not to mention suspiciously clean) in the hot, dusty frontier town, but she is a sight to behold. Sterling Hayden (1916–1986) and Dick Foran (1910–1979) capably provide the villainy. A suggestion that Hayden's character, too, is interested in Susan falls quietly by the wayside after a couple of early scenes.

A standout among the supporting cast is Henry Hull (1890–1977), whose performance shows both the sad drunk Judge Jeffers has become, and the upstanding, erudite man he could be once again. Mary Beth Hughes, as Stagecoach Nellie, has little to do, but is colorful and engaging in her few scenes, and has an amusing curtain line. Gabby Hayes, his role in this film less central to the story than it was in *Albuquerque*, provides adequate comic relief. As time goes on, Catherine Craig's assignments for the company are getting smaller; she's seen briefly as Sergeant Elkins' loyal wife.

While it might have been shortened slightly to its benefit, *El Paso* is a satisfying Western with a solid story underlining it. The screenplay manages to give Western fans the action they want, while ultimately coming down on the side of reason over vigilantism. The drama of the final battle royale is accented by a sandstorm. That sequence proved problematic when the city fathers of El Paso were shown the film prior to a scheduled premiere there. The local leaders thought the idea of a massive sandstorm bad for tourism, and insisted they didn't happen anyway. According to Thomas, they eventually accepted his explanation that "it's too late to tack on a new ending," and were taken aback when, "the night of the premiere, El Paso has its worst sandstorm in history."[27]

REVIEWS: "A slambang, outdoor feature … earmarked for a profitable ride through most of the situations it will play.… Lewis R. Foster has given lusty direction in action scenes to his own script." *Daily Variety*, February 28, 1949

"In terms of production effort, cast, camera work and general approach, *El Paso* does indeed emerge as a contender for deluxe theatre playing time, and suggests the future will bring bigger—and better—offerings from the new Pine-Thomas team. Where this picture falls short, however … is in its rigid adherence to stock situations and its failure to lend depth and conviction to its characters." *Motion Picture Daily*, March 2, 1949

Manhandled (1949)

CAST: Dorothy Lamour (*Merl Kramer*), Sterling Hayden (*Joe Cooper*), Dan Duryea (*Karl Benson*), Irene Hervey (*Ruth Bennet*), Philip Reed (*Guy Bayard*), Harold Vermilyea (*Dr. Redmond*), Alan Napier (*Alton Bennet*), Art Smith (*Lt. Bill Dawson*), Irving Bacon (*Sgt. Fayle*), Ian Wolfe (*Charlie*), Paul E. Burns (*Pawn Shop Owner*), Benny Baker (*Boyd*), James Edwards (*Henry*), Keye Luke (*Laundryman*), Maidie Norman (*Christine*), Robert Williams (*Fingerprint Man*), Morgan Farley (*Doc*), John George (*Newspaper Vendor*), Rose Plumer (*Flower Woman*), George Humbert (*Italian Restaurant Owner*), Garry Owen (*Police Photographer*), Ray Hyke (*Det. Phil Wilson*), Donald Kerr, Lee Roberts (*Reporters*)

CREW: Lewis R. Foster (*Director*), Lewis R. Foster, Whitman Chambers (*Screenplay*), L.S. Goldsmith (*Story*), Ernest Laszlo (*Director of Photography*), Lewis H. Creber (*Art Director*), Howard Smith (*Film Editor*), Edith Head (*Miss Lamour's Costumes*), Odette Myrtil (*Miss Hervey's Costumes*), William Fox (*Sound Recording*), Alfred Kegerris (*Set Decorator*), David Chudnow (*Music Supervision*), Darrell Calker (*Music Score*)

RELEASED May 1949. 98 minutes.

Writer Alton Bennet consults a psychiatrist, Dr. Redmond, describing a recurring dream in which he kills his wife Ruth with a quart-sized perfume bottle. As Redmond's confidential secretary, Merl Kramer, transcribes the session, Bennet admits that he needs money and despises his wife. Dr. Redmond advises his patient that the dream represents

Insurance investigator Joe Cooper (Sterling Hayden) is on the trail of stolen jewels in *Man-handled*, and Merl Kramer (Dorothy Lamour) is high on the list of suspects.

his subconscious impulses, and recommends that he sleep in the guest bedroom for the time being, just to be on the safe side.

In the home they share at the Crayford Arms Apartments, Bennet and his wife are barely civil to each other. Taking great pride in her jewel collection, insured for $100,000, Ruth enjoys evenings out, especially in the company of a handsome young architect, Guy Bayard, who's designing a beach house for the Bennets. In contrast to the Bennets' lavish life, the doctor's secretary Merl, who's been on the job only four weeks, lives modestly in a brownstone walkup. Downstairs is her friend Karl Benson, an ex-cop who runs a small detective agency. Karl is interested in Merl romantically, but the divorcee responds cautiously to his advances, saying she's already made one mistake.

When Merl tells him about her boss' client, and his wife's jewels, unscrupulous Karl sets a plan into motion. The next morning, Ruth is found murdered, and Karl takes her stolen jewels to his fence, Charlie. Told that Mrs. Bennet has been killed, Karl professes innocence of that crime. Charlie advises him that Mrs. Bennet's jewels are too hot to pawn, or resell, for the moment, so Karl hides them in his apartment.

Police Lieutenant Bill Dawson, investigating the homicide, is irked when insurance investigator Joe Cooper, representing the company that insured Mrs. Bennet's jewelry, horns in on his inquiries. The most obvious murder suspect, Alton Bennet, has a seemingly airtight alibi that he was knocked unconscious that night by an overdose of sleeping pills, which his butler verifies. Other suspects include Guy Bayard, who escorted Ruth to a nightclub a few hours before she died, Merl Kramer, whose references for her secretarial job are quickly recognized as forged, and Dr. Redmond himself, who is sporting a head wound the day after the murder.

When Merl finds a ring in her apartment, and innocently pawns it, she becomes of even stronger interest to the police in the investigation. Behind the scenes, at least one person is pulling strings to make certain she winds up holding the bag for the theft of the jewels, and the murder of Mrs. Bennet.

A lavish production by Pine-Thomas' 1940s standards, *Manhandled* is a top-flight murder mystery, with star names heading the cast, unusually careful and skilled cinematography (by Ernest Laszlo), and a witty, well-plotted script. Pine and Thomas take a rare "produced by" credit here, using their full names, rather than their usual "A Pine-Thomas Production." According to *Daily Variety* (November 9, 1948), the title *Manhandled* had to be cleared for use, after earlier adorning a silent Gloria Swanson film. Working titles for this film were "Betrayal" and "The Man Who Stole a Dream," the latter reportedly rejected after exhibitors found it "too long and suggestive of fantasy."[28] An item in *Daily Variety* (December 14, 1948) reported that Dorothy Lamour narrowly escaped injury in a scene set high atop a building when Dan Duryea, carrying her in his arms, nearly lost his footing, threatening to send her tumbling for real. A rare sight in P-T films of the 1940s was a credit for a costume designer; here, there are two, with the well-known Edith Head in charge of Dorothy Lamour's look.

Miss Lamour, top-billed as Merl, plays a character who is mostly low-key and rather glum in early scenes. The role gets substantially better as the film progresses, and she has some exciting moments to play in its last half-hour. Dan Duryea (1907–1968) is at his skeezy best as low-rent detective Karl Benson, whose geniality gradually gives way to something else.

Irene Hervey (1909–1998) gives verve to the character of Alton Bennet's trophy wife, making it a pity she's knocked off partway through the film. She trades cool, clipped barbs with Alan Napier's supercilious Bennet. Seeing that she's wearing easily half the contents of her jewelry box for her evening out, Napier purrs, "I wouldn't dream of depriving you of the opportunity of making a vulgar display of yourself. Go ahead, deck yourself out like some little carnival biddy." In turn, when he turns his acid tongue on his wife's slick, handsome escort, she comments calmly to Guy, "After four drinks, he's *really* detestable."

Having played the lead in Pine-Thomas' "Big Town" films, Philip Reed appears in a supporting capacity here, well-cast as the smoothie whose attentions to Ruth may have a sinister motivation. Art Smith (1899–1973) is a standout in his performance as the world-weary homicide cop. Two fine African American actors, James Edwards (1918–1970) and Maidie Norman (1912–1998), show up briefly as the butler and maid in the Bennet abode; Edwards' far better role of the year was in *Home of the Brave*. Keye Luke is wasted in a bit part as the smiling owner of a laundry.

The motion picture industry in 1949 was in the throes of a growing panic, as the encroachment of television, plus the antitrust, began to put a serious dent into studios' profits. According to Bill Thomas, *Manhandled* did not perform up to expectations for Paramount, and almost broke the producers' .1000 batting average. (Syndicated columnist Bob Thomas reported a few months after its release that it was "expected to limp out of the red ink.") It was the last movie lead for Lamour, excepting her appearance in *Road to Bali*.

REVIEWS: "A suspenseful film that will do well wherever played. It has fine performances and an interest-sustaining story; further it challenges the 'arm-chair detectives' who like to solve their mysteries before they are revealed on the screen. The top cast of players are all quite capable...." *Showmen's Trade Review*, April 16, 1949

"A sure-fire success on the murder mystery list. It boasts a clever plot that is refreshing because it has so many surprise switches and unexpected twists.... The entire cast is top flight. Dan Duryea almost steals the show with his characterization of the apparently good-natured but completely unscrupulous private eye.... Film looks like a solid boxoffice bet where melodrama and action fare are generally liked." *Hollywood Reporter*, April 12, 1949

Special Agent (1949)

CAST: William Eythe (*Johnny Douglas*), George Reeves (*Paul Devereaux*), Laura Elliot [Kasey Rogers] (*Lucille Peters*), Paul Valentine (*Edmond Devereaux*), Tom Powers (*Chief Special Agent Wilcox*), Carole Mathews (*Rose McCreary*), Frank Puglia (*Grandfather Devereaux*), Virginia Christine (*Mabel Rumpler*), Raymond Bond (*Sheriff Babcock*), John Hilton [John Hart] (*Frank Kent*), Walter Baldwin ("*Pop*" *Peters*), Jeff York (*Jake Rumpler*), Peter Miles (*Jake Rumpler, Jr.*), Jimmy Hunt (*Tim Rumpler*), Joseph Granby (*Sheriff Dodson*), Robert B. Williams (*Superintendent Phil Olmstead*), Morgan Farley (*Dr. Jerome Bowen*), Arthur Stone (*Tad Miller*), Thomas Browne Henry (*Detective Benton*), Mary Field (*Miss Tannehill*), Fred Santley (*Hardware Store Owner*), Walter Soderling (*Dan Simmons*), Alex Frazer (*Bookstore Owner*), Paul Harvey (*Mr. Travis*), Frank Cady (*Motorist*)

CREW: William C. Thomas (*Director*), Lewis R. Foster, Whitman Chambers (*Screenplay*), Milton Raison (*Story Material*), Ellis W. Carter (*Director of Photography*), Lewis H. Creber (*Art Director*), Howard Smith (*Film Editor*), Tom Lambert (*Sound Recording*), Alfred Kegerris (*Set Decorator*), Truman Bradley (*Narrator*)

RELEASED July 1949. 71 minutes.

New to his job as railroad detective, Johnny Douglas is restless in the quiet town of Santa Marta, where nothing much seems to happen. No sooner has he wished for a little excitement than word comes of a train robbery, in which four railroad employees were killed, and two mailbags stolen, one of which contains a $100,000 payroll. Working in the railroad office is pretty young Lucille Peters, whose father was the engineer killed in the robbery.

Leading a posse of investigators, including representatives from local law enforcement, the post office, and the railroad, Johnny soon determines that two men carried out the carefully planned ambush and robbery of the train. Their abandoned getaway car yields a few clues, including some articles of clothing and a copy of Tolstoy's *War and Peace*. The book proves to be an unexpectedly valuable clue, putting Johnny on the robbers' trail, as a bookstore owner remembers the two similar-looking men who bought it, and a jittery librarian tells him about the two roughly dressed men whose cleated shoes damaged the library floor. With the help of university criminologist Dr. Jerome Bowen's analysis of the clues (and his amazingly accurate sketches of the suspects), Johnny realizes he's on the trail of Paul Devereaux and his older brother Edmond.

The Devereaux boys live on a nearby ranch with their grandfather, but the family

William Eythe is flanked by his two beautiful co-stars in *Special Agent*: Carole Mathews (left) and Laura Elliot. Miss Elliot went on to have a successful TV career under the name Kasey Rogers.

has fallen on hard times, and most of their land has been repossessed. Paul agreed to the robbery plan, but is disturbed that his brother shot the railroad employees in carrying it out. After hiding out for quite some time as the chase for them goes on, Paul goes back to the site where he and Edmond hid the money-filled mailbag, allowing Johnny to pick up their trail. Paul's love for neighbor Rose McCreary first gives the Deveraux boys a much-needed heads-up when the law comes looking for them, but also proves costly when he can't resist the urge to see her again. Feeling a failure when the robbers slip away from the posse, Johnny expects to be fired from his job as a detective, but a lucky discovery by two little boys, sons of the murdered railroaders, finally puts him on the trail of his men.

Special Agent represents something of a departure for the Dollar Bills, a crime thriller told in the semi-documentary style popularized in the 1940s by bigger films like Fox's *The House on 92nd Street* (1945), which shared with this picture leading man William Eythe. Narrator Truman Bradley (1905–1974), who would go on to host the syndicated television series *Science Fiction Theatre* (1955–57) reminds us in the film's opening moments of the many passengers and much valuable property transported via the nation's railroads. "Few of us," he adds, "know anything about the great body of trained men who guard those millions of lives, and billions of dollars in property, by day and by night, the railroad detectives." The film, he says, documents "the greatest criminal manhunt in the history of California railroading."

Pine and Thomas assembled a most capable cast to tell the story, headed by Eythe as railroad detective Douglas. Newly signed to a Paramount contract, actress Laura Elliot (1925–2006), whose most famous film would be Hitchcock's *Strangers on a Train* (1951), appears as Eythe's love interest. After changing her professional name to Kasey Rogers in the early 1950s, Miss Elliot (or Elliott, as her name was sometimes spelled) would have a second successful career as a television actress, playing recurring characters in ABC's hit shows of the 1960s, *Peyton Place* and *Bewitched* (the latter as Louise Tate). Thomas took the directorial reins for the last time on a Pine-Thomas production.

The film's main curiosity value in the 21st century may be the casting of George Reeves (1914–1959), only a few years before he began starring in TV's *The Adventures of Superman*, as a railroad thief, albeit the more soft-hearted of the two. Reeves was credited by the *Los Angeles Times'* Edwin Schallert (July 22, 1949) with "a very sinister performance." Seen to good effect in smaller roles are Virginia Christine (1920–1996) as the grieving widow of a railroad man who dies in the robbery, Morgan Farley (1898–1988) as a university criminologist, the CSI man of his day, who gives Johnny a remarkably accurate idea of the suspects, and Carole Mathews (1920–2014) as Rose, whose love for Paul Devereaux entangles her in the manhunt.

Paramount publicity materials suggested various promotional stunts, including the placement of one or more money bags around town, with contestants who found them and brought them to the theater receiving free movie tickets. Publicists noted, "The showman has a wide choice of exploitation material. He can choose the 'right-out-of-the-headlines' angle, playing up the train robbery and the bandits' terrorizing; or he can call on the man-hunt factor; or the newly revealed story of the railroad special agents and their engrossing methods of detection."

Special Agent provides satisfying entertainment, making it a pity that the few prints currently in circulation are dreadful third or fourth-generation copies that render the cinematography murky and difficult to watch. At the time of its original release, it was frequently double-billed with *Manhandled*.

REVIEWS: "The story, though supposedly based in fact, offers nothing unusual. It is helped, however, by a fairly good semi-documentary treatment and by impressive outdoor scenic backgrounds…. The direction is good and the acting acceptable." *Harrison's Reports*, April 30, 1949

"The film is extremely well-made and crowded with fast-moving action, high-spots of drama and thrills…. William C. Thomas' skillful direction builds up the suspense and keeps the drama moving at a rapid tempo…. William Eythe gives an outstanding and convincing performance as the young special agent and Laura Elliot adds feminine charm and a dash of romance to the story." *Hollywood Reporter*, April 26, 1949

Captain China (1950)

CAST: John Payne (*Charles Chinnough*), Gail Russell (*Kim Mitchell*), Jeffrey Lynn (*Capt. George Brendensen*), Lon Chaney (*Red Lynch*), Edgar Bergen (*Mr. Haasvelt*), Michael O'Shea (*Trask*), Ellen Corby (*Miss Endicott*), Robert Armstrong (*Keegan*), John Qualen (*Geech*), Ilka Gruning (*Mrs. Haasvelt*), Keith Richards (*Alberts*), John Bagni (*Sparks*), Ray Hyke (*Michaels*), Walter Reed (*Martin*), Paul Hogan (*Speer*), Lawrence Tibbet [Tibbett], Jr. (*Wilkes*), Zonn Murray (*Gus*), Don Gazzaniga (*Tony*), Denver Pyle

(*Steve*), Wally Scott (*Scotty*), Lee Roberts (*Marsh*), Reed Howes (*Blake*), Charlie Regan (*Wade*)

CREW: Lewis R. Foster (*Director*), William H. Pine, William C. Thomas (*Producers*), Lewis R. Foster, Gwen Bagni (*Screenplay*), Gwen Bagni, John Bagni (*Story*), John Alton (*Photography*), Lewis H. Creber (*Art Director*), Howard Smith (*Film Editor*), William Fox (*Sound Recording*), Alfred Kegerris (*Set Decorator*), Alex Weldon (*Special Effects*), David Chudnow (*Music Supervisor*), Lucien Cailliet (*Music Score*), Josef Marcus (*Song,* "Oh Brandy Leave Me Alone"), Paul Stanhope, Harry Ray (*Makeup Artists*)

RELEASED January 1950. 97 minutes.

Experienced ship's captain Charles Chinnough (nicknamed "Captain China") awakens during a heavy storm to find himself locked in his cabin, an empty liquor bottle at his feet. Off course, the ship piles up on a reef, and Chinnough, washed overboard, is picked up by another vessel. After recuperating on a remote island, Chinnough learns that he has been stripped of his command, blamed for the crash. His former first mate, George Brendensen, provided the testimony that finished Chinnough's career, believing that the disgraced captain had been lost at sea.

Knowing that Brendensen connived against him, and was subsequently rewarded with a promotion to captain, Chinnough books passage to Manila on the *Crosswind*. The ship is under the command of Brendensen, who is unnerved to see his former captain as a passenger. Also on board are an older Swedish couple, the Haasvelts, and Miss Endicott, a mystery writer composing her latest tale.

Crew member Red Lynch, who conspired with Brendensen against "Captain China," gets into a fight with Chinnough. Watching is another passenger, a beautiful woman named Kim Mitchell. Kim, who has encouraged the friendly attentions of Brendensen, is interested in Chinnough, but tells him that she is on her way to Manila to marry a safe "solid citizen" she knows from her hometown of Council Bluffs, Iowa. Red, who was guilty of locking Chinnough in his cabin during the fateful storm, wants Brendensen to help him put their former captain out of commission, but the newly minted commander refuses to do so.

Brendensen's inexperience causes him to underestimate the importance of a storm that is brewing, until it has grown into a full-blown typhoon. With his ship in danger, the incompetent captain reluctantly comes to the conclusion that there's only one man aboard who can save him and his passengers.

Unlike some Pine-Thomas projects, *Captain China* took awhile to reach theaters. The producers originally acquired the rights to Gwen and John Bagni's story in late 1947. According to the *Los Angeles Times*' Edwin Schallert (December 11, 1947), it was first eyed as a vehicle for actor William Eythe. Director Lewis R. Foster revamped some of the Bagnis' material, sharing in the screenwriting credit for his contributions.

In its early scenes, *Captain China* concerns itself mostly with personal dramas. But the story builds to an impressively staged storm sequence that takes up most of the film's last half-hour. It is a bit jarring to see that, while the typhoon dumps gallons of water on deck, causing the ship to lurch from side to side, the passengers remain comfortably seated in a lounge below, the contents of their coffee cups not even sloshing as the storm worsens. (Payne's character is playing a leisurely game of solitaire, the cards sitting undisturbed on the table top in front of him.)

The strong chemistry between John Payne and Gail Russell is showcased much more

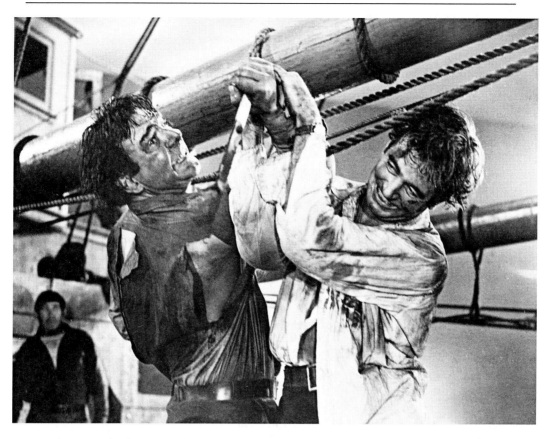

Lon Chaney and John Payne fight dirty in *Captain China*. Studio publicity called it "one of the most brutal fights ever filmed."

strongly here than it was in *El Paso*. Miss Russell is cast as a woman who has been around the block a few times, living her life seeking excitement and intrigue. Though she claims to be ready to settle down, Payne's character tells her, "You'd get awfully tired of one house and one man all your life." It's a bit sad to see this actress, whose real-world struggles with the bottle would shorten not only her career but her life, cast in a story that places such emphasis on alcohol, and the aftereffects of excessive drinking.

Ellen Corby (1911–1999) is delightful in her featured part as the twittery author of murder mysteries, who spends her time pondering various ways to do in her fictional characters, and doesn't let even a raging storm interrupt her work. Less successful is Edgar Bergen's somewhat pointless role as a fellow passenger, though he does get a funny exit line. Michael O'Shea (1906–1973) has a relatively small part as a sailor disciplined for drinking, who like Chinnough gets another opportunity to prove himself when trouble arises. Co-scenarist John Bagni also appears onscreen, seen briefly as the ship's radio operator (called "Sparks," of course).

On a publicity tour in North Carolina, Bill Thomas promised an interviewer that *Captain China* contained "one of the darndest fights you've ever seen. John Payne and Lon Chaney … wouldn't use doubles and took all the bumps themselves…. We shot the scenes right at the first of the picture and were scared someone was going to get hurt." Added Pine, "I guess if Payne had cracked a rib or something, we'd have had to throw him in the sea and let Jeffrey Lynn get the girl."[29] According to film historian Gene Freese, the brawl took five days to shoot, and did indeed leave both Payne and Chaney with injuries.[30]

At the film's world premiere in Roanoke, Virginia, star John Payne was honored as the city's "most famous native son." Promising audiences "a winner," Payne told a local reporter, "I'm sure that people of all ages will like *Captain China*. It is loaded with action, and besides it's got Gail Russell, who's one of the most appealing girls in pictures."[31]

REVIEWS: "Cram-jammed with action, this Pine-Thomas thriller will hold audiences spellbound.... The story, while somewhat far-fetched, is made altogether believable by the furious storm, good production, the generally excellent acting, and by the exceptionally good photography...." *Showmen's Trade Review*, November 5, 1949

"Pine-Thomas has a top money picture here.... Storm scenes have seldom been equalled [*sic*] in realism, and there's a vicious fight to please the most battle-scarred fan.... John Payne ... delivers sock performance, and both in his romantic scenes with Gail Russell and his more rugged struggle with the elements he scores tellingly." *Daily Variety*, October 31, 1949

The Eagle and the Hawk (1950)

CAST: John Payne (*Capt. Todd Croyden*), Rhonda Fleming (*Madeline Danzeeger*), Dennis O'Keefe (*Capt. Whitney Randolph*), Thomas Gomez (*Gen. Liguras*), Fred Clark (*Basil Danzeeger*), Frank Faylen (*Red Hyatt*), Eduardo Noriega (*Roberto*), Grandon Rhodes (*Gov. Lubbock*), Walter Reed (*Jones*), Margaret Martin (*Marguerita*)

CREW: Lewis R. Foster (*Director*), William H. Pine, William C. Thomas (*Producers*), Geoffrey Homes, Lewis R. Foster (*Screenplay*), Jess Arnold (*Story*), James Wong Howe (*Director of Photography*), Lewis H. Creber (*Art Director*), Robert Brower (*Technicolor Color Consultant*), Travis Banton (*Miss Fleming's Costumes*), David Chudnow (*Music Supervisor*), Rudy Schrager (*Music Score*), Howard Smith (*Editor*), William Fox (*Sound Recording*), Alfred Kegerris (*Set Decorator*), Charles Keehne, Mary Bowen (*Wardrobe*), Paul Stanhope, Harry Ray (*Makeup Artists*)

RELEASED May 1950. 104 minutes.

Captain Todd Croyden of the Texas Rangers is asked by the governor to help Whitney Randolph escape from the custody of an Army camp. Having done so, Todd, a loyal Confederate, is not happy to hear that the man he rescued, Whitney Randolph, is a Union spy. The governor explains that Whitney was on his way to Mexico, to investigate reports of a renegade army that threatens the safety of Texas. Todd is asked to help get Whitney safely across the Mexican border, so that he can learn the whereabouts of another Union agent, Brooks, who disappeared while investigating a town called Corales.

Todd and Whitney form an uneasy alliance as they travel together. Just after passing into Mexico, they come to the aid of beautiful Madeline Danzeeger, whose carriage overturned while crossing a stream. Upon arriving in Corales, they learn that the primary holder of local power is wealthy Basil Danzeeger, presumed by Todd to be Madeline's father, who claims to be an agent of Mexican General Juarez. Danzeeger is financing a renegade army that professes to support the efforts of Juarez to prevent Mexico from being overtaken by France. In fact, Danzeeger's army is actually designed to cross the

Rhonda Fleming makes her point at gunpoint in *The Eagle and the Hawk*, keeping John Payne in her sights.

border back into the U.S., while soldiers there are engaged in fighting the Civil War, and take possession of Texan lands.

Roberto, who has a shop in Corales making and repairing boots, confides in Todd and Whitney that Brooks was murdered, and that they will likewise be in danger if they arouse the suspicions of Danzeeger or his military leader, General Liguras. Foregoing his initial plan to drop off Whitney and leave Mexico, Todd decides to stay and help the cause. Dividing their efforts, Todd concentrates on ingratiating himself with Danzeeger, while Whitney tries to learn more about General Liguras, leader of the renegade army that is now some 1500 men strong.

Attracted to Todd, Madeline visits him late at night to warn him that he is in danger. Soon afterwards, he learns that Whitney failed to return from a visit to General Liguras' headquarters. Todd is caught at Danzeeger's storehouse, which contains munitions supplies from France, and some stolen from the United States. With Madeline's help, he escapes and makes his way to Liguras' compound, where Whitney is being held prisoner. The two men try to persuade a dubious Liguras that his employer is actually a French agent. When Liguras demands proof, Todd returns to Corales, but he falls into Danzeeger's hands and is slated for a particularly brutal death. Trying to bargain for his life is Madeline, who reveals that she is Danzeeger's wife, not his daughter.

Once again, John Payne is cast as a loyal Confederate, as he was in *El Paso* and will be again in *The Vanquished*. Screenwriters Foster and Homes adapted an original story, "A Mission for General Houston," by Jess Arnold. Filming began at Sedona, Arizona in August 1949.

In his first romantic scene with Madeline, Todd tells her, "I don't know anything about you, except you can tie a man's stomach in knots and make his tongue feel as thick as a saddle blanket." This is apparently a compliment, and leads to their first kiss. Later, he returns to the theme of linens, saying, "You could make a man forget a lot of things, like sentries outside his window and guards sleeping on his saddle blankets."

Making his Pine-Thomas debut, actor Dennis O'Keefe (1908–1968) is happily cast as the easygoing, somewhat whimsical Captain Whitney Randolph, a man who bears his responsibilities lightly. His deft comic touch (he dubs his dour traveling companion "Nursie") plays nicely off John Payne's more typically taciturn Western hero. According to *Daily Variety* (November 28, 1949), Pine and Thomas were sufficiently pleased with both actors' work on *The Eagle and the Hawk* to sign them for additional assignments— one film for O'Keefe, and three (over a three-year period) for Payne. Eduardo Noriega, previously seen in *El Paso*, is a strong, dignified presence in his supporting role as Roberto. The presence of character actor Thomas Gomez (1905–1971) becomes more significant in the film's final half hour.

REVIEWS: "Just about the best release [Pine and Thomas] have yet turned out for Paramount. It is beautifully done in Technicolor, has a western plot based in history to add an air of fact, the action is well-paced and the boxoffice outlook good.... The artful, mobile camera work used by James Wong Howe takes full advantage of every foot of film, both complementing and complimenting the entire story-telling." *Daily Variety*, February 3, 1950

"The yarn seldom rises above the level of pretentious make-believe, either in the lingo supposedly serving for the period or in the casting and characterization ... photographed in garish and indiscriminate Technicolor." *Los Angeles Times*, May 26, 1950

The Lawless (1950)

CAST: Macdonald Carey (*Larry Wilder*), Gail Russell (*Sunny Garcia*), John Sands (*Joe Ferguson*), Lee Patrick (*Jan Dawson*), John Hoyt (*Ed Ferguson*), Walter Reed (*Jim Wilson*), Guy [Herbert] Anderson (*Jonas Creel*), Lalo Rios (*Paul Rodriguez*), Maurice Jara (*Lopo Chavez*), Argentina Brunetti (*Mrs. Rodriguez*), William Edmunds (*Mr. Jensen*), Gloria Winters (*Mildred Jensen*), John Davis (*Harry Pawling*), Martha Hyer (*Caroline Tyler*), Frank Fenton (*Mr. Prentiss*), Paul Harvey (*Chief Blake*), Felipe Turich (*Mr. Rodriguez*), Ian MacDonald (*Al Peters*), Noel Reyburn (*Fred Jackson*), Tab Hunter (*Frank O'Brien*), Russ Conway (*Eldredge*), Robert Williams (*Boswell*), James Bush (*Anderson*), Julia Faye (*Mrs. Jensen*), Howard Negley (*Pete Cassell*), Gordon Nelson (*Cadwallader*), Frank Ferguson (*Carl Green*), Ray Hyde (*Motorcycle Cop*), Pedro de Cordoba (*Mr. Garcia*)

CREW: Joseph Losey (*Director*), William H. Pine, William C. Thomas (*Producers*), Geoffrey Homes (*Screenplay*), Roy Hunt (*Director of Photography*), Lewis H. Creber (*Art Director*), Howard Smith (*Editor*), John Carter (*Sound Recording*), Alfred Kegerris (*Set Decorator*), David Chudnow (*Music Supervision*), Mahlon Merrick (*Sound Recording*)

RELEASED June 1950. 83 minutes.

After a long week of work as fruit pickers, 19-year-old Paul Rodriguez and his pal, Lopo Chavez, are looking forward to a dance being held in the predominantly Mexican-American community of Sleepy Hollow. On their way home to the nearby town of Santa Marta, Paul and Lopo are involved in a fender-bender with several Caucasian boys, including Joe Ferguson, and a fistfight breaks out after one of them uses a racial slur.

Larry Wilder, new owner/publisher of the local newspaper, the *Morning Union*, attends the dance, having heard rumors that fights may break out. He meets lovely Sunny Garcia, editor of a Spanish weekly newspaper, *La Luz*. Though she tells him that the people of Sleepy Hollow have put a stop to fighting between two local gangs, trouble does break out when Joe and his friends show up, and begin harassing the young women guests. Jumping into the melee, Paul inadvertently hits police officer Al Peters. Panicking, Paul appropriates a nearby ice cream truck and flees. Jonas Creel, an ambitious young reporter for Larry's own paper, calls the story in to the wire service, exaggerating it into a riot. On the run, Paul is discovered by a young woman in her family's barn; when she bangs her head on a wooden beam and knocks herself out, he escapes. But local print and TV reporters take pretty, blonde Mildred at her word when she claims that Paul assaulted her.

Businessman Ed Ferguson, embarrassed by his son Joe's arrest, pays fines for all the boys involved in the fight, except for Paul, who's still running. Taken into custody by the police, Paul is brutalized by Al Peters, the angry cop he hit at the dance. A second policeman, distracted from his driving by Al's rough treatment of Paul, loses control of the car. Both Al and Paul escape from the car before it burns, but as the only surviving witness the policeman makes Paul's case worse. By the time Paul is caught a second time, he has been charged with a multitude of crimes, including Grand Theft Auto.

After a distinguished career as a crusading journalist and author, Larry Wilder moved to Santa Marta hoping for peace and quiet. Sunny, knowing his background, implores him to help. He courts controversy when he prints a defense of Paul's action, trying to point out that he was just a scared kid, and launching a fund for the teenager's legal defense. Mr. Jensen is infuriated by the implication that his daughter lied about the attack on her.

When Lopo visits Santa Marta to make a contribution to Paul's defense fund, he is attacked by a mob. The vigilantes first descend on the jail, where Paul is being moved to a safer location, and then to the newspaper office. There awaiting Larry's return is Sunny, who is injured as the angry mob destroys the equipment and furnishings of the *Union*. Refusing to press charges over the destruction, Larry says he is finished with Santa Marta, and will be leaving town. Ed Ferguson asks him to stay and rebuild, and pays for Paul to have the services of a good lawyer, but Larry isn't sure he wants to be part of the community any longer.

Forward-thinking for its day, *The Lawless* came along at a time when American filmmakers were beginning to challenge audiences to acknowledge the prejudices faced by minority and nonwhite populations. Following in the footsteps of films like *Gentleman's Agreement* (Fox, 1947) and *Pinky* (Fox, 1949), Pine and Thomas' *The Lawless* exposes the mistreatment of immigrants and their American-born offspring. The screenplay makes clear the wide divide between the way white residents live, and the conditions experienced by the Rodriguez family—getting ready for the dance, Joe Ferguson showers in a nicely appointed bathroom, while Paul rinses off the dirt of his manual labor under a hose in the backyard of his parents' shabby home. The men who do the hard, grimy work as pickers for low pay are described condescendingly by most white residents as "fruit tramps."

As an opening card says, "This is the story of a town and some of its people, who, in the grip of blind anger forget their American heritage of tolerance and decency, and become the lawless." It is also, secondarily, an examination of the ways in which a free press can be used—and misused—to further the cause of justice. While making its thematic points, the film also offers a rapid pace, plenty of suspense, and some good performances. If a few of the film's touches lack subtlety—we get several looks at a road sign that proclaims Santa Marta, despite its racial tensions, "The Friendly Town"—it was nonetheless a bold project more than six decades ago, and a credit to Pine and Thomas' filmography.

The Lawless was completed at a cost of approximately $435,000, with location shooting in the town of Marysville, California. Among the dozens of locals recruited to serve as extras and bit players in the film was the town's mayor, who earned $55 for a brief appearance as the mayor of Santa Marta.

Macdonald Carey (1913–1994) is subtly effective as Larry Wilder, a man of significant experience with the ugliness of the world, but one who initially balks at taking on a new crusade. Gail Russell, in her third Pine-Thomas film, is luminously beautiful and intelligent as the principled woman who quietly becomes a crusader on behalf of her people. Known to have a drinking problem, Russell was on suspension at Paramount when Pine and Thomas asked to use her in *The Lawless*. The studio agreed to the deal with the stipulation that the producers would be personally responsible for her salary—in the range of $30,000—if she failed to complete her assignment.

Lee Patrick, returning to the Dollar Bills' stable after an absence of several years, memorably portrays a cynical reporter. Herbert Anderson (1917–1994), billed here as "Guy," offers a portrayal far removed from his loving dad on TV's *Dennis the Menace*. Two up-and-coming young players, Tab Hunter and Martha Hyer, are seen in minor roles.

Newcomer Lalo Rios (1927–1973), previously employed as a carpenter, earned a reported $250 per week for his performance as Paul. According to syndicated columnist Hedda Hopper (June 25, 1950), Rios was discovered by director Losey, who "spotted him at a party and was struck by his sensitive face and expressive eyes." Pine and Thomas liked his performance well enough to decide that he should receive "introducing" credit on a separate card in the opening titles. Rios would win another lead in director Kurt Neumann's *The Ring* (1952).

To improve the chances of bringing their film home as a box-office winner, Pine and Thomas announced what *Daily Variety* (June 13, 1950) termed "a financial bombshell" when they "disclosed that 10 percent of net profits of *The Lawless* will be equally divided among the 240-odd members of the Paramount sales organization in the field … the fieldmen will receive quarterly statements and checks as long as they remain with Paramount."

In a show of confidence, Paramount vice-president E.K. O'Shea sent a memo to division and branch managers prior to general release, predicting that *The Lawless* would be "the box-office sleeper of the year." O'Shea instructed bookers, "If at this time you are unable to secure 'A' terms, 'A' theatres and 'A' playing time, we are perfectly willing to wait until the test engagements prove that we have not only an important motion picture but an equally profitable attraction at the box-office as well."[32] Among the publicity gimmicks recommended in Paramount's pressbook for the film: "Have an overturned, battered car (from the junk heap) in front of your theatre with a sign that reads, 'This is part of what happens when *The Lawless* are on the loose!'"

The strong box office and critical acclaim afforded to *The Lawless* amply demonstrated the old adage about success having many fathers. According to Thomas, the story idea originated with himself and Pine, and he recalled showing studio executive Y. Frank Freeman a newspaper clipping about a young Mexican-American war hero who prejudiced Texans denied burial in a "white" cemetery. Thomas later wrote, "Dan [Mainwaring] did not bring us an original story, as he would be the first to admit."[33] *The Lawless*, in his recollection, was written by Mainwaring to their specifications while a salaried Pine-Thomas employee.

However, the screenwriter asserted in a *New York Times* story (bylined under his Geoffrey Homes

According to studio publicity, Hollywood was "buzzing with excitement" over newcomer Lalo Rios, who made his film debut in *The Lawless*.

pseudonym) that he had approached Pine and Thomas with his screenplay, doubtful that they would be interested in taking on such a project. By his account, they agreed with alacrity to make a film about "a hero who isn't two-fisted, a heroine named Garcia, and a couple of boys who are kicked around because their skins have an olive tint."[34] Director Joseph Losey attributed the script's themes to Mainwaring, and later complained that Pine and Thomas had "corrupted" the film with their insistence on added action sequences. "All that business of the rape of the girl and the police car going up in flames were stuck in by them."[35]

Further confusing the authorship issue, several sources state that *The Lawless* was based on "The Voice of Stephen Wilder," a short story or novel supposedly written by Mainwaring as Geoffrey Homes. However, none of these sources offered details of when or where it was published. Bill Thomas told syndicated columnist Louella O. Parsons (December 17, 1948) that P-T had purchased a story by that title, which he said concerned "a man whose news column has such national influence that it almost causes a man he is after to get lynched. Then he has to turn around and try to defend the guy." A few weeks later, a brief newspaper blurb published in the *Salt Lake Tribune* (February 11, 1949) described "The Voice of Stephen Wilder" as an "action melodrama by Lewis R. Foster." The industry publication *Showmen's Trade Review* (August 20, 1949) also attributed the story to Foster, in a brief item announcing upcoming Paramount films.

Most likely, all of the above made substantial contributions to the film as it ultimately emerged. Though Mainwaring and Losey may have balked at Pine and Thomas' story suggestions, they almost certainly opened up the film to a wider audience than would otherwise have seen it. For the British market, it was released as *The Dividing Line*, emphasizing the sociological theme over the action element.

REVIEWS: "Every once in awhile [*sic*], there comes along an unpretentious little picture that delivers unexpected quality.... Produced by that redoubtable team of Pine and Thomas, it comes a long way from their early action 'quickies.' Not that it is an extravagant production, but it is a serious work of vital importance.... Under Losey's guidance, the members of the cast do themselves proud." *Independent Exhibitors' Film Bulletin*, April 10, 1950

"*The Lawless* is the finest picture ever turned out by the Pine-Thomas producing team ... it is a tense melodrama that puts the spotlight forcefully on an important social problem. The direction and acting are of the first order, with an exceptionally good performance turned out by Macdonald Carey...." *Harrison's Reports*, April 8, 1950

Tripoli (1950)

CAST: Maureen O'Hara (*Countess D'Arneau*), John Payne (*Lt. Presley O'Bannon*), Howard da Silva (*Capt. Demetrios*), Philip Reed (*Hamet Karamanly*), Grant Withers (*Sgt. Derek*), Lowell Gilmore (*Lt. Tripp*), Connie Gilchrist (*Henriette*), Alan Napier (*Khalil*), Herbert Heyes (*Gen. Eaton*), Alberto Morin (*Il Taiib*), Emil Hanna (*Interpreter*), Grandon Rhodes (*Commodore Barron*), Frank Fenton (*Capt. Adams*), Rosa Turich (*Seewauk*), Ray Hyke (*Crawford*), Walter Reed (*Wade*), Paul Livermore (*Evans*), Gregg Barton (*Huggins*), Don Summers (*Langley*), Jack Pennick (*Busch*), Ewing Mitchell (*Elroy*)

CREW: Will Price (*Director*), William H. Pine, William C. Thomas (*Producers*), Winston Miller (*Screenplay*), Winston Miller, Will Price (*Story*), James Wong Howe (*Director of Photography*), Robert Brower (*Technicolor Color Consultant*), Lewis H. Creber (*Art Director*), Alfred Kegerris (*Set Decorator*), Yvonne Wood (*Miss O'Hara's Costumes*), Bella Lewitzky (*Choreography*), David Chudnow (*Music Supervision*), Lucien Cailliet (*Music Score*), Howard Smith (*Editor*), Harold C. Lewis (Sound Recording), Nazih Massaad (*Technical Advisor*), Loyal Griggs (*Second Unit Photography*), Darrell A. Anderson, Alex Weldon (*Special Photographic Effects*), Charles Keehne, Mary Bowen (*Wardrobe*), James R. Barker, Harry Ray, Paul Stanhope (*Makeup Artists*)

RELEASED November 1950. 95 minutes.

In 1805, the United States is at war with the province of Tripoli, in the Mediterranean, where pirates have been demanding increasing ransoms of American merchant ships. For several months, the U.S.S. *Essex*, along with other vessels, has been barricading the capital city, preventing pirates from plying their trade. General William Eaton boards the *Essex* to announce President Jefferson's plan to conclude the war. He's looking for volunteers to undertake a mission that involves capturing the port city of Derna, part of a two-pronged attack on Tripoli, which is too heavily guarded to take. Lieutenant Presley O'Bannon, the highest-ranking Marine aboard, is chosen to take command.

The mission depends on the cooperation of Hamet Karamanly, deposed brother of the current leader of Tripoli, and friendly to U.S. interests. Hamet, in exile several hundred miles away, agrees to take part, and help assemble an army. His lady friend, a French-woman known as the Countess D'Arneau, does not want him to leave, as she covets a wedding ring on her finger, and the life of leisured exile she assumes will follow.

Having failed to prevent her lover from going on the mission, the Countess decides to come along as well, against Lt. O'Bannon's wishes. The journey across the desert is strenuous, with sandstorms, lack of water, and other travails, and at one point Hamet threatens to take his men and turn back. Stopped for rest near a waterhole, the company is joined by several men who claim to be merchants robbed by Tripolian forces. In fact, they have come with a secret message from Hamet's brother, who offers him a place alongside him if he helps defeat the American-led troops. Hamet plays one side against the other, convinced he'll come out fine either way. But he makes a tactical error when he confides the enemy's plan to the Countess, who is no longer as excited as she once was about marrying him.

At the end of the grueling journey, O'Bannon and his men reach the shoreline to find no sign of their Navy counterparts. Successfully stifling a threatened rebellion among his men, O'Bannon waits out the arrival of American ships, and plans go forward for the risky attack on the city.

Tripoli dramatizes the Battle of Derna, the first time U.S. forces ever raised an American flag in victory on foreign soil. While the story ultimately builds to an action-packed climax, the footage depicting the soldiers' trek across the desert proves to be a mild ordeal for the viewer as well, as little of interest happens while a substantial amount of film unspools.

John Payne relinquishes the top billing he will usually enjoy in Pine-Thomas films to Maureen O'Hara. Though the two stars' best-known collaboration was undoubtedly *Miracle on 34th Street* (1947), they had in fact worked together even earlier—on a film called *To the Shores of Tripoli*. For Miss O'Hara, the chief attraction of starring in Pine-Thomas' *Tripoli* was the chance to be directed by her then-husband, Will Price, and support his fledgling career behind the camera. Both the Countess and her lady-in-waiting, Henriette, are said to be Frenchwomen, though neither Miss O'Hara nor Connie Gilchrist offers an accent to back this up.

Philip Reed, as Hamet, has the film's best supporting role, as Hamet, who freely admits his own untrustworthiness. Offered the chance to betray O'Bannon and his forces, he's untroubled by the idea, saying, "Why risk my life for a whole kingdom when I can get half of one for nothing?" Howard da Silva (1909–1986), seen as Captain Demetrios, the Greek leader of a band of mercenaries that joins O'Bannon's mission, isn't given enough to do. Still, he has a few moments late in the film, as when he shows himself unimpressed with a stuffed-shirt Navy commodore who's throwing his weight around. Punctuating the officer's pompous speech with a timely (and loud) blow of his nose, Demetrios isn't fazed when the commodore snaps, "If you were under my command, Captain, you'd be court-martialed," replying, "If I was under your command, I'd be dead!"

According to the *Chicago Sun-Times'* columnist Irv Kupcinet (April 4, 1950), Pine and Thomas transported some 300 people, including both cast and crew, to Palm Springs to shoot desert scenes. "Not to mention," the columnist added, "50 horses, 25 camels and dozens of sheep and goats to create the necessary atmosphere. And if you have ever been close to camels, sheep and goats, you will ask how necessary is that kind of atmosphere?"

REVIEWS: "*Tripoli* combines an uninteresting plot with countless clichés. Net result, as might be expected, is poor film fare ... screenplay ... is a curious affair. Script continually talks of action, yet trite comedy dominates the footage.... Film's one shining technical credit is camera work of James Wong Howe." *Daily Variety*, October 5, 1950

"*Tripoli* is a satisfactory derring-do motion picture, although preliminaries leading up to the shooting prove a bit irksome to dyed-in-the-wool action fans ... the actual assault is done up in good style." *Los Angeles Times*, December 1, 1950

The Last Outpost (1951)

CAST: Ronald Reagan (*Capt. Vance Britton*), Rhonda Fleming (*Julie McQuade*), Bruce Bennett (*Col. Jeb Britton*), Bill Williams (*Sgt. Tucker*), Noah Beery [Jr.] (*Sgt. Calhoun*), Peter Hanson [Hansen] (*Lt. Crosby*), Hugh Beaumont (*Lt. Fenton*), Lloyd Corrigan (*Mr. Delacourt*), John Ridgely (*Sam McQuade*), Richard Crane (*Lt. Macready*), Ewing Mitchell (*Maj. Riordan*), Burt Mustin (*Marshal*), Iron Eyes Cody (*Mangas Coloradas*), John War Eagle (*Geronimo*), Chief Yowlachie (*Cochise*), Charles Evans (*Chief Gray Cloud*), Harold Goodwin (*Union Sergeant*), Chuck Roberson (*Confederate Corporal*)

CREW: Lewis R. Foster (*Director*), William H. Pine, William C. Thomas (*Producers*), Geoffrey Homes, George Worthing Yates, Winston Miller (*Screenplay*), David Lang (*Story Suggestion*), Loyal Griggs (*Director of Photography*), Robert Brower (*Technicolor Color Consultant*), Lewis H. Creber (*Art Director*), Howard Smith (*Film Editor*), Edith Head (*Miss Fleming's Costumes*), Harold C. Lewis (*Sound Recording*), Alfred Kegerris (*Set Decorator*), Charles Keehne (*Wardrobe*), Errol K. Silvera, Paul Stanhope (*Makeup Artists*), Kay Shea (*Hair Stylist*), Lucien Cailliet (*Music Score*)

RELEASED April 1951. 89 minutes.

Fort Point, near the town of San Gil, is an important watchpoint for the Union Army, as shipping of supplies for the war effort is dependent on access to the Santa Fe Trail. Colonel Jeb Britton arrives to take command of the fort just as several of its men have been robbed by Confederate rebels. Townsman Sam McQuade, proprietor of the local store, thinks the Union soldiers need to enlist the help of Indians to protect the town from Confederate forces, but Jeb rejects the notion.

Invited to McQuade's home for a drink, Jeb meets gorgeous Mrs. McQuade, and realizes she's the former fiancée of his brother Vance. Julie tells Jeb that his brother jilted her. She realizes that her husband mistook Jeb for the man Julie wanted to marry, and the realization that he tried to set up an awkward confrontation for her makes her decide to leave him once and for all.

Jeb is surprised to learn that Vance is one of the Confederate rebels who have been robbing Union supply shipments. Both believe that it would be unwise to enlist Indians in the battle between Union and Confederate soldiers. When Washington, at McQuade's instigation, sends Major Thomas Riordan to investigate the idea, Vance and his men intercept the emissary and steal his uniform.

Posing as Riordan, Vance visits the Indian camp, where he negotiates with the tribe's leaders, among them Chief Gray Cloud, a former Union soldier who abandoned the army when his marriage to an Indian woman wasn't accepted. The Indians tell Vance they will remain neutral in the North-South fight, provided he can get the leaders at Fort Point to release three of their tribe members from jail. The Indian captives robbed and killed Sam McQuade, but Gray Cloud says they did so because he sold them poisonous whiskey.

Arriving in San Gil, still posing as Major Riordan, Vance is reunited with Julie McQuade, and tries to make amends for breaking off their relationship. He schemes to get the Indian prisoners released, though the townspeople want them hung without a trial. Jeb is reluctant to blow his brother's cover, but warns him to get out of town.

Unaware he's been negotiating with an impostor, Chief Gray Cloud arrives in San Gil flying a truce flag. An impulsive townsman shoots and kills the Indian leader, provoking an Indian attack on the town, whose troops are greatly outnumbered. Vance and Jeb find themselves united in battle against the deadly onslaught.

Shot in vibrant Technicolor, *The Last Outpost* is well-made and packed with enough action to satisfy most Western fans, with a rousing showdown in the last 15 minutes. Both Union and Confederate leaders believe the Indians prone to violence; Vance doesn't think the distinction between sides will mean much to them, saying, "Their enemy is the whole white race." Still, the screenplay does provide motivation for the Indian attack, suggesting that they were not violent for violence's sake until they were provoked.

This was the first of Ronald Reagan's three films for Pine-Thomas. His film career past its peak, Reagan accepted a relatively modest $45,000 salary for the starring assignment. Reagan said in his memoirs that he welcomed the opportunity to play an action role after a string of domestic comedies and dramas (including *Louisa*, *Bedtime for Bonzo*, and *That Hagen Girl*). Another attraction of the job was the producers' arranging to let him ride his own horse, Tarbaby, in the film. It's a bit unexpected to find the 40-year-old star playing Bruce Bennett's irresponsible kid brother, who's fighting for the wrong cause. Carol Thomas Pantages remembered Reagan as "a really nice guy" who, because he avoided flying whenever possible, accompanied Carol's mother by train to the location shoot.

Rhonda Fleming has been nicknamed "The Queen of Technicolor," and it's easy to see why here. She is resplendent in Edith Head costumes that complement her flaming red hair; one of the Union men catches a glimpse of her and says with a wide grin, "That's a woman!" Her role in the film takes a back seat to gunplay, but she makes quite an impression nonetheless. Except for under-five players seen briefly, hers is the only female role in the film.

Bruce Bennett (1906–2007) fills the role of Reagan's older brother, Jeb, who shoots Eastern dandy Mr. Delacourt a withering look when the latter suggests that the Indians wouldn't be "foolhardy" enough to attack San Gil. "We killed their chief. They outnumber us fifty to one," Jeb points out. Seeing his point, Delacourt concedes, "They might be foolhardy."

Make of it what you will, cineastes, but Reagan's character Vance has a propensity for relieving other men of their clothes—all in the line of duty, of course. Vance and his rebels steal the uniforms of several Union soldiers while they are enjoying a brisk swim in their underwear, against orders. Later, he strips Major Riordan of his uniform, and gets a pompous Easterner out of his pants so that he can steal the key to the town jail. Richard Crane, in his third Pine-Thomas film, is unbilled for his brief (so to speak) appearance as the young leader who learns the hard way to keep an eye on his pants when he goes for a swim.

Making his film debut in a small part is character actor Burt Mustin (1884–1977), who, according to Bill Thomas, was recruited from a local theater troupe while the *Outpost* company was on location in Tucson. Impressed by Mustin's work, Thomas told him, "You're very good. You oughta go to Hollywood." When the actor followed his suggestion,

Thomas helped him get into the Screen Actors Guild and find an agent, preludes to a career that would last into the 1970s.[36]

REVIEWS: "Reagan and Bennett pair excellently as the opposing brothers.... Producing team takes advantage of some good Arizona location sites for outdoor values. Footage has been given a very good display through the color photography of Loyal Griggs." *Variety*, April 11, 1951

"Suitable for the action fans.... There is much movement throughout, but the story is ordinary and is lacking in human interest. The direction and acting are indifferent...." *Harrison's Reports*, April 14, 1951

Passage West (1951)

CAST: John Payne (*Pete Black*), Dennis O'Keefe (*the Rev. Jacob Karns*), Arleen Whelan (*Rose Billings*), Frank Faylen (*Curly*), Mary Anderson (*Myra Johnson*), Peter Hansen (*Michael Karns*), Richard Rober (*Mike*), Griff Barnett (*Emil Ludwig*), Dooley Wilson (*Rainbow*), Mary Field (*Miss Swingate*), Richard Travis (*Ben Johnson*), Mary Beth Hughes (*Nellie McBride*), Arthur Hunnicutt (*Pop Brennan*), Lillian Bronson (*Mom Brennan*), Ilka Gruning (*Mrs. Ludwig*), Estelle Carr (*Minna Karns*), Susan Whitney (*Lea Johnson*), Paul Fierro (*Ramon*), Clint Stuart (*Burk*), Howard Negley (*Mr. Brody*), Victor Kilian (*Messenger*), Jack Tornek (*Saloon Dealer*)

CREW: Lewis R. Foster (*Director/Screenplay*), William H. Pine, William C. Thomas (*Producers*), Nedrick Young (*Story*), Loyal Griggs (*Director of Photography*), Robert Brower (*Technicolor Color Consultant*), Lewis H. Creber (*Art Director*), Howard Smith (*Editor*), Hugo Grenzbach (*Sound Recording*), Alfred Kegerris (*Set Decorator*), Harry Ray (*Makeup Artist*), David Chudnow (*Music Supervisor*), Mahlon Merrick (*Music Score*)

RELEASED July 1951. 80 minutes.

In 1863, the Reverend Jacob Karns and members of his flock are traveling from Indiana by wagon train to begin new lives in California. While stopped to conduct a funeral service for a young member who died during the voyage, they are taken hostage by six escaped convicts. Leader of the convicts is hard-hearted Pete Black, who knows he is only a short distance ahead of pursuing authorities, and ruthlessly takes command of the wagon train. Reasoning that traveling with the wagon train will be slower, but safer, Pete pushes the church members relentlessly to speed up the trip. Jacob is troubled by the harshness of Pete's ways, but goes along with his demands so as not to put his members into further danger.

Along the brutal trip, livestock is lost, a baby dies for lack of milk, and the church members grow restless as the preacher shows no signs of going against Pete's demands. Rose Billings, a headstrong young woman who the preacher has been courting, is, against her better judgment, intrigued by the violent Pete. When Pete finally pushes the travelers too far, Jacob takes him on in a fistfight, showing more bravery and strength than even his own flock knew he had.

Curly, one of Pete's men, proposes that they steal the cash in the travelers' strongbox and abandon the wagon train. The next morning, Pete and his men are missing, as well as the money. Just as the loss is discovered, Pete returns, having been shot in the back by Curly. Jacob and his followers care for Pete's wounds, despite his prior treatment of them.

When the travelers finally arrive in California, Pete means to leave the church members behind, taking his fellow escapees with him. Jacob still hopes that Pete may be touched by God, and see what's wrong with the life he's been leading. Not anticipating any further contact with the outlaws, Jake and his flock build a small church and a primitive settlement. But when "Wanted" posters begin appearing for Pete and his cohorts, they decide they'd be safer hiding out with the settlers. Pete and the other escapees help the settlers build their new town, until the unexpected discovery of gold threatens to bring on a violent confrontation.

For nearly half the film, *Passage West* is relentlessly downbeat, depressing to watch as the innocent travelers suffer one heartbreak after another. There's little or no humor, aside from the slightly macabre moment when an undertaker proudly boasts to the weary travelers of having "the only silk-lined hearse west of Independence."

Originally announced as "Passage Westward," this project was reportedly viewed by Paramount executives as a potential vehicle for William Holden. Instead, it was Pine and Thomas' favorite hero of the 1950s, John Payne, who was ultimately cast. Going over to the dark side, Payne demonstrates that playing a villain is within his repertoire as well. He's teamed once again with Dennis O'Keefe; the two paired to strong effect in *The Eagle and the Hawk*. Though their characterizations here are quite different, they play effectively off each other as two men whose differing beliefs slowly give way to grudging respect:

PETE: People are what they are, Preacher. You can't change 'em.

JACOB: I can't accept that. There's a reason our paths crossed.

There's a good part in most Pine-Thomas productions for an independent-minded, beautiful redhead, and here it goes to Arleen Whelan (1914–1993) as the foolish Rose. It's not the actress' fault that her character looks like a prize idiot, given her unfathomable infatuation with the violent Pete Black, who as Rose herself says, seems to be "rotten all the way through." According to Bill Thomas, "it was no accident" that Miss Whelan, the wife of a Paramount publicity executive, was cast, nor was it happenstance that the picture received better-than-average ballyhoo and attention when it was sent out for release.[37]

Mary Beth Hughes stands out in her featured role as Nellie McBride, an entertainer who's along for the ride with the church members. Fond of eye-catching clothes, she knows they're pivotal to her success as a saloon singer, explaining, "The way I sing, a gal's legs are much more important than her voice." Dooley Wilson (1886–1953), always remembered for his appearance in *Casablanca*, gives his final film performance here as Rainbow, a slave who was one of Payne's fellow escapees. Offered a chance to be cut in on the theft of the travelers' money, Rainbow says with painful awareness, "Slaves ain't allowed to have shares of nothin.'"

Demonstrating that Pine-Thomas budgets had gone up substantially in recent years, the producers employed more than 100 extras and bit players in one saloon sequence for *Passage West*. The film was retitled *High Venture* for British audiences.

REVIEWS: "This pioneer drama of the early west blends a theme of simple religious faith with its outdoor action ingredients.... General audiences will wish for more action scenes but there are enough to put the film in the action classification. Both Payne and O'Keefe are excellent as the male leads.... Scripting and direction are able, although Foster permits the film to become laborious during the wagon train's overlong journey across a desert." *Variety*, May 30, 1951

"William H. Pine and William C. Thomas have made a rough and ready feature ...

its cruelties somewhat overshadow its purposefulness. It attempts to stress the power of religion, though the melodrama is what holds the fort in the long run." Edwin Schallert, *Los Angeles Times*, July 13, 1951

Crosswinds (1951)

CAST: John Payne (*Steve Singleton*), Rhonda Fleming (*Kay Shelley*), Forrest Tucker (*Gerald "Jumbo" Johnson*), Alan Mowbray (*Sir Cecil Daubrey*), John Abbott (*Algernon "Mousey" Sykes*), Robert Lowery (*Nick Brandon*), Frank Kumagai (*Bumidai*)

CREW: Lewis R. Foster (*Director*), William H. Pine, William C. Thomas (*Producers*), Lewis R. Foster (*Screenplay*), Thomson Burtis (*Adaptation, from his novel "New Guinea Gold"*), Loyal Griggs (*Director of Photography*), Richard Mueller (*Technicolor Color Consultant*), Lewis H. Creber (*Art Director*), Howard Smith (*Film Editor*), Edith Head (*Miss Fleming's Costumes*), Harold C. Lewis (*Sound Recording*), Alfred Kegerris (*Set Decorator*), Charles Keehne (*Wardrobe*), Norman Pringle (*Makeup Artist*), Kay Shea (*Hair Stylist*), Lucien Cailliet (*Music Score*)

RELEASED October 1951. 95 minutes.

Owner and operator of his own schooner, the *Seeker*, Steve Singleton docks at Port Moresby in New Guinea, seeking a paying job. Local operator "Jumbo" Johnson tells him he has the necessary permits to harvest a rich cache of pearls in a remote spot. Johnson and Singleton agree to a partnership, in which the latter will use his boat while Johnson furnishes the crew, and the two men split the pearl harvest 50/50.

While hashing out the deal, Steve sees pilot Nick Brandon having drinks with beautiful Kay Shelley. Steve, recognizing Nick as someone he knew in the war, promptly slugs him, repaying an old grudge. Nick is trying to romance Kay, but she refuses to take any man seriously, and, according to local rumor, has a distinct fondness for the grape. Unhappy with her life, Kay persuades Steve to let her ride downriver with him as far as the site where he will meet Johnson to load supplies. They discover they share a mutual belief that a boat offers people the chance to escape the cares and worries of the day-to-day world.

After nearly two weeks diving for pearls, with scant results, Steve's expedition is brought to a halt when an Australian naval inspector informs him that the permit papers he was furnished by Johnson are forgeries. When Johnson refuses to corroborate Steve's story, the seaman is sentenced to jail time and a fine, and the *Seeker* is sold at public auction to pay his debt. Steve is infuriated to learn that Johnson bought the *Seeker*.

After his sentence is commuted, Steve joins forces with two disreputable Englishmen, Sir Cecil Daubrey and Sykes, known as "Mousy." They offer him a job piloting their decrepit boat, the *Susan*, but he is warned by the local magistrate that the two men are likely crooks, who may have disposed of their last captain. Steve learns that, not long after he left Port Moresby, Kay accompanied Nick on his last flight, which was carrying a fortune in gold bullion. The plane was lost at sea, and both Nick and Kay are believed dead. He's also told that Kay is a widow, whose husband was shot down over England only two weeks after they married, and that she had lived aimlessly, drinking too much, ever since.

Daubrey believes he can make an educated guess as to where the plane went down, and Steve agrees to pilot the *Susan* there, though he remains wary of whether the two

Englishmen can be trusted. Indeed, reluctant to give the government the two-thirds share of the gold it is entitled to receive, Daubrey and Mousey plan to hide the bullion and get rid of Steve, so they won't have to cut him in. Steve soon learns that Johnson, too, plans to locate the downed plane and the fortune.

En route, the travelers find a drifting raft containing Nick's body, and see that there is a band of headhunters nearby. Steve realizes that the headhunters are holding Kay captive, and comes to her rescue. Spotting the *Seeker*, Steve boards and confronts Johnson, offering a deal since he is a skilled diver, and has Kay, who knows exactly where the plane crashed. Though grateful to Steve for her rescue, Kay is led to ponder his motives when Daubrey and Mousey imply that her ability to pinpoint the location of the wreckage was uppermost in the men's minds.

After drinking herself into a stupor, Kay nonetheless leads the men to the treasure. As Steve and Johnson bring the gold up from the water, the men began to eye each other with increasing suspicion, each wondering whether any of the others can be trusted not to pull a double-cross and harvest a bigger bounty. Steve, determined to bring Johnson back into port to face justice, must carefully play the angles in order to survive and emerge victorious.

Crosswinds filled the bill nicely for moviegoers who wanted to see plenty of adventure, with sword-throwing headhunters, gunplay, undersea diving, jungle wildlife, and a grisly death by crocodile thrown into the mix. Though set in New Guinea, the film's outdoor scenes were filmed primarily in Florida, along the banks of the Homosassa River. According to Bill Thomas, it was a trouble-plagued shoot, due in part to unseasonably cold weather. "We were afraid the players would show blue in Technicolor," he later cracked.[38] The opening credits acknowledge the Weeki Wachee Springs Park for production assistance; the site was used to film the undersea diving scenes. Jay Livingston and Ray Evans contributed the film's title song. Thomson Burtis' novelette was originally serialized in *Adventure* magazine between July and September 1945.

Aside from the rich Technicolor and vivid scenery, most viewers can find a little eye candy with the sight of stars Payne and Fleming, although some may be disappointed to find that he logs substantially more swimsuit time than she does. Brawny Payne has another physically demanding role here.

Although there are few dramatic opportunities here for Rhonda Fleming—her character's slide into alcoholism is talked about, but little seen—she shows both beauty and pluck. In some of her Pine-Thomas films, Miss Fleming will be on the sidelines during most of the action scenes; here, she dives right in, with Kay proving to be a handy shot with a rifle. As Kay, she explains, "A boat's the only place left in this cockeyed world where a person can plant his two feet and know he's free. Free to go where he wants to go, think what he wants to think, and fear nothing."

Robert Lowery, one of Pine-Thomas' favorite leading men of the 40s, is seen in a smallish supporting role as Nick. Not until fairly late in the film do we learn the motivation behind Steve's impromptu attack on him, for which Lowery takes a convincing dive. John Abbott (1905–1996) and Alan Mowbray (1896–1969) have strong featured parts as the men Steve describes as "two of the scummiest waterfront rats that ever put a knife in a man's back." Abbott's character here could be a distant cousin of Huish, whom he played in *Adventure Island*. Mowbray gives a colorful performance as his fellow scoundrel, who remarks, "I do rather pride myself on employing a certain integrity in my skullduggery."

Like other Pine-Thomas films, this one gives an in-joke nod onscreen to a crew member, in this case set decorator Alfred Kegerris. Nick and Kay's grouchy boss at the mining company (played by an unbilled actor) is addressed by both as Mr. Kegerris.

REVIEWS: "An engaging bunch of scoundrels have been brought together in this South Seas adventure yarn filmed in splashy Technicolor.... Exhibitors whose audiences like their adventure pictures spiced with humor will not go wrong with this Paramount release." *Motion Picture Daily*, August 3, 1951

"The action moves briskly from start to finish, and the contrived tale has plenty of thrills.... There is no human interest, and no sympathy is felt for any of the characters, including the hero and heroine.... Pictorially, the picture is a treat to the eye." *Harrison's Reports*, August 11, 1951

Hong Kong (1952)

CAST: Ronald Reagan (*Jeff Williams*), Rhonda Fleming (*Victoria Evans*), Nigel Bruce (*Mr. Lighton*), Marvin Miller (*Tao Liang*), Danny Chang (*Wei Lin*), Lowell Gilmore (*Danton*), Claud Allister (*Hotel Manager*), Mary Somerville (*Mrs. Lighton*), James Craven, Arthur Tovey (*Customs Officers*), Keye Luke (*Cab Driver*), Kenner G. Kemp (*Detective*), Kam Tong (*Jewelry Store Clerk*), Victor Sen Yung (*Mr. Howe*), Spencer Chan (*Vendor*), Lane Nakano (*Pilot*), Paul Bradley (*British Captain*)

CREW: Lewis R. Foster (*Director*), William H. Pine, William C. Thomas (*Producers*), Winston Miller (*Screenplay*), Lewis R. Foster (*Story*), Lionel Lindon (*Director of Photography*), Robert Brower (*Technicolor Color Consultant*), Lewis H. Creber (*Art Director*), Howard Smith (*Film Editor*), Edith Head (*Miss Fleming's Costumes*), Harold C. Lewis, Walter Oberst (*Sound Recording*), Alfred Kegerris (*Set Decorator*), Charles Keehne (*Wardrobe*), Norman Pringle (*Makeup Artist*), Kay Shea (*Hair Stylist*), Lucien Cailliet (*Music Score*)

RELEASED January 1952. 90 minutes.

After three unsuccessful years trying to run a war surplus business in China, ex–GI Jeff Williams is ready to bail out, one step ahead of the new Communist regime. Making his way toward Hong Kong, he hails a canoe that proves to contain a dead man at the helm, and a four-year-old Chinese boy. Reluctantly taking the boy in tow, Jeff continues his journey until he encounters a small band of refugees, being led by Red Cross schoolteacher Victoria Evans.

Victoria has paid $2000 for a flight to Hong Kong, and allows Jeff and the boy, Wei Lin, to come along. While on board, Jeff and Victoria are surprised to see that Wei Lin has in his possession what looks like an extremely valuable jeweled idol. Landing in Hong Kong after a failed engine en route nearly results in tragedy, Jeff bluffs his way into hotel accommodations in the overcrowded city, forcing Victoria to pose as his wife to give her and the boy shelter.

A less-than-scrupulous dealer, Tao Liang, tells Jeff the jeweled idol he described is worth $100,000 on the black market. Booking passage on a ship bound for America, Jeff plans to collect the money while leaving Victoria and the boy behind, but when the moment arrives he can't bring himself to do it. Jeff comes clean to Victoria, and things are looking up for the two, who are growing closer.

Mr. and Mrs. Lighton, whom Jeff and Victoria have been impersonating, show up to claim the hotel suite that's rightfully theirs. The Lightons prove to be surprisingly understanding, but the cutthroats to whom Jeff arranged to sell the idol are less so. Mistaken for Jeff, the elderly Mr. Lighton is stabbed, and Wei Ling is kidnapped. With the police dubious about their story, Jeff and Victoria must act quickly, and put themselves at risk, in order to recoup the stolen idol and rescue the boy they've grown to love.

Ronald Reagan and Rhonda Fleming team for their second Pine-Thomas film, after *The Last Outpost,* which had been a box office success. Reagan has some amusing moments as the cynical, blunt Jeff, who barges his way into Victoria's camp and demands of one Chinese man, "What kind of a clambake is this?" He's a rough-hewn, down-to-earth guy, as we see when Victoria mentions Rachmaninoff, to which Jeff barks, "Rock who?" "I was grateful to [Pine and Thomas] for letting me do a sword and saddle role," Reagan later recalled.[39]

Nigel Bruce (1895–1953), remembered always as Dr. Watson in the Sherlock Holmes film series of the 1940s, is third-billed for what is little more than a cameo as the real Mr. Lighton, one of his typical blustery upper-class Englishmen who's a bit slow on the uptake. Mary Somerville (1883–1972, real-life mother of actor Peter Lawford) is endearing as his feather-brained wife, who assumes that Jeff and Victoria are from a branch of the Lighton family she hasn't yet met. Cast as the chief villain of the piece is Missouri native Marvin Miller (1913–1985) in yellowface. Four-year-old Danny Chang (born 1947) is a cute little boy, which is all the role really demands. He went on to play smaller parts in other films of the era, including *Blood Alley* (1955). According to Bill Thomas, it was fellow cast member Keye Luke who located young Chang for the producers. Studio publicity quoted Ronald Reagan as saying, "I've worked with a lot of scene stealers, but Danny is the greatest of them all. It was great being in *his* picture."

In his opening narration, Reagan's character describes the city of Hong Kong as "a haven for political refugees, outmoded Manchurian warlords, and homeless Chinese peasants from the mainland ... almost everybody's running away from something." Art director Lewis H. Creber and set

Top-billed Ronald Reagan gives a boost to four-year-old scene-stealer Danny Chang in *Hong Kong.*

decorator Alfred Kegerris do a fine job creating the ambience of the region, though it's evident (especially in the final reel) that Mr. Reagan and Miss Fleming didn't get a free trip overseas as part of their assignments.

According to Bill Thomas, *Hong Kong* "has been our biggest grosser since we organized the [Pine-Thomas] unit 12 years ago.... [It] has established boxoffice records and has definitely convinced us that the public wants adventure dramas, especially pictures that feature action, romance and intrigue."[40] Upon its rerelease in the early 1960s, *Hong Kong* was retitled *Bombs over China.*

Reviews: "Neat footage is dished up in Pine-Thomas' *Hong Kong*, which is among the Paramount producing team's best pix to date.... Reagan and Miss Fleming, with well-defined characters to work with, turn in likeable and authoritative performances.... Production job ... is a thorough and commendable one." *Daily Variety*, November 13, 1951

"A fairly good mixture of adventure, romance and intrigue. It should please undiscriminating movie-goers as well as those who enjoy the mysticism of an oriental [*sic*] atmosphere." *Harrison's Reports*, November 17, 1951

Caribbean (1952)

Cast: John Payne (*Dick Lindsay*), Arlene Dahl (*Christine*), Sir Cedric Hardwicke (*Capt. Francis Barclay*), Francis L. Sullivan (*Andrew MacAllister*), Willard Parker (*Shively*), Dennis Hoey (*Burford*), Clarence Muse (*Quashy*), William Pullen (*Robert MacAllister*), Walter Reed (*Evans*), Ramsay Hill (*Townsend*), John Hart (*Stuart*), Zora Donahoo (*Elizabeth*), Woody Strode (*Esau*), Ezeret Anderson (*Cudjo*), Kermit Pruitt (*Quarino*), Dan Ferniel (*Caesar*), Rosalind Hayes (*Sally*), Richard Hale (*Ship's Doctor*), Diana Sands (*Native Woman*)

Crew: Edward Ludwig (*Director*), Frank L. Moss, Edward Ludwig (*Screenplay*), Ellery H. Clark (*Novel*), Lionel Lindon (*Director of Photography*), Monroe W. Burbank (*Technicolor Color Consultant*), Hal Pereira, Earl Hedrick (*Art Directors*), Howard Smith (*Film Editor*), Edith Head (*Miss Dahl's Costumes*), Harold C. Lewis, Walter Oberst (*Sound Recording*), Bertram Granger (*Set Decorator*), Henry West (*Wardrobe*), Norman Pringle (*Makeup Artist*), Kay Shea (*Hair Stylist*), Lucien Cailliet (*Music Score*)

Released September 1952. 91 minutes.

Adventurer Dick Lindsay is taken captive by internationally renowned pirate Captain Francis Barclay and his men. For more than 20 years, Barclay has been planning a vendetta against his rival and ex–business partner, Andrew MacAllister. Trading on a longstanding family feud, Captain Barclay has on his ship MacAllister's nephew Robert, who pledges his loyalty to his uncle's opponent. Noting Dick Lindsay's grit and determination, Barclay offers him a sizable reward if he can pull off a nearly-impossible stunt—infiltrating the heavily guarded island in the Caribbean where the wealthy trader MacAllister lives. Barclay has been embittered against MacAllister ever since the latter sold him into slavery, abducted his wife, and kept Barclay's infant daughter Christine for his own. Instead of trusting the real Robert MacAllister with this mission, finding him unsatisfactory, Barclay enlists Dick Lindsay, who is forcibly given a facial scar to make him resemble the man he's impersonating.

After Barclay and his crew attack one of MacAllister's ships, the *Shark*, Dick is set

Pine and Thomas sometimes used contests to stimulate more aggressive promotion of their movies by exhibitors, as seen in this trade ad for *Caribbean*.

adrift near the island in a small rowboat, accompanied only by the corpses of a few crew members from the *Shark*. Christine's adoptive father, MacAllister, accepts that Dick is his long-absent nephew, but tells him he is nonetheless not welcome on the island. With the approval of his second-in-command, Shively, who clearly aspires to be heir to MacAllister's fortune, Dick is given a grueling job at the island mill.

On short acquaintance, Dick is less than enchanted with the bratty, entitled Christine, though (despite their supposed cousinship) she's attracted to the handsome newcomer. Looking forward to being introduced into society in a sophisticated city environment, she asks Dick coyly, "Will the gentlemen like me?"

DICK: Yes, until they get to know you.

CHRISTINE (angrily): What's wrong with me?

DICK: I'm afraid I won't be on the island long enough to tell you.

MacAllister sees that, put in charge of the slaves at the mill, Dick achieves better productivity with his humane treatment than Shively did with cruelty. Though they are initially at odds, Dick and Christine are drawn to one another, and she entreats him to take her away from MacAllister's island. But when the real Andrew's body washes up on shore, the island kingpin recognizes that there is a traitor in their midst.

Originally planning a knife fight between two of the slaves, for the entertainment of visiting buyers, MacAllister announces that instead the combatants will be Shively and Dick. Meanwhile, the slave uprising begins. Soon, much of MacAllister's property is in flames. Offshore, Barclay watches for the best moment to come ashore, avenge himself on MacAllister, and be reunited with Christine.

Initially set to go before the cameras in September 1951, filming of *Caribbean* was delayed until early 1952 when Paramount executives advised Pine and Thomas that a backlog of more than 20 unreleased features made it necessary to slow production activities. Ellery H. Clark's novel, *Carib Gold,* from which the screenplay was adapted, was originally published in 1926. The film was originally announced in trade papers as *Caribbean Gold,* and that title was retained for the British market.

Sir Cedric Hardwicke (1893–1964) anchors the film's first half hour with his assured performance as the coldly menacing Barclay. Hardwicke knows precisely how to make his performance rich and colorful, without letting it descend into camp. When he disappears from the story for a spell, Francis L. Sullivan takes over, just as malevolent or more so. Sullivan (1903–1956) had worked in films on both sides of the Atlantic for some years, but may be best-known for his Tony-winning performance in Agatha Christie's play *Witness for the Prosecution.*

Arlene Dahl (born 1925), tasked with playing a spoiled character, is glorious in her Edith Head costumes, though she's occasionally in danger of being upstaged by the nearly as opulent attire with which Sullivan, as MacAllister, is clad. While she and John Payne make a charismatic pair, Miss Dahl admitted that she was not impressed with her leading man. "He didn't believe in rehearsals," she said. "He was a one-shot actor. It was like working with a glass of water."[41] She, Francis L. Sullivan, and Willard Parker will work together a second time a year or so later, in *Sangaree.* Clarence Muse (1889–1979), in the first of his two films for the Dollar Bills, plays a leader among the enslaved population who becomes Dick's ally.

REVIEWS: "A rousing saga of high adventure and rugged heroics, all of which emerge as solid entertainment. The lusty yarn is given the full Pine and Thomas treatment: A fine cast, lavishly gorgeous sets and beautiful photography attractively lensed in exquisite colors.... Payne handles his role in a rugged, rather taciturn style that is tremendously effective." *Hollywood Reporter,* August 1, 1952

"A good large-scale adventure melodrama, photographed in Technicolor ... packed with excitement and fast-moving action, It should easily satisfy those who enjoy pirate and bandit costume pictures…. As the villains, Francis L. Sullivan and Willard Parker hit below the belt with obvious relish." *Harrison's Reports*, August 2, 1952

The Blazing Forest (1952)

CAST: John Payne (*Kelly Hansen*), William Demarest (*Syd Jessup*), Agnes Moorehead (*Jessie Crain*), Richard Arlen (*Joe Morgan*), Susan Morrow (*Sharon Wilks*), Roscoe Ates (*Beans*), Lynn Roberts (*Grace Hansen*), Walter Reed (*Max*), Ewing Mitchell (*Walt*), Edward Earle (*Mr. Simpson*), Keith Richards (*Mac*), Allene Roberts (*Milly*), Harold Goodwin (*Mac*), Lester Dorr (*Train Conductor*), Steve Darrell (*Sheriff*), Robert Williams (*Forest Ranger*)

CREW: Edward Ludwig (*Director*), Lewis R. Foster, Winston Miller (*Screenplay*), Lionel Lindon (*Director of Photography*), Richard Mueller (*Technicolor Color Consultant*), Lewis H. Creber (*Art Director*), Howard Smith (*Film Editor*), Harold C. Lewis, Gene Garvin (*Sound Recording*), Alfred Kegerris (*Set Decorator*), Alex Weldon (*Special Effects*), Charles Keehne, Adele Parmenter (*Wardrobe*), Kay Shea (*Hair Stylist*), Lucien Cailliet (*Music Score*)

RELEASED December 1952. 90 minutes.

Living deep in the Nevada forest, widowed Jessie Crain recognizes that her niece, Sharon Wilks, whom she raised from a child, needs an opportunity to go out into the world and make a place for herself. Jessie's most valuable asset is the more than 200 acres of land left to her by her late husband, which is thickly forested with timber. But the remote location of the property makes it difficult to reap the rewards of logging it.

Jessie reaches out to an old friend, Syd Jessup (once one of her suitors), seeking advice on how to proceed. Syd, getting older, is not ready to go back to active logging, since he was injured on his last job. But logging boss Kelly Hansen, working some miles away on another job, offers to work Jessie's land for 25 percent of the profits. Syd provides most of the startup funds for the project, and agrees to serve as foreman, though he's not happy to learn that he'll be working alongside Kelly, who was the boss on his previous job.

Kelly's reputation as a logger is that of a man who pushes his crews hard, producing results but sometimes making enemies. Arriving to see the crew Syd has assembled, Kelly is none too pleased to see a man who introduces himself as Joe Morgan, with whom he shares a history. When Sharon notices the animosity between the two men, Joe, who takes an immediate shine to her, explains, "I'm his brother."

Kelly lives up to his notoriety, demanding that his crew work in the midst of a pouring rain. Even after one man is injured as a result, he refuses to slow down. Aside from the tight deadlines faced by Jessie, Kelly is also working to raise money to pay off one of his ne'er-do-well brother Joe's debts, in hopes of keeping him out of jail. Sharon refuses to admit that she is interested in Kelly, but she's deeply disappointed when she follows him to town on a Saturday night and sees him with another woman. She soon learns that the woman is actually Joe's estranged wife, who hopes to be reunited with her husband, but is heartbroken to find him drunk after attending a dance and hitting on Sharon.

After a disagreement with Kelly, Syd takes a carelessly loaded logging truck and starts for town, stopping along the way to pick up Joe, whose brother fired him. Angry and reckless, Syd sends the truck hurtling over the edge of a cliff. The resulting explosion leaves both occupants of the truck hurt, and struggling to survive amidst the fire that breaks out in the forest, threatening the lives and livelihoods of Kelly, Jessie, Sharon, and their crew members.

Originally announced as "The Lumberjack and the Lady," *The Blazing Forest* tries to offer something for almost everyone in the ticket-buying audience. It's primarily an action-oriented thriller, but adds elements of romance and family drama to the mix, in some ways anticipating the *Towering Inferno–type* disaster movies that would be big box office in the 1970s. The Dollar Bills shot in Technicolor so as to make the most of the fire effects. Working titles during pre-production included "Green Gold of Nevada" and "Big Timber." Shooting began in the late summer of 1951. According to *Variety* (August 29, 1951), "a 22-acre forest fire among the tall timber in the Feather River area" would be utilized to shoot the climactic scenes. "Blaze will be confined to that space," the report noted, "through precautions taken by Alex Weldon, head of the company's special effects department, in cooperation with forest rangers."

This is the first of two films the fine actress Agnes Moorehead (1900–1974) made for the Pine-Thomas unit. Though another director might have elicited a more nuanced, consistent performance from Moorehead, she's always capable of holding her own, and she certainly does so here. Playing Jessie, a plain-spoken woman used to a hardscrabble life, she casts her eyes on the motley crew of men Syd hired as loggers, and says, "Better spray 'em good for bedbugs." The widowed Jessie is being pursued romantically by William Demarest's Syd, but proves resistant to his charms, saying, "One logger with a musical saw's enough in a woman's life. I'm gonna get me a phonograph—you can always turn it off, and you don't have to cook it any meals." Leading man John Payne told columnist Hedda Hopper (April 13, 1952) that Miss Moorehead was "a great trouper" during the location shoot: "Life there was plenty rough, but Aggie took it without complaint."

Susan Morrow (1931–1985), still a relative newcomer to movies, acquits herself well in the role of Jessie's spirited niece, who gets the unenviable task of looking Miss Moorehead in the eye and saying, "And look at you. Old before your time." Richard Arlen, moving into support after his many starring turns in P-T films of the 40s, has some effective scenes as Kelly's brother Joe, who has a certain charm that's getting a little rough around the edges from wear and tear.

The film was undoubtedly a hard, grubby shoot for the cast and crew, but the result was a picture Pine and Thomas had every reason to believe would lure viewers away from their black-and-white television sets and into a theater. Its premiere was held in Reno, Nevada, with John Payne, William Demarest, and (though she didn't appear in the picture) Rhonda Fleming in attendance.

REVIEWS: "While it follows a familiar plot pattern, *The Blazing Forest* has enough action, interest, and some surprisingly good by-play to make it a solid attraction…. There isn't much in the way of romance, as handled by John Payne and Susan Morrow, and what there is comes off painlessly enough to prevent squirming by the action fans." *Independent Exhibitors' Film Bulletin*, October 20, 1952

"When the giant pine forest in this color by Technicolor creation gets to blazing it burns all the other fire pictures ever made right out of memory…. Maybe because of the way it's worked into the story, maybe because it's a genuine forest fire in the Nevada Sierras instead of a phony on a miniature set, or maybe because Technicolor and technology have never collaborated more congenially in the interests of melodrama, the fire section of the film is the best ever produced." *Motion Picture Daily*, September 26, 1952

Tropic Zone (1953)

CAST: Ronald Reagan (*Dan McCloud*), Rhonda Fleming (*Flanders White*), Estelita [Rodriguez] (*Elena Estebar*), Noah Beery [Jr.] (*Tapachula Sam*), Grant Withers (*Bert Nelson*), John Wengraf (*Lukats*), Argentina Brunetti (*Tia*), Maurice Jara (*Macario*), Rico Alaniz (*Capt. Basilio*), Pilar Del Rey (*Victoriana*), Charles Stevens (*Macario's Grandfather*), Jack Tornek (*Plantation Owner*), Manuel Paris (*Headwaiter*), Stephen Chase (*Captain*), Nacho Galindo (*Christopher*), Max Wagner (*First Mate*)

CREW: Lewis R. Foster (*Director and Screenplay*), Tom Gill (*Novel*), Lionel Lindon (*Director of Photography*), Monroe W. Burbank (*Technicolor Color Consultant*), Hal Pereira, Earl Hedrick (*Art Directors*), Howard Smith (*Editor*), Farciot Edouart (*Process Photography*), Sam Comer, Ray Moyer (*Set Decorators*), Lucien Cailliet (*Music Score*), Edith Head (*Miss Fleming's Costumes*), Jack Baker (*Choreography*), Wally Westmore (*Makeup Supervisor*), Harold Lewis, John Cope (*Sound Recording*),

RELEASED January 1953. 94 minutes.

Battered and bloodied, American adventurer Dan McCloud is on the run from the police in a small South American country, Guatara. He staggers into the hotel room of singer Elena Estabar, who takes a liking to him, and persuades her pilot friend Tapachula Sam to transport all three of them to nearby Puerto Barrancas.

There, Dan meets beautiful Flanders White, who is struggling to keep her late father's plantation up and running. Seeing that her hard-drinking foreman Bert Nelson is taking advantage of Flanders, Dan agrees to go for work for her, using his prior experience on a banana plantation to make her operation more efficient and productive. Flanders, and most of the other small farmers nearby, are dependent on local businessman Lukats to transport their harvests to market. But Lukats, who wants to take over Flanders' plantation, knows that Dan is a fugitive from justice, and uses blackmail to demand his help. Bert Nelson, whom Flanders fired after his latest drunken escapade, is happy to assist Lukats as well.

Dan and Flanders are clearly attracted to each other, but a vindictive Bert tells her that Dan is involved with Elena, who does pine for him. Lukats arranges for several of his henchmen to torch the workers' village at Flanders' plantation, with Dan's task to keep her occupied elsewhere. When she insists on going to the village that night, Dan, horrified to see it going up in flames, gives her his allegiance, fighting off Lukats' planned attack.

Lukats, with help from Bert Nelson, continues to undermine the White farm. While Dan and Flanders cope, Sam is dispatched to seek a lucrative contract from a big vendor for her farms and the adjoining ones, which will break Lukats' stranglehold on the town. Sam comes back with news of a lucrative contract, if Dan and Flanders can triumph over the opposition.

Tropic Zone was adapted from Tom Gill's 1939 novel *Gentleman of the Jungle*, "a blazing story of the lush tropics." The screenplay retains the novelist's names for several key characters (Flanders White, Tapachula Sam, Bert Nelson), but Gill's hero Dexter Cloud, said to be in his late 20s, is rechristened Dan McCloud by the screenwriters. In both novel and film, Flanders White is a stunning redhead, one Gill described as having "a mass of hair so deeply red it glowed coppery in the sun."[42]

Unable to secure access to a working banana plantation where the film could be shot, Pine and Thomas purchased enough bananas to build their own, and put art director Hal Pereira to work. The resulting set looked good, but as shooting progressed ceased to smell good, the fruit beginning to rot under hot lights. Thomas later wrote, "As the fermenting bananas mellowed, *Tropic Zone* was the most talked-about picture on the Paramount lot. Gamblers took even-money bets on which would go first—the actors or bananas. The actors wouldn't touch the bananas, and they *wanted to go!*"[43] The fiery sequence in the native village is one of the film's key action spots, and is well-staged, though a few of the bad guys line up a bit too obligingly for Reagan to punch out one by one.

Reagan later considered this easily the worst of the three films he made for Pine-Thomas, calling the script "hopeless." He said it was only his gratitude for previous assignments like *The Last Outpost* that made him accept the Dollar Bills' "sand and banana epic."[44] In 1954, the year after its release, Reagan began his lengthy stint as host and occasional star of television's *General Electric Theater*.

Rhonda Fleming plays perhaps the world's nicest plantation owner, one who gives her native workers bonuses, and educates their children in an onsite schoolhouse. For all her efforts, it seems that everyone around her has a sour comment to make about poor Flanders and her work. Seeing her dressed in jodhpurs for a day's toil, her housekeeper Tia complains, "I raised you to be a lady! Every day you look and act more like a man." The condescending Bert sneers, "Patron saint, mother confessor, guardian of the people's health, rights, and education. You sure that isn't too big a job for one woman?" At their first meeting, Dan, not to be outdone, says, "Only a good-looking dame could

Tapachula Sam (Noah Beery, Jr.) cozies up to Latin bombshell Elena (played by Estelita) in *Tropic Zone.*

kill off a banana grove as cold-bloodedly as this one's being murdered." Even after he and Flanders recognize their mutual attraction, his courting technique leaves a little something to be desired, as when he tells her, "You look like a stem of underripe bananas." In later years, Miss Fleming would remember *Tropic Zone* and some of her other roles of the period as "fun, and good clean entertainment," praising her leading man Reagan as "a very wonderful, nice, kind guy."[45]

Estelita (1928–1966), perhaps best-known for *Rio Bravo* (1959), is not only sexy and appealing, but displays a welcome comic touch as Elena, making her childlike character endearing. "You try to take my Danny away from me, and I think I kill you!" she says spiritedly to Fleming's character. Noah Beery gives a low-key charm to the character of Sam, seemingly laconic but ready to come to a buddy's aid when needed, and wishing Elena would look more favorably on him. Argentina Brunetti (1907–2005) has a sizable featured role here as Tia, housekeeper on the plantation, who clearly likes Dan McCloud's style. She makes the stereotyped character likable, despite dialogue that calls her to say things like, "I'm not so good at thinking, Chiquita!"

REVIEWS: "A typical western plot is transported to a tropical banana-growing country for this round of love and adventure offered under the Pine-Thomas banner…. Reagan and Miss Fleming, the latter very attractive in Technicolor and several brief outfits designed by Edith Head, make a pleasing hero-heroine team. Estelita as a fiery café entertainer with a big yen for Reagan gives Miss Fleming some competition." *Variety*, December 17, 1952

"William Pine and William Thomas have fashioned another of their smooth, actionful productions … that utilizes handsome island settings…. The film has plenty of brawls and under the skillfull [*sic*] direction of Lewis R. Foster there is a neat blending of action, romance and song. There are sufficient merchandising angles to garner ample box-office returns." *Motion Picture Daily*, December 17, 1952

Jamaica Run (1953)

CAST: Ray Milland (*Patrick Fairlie*), Arlene Dahl (*Ena Dacey*), Wendell Corey (*Todd Dacey*), Patric Knowles (*William Montague*), Laura Elliot [Kasey Rogers] (*Janice Clayton*), Carroll McComas (*Mrs. Dacey*), William Walker (*Human*), Murray Matheson (*Inspector Mole*), Clarence Muse (*Mose*), Michael Moore (*Robert Clayton*), Rex Evans (*Judge Henry*), Robert Warwick (*Magistrate*), Lester Matthews (*Willoughby*), James Fairfax (*Mousey*)

CREW: Lewis R. Foster (*Director/Screenplay*), Max Murray (*Novel*), Lionel Lindon (*Director of Photography*), Richard Mueller (*Technicolor Color Consultant*), Hal Pereira, Earl Hedrick (*Art Directors*), Howard Smith (*Editor*), Farciot Edouart (*Process Photography*), Sam Comer, Grace Gregory (*Set Decorators*), Howard Pine (*Assistant Director*), Lucien Cailliet (*Music Score*), Edith Head (*Costumes*), Wally Westmore (*Makeup Supervisor*), Harold Lewis, John Cope (*Sound Recording*)

RELEASED April 1953. 92 minutes.

Patrick Fairlie, using his dilapidated schooner *Dolphin*, runs an intra-island trading business in the Caribbean. He is in love with beautiful Ena Dacey, the only sensible member of an eccentric family that lives in Jamaica. The Daceys—Ena, spoiled brother Todd, and their flighty mother—live at Great House, a lavish mansion that has been in the family for more than 100 years.

After a hitch in the Navy, Patrick pays a visit to Great House, where he learns that the family is continuing to live high on the hog despite dwindling finances. An investor, William Montague, is interested in purchasing some of the Daceys' beachfront property to build a hotel, but the family matriarch refuses to sell.

Trying another angle, Montague aims to demonstrate that the rightful ownership of the property is in question. Decades earlier, a sale of the house and land was imminent when a Dacey ancestor's ship sank off the Jamaican coast. Montague tracks down the young

Janice Clayton and William Montague (Laura Elliot and Patric Knowles, squatting) find an uncertain reception at the home of the Daceys in *Jamaica Run*. Pat (Ray Milland) and Ena (Arlene Dahl) aren't sure who can be trusted.

cousins of Ena and her family, and hires Patrick to dive for the remains of the sunken ship, where the industrialist hopes to find evidence that the property changed hands.

The Daceys' kin, brother and sister Robert and Janice Clayton, pay a visit while the hunt for the sunken ship is underway. Both Todd Dacey and Montague offer Janice their romantic attentions, but after a tense family reunion she is uncertain whom she can trust. Janice narrowly escapes drowning in a cave at high tide, and shortly afterwards Robert is found dead, throwing the Dacey family and their associates into a murder investigation.

For much of its running time, *Jamaica Run* can't seem to decide what it wants to be, scrambling elements of undersea adventure, murder mystery, and family saga; the failure to establish a consistent tone works against it. The home life of the Dacey family, especially the antics of its matriarch, too often resemble drawing-room comedy. Near the halfway point, a stagey murder mystery begins to play out, with the requisite British-accented inspector expected to untangle the complications of the family relationships. There's not much rooting value to be found in its characters; in early scenes, Pat Fairlie doesn't seem to care a great deal one way or the other whether he wins Ena's heart, and viewers are likely to be similarly disinterested.

Despite the improved budgets of Pine-Thomas' films in the 1950s, the producers often chose more economical means than location shooting in depicting the exotic locales in which the stories took place. That's more than usually evident in *Jamaica Run*, which relies heavily on rear-screen projection to place its leading actors on the Caribbean coast, or at sea. Lionel Lindon's cinematography is quite good, but can't hide the fact that many of the outdoor scenes are simulated. According to leading lady Arlene Dahl, her scenes for *Jamaica Run*, like her other two Pine-Thomas films, were shot entirely on the Paramount lot. As with *Albuquerque* (1948), Pine and Thomas don't take a producing credit here, which they would do in most of their 1950s films. Instead, their company, Clarion Productions, is listed in the opening titles.

Unusually for the Dollar Bills, the casting of *Jamaica Run* is off. Star Ray Milland (1907–1986) is too mature and dignified for the character of free-wheeling adventurer Pat Fairlie, and is ill-matched with Arlene Dahl, nearly a generation younger than he. Stage actress Carroll McComas (1886–1962), in one of her few sizable film roles, makes Mrs. Dacey a caricature (with considerable help from the script). Not until the last 20 minutes or so does the humanity of her characterization shine through, by which time audience sympathy has long since wandered. African American actor William Walker (1896–1992) is seen as the Daceys' longtime servant ("Human"), loyal to an extreme made clear only in the final reel. Clarence Muse is largely wasted as a crew member on Pat's schooner. Young Paramount contract player Laura Elliot, previously seen in P-T's *Special Agent*, is showcased here as well as anyone, and comes closest to playing a character with whom viewers can empathize.

Jamaica Run was adapted from *The Neat Little Corpse*, a 1950 novel by Australian-born mystery writer Max Murray (1901–1956). The story had previously been serialized in *The Saturday Evening Post* as "The Corpse in the Sea." All of Murray's 11 published murder mysteries contained the word "Corpse" in the title; others included *The Voice of the Corpse* and *Good Luck to the Corpse*. Murray's novel is structured as a traditional murder mystery, more so than Lewis R. Foster's screenplay, opening with the discovery of the body. Foster omits one key character from the novel, a seven-year-old boy who is Patrick Fairlie's ward, named Robert but known to his guardian as "Captain Bloodshot."

Syndicated columnist Harrison Carroll (October 7, 1952) was visiting the set on the day that a key fire scene was shot, and shared a few of the crew's secrets. "The area to be burned ... is sprayed with a mixture of kerosene and rubber cement. Augmenting this will be fire from concealed gas jets.... In the hallway, another man, using a rope over a pulley, is hauling a bundle of charred timbers so they can be ignited and allowed to crash to the floor as [Ray] Milland and [Wendell] Corey dash through the flames." Once the scene was completed, Milland joked to Carroll, "I finally got the hair out of my ears. It was burned out!"

REVIEWS: "The screenplay ... wanders along without providing enough excitement or suspense to wholly satisfy devotees of adventure fare, who prefer action rather than the welter of talk provided here ... [the film] will need strong selling in the later runs to offset lack of audience enthusiasm." *Film Bulletin*, April 20, 1953

"The story is unpleasant and unconvincing ... not one of the characters is particularly sympathetic ... there are some underwater scenes, a murder, and a huge fire at the end, but these all seem to lack a melodramatic punch. Even the romances are of mild interest." *Harrison's Reports*, April 11, 1953

Sangaree (1953)

CAST: Fernando Lamas (*Dr. Carlos Morales*), Arlene Dahl (*Nancy Darby*), Patricia Medina (*Martha Darby*), Francis L. Sullivan (*Dr. Bristol*), Charles Korvin (*Felix Pagnol*), Tom Drake (*Dr. Roy Darby*), John Sutton (*Harvey Bristol*), Willard Parker (*Gabriel Thatch*), Charles Evans (*Judge Armstrong*), Lester Mathews (*Gen. Darby*), Roy Gordon (*Dr. Tyrus*), Lewis L. Russell (*Capt. Bronson*), Russell Gaige (*McIntosh*), William Walker (*Priam*), Voltaire Perkins (*Dr. Crowther*), Sam McDaniel (*Nancy's Coachman*), Felix Nelson (*Billy*), Ethan Laidlaw (*Warehouse Guard*), Emile Meyer (*Townsman*), Don Megowan (*River Pirate*), Walter Reed (*Conspirator*), Franklyn Farnum (*Board Member*)

CREW: Edward Ludwig (*Director*), William H. Pine, William C. Thomas (*Producers*), David Duncan (*Screenplay*), Frank Moss (*Adaptation*), Frank G. Slaughter (*Novel*), Lionel Lindon, Wallace Kelley (*Directors of Photography*), Richard Mueller (*Technicolor Color Consultant*), Hal Pereira, Earl Hedrick (*Art Directors*), Howard Smith (*Editor*), Farciot Edouart (*Process Photography*), John P. Fulton, Paul Lerpae (*Special Photographic Effects*), Sam Comer, Ross Dowd (*Set Decorators*), Herbert Coleman (*Assistant Director*), Lucien Cailliet (*Music Score*), Edith Head (*Costumes*), Wally Westmore (*Makeup Supervisor*), Harold Lewis, John Cope (*Sound Recording*)

RELEASED May 1953. 94 minutes.

In 18th century Georgia, with the Revolutionary War over, General Darby lies near death. He summons Dr. Carlos Morales, a young doctor who was the son of an indentured servant on Darby's estate, Sangaree. Although Dr. Morales tries to decline, General Darby presses him to take on managing Sangaree, and the family wealth, after the patriarch dies. General Darby's son, Dr. Roy Darby, is amenable to the plan, but they agree that Roy's sister Nancy, whom Carlos has not yet met, will be firmly opposed.

Heading for Savannah to take up his duties, Carlos meets a young woman who introduces herself as Nancy Darby's maid. The woman is actually Nancy herself, which Carlos eventually realizes, playing a ruse in order to size up her new nemesis. The attraction between the two is obvious, though she coyly rebuffs his advances.

In Savannah, Carlos undertakes the work assigned to him in General Darby's will, including the establishment of a free clinic for the children of slaves and indentured servants. He learns that the city is beginning to experience an outbreak of bubonic plague, although wealthy merchants like Dr. Bristol don't take the warnings seriously. With the help of her fiancé, lawyer Harvey Bristol, Nancy takes Carlos to court, seeking to overturn the will. Carlos emerges victorious by making Nancy herself disprove her lawyer's assertion that the late general was not of sound mind.

Fernando Lamas and Arlene Dahl, then enjoying "a big romance" offscreen, had no trouble turning up the heat for the cameras in *Sangaree*.

Under Carlos' leadership, the business of the Darby company prospers, and he is elected health officer for the city, but his relationship with Nancy remains cool. Carlos' former lover, Martha, now the wife of Nancy's brother Roy, wants to resume her relationship with him, but Carlos will not be disloyal to her husband.

With company products ready to be transported out of Savannah, it becomes clear that someone is providing insider information about ship movements to pirates, with Frenchman Felix Pagnol identified by Martha as being at the forefront of the illegal activities. Carlos, with the help of his friend and lawyer Gabriel Thatch, succeeds in staving off the attack of a pirate ship, but he is saddened when it appears that his treacherous enemy is Nancy herself, with whom he has just began to establish a truce.

Sangaree was adapted from Frank G. Slaughter's 1948 bestseller of the same title, although the film version was originally announced as "Thunderbolt." In general, the screenplay tracks the novel fairly closely, but the casting of Fernando Lamas (1915–1982) as the male lead necessitated some changes in the conception of the main character. In Slaughter's book, the character was Dr. Toby Kent, and Pine and Thomas had originally considered John Payne for the role.

According to leading lady Arlene Dahl, it was she, upon reading the script, who suggested that Lamas be offered the male lead in *Sangaree*. "We were having a big romance," she explained (they would marry in 1954), and the producers "jumped at the chance" to sign the former MGM leading man. Miss Dahl, whose name seemed to be listed in the Pine-Thomas casting files under "Tempestuous Bad Girl in Need of Taming," had no difficulty generating sparks with Lamas on-screen. From the time Dahl's character haughtily tells Carlos, "I'll never acknowledge you as my master in any way!" we know pretty well what to expect of the pairing. Thomas admitted that the "torrid love scene" between stars Lamas and Dahl flirted with Production Code difficulties. "It got past the censors," he said. "Thank goodness!"[46] Still, the National League of Decency classified *Sangaree* as "B" due to a "suggestive sequence."

Stunning Patricia Medina (1919–2012) gives Miss Dahl some stiff competition in terms of beauty, and is gorgeously costumed, but her part is distinctly secondary, though she has a strong dramatic scene that figures into the climax. Willard Parker (1912–1996), effectively slimy in *Caribbean*, shows a more heroic side of himself here.

In producer Adolph Zukor's autobiography, *The Public Is Never Wrong,* he wrote that the overnight sensation caused by *Bwana Devil* in 3-D was a clear indication of audience interest in the new technology, and persuaded other Paramount executives to convert *Sangaree* to the format after filming was already underway. "We had to shoot two pictures," Miss Dahl said of the change. "We got paid for one film, but we shot twice: one for Paramount's VistaVision and one for 3-D." Key scenes such as a barroom brawl were staged so as to play to the potential of 3-D. Thomas told a reporter that, when it came to the new technology, his and partner Pine's philosophy was, "Use it, but not abuse it.... We decided not to just throw third dimension at the audience. We felt we had a good story and good stars, and we wanted to let the 3-D be a nice addition to the picture, like Technicolor."[47]

Sangaree was a substantial box office hit, rivaling other Paramount films like *Shane, Roman Holiday*, and *War of the Worlds* for ticket sales. The Pine-Thomas film made *Motion Picture Herald*'s list of "Box Office Champions" for July 1953, "on the basis of the gross revenue at key city theatres throughout the country."

REVIEWS: "A beautifully mounted production [with] a number of tempestuous love scenes, a hair-raising brawl, and beautiful Arlene Dahl.... The element of 3-D in the film is not used for 'gimmick' purposes, but is interwoven as a natural medium for the story ... however, the screenplay ... appears overloaded with dialogue and contrived situations." *Motion Picture Daily*, May 27, 1953

"Pine and Thomas have a solid hit in *Sangaree*, a rousing adventure yarn that benefits by being in 3-D, but would be exciting entertainment in any process.... There are excellent performances from a fine cast in what must rate as the best picture from the Pine and Thomas banner to date." *Hollywood Reporter*, May 27, 1953

The Vanquished (1953)

CAST: John Payne (*Rockwell Grayson*), Jan Sterling (*Rose Slater*), Coleen Gray (*Jane Colfax*), Lyle Bettger (*Roger Hale*), Willard Parker (*Capt. Kirby*), Roy Gordon (*Dr. Colfax*), John Dierkes (*Gen. Morris*), Charles Evans (*Gen. Hildebrandt*), Ellen Corby (*Mrs. Barbour*), Russell Gaige (*the Rev. Babcock*), Karen Sharpe (*Lucy Colfax*), Sam Flint (*Connors*), Louis Jean Heydt (*Luke Taylor*), Leslie Kimmell (*Col. Ellensby*), Freeman Morse (*Randy Williams*), Paul Newlan (*Blacksmith*), Richard Shannon (*Lt. Adams*), Matthew Beard (*Stableboy*), Pete Kellett (*Orderly*)

CREW: Edward Ludwig (*Director*), William H. Pine, William C. Thomas (*Producers*), Winston Miller, Frank L. Moss, Lewis R. Foster (*Screenplay*), Karl Brown (*Novel*), Lionel Lindon (*Director of Photography*), Richard Mueller (*Technicolor Color Consultant*), Hal Pereira, Earl Hedrick (*Art Directors*), Frank Bracht (*Editor*), Sam Comer, Ross Dowd (*Set Decorators*), Lucien Cailliet (*Music Score*), Edith Head (*Costumes*), Wally Westmore (*Makeup Supervisor*), Howard Pine (*Assistant Director*), Harold Lewis, Walter Oberst (*Sound Recording*)

RELEASED June 1953. 84 minutes.

With the Civil War over, former Confederate Captain Rockwell Grayson returns to his hometown, Galeston, which is being tightly run under martial law by Union-appointed civil administrator Roger Hale. Hale, though Southern by birth, is ruling Galeston with an iron fist, backed by enforcement from Union soldiers. He has taken over the Graysons' former family estate, uses his power to personally profit by buying up foreclosed properties, and has a hangman's rope ready for anyone who argues.

Rock Grayson tells the people of Galeston that the war is over, and they should accept the new circumstances. Weary after five years at war, including time spent recuperating in a military hospital, he is short on money and says he has no appetite for another fight. Hearing this, Roger Hale offers him a job as tax collector, which Rock accepts. Rock's childhood friend Jane Colfax, who has always had a crush on him, is appalled by his willingness to join Hale's team. Roger's lady companion, Rose Slater, daughter of the Graysons' former seamstress, is thoroughly enjoying her newfound wealth, but has a yen for Rock's attentions as well.

No one in town knows that, before he even arrived, Rock carried the town's cries for help to Union General Hildebrandt, who told him solid evidence of Hale's misdoings would be needed. Though he becomes a pariah to the townsfolk, Rock continues to work as Hale's lieutenant, collecting delinquent taxes and posting eviction notices on properties in default. He quickly becomes a trusted member of Hale's inner circle, so much so that Rose suggests he be given a partnership. But when General Hildebrandt arrives in town for an unannounced inspection visit, he confides to Hale's assistant Captain Kirby that he's there to inspect the financial ledgers, and see any damaging information that Rock has collected.

Hale hastily prepares some dummy ledgers, but panics when General Hildebrandt says he will take them along for an audit. Seeing his lucrative fiefdom in jeopardy, Hale plots to have Hildebrandt shot and killed before he can leave town, and Rock Grayson left holding the bag for the crime.

An opening card proclaims that the film's story is based on real-life happenings during Reconstruction—"many Southern towns were occupied by Union forces and civil administrators were appointed to carry out the terms of peace. In some instances, those administrators were just; in others, cruel and despotic. This is the story of such an occupied town." Production began in August 1952, with working titles during pre-production including "The Rebel" and "Violence at Thunder Run."

A strong basic premise and a serviceable screenplay are supported by capable performances in *The Vanquished*. While action fans may criticize its shortage of gunplay, explosions, and the like, the story is absorbing, and the pace is good. John Payne is well-suited to his lead role as a Confederate gentleman from a good family, one who is conscious of social niceties, but nonetheless not a man with whom to trifle.

Second-billed Jan Sterling (1921–2004) provides a strong characterization as Rose Slater, whose loyalties are never entirely clear, but whose hunger for money and respect are formidable. Leading ladies Sterling and Coleen Gray (1922–2015) scarcely cross paths until late in the film. But when they do meet up, the memorable scene shows us that Miss Gray's character may go further than we would expect in defending her man's interests. Lyle Bettger (1915–2003) effectively underplays Roger Hale, another eager sellout in a town that seems to be full of them. Ellen Corby has a noteworthy, if brief, character role in the first reel as the soon-to-be-widowed Mrs. Barbour, who watches in horror as her husband is hanged for resisting Hale's rule. (It does seem a bit odd that she apparently brought along the kids, and made sure they had a good vantage point from which to watch Dad swing.)

"A splashing action drama ... enhanced by a good flow of action and a large cast that includes John Payne, Jan Sterling, Coleen Gray and Lyle Bettger." *Motion Picture Daily*, May 7, 1953

"A mild round of costumed program entertainment [that] puts the emphasis more on talk than action.... Edward Ludwig's direction of story is unevenly paced. Several action sequences come through in okay fashion, but generally he isn't able to whip the routine scripting.... There's eye appeal in the color lensing, settings and costuming, to which the two lead femmes bring ample curves." *Variety*, May 13, 1953

Those Redheads from Seattle (1953)

CAST: Rhonda Fleming (*Kathie Edmonds*), Gene Barry (*Johnny Kisco*), Agnes Moorehead (*Mrs. Edmonds*), Teresa Brewer (*Pat Edmonds*), Guy Mitchell (*Joe Keenan*), The Bell Sisters (*Connie and Nell Edmonds*), Jean Parker (*Liz*), Roscoe Ates (*Dan Taylor*), John Kellogg (*Mike Yurkil*), Frank Wilcox (*Vance Edmonds*), Walter Reed (*Whitey Marks*), William Pullen (*the Rev. Louis Petrie*), Ewing Mitchell (*Mr. Fawcett*), Paul E. Burns (*Hotel Manager*), Stanley Andrews (*Sheriff*), Sheila James (*Girl on Boat*), Edwin Rand (*Jacobs*)

CREW: Lewis R. Foster (*Director*), William H. Pine, William C. Thomas (*Producers*), Lewis R. Foster, Geoffrey Homes, George Worthing Yates (*Screenplay*), Lionel Lindon (*Director of Photography*), Wallace Kelley (*Second Unit Photography*), Richard Mueller (*Technicolor Color Consultant*), Hal Pereira, Earl Hedrick (*Art Directors*), Farciot Edouart (*Process Photography*), John P. Fulton, Paul K. Lerpae (*Special Photographic Effects*), Sam Comer, Roy Moyer (*Set Decorators*), C.C. Coleman, Jr. (*Assistant Director*), Archie Marshak (*Editor*), Edith Head (*Costumes*), Wally Westmore (*Makeup Supervisor*), Howard Lewis, John Cope (*Sound Recording*), Leo Shuken, Sidney Cutner (*Music Score*), Joseph J. Lilley (*Vocal Adaptations*), Jack Baker (*Choreography*)

RELEASED September 1953. 90 minutes.

In the Yukon Territory of the late 19th century, some residents of the town of Dawson look disapprovingly on the Klondike Club, a raucous joint operated by Johnny Kisco. Among its vocal critics is Vance Edmonds, publisher of the local newspaper, the *Daily Bonanza*. Tensions escalate after the newspaper's warehouse mysteriously catches fire. When that fails to discourage Edmonds, Kisco's club manager Mike Yurkil takes the publisher down with two well-placed shots, a tactic that draws his boss' disapproval.

Back in Seattle, Edmonds' wife and their four daughters are waiting to join him.

Strait-laced Mrs. Edmonds has tried to bring up her pretty daughters to live a quiet, dignified life, but they are eager for new experiences. A letter Edmonds wrote just before being shot advises them to stay in Seattle for the time being. But Mrs. Edmonds, reading between the lines, decides that her husband needs his family, and books passage for the Yukon Territory.

When the Edmonds find themselves stranded, still several hundred miles short of Dawson, their fellow ship's passenger Joe Keenan offers to help. Joe, an entertainer who's known professionally as "Spats," is an old buddy of Johnny Kisco, and entreats him to help the ladies reach their destination. Neither man is eager to tell the ladies that Mr. Edmonds was seriously injured, and they agree to postpone the bad news until later.

Along the ten-day trip by dogsled, Johnny takes a shine to lovely Kathie Edmonds. Arriving in Dawson, Mrs. Edmonds and her daughters are grieved to learn that Mr. Edmonds has died. Mrs. Edmonds is eager to leave the "heathenish" town as soon as possible, but runs into difficulty selling her late husband's newspaper.

The ladies of the Edmonds family try their hands at dressmaking, nursing, and typing to earn a living while staying in Dawson. Unbeknownst to them, most of their customers are being sent by Johnny. When Mr. Edmunds' former employee spills the beans about the killing, and puts the blame squarely on Johnny's head, the romance between Kisco and Kathie comes to an abrupt halt. However, Pat, eager to establish herself as a singer and dancer, refuses to give up her new job performing at the Klondike Club, although it causes a break with her family.

Unwilling to accept any more of Johnny's help, Kathie persuades her mother that the only viable option is to resurrect the *Bonanza*. As editor, Kathie publishes scathing articles about her former lover Johnny and the Klondike Club. Meanwhile, she accepts a wedding proposal from a more proper suitor, the local minister. Fed up, Johnny sells the Klondike Club, and sets out for Fairbanks, the last place that murderous Mike Yurkil was seen, while Kathie has second thoughts about letting him go.

The film's working title was "Those Sisters from Seattle." Leading lady Rhonda Fleming later said, "*Redheads* is a picture people still mention to me and I shiver, because I was always trying to get into another big-budgeted musical and this wasn't it."[48] Agnes Moorehead gets substantially better treatment from the wardrobe and makeup departments than she did in *The Blazing Forest,* though her character favors modest clothes, and wears mourning for a number of scenes. She has a few effective dramatic scenes, mostly in the film's second half.

Pop singers Teresa Brewer (1931–2007) and Guy Mitchell (1927–1999), both making their film acting debuts here, have roles that call for acting abilities as well as singing voices, and both do fine. Brewer's song "Baby, Baby, Baby," heard in the film, made the *Billboard* charts once *Those Redheads* went into wide release. Mitchell continued to act occasionally, being a regular in the short-lived TV series *Whispering Smith* (1961), but Brewer stuck to singing afterwards. Carol Thomas Pantages recalled that Brewer and Mitchell were popular with young people. She arranged for some school friends to be on set during the shoot, saying, "All my friends were so excited to go see them."

Two of the four Edmonds sisters are played by real-life singing siblings Cynthia and Kay Bell, who used their mother's maiden name professionally instead of their actual family name, Strother. The duo was under contract to RCA in the early 1950s, earning a gold record for their 1952 single "Bermuda." According to her son Keven, Cynthia

Bill Thomas takes a hasty lunch break during location filming of *Those Redheads from Seattle* **at Aspen, Colorado. At upper left is co-star Gene Barry.**

remembered Pine and Thomas some 60 years later as "very positive, happy, knowledgeable and instrumental in getting their movie into 3-D."[49]

Reliable character actor Frank Wilcox (1907–1974) has a good role as crusading newspaper publisher Vance Edmonds—for about five minutes. Longtime Pine-Thomas player Jean Parker returns to the fold after a nine-year absence. Only in her late 30s, she has been reduced to support here, though her scenes as cynical Liz, one of the employees at the Klondike Club, have their moments. She has an amusing exchange with Agnes Moorehead, when Johnny sends Liz to buy a dress. Liz wants the skirt so short that Mrs. Edmonds disapproves, saying, "A lady never shows her ankles." Unperturbed, Liz retorts, "So I ain't a lady!"

Director Lewis R. Foster stages scenes large and small so as to make them more attention-getting in 3-D. A dramatic snow slide serves the gimmick well, as do small moments like a bartender's sliding a glass of beer down the length of a bar, where it comes to rest in the center of the frame.

The film's world premiere was held, not surprisingly, in Seattle, with Gene Barry, Rhonda Fleming, and the Bell Sisters making personal appearances.

REVIEWS: "This first 3-D musical appears to prove the point that the three-dimensional medium should have been introduced in musicals rather than in horror, slugfest and jungle films … a very good offering [that] stands to make a great deal of money.… Agnes Moorehead's performance is, naturally, the best in the picture, but isn't it always?" *Motion Picture Daily*, September 24, 1953

"Under Foster's direction, the lightweight story comes off acceptably, combining some action with the musical interludes for a satisfactory pace.… The tunes are good, some already being heard from on the pop music front, and platter artists Teresa Brewer, Guy Mitchell and the Bell Sisters work them over expertly." *Daily Variety*, September 23, 1953

Jivaro (1954)

Cast: Fernando Lamas (*Rio Galdez*), Rhonda Fleming (*Alice Parker*), Brian Keith (*Tony*), Lon Chaney (*Pedro Martines*), Richard Denning (*Jerry Russell*), Rita Moreno (*Maroa*), Marvin Miller (*Chief Kovanti*), Morgan Farley (*Vinny*), Pascual Pena (*Sylvester*), Nestor Paiva (*Jacques*), Charlie Lung (*Padre*), Gregg Barton (*Edwards*), Kay Johnson (*Umari*), Rosa Turich (*Native Woman*), Marian Mostick (*Sylvester's Wife*), Eugenia Paul (*Indian Girl*)

CREW: Edward Ludwig (*Director*), William H. Pine, William C. Thomas (*Producers*), Winston Miller (*Screenplay*), David Duncan (*Story*), Lionel Lindon (*Director of Photography*), Richard Mueller (*Technicolor Color Consultant*), Howard Smith (*Editor*), Wallace Kelley (*Second Unit Photography*), John P. Fulton (*Special Photographic Effects*), Farciot Edouart (*Process Photography*), Sam Comer, Grace Gregory (*Set Decorators*), Edith Head (*Costumes*), Wally Westmore (*Makeup Supervisor*), Harold Lewis, Gene Garvin (*Sound Recording*)

RELEASED February 1954. 82 minutes.

Rio Galdez operates a small South American trading post in the village of Pedrone, as well as captaining a rather rundown ship he uses primarily to transport supplies up and down the Amazon River. On his way home from a buying trip, he meets glamorous, beautiful Alice Parker, an American who has come to Brazil to marry her fiancé, Jerry Russell. Unfortunately, Galdes is only too familiar with Jerry, who after nearly two years in South America has given way to drink and dissolution, occupying his time with fantastic schemes to locate lost treasure in the jungle.

During the two-day return trip, Rio and Alice become friendly, but he can't bring himself to warn her what has become of the man she's expecting to make her the mistress of her own plantation. Upon arrival, Rio learns that Jerry is off on a treasure hunt, believing a cache of gold has been secreted in a place known as the Valley of the Winds. Awaiting his return, Alice nearly falls prey to the unwanted advances of sleazy Tony, who promises to show her Jerry's nonexistent plantation, but Rio once again comes to her rescue.

The local priest brings to Rio a piece of jewelry that belonged to Jerry, suggesting that he may have fallen victim to the Indians native to the region, who are cannibalistic headhunters. Rio assembles a search party to track down Jerry and his cohorts; Alice insists on coming along.

After finding the body of one of Jerry's men, Rio offers to take Alice back to town, but she wants to continue until she learns the truth about Jerry. She admits to Rio that she has come to the realization that Jerry's letters to her were full of exaggeration. But now both need to know, for reasons of their own, what has become of the man Alice loved.

Fernando Lamas and his bare chest play the lead roles in *Jivaro*; his shirt is either unbuttoned, or absent altogether, for most of the film's first hour. Rhonda Fleming, in her final Pine-Thomas appearance, works well with him as the city-bred but brave Alice. By any standard, Rio proves to be a handy man to have around, as at various times he saves the heroine from a would-be rapist, the alligator-infested waters of the river, and various other perils large and small.

Richard Denning, previously the leading man of Pine-Thomas' *Seven Were Saved* (1947), has an atypical character assignment here as the gone-to-seed Jerry. *Jivaro* was released only a few weeks before Denning and his cohorts discovered the *Creature from the Black Lagoon*. The chief bad guy here (aside from the headhunters themselves) is a young Brian Keith (1921–1997), who plays the sleazy, opportunistic Tony. He and Lamas have a vigorous fight scene about an hour into the film.

Lon Chaney (1906–1973), fourth-billed for his appearance as a duplicitous shop-keeper who tries to swindle the natives, has little more than a cameo here; in his few moments onscreen he takes a punch from Lamas' character. Twenty-two-year old Rita Moreno (born 1931) is seen in a minor role as a jealous "native girl."

A few stock shots of wildlife are integrated into the original footage, occasionally with a jarring difference in color or film quality. *Jivaro* was filmed in the 3-D process, but released "flat"; Paramount and the producers decided that the popularity of 3-D had passed, and opted not to incur the extra expenses associated with sending out prints in that format. For the British marketplace, the film was retitled *Lost Treasure of the Amazon*.

REVIEWS: "Direction by Edward Ludwig is rugged enough to overcome the stereotyped aspects of plot, and his use of the Amazon footage contributes to the melodramatic effect.... Lamas projects his hard-hitting character successfully, and Miss Fleming, beautiful in tints, is an acceptable heroine, benefiting by some slick closeups. Co-starred is an interesting newcomer, Brian Keith." *Variety*, January 20, 1954

"Producers William H. Pine and William C. Thomas have a bundle of potential box-office dynamite in *Jivaro*, a combination of romance, adventure, action and sex all wrapped up in beautiful Technicolor. The picture is long on romance and action and short on story values, but nevertheless [makes] a highly acceptable piece of cinematic entertainment." *Hollywood Reporter*, January 18, 1954

Hell's Island (1955)

CAST: John Payne (*Mike Cormack*), Mary Murphy (*Janet Martin*), Francis L. Sullivan (*Barzland*), Eduardo Noriega (*Inspector Peña*), Arnold Moss (*Paul Armand*), Walter Reed (*Lawrence*), Sandor Szabo (*Johann Torbig*), Pepe Hern (*Lalo*), Robert Cabal (*Miguel*), Paul Picerni (*Eduardo Martin*), Mario Siletti (*Surgeon*), Ralph Dumke (*Drunk at Las Vegas Casino*), Matty Fain (*Pit Boss*), Nacho Galindo (*Carlos Penasco*), Lillian Molieri (*Girl at Juke Box*), Argentina Brunetti (*Pottery Maker*)

CREW: Phil Karlson (*Director*), William H. Pine, William C. Thomas (*Producers*), Maxwell Shane (*Screenplay*), Martin Goldsmith, Jack Leonard (*Story*), Lionel Lindon (*Director of Photography*), Richard Mueller (*Technicolor Color Consultant*), Hal Pereira,

Leading lady Rhonda Fleming initially fails to appreciate co-star Fernando Lamas' bare chest in *Jivaro*.

Al Roelofs (*Art Directors*), Archie Marshek (*Editor*), John P. Fulton (*Special Photographic Effects*), Farciot Edouart (*Process Photography*), Sam Comer, Otto Siegel (*Set Decorators*), Irvin Talbot (*Music Supervisor*), Edith Head (*Costumes*), Wally Westmore (*Makeup Supervisor*), Michael D. Moore (*Assistant Director*), Harry Lindgren, Gene Garvin (*Sound Recording*)

RELEASED May 1955. 84 minutes.

Mike Cormack, formerly a deputy district attorney in Los Angeles, is now working a subsistence job as "a high-class bouncer" at a Las Vegas casino. He sabotaged his legal career by going on "the granddaddy of all binges" after being dumped by his fiancée, Janet.

At the casino, Mike is introduced to a wealthy older man, Barzland, who wants to hire him to retrieve a valuable ruby that was stolen from him. Having done his homework, Barzland knows that the man he suspects of the theft, Eduardo Martin of the Caribbean republic of Puerto Rosario, is now married to Mike's former fiancée. Mike accepts a $1000 retainer, with the promise of an additional $4000 if he can lead Barzland to his ruby, which the latter believes Janet's husband stole. Mike resents the assumption that he will trade on his relationship with Janet to secure the gem, but can't resist an opportunity to see her again.

Arriving in Puerto Rosario, Mike sees Janet at the local marketplace, where she initially runs when she spots him. Shortly afterwards, however, he is summoned by car to the Martins' palatial home, where Janet tells him that her husband is serving a life sentence in an offshore penal colony. Eduardo was found guilty of murdering a business rival, one who took away the airplane he needed to run his charter business. The plane crash that killed Mike's rival was attributed to tampering with the gas tank, for which Eduardo was blamed.

Unable to resist Janet's appeals, Mike tracks down Carlos Penasco, the mechanic who frequently worked on the plane, at a cockfight. Just as the fight begins, the lights go out; when they come back on, Carlos is dead, a steel spur jammed into his body. Mike is interviewed by the local police inspector, who tells him that the case against Janet's husband was more than just circumstantial, that he was caught in the act of trying to cover up the tampering after the fact. Inspector Pena mentions the name of Paul Armand, who turns out to be Eduardo's former business partner, and proprietor of a local shop. Paul denies that Eduardo was the type to commit a murder.

Insisting she knows nothing about the ruby, Janet implores Mike to rescue her husband from the island penal colony. She claims that she actually tampered with the plane, and that Eduardo took the rap for her. Sneaking back onto her estate late at night in search of answers, Mike finds a dying Miguel, Janet's houseboy, who's been attacked. Outside, Mike himself is knocked out in a surprise attack, and awakes sometime later to find himself being held prisoner by Barzland.

Barzland believes that Mike has "obviously gone over to the other side," telling him that Janet and Paul are plotting an escape from the country. After overpowering one of Barzland's stooges, Mike gets away. He demands answers from Janet and Paul, and she confesses that Eduardo hid the ruby, and that they have devised a plan for Mike to help her husband break out. Before the night is over, Mike successfully infiltrates the prison, but his meeting with Eduardo offers only the first of a series of deadly surprises.

Although it has some draggy spots, overall *Hell's Island* is a diverting melodrama with some intriguing plot twists, and an exciting finale. The film opens with an interesting framing device in which a key scene from the climax is previewed under the opening titles. Mike's treatment in the hospital for a gunshot wound, which leads into the flashback that is the film's main story, offers a laugh that may or may not have been intentional. When the doctor is asked if his patient can smoke while he's on the surgical table, the nonchalant answer is, "Why not?" Mercifully, we see very little of the cockfight at which a murder is committed.

Star John Payne is reunited with director Phil Karlson (1908–1985), three years after they'd first teamed for the influential *film noir Kansas City Confidential* (1952). The star-director duo worked on three films together (this being the only one for Pine-Thomas), with Karlson, according to author David J. Hogan, bringing out Payne's "boldly declarative line readings, the physique of a trained athlete, and the intimidating handsomeness of his face—which looked best when locked in a scowl."[50]

Mary Murphy (1931–2011), best-known for co-starring with Marlon Brando in *The Wild One* (1953), is cast as the alluring Janet, who may or may not be the kind of girl you take home to Mother. Though the nearly 20-year age difference between Miss Murphy and her leading man is distracting, she gives a solid performance in a role that calls for nuance and ambiguity.

Although his character's name is on everyone's lips for much of the film's running time, Paul Picerni (1922–2011) doesn't actually put in an appearance as Eduardo until the last 15 minutes. He's colorful and engaging, enacting a character who proves to be not what Mike expected. Francis L. Sullivan, in his second Pine-Thomas appearance, makes the most of his relatively few scenes.

The film was originally to be called "The Ruby Virgin." After censors raised objections, it was renamed *Hell's Island*. That title had previously been used by Columbia Pictures some 25 years earlier, for a melodrama about a soldier from the French Foreign Legion sent to a rough penal colony.

REVIEWS: "This minor melodrama is chiefly for the action houses…. Story is mildly suspenseful, but the action is too often slowed down by long stretches of dialogue and far-fetched motivations." *Independent Exhibitors' Film Bulletin*, May 16, 1955

"Phil Karlson gives narrative a hard glossing in his direction, generally delivering a briskly told tale. Capable players lend realism to colorful characters…. Carries enough interest to rate good returns in the action market." *Daily Variety*, May 2, 1955

Run for Cover (1955)

CAST: James Cagney (*Matt Dow*), Viveca Lindfors (*Helga Swenson*), John Derek (*Davey Bishop*), Jean Hersholt (*Mr. Swenson*), Grant Withers (*Gentry*), Jack Lambert (*Larsen*), Ernest Borgnine (*Morgan*), Ray Teal (*Sheriff*), Irving Bacon (*Scotty*), Trevor Bardette (*Paulsen*), John Miljan (*Mayor Walsh*), Gus Schilling (*Doc Ridgeway*), Denver Pyle (*Harvey*), Emmett Lynn (*Bartender*), Phil Chambers (*Robber*), Bob Folkerson (*Hughes*), Emerson Treacy (*Bank Clerk*), Harold J. Kennedy (*Devers*), Joe Haworth (*Larry*)

CREW: Nicholas Ray (*Director*), William H. Pine, William C. Thomas (*Producers*), Winston Miller (*Screenplay*), Harriet Frank, Jr., Irving Ravetch (*Story*), Daniel Fapp (*Director of Photography*), Richard Mueller (*Technicolor Color Consultant*), Hal Pereira, Henry Bumstead (*Art Directors*), John P. Fulton (*Special Photographic Effects*), Farciot Edouart (*Process Photography*), Sam Comer, Frank McKelvy (*Set Decorators*), Wally Westmore (*Makeup Supervisor*), Gene Merritt, John Cope (*Sound Recording*), Howard Jackson (*Music Score*), Howard Jackson, Jack Brooks (*Song*, "Run for Cover"), Howard Smith (*Editor*), Edith Head (*Costumes*), Francisco Day (*Assistant Director*)

RELEASED May 1955. 92 minutes.

Middle-aged Matt Dow and 20-year-old Davey Bishop don't exactly hit it off on their first meeting; suspicious Dow pulls a gun on the younger man when they meet unexpectedly alongside a river stream. Past that first hurdle, they establish more friendly relations. Both are headed to the town of Madison, where the orphaned Davey lives, so they agree to ride together.

On the outskirts of town, they are mistaken for train robbers, and a posse led by Madison's incompetent sheriff shoots first and asks questions later. Keeping a cool head, Matt manages to persuade the bloodthirsty townspeople that the railroad men were mistaken. While Matt's wounds are mild, Davey is badly injured, and it's uncertain whether he'll live. Recuperating at the nearby farm of a Swedish immigrant, Mr. Swenson, and his daughter Helga, Davey is kept company by Matt, who has taken a fatherly interest in him. He confesses to the kindly Helga that he is divorced, and his own son died at around Davey's age some ten years earlier. Davey slowly regains his health, though his leg remains injured and his ability to walk impaired. While helping the Swensons on their farm, Matt is asked by the mayor to take the job of sheriff. He agrees to do so if Davey can be hired as his deputy, sensing that, on the verge of manhood, Davey needs a positive direction for his life. Before Matt leaves the farm, he and Helga acknowledge their mutual attraction with a kiss.

At first, the town remains quiet. But when two robbers on the lam are spotted at the local bank, and the banker is shot in the resulting mayhem, Matt goes after Morgan, the crook who got away. Leaving Davey to take charge of the injured second would-be holdup man, Matt captures Morgan. On his return to town, he learns that a lynch mob has carried out its own justice against the second robber, who swings from a nearby rope. Davey, unable to prevent the violence, offers to turn in his badge. Matt, giving him another chance, assigns him to escort Morgan to the county seat to await trial, but once again the results are unsatisfactory.

With Davey gainfully employed at the local hardware store, Matt feels settled enough to make Helga his wife, and settle permanently in Madison. But on Easter Sunday, another bank holdup leaves one man dead, and the townspeople newly aware of the years Matt spent in prison. The robbers have escaped with $85,000 of the town's money, but Matt encounters resistance when he tries to form a posse and take off in pursuit.

Run for Cover is a well-made Western drama for those who appreciate some detail to characterization, and motivated action scenes. It includes striking location footage shot in the Aztec, New Mexico region. Daniel Fapp's cinematography captures the beauty of snow-tipped mountaintops, and vividly blue skies. It's interesting to see a Western story in which a character is not killed outright in a gun battle, but survives it with injuries that change the course of his life. Advance publicity indicated a $1.6 million budget.

Nearly 25 years after his first starring roles, James Cagney (1899–1986) is older and grayer, befitting the character he plays, a man who's learned from his life experiences and wants to see that others do as well. According to Bill Thomas, Cagney pocketed $200,000 for the gig, well more than the entire budgets of early Pine-Thomas films. He's paired nicely with Swedish-born actress Viveca Lindfors (1920–1995), who'd first been brought to Hollywood nearly ten years earlier by Warner Brothers. Production of *Run for Cover* got underway in May 1954, but the film wasn't released until nearly a year later. Movie-goers would see quite a bit of Cagney in 1955, who along with this film had leading roles in *Mister Roberts* and *Love Me or Leave Me*. According to *Daily Variety* (February 23, 1955), Cagney went on the first cross-country publicity tour of his career in conjunction with *Run for Cover*.

John Derek (1926–1988), later better known as the director who guided the career of his wife, Bo Derek, plays Davey. Derek isn't sufficiently nuanced as an actor to fully depict the character's complexities, but his scenes with Cagney mostly play well.

Ray Teal (1902–1976), who would later be cast in the recurring part of Sheriff Coffee on TV's *Bonanza*, here plays a lawman who's thoroughly incompetent. Irving Bacon (1893–1965) is seen to good effect as the town's voice of reason and conscience, while Gus Schilling (1908–1957) plays the town doctor, who may have the world's worst bedside manner. Playing the last film role of his career, Jean Hersholt (1886–1956), best-known as Dr. Christian from his radio and film series of the 1940s, has a few good moments as Lindfors' father. Cagney and Hersholt's quiet scene over a chessboard, with Matt ready to ask for Helga's hand in marriage, is subtly effective.

Nicholas Ray directed *Run for Cover* just a few months before making his most famous film, *Rebel without a Cause*. The previous year, he had directed another Western, the oddball *Johnny Guitar*, starring Joan Crawford and Mercedes McCambridge. Much later, Cagney told his biographer that he was disappointed with the finished film. "Both Nick Ray and I had put in some ingenious touches. But the assholes who cut the picture were unhappy with anything they hadn't seen before … anything that was novel was out. It became just another programmer."[51]

REVIEWS: "A story filled with human interest, intrigue and suspense … with James Cagney in the kind of role that has established him as an all-time favorite add up to a worthwhile box office attraction…. Scenic wonders of New Mexico are impressively reproduced by VistaVision and Technicolor to become an important asset of the film." *Motion Picture Daily*, March 18, 1955

"*Run for Cover* is handicapped by a sprawling story and by plot inconsistencies, but on the whole it emerges as a better-than-average Western melodrama … it moves along for the most part at a leisurely pace and is concerned more with characterization than with riding, shooting and fighting…. Derek is not too convincing in his role, for the manner in which he fluctuates between good and bad makes the characterization confusing. Viveca Lindfors is warm and sympathetic as a Swedish immigrant." *Harrison's Reports*, May 7, 1955

The Far Horizons (1955)

CAST: Fred MacMurray (*Capt. Meriwether Lewis*), Charlton Heston (*Lt. William Clark*), Donna Reed (*Sacajawea*), Barbara Hale (*Julia Hancock*), William Demarest (*Sgt. Gass*), Alan Reed (*Charbonneau*), Eduardo Noriega (*Cameahwait*), Larry Pennell (*Wild Eagle*), Herbert Heyes (*Pres. Thomas Jefferson*), Lester Matthews (*Mr. Hancock*), Ralph Moody (*Le Borgne*), Helen Wallace (*Marsha Hancock*), Argentina Brunetti (*Old Crone*), Julia Montoya (*Crow Woman*), Walter Reed (*Cruzatte*), Vernon Rich (*Collins*), Bill Walker (*Tom*), William Phipps (*Camp Sentry*), Robert Hinkle (*Jake*)

CREW: Rudolph Maté (*Director*), William H. Pine, William C. Thomas (*Producers*), Winston Miller, Edmund H. North (*Screenplay*), Della Gould Emmons (*Novel*, "Sacajawea of the Shoshones"), Daniel Fapp (*Director of Photography*), Richard Mueller (*Technicolor Color Consultant*), Hal Pereira, Earl Hedrick (*Art Directors*), Frank Bracht (*Editor*), William Williams (*Second Unit Photography*), John P. Fulton (*Special Photographic Effects*), Sam Comer, Otto Siegel (*Set Decorators*), C.C. Coleman, Jr. (*Second Unit Director*), Edith Head (*Costumes*), Wally Westmore (*Makeup Supervision*), William McGarry (*Assistant Director*), Donald R.O. Hatswell (*Technical Advisor*), Gene Merritt, Gene Garvin (*Sound Recording*), Hans Salter (*Music*)

RELEASED May 1955. 107 minutes.

In 1803, the Louisiana Purchase, championed by President Jefferson, nearly doubles the size of the United States. Jefferson's secretary, Captain Meriwether Lewis, is summoned back from vacation and asked to assume command on a military expedition to explore and map the newly acquired land. Lewis suggests a friend from his Army service, Lt. Bill Clark, to share the command. Their work gets off to an awkward start shortly before departure, when Clark proposes marriage to a woman, Julia Hancock, unaware that Lewis was also in love with her. Still, the men pledge to work together on the expedition.

Trade-paper ad for *The Far Horizons*, emphasizing its star power. Not pictured is Barbara Hale, whose role was substantially smaller than those of MacMurray, Heston, and Reed.

Not long after the expedition enters the Louisiana Territory, Lewis and Clark's company sees that they are being observed by Indians. As President Jefferson suggested, the expedition leaders try diplomacy first, approaching Le Borgne, chief of the Minitari tribe, with gifts and offering friendship. Captain Lewis asks Le Borgne to appoint a guide to help his company navigate the unfamiliar territory, but the Indian chief is angered by the announcement that they are now under the leadership of the United States. A young Indian woman, Sacajawea, surreptitiously approaches Lewis and Clark offering to serve as their guide, explaining that she is a Shoshone who has been enslaved by the rival tribe. Clark, more experienced in fighting Indians, does not believe she can be trusted, and her help is refused.

Instead, Le Borgne appoints French tradesman Charbonneau as the expedition's guide. Charbonneau, who doesn't wish to share his lucrative trading territory with newcomers, pretends to be of help while luring Lewis and Clark into a trap. Sacajawea, knowing the Minitari Indians are preparing to attack the expedition, escapes from the camp, reaching Lewis and Clark in time to warn them. After they successfully ward off the Indian attack, she is offered the chance to join the expedition.

As they head westward, Clark falls ill, and Sacajawea, whom he has nicknamed "Janey," nurses him back to health. Their growing closeness is protested by Charbonneau, who claims ownership of her. After Clark defends her honor in a fight with the Frenchman, Sacajawea tells him she now belongs to him. He hesitates to tell her that a fiancée awaits him back home, as he is falling in love with her.

At the far edge of the Louisiana Territory, Sacajawea is reunited with the Shoshone tribe of which her brother Cameahwait is chief. With her help, the explorers and the Indians agree to friendly relations. But Wild Eagle, an Indian brave who wants Sacajawea for himself, undermines the peace efforts. As the expedition heads on, aiming to reach the Pacific Ocean, the growing animosity between Lewis and Clark threatens the success and safety of the voyage.

The Far Horizons is an odd combination of historical accuracy (mostly in minor details) and complete fiction. Falling into the latter category is Clark's romance with Sacajawea. In the film, Sacajawea escapes the Indian village in part because the chief has promised her to Charbonneau, as a reward for his treachery against the expedition members. In reality, Sacajawea was already the bride of Toussaint Charbonneau, and pregnant with his child when she joined the expedition. Screenwriter Winston Miller later admitted, "I took great liberties with history. I hope they never show that film in schools. Sacajawea did not look like Donna Reed."[52]

For a modern-day viewer, the most glaring problem with the film is indeed the miscasting of Miss Reed (1921–1986) as the Native American heroine. Makeup and costuming can go only so far to make her look like anything but her white-bread self. Not helping her cause is some of the corny dialogue she's given to recite, as when she tells Clark after his fight with Charbonneau, "I belong to you, as if you had bought me. It is the custom." (For a woman who grew up living among Indians in previously uncharted territory, she speaks remarkably good, albeit slightly stilted, English.) According to Reed's biographer, Jay Fultz, however, she took the role of Sacajawea seriously, and "read everything available about the Shoshone guide," and even "hoped to make a movie of the entire life of Sacajawea."[53]

Fourth-billed Barbara Hale (1922–2017) has a disappointingly small part to play, seen only in the film's opening and closing segments. Fred MacMurray (1908–1991), in his only film for the Dollar Bills, is a bit long in the tooth to play Meriwether Lewis, who was still shy of his 30th birthday when the expedition took place. He plays the character with his usual competence, if not an overabundance of energy or passion. Charlton Heston will make two films for Pine-Thomas in 1955.

More than some of Pine-Thomas' then-recent historical epics, *The Far Horizons* benefits from significant location shooting, relying less heavily on process photography. Rudolph Maté's direction makes it clear that the principal cast members plunged into the action. In its early stages, the film was known as "Blue Horizons." Both this and *Lucy Gallant*, which followed, employed Paramount's wide-screen process dubbed VistaVision.

In a memo to Paramount president Barney Balaban, studio executive George Weltner thought *The Far Horizons* showed potential to match "the enormous success in the foreign field of *Naked Jungle*" (the 1954 action-adventure starring Charlton Heston and Eleanor Parker). Weltner enthused, "*Far Horizons* will take its place in the parade of hits that is now coming out of our studio. Our job will be to absorbe [*sic*] the very rich diet that we are now receiving. Our people are trained and ready."[54]

REVIEWS: "A fairly good historical outdoor melodrama … though the story and some of the dialogue is on the stilted side, it moves along at a satisfactory pace…. Among the exciting highlights are a vicious knife duel and several battles with Indians." *Harrison's Reports*, May 21, 1955

"Scenically, the … production has magnificent values, thanks to the location lensing in the Jackson Hole country of Wyoming. However, these pictorial splendors aren't sufficient to overcome the cliché scripting and direction … not enough action to sustain the long 107 minutes of footage." *Daily Variety*, May 20, 1955

Lucy Gallant (1955)

CAST: Jane Wyman (*Lucy Gallant*), Charlton Heston (*Casey Cole*), Claire Trevor (*Lady Macbeth*), Thelma Ritter (*Molly Basserman*), William Demarest (*Charles Madden*), Wallace Ford (*Gus Basserman*), Tom Helmore (*Jim Wardman*), Gloria Talbott (*Laura Wilson*), James Westerfield (*Harry Wilson*), Mary Field (*Irma Wilson*), Gov. Allan Shivers, Edith Head (*Themselves*), Joel Fluellen (*Summertime*), Roscoe Ates (*Clem Anderson*), Lyle Latell (*Oil Rigger*), Diane Brewster (*Salesgirl*), Nicky Blair (*Intern*), Jay Adler (*Sam*)

CREW: Robert Parrish (*Director*), William H. Pine, William C. Thomas (*Producers*), John Lee Mahin, Winston Miller (*Screenplay*), Margaret Cousins (*Novel*), Lionel Lindon (*Director of Photography*), Monroe W. Burbank (*Technicolor Color Consultant*), Howard Smith (*Editor*), John P. Fulton (*Special Photographic Effects*), Sam Comer, Grace Gregory (*Set Decorators*), Wally Westmore (*Makeup Supervisor*), William McGarry (*Assistant Director*), Van Cleave (*Music Score*), Edith Head (*Costumes*), Jack Baker (*Fashion Show Staging*), Hugo Grenzbach, Gene Garvin (*Sound Recording*)

RELEASED October 1955. 104 minutes.

An enterprising woman of the early 1940s, Lucy Gallant is stuck overnight in a formerly quiet Texas town—White Sage Junction, recently renamed New City—that's in the midst of an oil boom. Accommodations are in short supply, but rancher Casey Cole arranges for her to use his room at Molly Basserman's boardinghouse. Lucy, a New Yorker dressed in the height of fashion, notices that lucky oil strikes have left many of the local residents flush with money. She sets up a temporary storefront and sells several suitcases full of clothes she brought on her trip, clearing more than $4000 in a quick turnaround.

Seeing a ready market awaiting her in the drab town ("Women can't wear derricks"), Lucy decides to stay and open a store called Gallant's. She obtains a loan from banker Mr. Madden, bargains with the proprietress of a local saloon to obtain space for the shop, and, despite Casey's friendly skepticism, watches her business flourish. She admits to Casey, with whom she shares a mutual attraction, that the first batch of clothes she sold were her own never-used trousseau, but offers no details.

Casey's ranch is believed to be another potentially lucrative site for oil, but he's in no hurry to sell out. As they grow closer, Lucy explains that her wedding to another man was called off just before it took place, when her father was charged with fraud. After her disgraced father committed suicide, Lucy set out to make her own way in the world, not relying on a man to take care of her.

When news of the attack on Pearl Harbor reaches the town, Casey enlists in the military, where he's wounded in action, but ultimately returns to New City after a four-year absence. Lucy and Casey are ready to acknowledge their love for each other, but he expects her to give up her business interests if they are wed.

After the breakup, Casey prospers as an oilman, while Lucy faces a serious setback when her store goes up in flames. Without telling Lucy, Casey persuades a reluctant Mr. Madden to bankroll her newer, larger establishment. Although Casey becomes engaged to a Parisian model, and Lucy is being escorted by her store's manager, Jim Wardman, they clearly still have eyes for each other. Matters both romantic and fiduciary come to a head at a lavish fashion show held to celebrate the anniversary of Lucy's business enterprise, just as she's told she's about to lose it.

Lucy Gallant was based on a novelette, "The Life of Lucy Gallant," which appeared in *Good Housekeeping*'s May 1953 issue. Author Margaret Cousins (1905–1996), also the magazine's managing editor at the time, told "the story of a woman who was in love with her work, and of the man who came between them." For the purposes of the screenplay, the setting was changed from Oklahoma to Texas.

The film adaptation landed in theaters several months after the phenomenal box-office success of *Magnificent Obsession*, one of the biggest hits of Jane Wyman's career. In the mid–50s, Wyman's name will be firmly associated with romantically oriented melodramas, often ones that pair her with a younger leading man like Rock Hudson.

Bill Thomas later recalled that he initially pitched *Lucy Gallant* to Joan Crawford, whom he had known since she was a young starlet. The actress liked the script, owed a picture commitment to Paramount, and tentatively accepted the part. Unfortunately, when Wyman became available, Pine and Thomas agreed that she was then a better box-office draw, and argued over who would take on the awkward assignment of informing Crawford she had lost the job. Thomas ultimately decided to let agents at MCA, who represented him as well as both actresses involved, handle the delicate situation. "I received a sweet letter from Joan stating that she was sorry it didn't work out and she would like to do a picture with us someday. The next time I saw Joan—she was friendly as ever."[55]

After making dozens of films targeting male, action-loving moviegoers, Pine and Thomas went after the female ticket buyers with this lush romantic drama, made on a reported budget of $1,750,000. Veteran P-T action fans may have been confused, waiting in vain to see Casey hanging by one arm from the uppermost reach of an oil rig, or

Lucy Gallant (Jane Wyman, right) gets a word of advice from pal Molly (Thelma Ritter).

working with seconds to spare to avoid an explosion. However, the producers do get to level Lucy's store in a fire in the film's final half-hour. They should have resisted the temptation to underline her downfall by having her name from the store's sign crumble at her feet in the aftermath.

Studio ads in trade journals called the heroine of *Lucy Gallant* "a boxoffice name to remember with Mildred Pierce or Scarlett O'Hara...." But although it purportedly tells the story of a woman ahead of her time, almost single-handedly building a business empire, *Lucy Gallant* is in some ways a feminist viewer's nightmare, as the ultimate lesson to be learned by its central character is quite plain. The lovebirds reach an impasse minutes after they are reunited, and ready to get married, when Lucy makes it clear she wants to keep working.

CASEY: I kinda thought being married was a full-time job.

LUCY: Haven't I the right to do two jobs at once?

CASEY: Not these two.

Lucy's buddy Molly comes down clearly on the side of l'amour, shrugging over the success of "this glorified dry goods store." When Lucy protests, "But it's my big dream!" Molly retorts, "Well, wake up! Having your own man is better." Margaret Cousins' novelette, while also depicting Casey as initially dubious about Lucy's career, presents a more progressive outcome than the film, with her man ultimately telling her, "If you want the store, you can have it. Finally came to me that if you care enough for somebody you want them to be happy the way they want to be, instead of setting such store by your own stubbornness."

Leading man Charlton Heston (1923–2008), looking back on the film when he wrote his memoirs some 40 years later, commented that *Lucy Gallant* "wasn't very good, I'm afraid, though I thought Jane was.... It shows up on TV frequently, but I wouldn't recommend it."[56]

Thelma Ritter (1902–1969), though she looks a bit out of place in Texas, is well-suited to the role of Molly. Like most Ritter characters, Molly is plain-spoken, down-to-earth, and no-nonsense, but her husband's rich oil strike gives her life a fast makeover. The actress skillfully conveys Molly's lack of ease with the twist of fate that unexpectedly bestows her with a huge house, glittery party dresses, and multiple fancy cars in the garage. Sporting a glamorous green gown at a party, she tells one onlooker laconically, "Lucy whipped it up. I'm supposed to wear it to picnics and barbecues."

The slightly faulty construction of the screenplay leaves too many characters hanging around the edges of the film. The script goes to some trouble to introduce us to the Wilson family early on, possibly setting up Gloria Talbott (1931–2000) to be a romantic rival to Lucy, before they fade into the background with no explanation.

Likewise, despite her prominent billing, Claire Trevor (1910–2000) is disappointingly absent from large chunks of the film. Viewers may well have forgotten about her character before she resurfaces to play a significant role in the last act. She does, however, get what may be the single best wisecrack in the screenplay. Twitting Casey about his aborted romance with a model, Trevor cracks, "What happened? Didn't she look enough like Lucy when you turned on the lights?"

The elaborate fashion show in the film's last reel gives a small speaking role to Allen Shivers, then the real-life governor of Texas, who shows up to congratulate Lucy on her business enterprise. Shivers issued official proclamations declaring both Pine and Thomas to be "Honorary Texans." In turn, Thomas told a local reporter, "The movies lost a great actor when Gov. Shivers went into politics. He can get a contract from Bill Pine and me anytime he wants one."[57] Edith Head (1897–1981), in addition to being the film's costume designer, appears onscreen as herself, declaring that Lucy has made this Texas city "the real fashion center of the world."

This was the final film on which William H. Pine worked prior to his death in April 1955, and Pine-Thomas' final release for Paramount after a 14-year association.

REVIEWS: "A fairly entertaining, but routine drama. It's all been seen before, but Jane Wyman and Charlton Heston are appealing personalities, and their thesping keeps interest aroused.... Chief appeal of this Paramount offering will be to the fem trade." *Independent Exhibitors' Film Bulletin*, October 3, 1955

"The acting 'thunder' is stolen from the principals by veteran character performers Thelma Ritter, William Demarest and Wallace Ford, all of whom contribute many laughs, even though this film is not a comedy." *Motion Picture Daily*, September 29, 1955

Nightmare (1956)

CAST: Edward G. Robinson (*Rene Bressard*), Kevin McCarthy (*Stan Grayson*), Connie Russell (*Gina*), Virginia Christine (*Sue Bressard*), Rhys Williams (*Deputy Torrence*),

Gage Clarke (*Belknap/Harry Britten*), Marian Carr (*Madge Novick*), Barry Atwater (*Captain Warner*), Meade "Lux" Lewis (*Meade*), Ralph Brooks (*Oscar*), Sol Gorss (*Bob Clune*), Billy May and His Orchestra

CREW: Maxwell Shane (*Director/Screenplay*), Cornell Woolrich (*Novel*), Joseph F. Biroc (*Director of Photography*), Frank Sylos (*Art Director*), George Gittens (*Editor*), Howard A. Anderson (*Special Photographic Effects*), Edward Boyle (*Set Decorator*), Norman Pringle (*Makeup Artist*), Myrl Stoltz (*Hair Stylist*), Frank Beetson, Fay Moore (*Wardrobe*), Robert Justman (*Art Director*), Jack Soloman, Roger Heman (*Sound Recording*)

RELEASED May 1956. 89 minutes.

Musician Stan Grayson wakes from a vivid dream in which he killed a man, only to find evidence in the real world that the incident actually happened. He confides in his brother-in-law, Detective Rene Broussard, who refuses to believe his story. On a picnic with Rene, Stan's sister Sue, and his girlfriend Gina, Stan leads them to a house where he finds the mirrored room from his dream.

Nine years after Pine-Thomas released the thriller *Fear in the Night,* writer/director Maxwell Shane had a second chance to tell the story, with bigger-name actors and a more substantial budget. Because the remake tracks the original so closely, a lengthy synopsis isn't necessary here, as it is easier to point out the differences between the two.

Nightmare transfers the action to New Orleans, and makes the lead character a musician, rather than a bank employee. His first name has been changed, from Vince to Stan. Some latter-day viewers of the original film have interpreted Grayson's neurosis, and the source of his sister's fears about him, as latent homosexuality. That reading isn't as well supported by this version of the story. One of the major departures from the original script comes when Stan Grayson picks up beautiful blonde Madge at a bar (after she makes her availability quite plain), and willingly goes to her apartment for a tryst—albeit one he cuts short when he's tormented by a flashback from his dream. The screenplay in this instance has been modified in small ways to build up the basically secondary role of Stan's brother-in-law, for which Edward G. Robinson is billed above the title.

In theory, more money, bigger-name actors, and a longer shooting schedule should have resulted in *Nightmare* being an improvement on *Fear in the Night*. The enhanced budget allowed for location shooting in New Orleans. That, along with the crisp, clear photography of cinematographer Joseph F. Biroc, later an Oscar winner for *The Towering Inferno* (1974), gives definition to Stan's daytime world that was lacking in the original. However, the result is to somehow make a sharper delineation between dreams and reality, which actually works against the film's suspense and mood.

At the time of this film's original release, many moviegoers still had fresh in their minds Kevin McCarthy's performance as Dr. Miles Bennell in *Invasion of the Body Snatchers,* released only a few months earlier. McCarthy (1914–2010) is always a capable leading man, but his performance as Stan Grayson doesn't come off as effectively as DeForest Kelley's version in the 1947 original. McCarthy's bug-eyed reaction to his frightening dream is overdone, and his leading-man looks tip us off too early that he is eminently sane and sensible, despite his baffling predicament.

Virginia Christine rarely, if ever, gave a bad performance, even in bad films, and she's completely satisfactory as Robinson's love interest. However, the chemistry that Paul Kelly and Ann Doran created in the original is largely absent here. Robinson, well into

A seemingly deserted house holds the key to Stan Grayson's *Nightmare*. Pictured (left to right) are Connie Russell, Kevin McCarthy, Virginia Christine, and Edward G. Robinson.

his 60s, is too old to be playing a man about to become a father after nine years of marriage. No matter how big a star plays Stan's brother-in-law, it's a secondary role, though Robinson makes the most of it. Like many players who found themselves in Pine-Thomas films, he had been knocked down a peg or two by career difficulties. In his case, a brush with the House Un-American Activities Committee had threatened to interrupt his acting career, and he was also in the process of negotiating an expensive divorce.

Still, Robinson held to his professional standards, and initially balked when co-producer Thomas asked him to work past his contractually stipulated 6 p.m. quitting time one night. After a brief negotiation, Robinson agreed to an extra 40 minutes of shooting, in exchange for the three custom-made suits that comprised his *Nightmare* wardrobe. Thomas readily accepted the offer, not telling the star he'd planned to make a gift of them anyway. "Hell, they wouldn't fit me!" Thomas later noted.[58]

One other key difference between *Nightmare* and its 1947 predecessor is the characterization of Stan's girlfriend. Here, the producers have cast singer Connie Russell (1923–1990) in the part, making the character a nightclub performer so that Miss Russell can warble two numbers. The second of them interrupts the momentum of Rene Bressard's reconstruction of the crime, making it an annoying distraction. Otherwise, the part (here renamed Gina, rather than Betty) is no more important to the story than it ever was, though Russell snagged co-star billing for her efforts. Director Shane allows featured player Rhys Williams (1897–1969) to hoke up the character of Deputy Torrence as a rube, injecting a comedic note that's out of place.

The trade journal *Harrison's Reports*, in its May 1956 review of *Nightmare*, recommended that theater managers "exercise caution in booking this picture," pointing out that *Fear in the Night* was then receiving regular television showings. "The danger faced by the exhibitors who buy these remakes," the publishers editorialized elsewhere in the same issue, "lies mainly in the fact that the titles are different from the originals and give no indication to the unsuspecting movie-goers that they are new versions of old pictures…. [The customer's] justifiable wrath will know no bounds and, even if he demands his money back and gets it, he will bear a grudge against the motion picture industry in general…."

REVIEWS: "*Nightmare* is a program thriller that should serve out its playing time as a companion feature in the regular dual market…. Along with the changes made [from the original], 18 more minutes of footage has been added, resulting in a slowly-paced unfoldment unnecessarily prolonged." *Daily Variety*, May 11, 1956

"An exciting and absorbing film … a gripping picture that will have many fans jumping off the edges of their seats." *Syracuse* (NY) *Herald-Journal*, June 28, 1956

The Big Caper (1957)

CAST: Rory Calhoun (*Frank Harper*), Mary Costa (*Kay*), James Gregory (*Flood*), Robert [H.] Harris (*Zimmer*), Roxanne Arlen (*Doll*), Corey Allen (*Roy*), Paul Picerni (*Harry*), Patrick McVey (*Sam Loxley*), Louise Arthur (*Alice Loxley*), James Nolan (*Sgt. Waldo Harrington*), Roscoe Ates (*Falkenburg*), Jack Shea (*Joe Stancil*), Ray Teal (*Real Estate Broker*), Terry Kelman (*Benny Laxley*), Valentin de Vargas (*Gas Station Attendant*)

CREW: Robert Stevens (*Director*), William C. Thomas, Howard B. Pine (*Producers*), Martin Berkeley (*Screenplay*), Lionel White (*Novel*), Lionel Lindon (*Director of Photography*), Albert Glasser (*Music Composer/Conductor*), Frank Sylos (*Art Director*), George Gittens (*Editor*), Alfred Kegerris (*Set Decorator*), Alvena Tomin (*Costumes*), Norman Pringle (*Makeup Artist*), Myrl Stoltz (*Hair Stylist*), Jerry Bos, Fay Moore (*Wardrobe*), Frank Fox (*Assistant Director*), Fred Lau, Roger Heman (*Sound Recording*)

RELEASED March 1957. 83 minutes.

A tough, middle-aged bunco artist named Flood is happily reaping the rewards of his criminal empire—a big house with a swimming pool, and a beautiful girlfriend, Kay. Flood's young cohort, Frank Harper, who's broke after his latest loss at the racetrack, is threatening to get a job and go straight. He's dissuaded from doing so when Flood agrees to plan and bankroll a daring caper—stealing a million-dollar military payroll from a small-town bank where it's stored on certain weekends.

Laying the groundwork for the caper, Frank buys a service station in the quiet little town of San Felipe, and moves into a suburban house, with Kay recruited to pose as his wife. Meanwhile, Flood, although he professes to dislike violent crime ("I don't like being shot at"), recruits a gang of helpers with skills in safecracking, explosives, and other specialties that the job will require.

Frank and Kay try to maintain the fiction of a happy young married couple in the suburbs, though he grows stir crazy waiting out the time that Flood decreed was necessary

Kay (Mary Costa) and Frank (Rory Calhoun) find life in suburbia a bit of an ordeal in *The Big Caper*.

to establish them as well-liked local residents. Kay, meanwhile, is ready to break off her relationship with Flood, after a taste of a quieter life—and spending time with Frank— prove unexpectedly appealing to her.

Flood's carefully-laid plans for robbing the bank begin to unravel a day or two before the planned heist, when he and his cohorts arrive at Frank and Kay's house. Petty arguments among the conspirators, as well as the tension between Flood and Frank over Kay, threaten to unravel the precision timing and mutual trust needed to pull off the job. When Frank and Kay learn that, unbeknownst to the others, the high school they plan to blow up will be full of schoolchildren that night (rehearsing a play), they fear that it's too late to extricate themselves from a crime that has spiraled well beyond what they bargained for.

The little-known *The Big Caper* is a workmanlike thriller that tells a fast-moving story on a modest budget, with a cast boasting few marquee names. Lionel White's novel, published as a paperback original by Fawcett Crest in 1955, took place in Florida, rather than California. Although the locale and several character names have been changed, Martin Berkeley's screenplay is for the most part a faithful adaptation of the novel. After being submitted for Production Code approval, it underwent a few changes, as officials there were concerned that juvenile delinquents might be encouraged to mimic the acts of arson depicted. Revisions put additional emphasis on the function of explosives, and the level of expertise needed to use them. *The Big Caper* arrived in theaters one year after Stanley Kubrick's critically acclaimed *The Killing* (1956), also adapted from one of White's novels, *Clean Break*.

When the film was first announced, in the summer of 1955, Pine and Thomas were said to be envisioning John Payne in the lead. Instead, leading man Rory Calhoun returned to the Pine-Thomas stable ten years after getting an early career break in *Adventure Island*. Billed above the title here, he's well-cast as the edgy small-time criminal who may not yet be completely beyond redemption. By the time of this film's release, most of Calhoun's fans knew that he had had brushes with the law as a young man, and served a three-year prison sentence for robbery and auto theft.

James Gregory (1911–2002), familiar to latter-day audiences as Inspector Luger on TV's *Barney Miller*, offers a strong portrayal of boss-man Flood. As Frank remarks, Flood is most worrisome when he's offering a smile his associates would be wise not to trust. Actress-singer Mary Costa (born 1930) plays Kay's varied moods and emotions skillfully, without exaggeration. Costa is best-known for her musical contribution to *Sleeping Beauty* (1959); this film offers her a substantial acting role, but doesn't take advantage of her singing voice. She was at this time married to director and screenwriter Frank Tashlin.

Flood's band of associates are indeed a motley crew, animated by some lively performances. Not generally given to subtlety as an actor, Robert H. Harris (1911–1981) goes full-out as jittery, twitchy boozehound Zimmer, whom Frank describes as "the kind that starts fires for kicks." Given a ride around by town so that he can case San Felipe, Zimmer salivates at the sights of buildings that he longs to set ablaze, and is reduced to whiny pleading when he's denied the gin bottle for more than a few hours. Still, when push comes to shove, Frank's contempt for Zimmer leads him to underestimate his menace. Corey Allen (1934–2010) is not quite as manic as Harris, but radiates nervous intensity as muscle-bound, milk-drinking Roy, who quivers in fear when Flood is dissatisfied with his work, but can also commit a violent murder without flinching. Roxanne Arlen (1931–1989) beautifully embodies the bimbo Doll, described by Flood as "some cheap floozy Harry picked up in a bar," who foolishly tries to cut herself in on the action. Paul Picerni, who will soon be on the right side of the law as Agent Hobson on TV's *The Untouchables*, is another gang member.

Occasional touches of humor and irony add spice to the story, without detracting from the tension. The script and direction take a few satirical digs at the charms of life in the suburbs, contrasting the ensuing robbery with a chorus of schoolchildren nearby singing "America the Beautiful." Kay, the sexy girlfriend of a career crook, transforms herself overnight into a young Stepford Wife. She and Frank have the neighbors over for a game of Scrabble, and, when they get ready to call it a night, chirps, "Not till you taste this angel food cake!" Behind the façade, she's distinctly lacking in the skills expected of a 1950s housewife, leaving a sink piled with dirty dishes, and having to get a lesson in making hotcakes from Calhoun's Frank.

Director Robert Stevens (1920–1989) was best-known for his work in television, where he won an Emmy for his work on *Alfred Hitchcock Presents*. He frames some interesting shots in *The Big Caper*, including one of a man being pushed forcibly into a ravine with a road sign in the foreground that warns, "No Dumping." Martin Berkeley (1904–1979), author of the screenplay, was at this time practically a specialist in sci-fi and big-bug movies, having penned *Revenge of the Creature*, *Tarantula* (both 1955), and *The Deadly Mantis* (1957). According to an item in *Daily Variety* (September 4, 1956), Pine and Thomas allowed star Rory Calhoun to "make his debut as a motion picture director" by taking the reins for one scene that centered on his leading lady, Mary Costa.

Newspaper ads for *The Big Caper* strongly emphasized the sex appeal of Miss Costa,

Pressbook ad for *The Big Caper* promises gunplay, fistfights, and feminine pulchritude.

"the big blonde," whose character Kay, according to ad copy, "just likes people ... men-people!" The film's pressbook suggested that theater managers decorate their concession stands with "Wanted" posters borrowed from the local post office, especially those pertaining to bank robberies, "with appropriate signs calling attention to your 'Big Caper' playdate."

REVIEWS: "Arson, death by strangling, purposeless floggings, bombing of a school, a detailed study of the robbing of a bank vault, and tender romance are the diverse ingredients of this venture into crime.... The atmosphere of realism is spoiled by the overdrawn characters and the emphasis on unmotivated cruelty." *Motion Picture Daily*, April 16, 1957

"Other than Rory Calhoun's, the star and feature names aren't too familiar ... but all are satisfactorily cast to type so the meller [melodrama] entertainment ... is maintained.... Robert Stevens' direction, while handicapped at times by Martin Berkeley's script, still develops a growing suspense as the story moves toward the not unexpected payoff." *Variety*, April 3, 1957

Bailout at 43,000 (1957)

CAST: John Payne (*Maj. Paul Peterson*), Karen Steele (*Carol Peterson*), Paul Kelly (*Col. Hughes*), Richard Eyer (*Kit Peterson*), Constance Ford (*Frances Nolan*), Eddie Firestone (*Capt. Mike Cavallero*), Adam Kennedy (*Lt. Ed Simmons*), Gregory Gaye (*Dr. Franz Gruener*), Steven Ritch (*Maj. Irv Goldman*), Richard Crane (*Capt. Jack Nolan*), Barbara Eden (*Mike's Date*), Jack Chefe (*Headwaiter*), Bing Russell (*Flyer at Bar*), Bert Stevens (*Officer*)

CREW: Francis D. Lyon (*Director*), William C. Thomas, Howard B. Pine (*Producers*), Paul Monash (*Screenplay*), Lionel Lindon (*Director of Photography*), Albert Glasser (*Music Composer/Conductor*), Frank Sylos (*Art Director*), George Gittens (*Editor*), Alfred Kegerris (*Set Decorator*), Alvena Tomin (*Costumes*), Norman Pringle (*Makeup Artist*), Myrl Stoltz (*Hair Stylist*), Jerry Bos, Fay Moore (*Wardrobe*), Frank Fox (*Assistant Director*), Frederick Hartsook (*Dialogue Supervisor*), Hazel W. Hall (*Script Supervisor*), Fred Lau, Roger Heman (*Sound Recording*)

RELEASED May 1957. 78 minutes.

Korean War veteran Paul Peterson, back on active Air Force duty after a stint in civilian life, is on a team with the Air Research and Development Command, under the supervision of Colonel Hughes. The team is testing a new type of ejection seat that will allow pilots to safely bail out of a B-47 bomber at a height of some six miles above the ground. After doing as much testing as possible with crash dummies, the time has come to determine whether a live human can withstand the fall. Major Peterson, who has a wife, Carol, and a little boy, Kit, is both relieved that he isn't initially chosen to test the device, and simultaneously ashamed of that relief.

A malfunction during the first full test, in which the automatically-controlled parachute opens too early, leaves Captain Mike Cavallero hospitalized with a broken neck. Paul and his colleague, Lt. Ed Simmons, hope that their superior officer will call off the experiment, but Colonel Hughes is determined to press on.

The death of a pilot in a crash, which he might have survived had the ejector seat been ready to use, only serves to underscore the urgency of the work Peterson and his colleagues are doing. When Ed is sidelined with an attack of appendicitis, Paul is told he will be making the test the next day. After a panicky Carol tries to intercede, Colonel Hughes offers Paul the choice of backing out if he needs to do so. But Paul is determined to prove his bravery, and that his superior officer's faith in him is justified.

Something of a throwback to the Pine-Thomas programmers of the 1940s, this is another story about servicemen risking their lives in order to complete a dangerous assignment—not to mention, yet another drama playing on a fear of heights. It opens with a card thanking members of the real-life Air Force Research and Development Command for technical assistance and cooperation. The story was adapted from Paul Monash's teleplay, which aired in December 1955 as an episode of the anthology series *Climax*. The

Bill Thomas relaxes on the set of *Bailout at 43,000* with leading lady Karen Steele.

TV version starred a young Charlton Heston as Paul Peterson, with Richard Boone as Colonel Hughes.

While well-suited to a one-hour television show, the story thread here is a bit thin to sustain a 90-minute feature. However, the TV drama lacked the production resources brought to bear on this telling of the story. Performances are generally good, with Constance Ford (1923–1993) standing out in her brief appearances as a pilot's wife. It's fitting that Paul Kelly, after nearly a decade's association with the Dollar Bills, gave his final performance in a P-T feature. Bill Thomas would serve as a pallbearer at his November 1956 funeral. John Payne doesn't seem quite the type to play a man worried he's "gone soft" in peacetime. (According to columnist Sheilah Graham, Pine and Thomas had originally offered Payne's role to Richard Boone, who declined it.) Karen Steele (1931–1988) was borrowed from producer Samuel Goldwyn, Jr., with whom she was under contract at the time of filming.

Bailout at 43,000 was the recipient of a "Certificate of Award" from the Southern California Motion Picture Council, which designated it as "a picture of outstanding merit." This was the final feature film produced in the 1950s by the company that had become Pine-Thomas-Shane Productions.

REVIEWS: "A fair little thriller about parachute testing for jet bombers ... the acting of the cast is competent [although] Constance Ford is wasted...." *Motion Picture Daily*, April 26, 1957

"Fairly suspenseful.... Payne moves through his role with ease and assurance, while Karen Steele is okay in the rather thankless part of his wife. Film is last for the late Paul Kelly, and his performance here is a good one.... Lionel Lindon's camera work tops the list of good technical contributions." *Variety*, May 15, 1957

Cat Murkil and the Silks (1976)
a/k/a Cruisin' High

CAST: David Kyle (*Eddie "Cat" Murkil*), Steve Bond (*Joey Murkil*), Kelly Yaegermann (*Claudine*), Rhodes Reason (*Lt. Harder*), Meegan King (*Marble*), Don Carter (*Bumps*), Derrel Maury (*Punch*), Ruth Manning (*Mrs. Murkil*), Douglas McGrath (*Det. Al Lambert*), Mike Tucker (*Pluto*), Joe Renteria (*Carlos Garvanza*), John Ashton (*Coach Larkin*), Ricardo Militi (*Edward "Moss" Peters*), Jamie Jotelloh (*Spooner*), Gary Wild (*James "Bright" Sturgis*), Jackie Chapman (*Miss Plimpton*), Felicity Tagliabue (*Mrs. Plimpton*), Gregory Castillo (*Davila*), Ben Polando (*Garcia*), Buddy Kling (*Principal Leeds*), Lee Turnmire (*Mr. Foster*), Rich Evans (*Cutter*), Enoch Johnson (*Needle*), Doodles Weaver (*Kelso*), Vicki Risk (*Landlady*), Pat Geiger (*Mrs. Crocker*), Bill Long (*Watchman*), Myron Griffin (*Minister*), John Holbrook (*TV Announcer*)

CREW: John Bushelman (*Director*), William C. Thomas (*Producer/Screenplay*), Bruce Logan (*Photography*), Jeff Bushelman (*Editor*), Bernie Kaai Lewis (*Music*), Peter MacGregor-Scott (*Production Manager*), Larry Hilbrand (*Dialogue Director*), Buddy Kling (*Production Coordinator*), Miles Tilton (*Second Assistant Director*), Paul Hipp (*Camera Operator*), Ron Johnson (*Assistant Cameraman*), Brent Kruse (*Second Assistant Cameraman*), James DePerna (*Gaffer*), Brink Brydon (*Best Boy*), William Kaplan (*Sound Mixer*), Earl Sampson (*Boom Operator*), Bob McVay (*Grip*), Jeff Gilliam (*Best Boy*), Jean Said (*Script Supervisor*), Llandys Williams (*Wardrobe*), Pat Hutchence, Tina Lewis (*Makeup*), Gino Wernikoff (*Property Master*), Ron Stein (*Stunt Coordinator*), Roger George (*Special Effects*), Barbara Hoddus (*Production Secretary*), Jose Marquez (*Production Assistant*)

Song: "Slow Down, Baby": words and music, Mark Hollingsworth, Bernie Kaai Lewis, William C. Thomas

RELEASED July 1976. 103 minutes.

The Silks are a teenage gang in Los Angeles, specializing in mostly petty crimes like car stripping and shoplifting. When a showdown with a rival gang turns violent, Silks member Eddie Murkil, known as "Cat," takes advantage of the ensuing confusion to shoot and kill his own gang's leader, Punch. Cat steps into the shoes of the man he murdered, assuming leadership of the Silks while blaming Punch's death on their rivals.

Two younger members of the Silks, Moss and Bright, are assigned to avenge Punch's death by stabbing two members of the rival gang in a steamy shower room at the nearby school they attend. Lieutenant Harder investigates the crime, which becomes a murder case when Davila dies of his injuries. A school coach tentatively identifies Moss, but he produces an alibi when his terrified English teacher, Miss Plimpton, whose home the gang invaded, claims he was in class at the time.

Cat, feeling invincible after taking over leadership of the Silks, visits his older brother Joey in prison. Cat looks forward to teaming up with Joey, who is soon to be released. But

Joey fully intends to avoid any activities that might violate his parole. Angered, Cat tells Joey's wife Claudine, whom he wants for himself, that Joey wants nothing more to do with her.

When the rival gang counterattacks during a party, Cat panics and runs away, losing the respect and loyalty of his fellow Silks. Trying to take the place of his brother in Claudine's life, Cat is humiliated when she rebuffs him, and he is beaten by Joey's old rival, her new lover. Spiraling out of control, an armed Cat proceeds to unleash a violent revenge on those who have crossed him, just as brother Joey comes home from prison.

Half of the Pine-Thomas duo returned to film production after a nearly 20-year hiatus with this low-budget melodrama about gang violence in L.A. William C. Thomas both produced the film and wrote

David Kyle makes a rather unconvincing gang leader in *Cat Murkil and the Silks*.

the screenplay, and gives his late partner the tribute of calling this a Pine-Thomas production. The script depicts the tensions between the all-white Silks gang and their rival gang, whose members are Latino. Thomas, a member in good standing of ASCAP, even collaborated on "Slow Down, Baby," the picture's title song. Director John Bushelman (1915–2013) was more often employed as a film or sound editor.

Aside from an emphasis on action sequences, there's not much about *Cat Murkil and the Silks* that recalls the heyday of Pine-Thomas Productions. The film opens with a quote from then–Chief of the Los Angeles Police Department, Edward M. Davis: "Juvenile gang violence is a corrosive acid eating away at the structure of our society." Like many of the 1950s dramas about juvenile delinquency, *Cat Murkil and the Silks* presents itself as an expose of gang life, then proceeds to depict it in lavish detail that labels the film as drive-in exploitation. Elements not available to Pine and Thomas 20 years later are now acceptable on movie screens, and the film makes liberal use of profanity, racial epithets, gore, sex, and nudity to tell its story. It received an "R" rating from the Motion Picture Association of America.

Aside from the expected array of 70s lingo (jive, heavy, chicks, etc.), the dialogue also serves as an amusing time capsule of pop culture. One policeman is taunted by a gang member with, "You must think you're Kojak or something!" Joey's wife Claudine, eking out a dismal living as a dancer at the low-rent Kit Kat Club, says sarcastically of her sleazy working environment, "I wouldn't trade it for a date with Mick Jagger!" The policeman, of course, are all "pigs" to the young miscreants.

Casting is erratic. Baby-faced David Kyle, who receives top billing, is not credible as a gang leader. The young newcomer, his experience limited to a few TV commercials and extra work, later described *Cat Murkil* as "a horrible script," complaining that John Bushelman "did not give me one word of direction."[59] Be that as it may, Bill Thomas retained in his personal scrapbook a handwritten note from star Kyle, offering "many thanks for a marvelous opportunity. Especial salutations to Bill and John [Bushelman] for putting some magic in such a young career as mine." Some years later, Kyle turned his back on Hollywood, undergoing a religious conversion and beginning a new life as a minister under his birth name, David Kyle Foster.

For several of the younger players, this film is the only credit on their IMDb filmographies, and in some cases don't seem to be professional actors. One of the more recognizable performers, Derrel Maury (born 1954), is killed off in the first 20 minutes, while Steve Bond (born 1953), later a regular on TV's *General Hospital*, has more to do in the second half, as Cat's brother. A veteran publicity man like Thomas surely appreciated the PR value of Bond's then-recent nude centerfold in *Playgirl* magazine, although, as columnist Army Archerd noted in *Variety* (September 29, 1975), Bond would appear on movie screens "with threads."

Professionals Rhodes Reason and Ruth Manning are among the adult performers earning a paycheck here, and giving adequate performances. Actor Mike Tucker, seen as Pluto, a junior recruit to the Silks, is billed as Mike Turner in the closing credits. Likewise, actor Joe Renteria has his name spelled correctly in the beginning, and misspelled at the end. Bill Thomas' wife Louisa appears briefly as a clerk at the Department of Motor Vehicles.

Filming began in the summer of 1975, with additional shooting days in September and October. Thomas' company spent several days shooting in and around Santa Maria, California, using the local high school as its principal location. Shonda Holm Croly, who attended the school in the 1970s, recalled some years later that the production company set up a casting office at a local hotel, and recruited students on summer vacation to work as extras in the film. Base pay for the teenage atmosphere players was $15 a day, paid out in cash, with supplementary stipends for those who spoke a line of dialogue, or took part in one of the fight scenes.[60]

Cat Murkil and the Silks' original release mostly found it playing drive-ins, frequently on a double bill with Jack Hill's *Switchblade Sisters* (1975). Not a box office success under its original title, Thomas' film was reissued a year or so later, with some of the more violent scenes trimmed, and rechristened *Cruisin' High*. That title was retained for its videocassette release.

REVIEWS: "The film, in all respects save color printing, is dismally amateurish when not being gratuitously violent…. Script, direction, performances, scoring and photography are below going standard for even the most inexpensive claim to professional production. At 102 minutes, pic's running time seem[s] interminable." *Variety*, June 16, 1976

"The new P-T production … might well be a camp classic someday because of the inept acting of the youthful cast … has a high violence content [and] a fair share of laughs, not always intentional…." *Boxoffice*, June 21, 1976

High Seas Hijack (1977)

CAST: Tetsurô Tanba [Tamba] (*Capt. Munekata*), Hiroshi Fujioka (*Jiro Tate*), Peter Graves (*Elliott Rhoades*), Gigi Perreau (*Patricia Haber*), K. Amoha (*Samba*), Willy Dorcey

(*Zamba*), Tappei Shimokawa (*Terada*), Kei Suzuki (*Fukami*), Ken Saunders (*Kifal*), Hiroshi Kanai (*Dr. Hatsuyama*), Joe Shishudo (*Kusai*), Mizuho Suzuki (*Katsuragi*), Ryoki Uchida (*Nishizawa*), Yutaka Mizutani (*Munk*), Fumio Watanabe (*Tatsuya Iwado*)

CREW: Katsumune Ishida (*Director, Japan*), John Bushelman (*Director, U.S.*), Tomo-yuki Tanaka (*Executive Producer*), William C. Thomas (*Producer*), Yasuko Ono, Toshio Masuda (*Screenplay*), Koji Tanaka (*Original Story*), Osamu Tanaka (*Associate Producer*), Terayoshi Nakano (*Director of Special Effects*), Tsukuru Kaburagi (*Music*), Nobuo Ogawa (*Film Editor, Japan*), Hashino Muraki (*Art Director, Japan*), Shin Watarai (*Sound Recorder*), Toshio Takashima (*Lighting*), Takashi Nakai (*Stillman*), Ippei Imamura (*Assistant Director*), Hisayuki Murakami (*Unit Production Manager*), Reilly Jackson (*Dialogue Director, U.S.*), Normand Hole (*Art Director, U.S.*), Jeff Bushelman (*Film Editor, U.S.*)

A Japanese oil tanker, the *Arabian Light*, is hijacked by six armed men who make their way aboard by posing as shipwreck victims. Once they have assumed control of the ship, the hijackers explain that they represent a multinational organization called PAVDOR ("the organization to promote fair distribution of resources in the world"). The terrorists claim that Japan, the United States, and other prosperous countries have refused to lend assistance to other countries that are impoverished and that "the wealth of the world must be redistributed, by force if necessary."

Planting explosives among the ship's cargo of highly flammable oil, the hijackers issue their demands. The Japanese government must agree to detonate and destroy oil tanks at Kyama that represent one-sixth of the country's reserves, and broadcast the results on television. If this is not done by the deadline set by the hijackers, they will detonate the bombs on the *Arabian Light* at the Tokyo coastline, causing mass destruction and a huge death toll. Dealing harshly with the crew of the *Arabian Light*, the terrorists show that they are quite willing to resort to violence if their orders are not followed.

Patricia Hagan, an ambitious young journalist bored with her unimportant assignments for the Tokyo bureau of FBS, an American television network, is eager to pursue the story of the hijacking, calling it "potentially the biggest story to hit this town since Hiroshima!" Her boss, bureau chief Elliott Rhoades, urges her to use caution, but allows her to proceed.

Facing an impossible choice, officials of the Japanese Army Reserve call on members of the news media to announce (falsely) that Japan will destroy the oil tanks as demanded. But while seemingly making the necessary preparations, Japanese officials are meeting with motion picture special effects experts to determine if the detonation can be faked for the television broadcast, leading to the safe release of the *Arabian Light* hostages without crippling the country's economy. Working her informants, and doing her best to infiltrate the government reserve at Kyama, Patricia realizes that the story being given to the media is false, and keeps investigating despite being warned of the danger to herself.

High Seas Hijack was an Americanized version of the Toho studio's 1975 thriller *Tôkyô-wan enjô* ("The Burning of Tokyo Bay"). The original film offered action footage and special effects that would have been difficult to replicate for a low-budget American film. Top-billed in the original film was actor Tetsurô Tamba (1922–2006), playing the calm, intelligent captain of the oil tanker.

Though Pine-Thomas publicity depicted it as a co-production with Toho, the

A rare ad mockup for *High Seas Hijack,* Bill Thomas' Americanized version of a Japanese thriller.

American contribution in the finished film consists primarily of a small amount of additional footage with actors Peter Graves (1926–2010) and Gigi Perreau (born 1941), neither of whom seems to have left Southern California to complete the assignment. Graves, apparently hired for one day of shooting, makes his entrance about 15 minutes into the film. His handful of brief scenes, emerging at ten- to 15-minute intervals for the remainder of the running time, have all been shot on one of two sets—a nondescript office, and a modest studio backdrop from which he delivers his live newscasts for the FBS network. The screenplay depicts him as a sexist boss who, discussing the "legwork" Patricia will need to do, admiringly takes in her legs and remarks, "I can't think of anyone better qualified." Later, as if unsure he's been sufficiently offensive, he terms Patricia "the employee who put the broad into broadcasting."

Former child star Perreau, cast as the tenacious young reporter, has a little more to do. She is cut into a few scenes already shot for the Japanese market, including one in which an insert shot places her at a press conference. Her shots outdoors, though not outrageously mismatched with the Japanese footage, still look more like Southern California than the outskirts of Tokyo. Her outdoor footage finds her meeting with her informants, or trying to infiltrate the alleged bombing site at Kyama. Perreau told syndicated columnist Dorothy Manners (September 28, 1976) that she was initially uncertain about taking the job, because of the violent content. "But my own kids saw it and didn't blink an eye," she said. John Bushelman, who'd directed *Cat Murkil and the Silks*, was called upon to shoot the additional scenes for American release, and edit them into Toho's film.

Only a few months later, *Daily Variety* (August 24, 1976) reported that Pine-Thomas "has completed postproduction on *High Seas Hijack* … and is now seeking a distrib[utor]." Newspaper ads promised ticket buyers "a daring suicidal mission with a nation held in ransom." However, the film never made it into wide release, and played few, if any, dates outside drive-ins.

SHORT SUBJECTS

In 1942, the motion picture industry's War Activities Committee announced plans to release a series of patriotic short films, in conjunction with the United States Office of War Information. Major studios, including Paramount, agreed to take part in the project, with the films to be produced on a nonprofit basis. Pine and Thomas were assigned to the project by studio executives, and contributed four shorts. According to *Motion Picture Herald* (August 1, 1942), "All theatres, regardless of run, will pay the same price, $1 per day per short. The shorts are available to all theatres and all intervals of clearance have been waived."

After screening the first two (*A Letter from Bataan* and *We Refuse to Die*), Paramount studio chief Y. Frank Freeman, in a letter to Pine and Thomas, wrote, "I do not see how a better job could have been done. Both are outstanding in their particular fields." He congratulated the producers on "delivering such a potent message at a time when it is most needed."[61]

While their experience with modest budgets was undoubtedly a factor in Paramount's choice of Pine and Thomas to produce the shorts, they turned out a product that won critical acclaim nonetheless. Their film *We Refuse to Die* was a nominee for the Academy Awards, as Best Documentary of 1942.

Though not part of the Paramount Victory Shorts series, Pine and Thomas were also commissioned by the DuPont Company to make another patriotic short film, *Soldiers of the Soil*. It was made available to theaters for free screenings, and used in classrooms as well.

A Letter from Bataan (1942)

CAST: Richard Arlen (*Johnny Lewis*), Susan Hayward (*Mary Lewis*), Jimmy Lydon (*Chuck Lewis*), Joe Sawyer (*Roy*), Janet Beecher (*Mrs. Lewis*), Keith Richards (*Pete*), Esther Dale (*Mrs. Jackson*), Will Wright (*Postman*)

CREW: William H. Pine (*Director*), William C. Thomas (*Producer*), Maxwell Shane (*Screenplay*), Fred W. Jackman, Jr. (*Director of Photography*), F. Paul Sylos (*Art Director*), Ben Berk (*Set Dresser*), Howard A. Smith (*Editor*), Earl Sitar (*Sound Recording*), Daniele Amfitheatrof (*Music Score*)

13 minutes. [Paramount Victory Short, #T2-1]

American soldiers Johnny and Pete fall victim to enemy gunfire while on anti-aircraft duty in the Philippines. After Pete succumbs at the scene, Johnny is transported to a military hospital, where he dies due to complications from a leg amputation. Both suffered from night blindness (due to a lack of proper nutrition), which contributed to their vulnerability while on duty.

Johnny's family, including the wife he married just before enlisting, receives his final letter home, in which he explains how "lack of food and equipment and medicine" are hindering soldiers' efforts to win victory. A ghostly apparition of Johnny hovers as his family receives the letter, explaining how civilians must conserve rubber, scrap metal, and other items needed in the war effort, and not hoard food. Just as the family finishes reading the letter, a telegram brings the news of Johnny's death.

REVIEWS: "An excellent screenplay by Maxwell Shane, as well as the capable direction of William H. Pine and the high production values accorded the subject by William C. Thomas have made ... an impressive and convincing appeal that drives itself home to the heart of the spectator." *Showmen's Trade Review*, October 3, 1942

"The need for conservation and self-sacrifice by the civilian population ... is illustrated dramatically in this short. The film, done in a manner that would do justice to a feature production, conveys the gravity of its message with a simplicity and a clarity that are most commendable.... This short deserves heavy playing time in every theater in the land." *Film Daily*, October 8, 1942

We Refuse to Die (1942)

CAST: Barry Sullivan (*Paul*), Henry Victor (*Reinhard Heydrich*), Ellen Drew (*Kathy*); Lionel Royce, Henry Rowland

CREW: William H. Pine (*Director*), William C. Thomas (*Producer*), Maxwell Shane (*Screenplay*)

14 minutes. [Paramount Victory Short, #T2-2]

The citizens of Lidice, Czechoslovakia suffer under Nazi occupation, with food scarce, communication with the outside world restricted, and a violent response to any resistance. Reinhard Heydrich, known as "The Hangman," rules over the entire town, until he is killed by a bomb under the cover of night. In retaliation, the Nazis order the village and its people destroyed. Once the men of Lidice have been machine-gunned to death, its women and children sent to labor camps, and the town itself burned, a German general sent to oversee the massacre dreams that the men killed come back to life. The film's narrator, Paul, one of the victims, is seen telling the Nazi, "You meant to wipe Lidice from the memory of man. In your stupid arrogance, you have made us *live*. By this very outrage you have only fanned higher the flames of purpose in the lands where men are still free. Night and day, minute after minute, they prepare your destruction...."[62]

Newsreel footage and stock shots from previous Paramount films are used to flesh out the story. Maxwell Shane subsequently adapted his screenplay for a radio drama starring Madeleine Carroll and Joseph Schildkraut.

REVIEWS: "A moving reenactment of the story of Lidice, Czechoslovakian village utterly destroyed by the Nazis.... Much of its power stems from the acting of Barry Sullivan ... who narrates the story as one of the villagers." *Motion Picture Herald*, October 10, 1942

"Here is a subject that grips, that entertains, that projects a strong appeal to the spectator.... Mere words won't do the subject justice; one must see it to appreciate its power. Director William H. Pine and Producer William C. Thomas have carried out their respective assignments magnificently." *Showmen's Trade Review*, October 3, 1942

The Price of Victory (1942)

CAST: Vice-President Henry A. Wallace
CREW: William H. Pine (*Director*), Howard J. Green (*Adaptation*)
13 minutes. [Paramount Victory Short, #T2-3]

Vice-President Henry A. Wallace delivers an abridged version of a speech he originally presented to the Free World Association in May 1942. "Through the leaders of the Nazi revolution, Satan now is trying to lead the common man of the world back into slavery and darkness.... We shall fight for a complete peace, as well as for a complete victory."

REVIEWS: "The Vice-President seems quite at ease before the cameras, speaks in a manner that compels full attention.... William Pine and William Thomas deserve credit for fine production treatment, and Pine has performed a capable directorial job." *Showmen's Trade Review*, November 21, 1942

"Paramount has made a powerful and moving short that should do as much as any motion picture possibly can to crystalize the objectives of this war so that we can all know for what we are fighting." *The Exhibitor*, December 2, 1942

The Aldrich Family Gets in the Scrap (1943)

CAST: Jimmy Lydon (*Henry Aldrich*), John Litel (*Sam Aldrich*), Olive Blakeney (*Alice Aldrich*), Charles Smith (*Dizzy Stevens*), Martha O'Driscoll (*Mary Aldrich*), Diana Lynn (*Phyllis Michael*)
CREW: Frank McDonald (*Director*), William H. Pine, William C. Thomas (*Producers*), Howard J. Green (*Screenplay*)
11 minutes. [Paramount Victory Short, #T2-4]

Appointed head of the local salvage committee, Sam Aldrich leads the effort to have Centerville citizens collect more scrap metal than the residents of neighboring towns. Centerville teenagers compete, boys against girls, in a race to see which will be awarded a silver cup for the largest collection, with Henry Aldrich leading the boys' team ("The Minute Men.")

According to an article in *The Exhibitor* (March 17, 1943), two cities in New Jersey, Camden and Paterson, competed to host the film's opening: "The city collecting the most tin can salvage during the period of February 15 to March 15 is to be awarded a miniature Hollywood world premiere, with leading government officials and screen celebrities present."

REVIEWS: "The business of collecting scrap for use in the war against the Axis gets a boost from the Aldrich family.... The picture, a Pine-Thomas production, serves its purpose entertainingly." *Film Daily*, March 8, 1943

"Better than a hundred written appeals ... this eleven-minute subject, through its average-folk characterizations and humorous situations, impresses one with the importance of 'getting in the scrap.'" *Showmen's Trade Review*, March 6, 1943

Soldiers of the Soil (1943)

CAST: Carroll Nye (*David Landis*), Russell Hayden (*John Landis*), Irving Bacon (*Samuel Landis*), Fay Helm (*Mary Landis*), Mady Correll (*Grace Landis*), Teddy Infuhr (*Joey Landis*); Grant Withers, Edward Earle

CREW: William Berke (*Director*), William H. Pine, William C. Thomas (*Producers*), L.B. Merman (*Associate Producer*), William S. Dutton, Maxwell Shane (*Screenplay*)

40 minutes.

Marine Sergeant David Landis returns to his family's farm after being wounded at Guadalcanal. His loved ones are grieved to learn that his injuries left him blinded. David's brother John feels compelled to enlist in the Marines, although their older brother Richard tells him, "Everybody can't fight. Food's important, too. Your place is on the farm."[63]

David is asked to address his church congregation, and describe his war experiences. As he speaks, flashbacks show his how his family struggled to establish and sustain their farm. David tells the members of the congregation, "We, the soldiers of America, fighting for you abroad, salute you, the farmers of America—fighting for us at home! You are soldiers of the soil!"[64] Afterwards, John thanks his brother, and says he will continue his work on the farm.

This short financed by the DuPont Company dramatizes the critical role played by farmers in the war effort.

REVIEW: "An inspiring message to the farmers of America ... excellent cast." *Film Daily*, September 27, 1943

"Highly recommended for secondary and college classes in agriculture and social studies, and for school assembly and adult meetings concerned with the importance of agriculture in winning the war." *Educational Screen*, November 1943

APPENDIX I:
PINE-THOMAS PLAYERS

Even a cursory review of Pine and Thomas' films makes it obvious that the producers were loyal to some of their favorite performers. This was especially true in the 1940s, when the rapid-fire production of B pictures called for actors who could produce good work amidst sometimes challenging circumstances. While they had no established stock company, per se, Thomas wrote, "Whenever possible, Bill Pine and I used players who worked competently and congenially for us in earlier pictures.... I knew their work and they knew my ways."[1]

Below are brief biographical sketches of actors who appeared in at least eight Pine-Thomas films. The producers' first star, Richard Arlen, holds the record for most appearances, appearing in 13 P-T features, and one short film. He's not far ahead of leading lady Jean Parker, who racked up roles in an even dozen. Both were in from the beginning, playing the starring parts in *Power Dive* (1941). The last of the prolific Pine-Thomas players to arrive on the scene was actor John Payne, who would become their most frequently used action star of the 1950s.

Aside from booking the same star players, Pine and Thomas also found work multiple times for some of their favorite character actors, including Will Wright and Ralph Sanford. Others who appeared in at least five Pine-Thomas films included Roger Pryor, Dick Purcell, Byron Foulger, Byron Barr, and Grant Withers.

Richard Arlen

BORN: September 1, 1899, St. Paul, Minnesota
DIED: March 28, 1976, North Hollywood, Calif.

Born as Sylvanus Richard Mattimore, Arlen entered the motion picture industry during the silent era. Having served in the Royal Canadian Flying Corps during World War I, he maintained a lifelong interest in aviation.

Arlen purportedly received his first break in motion pictures by breaking a limb. "He was delivering some film to the old David Griffith studios on a motorcycle when he had an accident and broke his leg. He delivered the film, and went to a hospital where studio officials called to thank him. And because he was out of a job, he was put on the

Three of the Dollar Bills' favorite players: (left to right) Chester Morris, Jean Parker and Richard Arlen.

rolls as an extra."[2] Handsome and personable, he was soon entrusted with larger roles. In 1927, Arlen had one of the biggest successes of his career with the aviation drama *Wings*, co-starring Buddy Rogers and Clara Bow. It was on the set of that film that Arlen (already divorced after a brief first marriage) met his second wife, actress Jobyna Ralston. They divorced in 1946.

Bill Thomas first became friendly with Arlen while doing publicity for the actor's Paramount film *Island of Lost Souls* (1932). Arlen's commitment to appear in the first Pine-Thomas films was a key factor in the producers' success getting started. Some years later, Arlen said good-naturedly, "The reason they wanted me was that they wanted to make three air films first, and I just happened to have an air school and a few planes lying around. They wanted an actor who could furnish his own propellers."[3]

To some, Richard Arlen was old news by 1940, especially in a town always to ready to promote "new faces." Yet, as syndicated columnist Hedda Hopper pointed out (August 13, 1940), Arlen "does six pictures a year at Universal, makes around $90,000, has four months vacation, and no worry." She noted that he continued to be a ticket seller: "Just give him a good part and watch his smoke; he has a following."

Journalist Robbin Coons described Arlen as "a durable fellow who seemingly will be around as long as scripts call for two-fisted characters." Coons added, "He never studied to be an actor and never expected to be one. But when he got out of the University of Pennsylvania he gravitated to Hollywood and cracked the movies. He did some 'jazz age' and 'flaming youth' silents, and crashed the big time in *Wings*.... He's brushing 40—

or has brushed it—and he's still a fellow who gets around on the screen, fast, in action pictures."[4]

After working in several Pine-Thomas films, Arlen told a journalist that it had been a learning experience. "The point is, they've got no time to remove wrinkles from actors' faces with fancy lighting. They can't wait for an actor to learn his lines.... They haven't even got time to monkey with stunt men."[5] An actor like Arlen who could easily handle most of his own action scenes was a double-barreled asset to the Dollar Bills.

By the mid–1940s, however, Arlen was itching to break out of B movies, and proclaimed that he would accept no more such assignments. He starred on Broadway in the 1945 comedy *Too Hot for Maneuvers,* but the show was a flop, closing after five performances. Though he continued to work in films, he had little success getting beyond lower-budgeted features. In 1948, he returned to the Pine-Thomas fold, starring in *Speed to Spare,* and, a few years later, accepted a supporting role in *The Blazing Forest.*

Like several other Pine-Thomas alumni, Arlen appeared frequently in the modestly budgeted 1960s Westerns of producer A.C. Lyles. Lyles, who'd served as Pine-Thomas' publicity man, learned well from his former bosses, and adapted many of their principles to making inexpensive pictures. According to Lyles, he had been working in the Paramount mailroom when he first met Arlen. The actor, impressed with the young upstart, had said, "Some day you'll be a big producer—and when you are I want to be in every picture you ever make."[6]

Arlen died of emphysema in 1976. He was survived by third wife Margaret, whom he met on a Pine-Thomas shoot. Other survivors included a daughter and a son, as well as two grandchildren and two great-grandchildren.

PINE-THOMAS FILMOGRAPHY: *Power Dive* (1941); *Forced Landing* (1941); *Flying Blind* (1941); *Torpedo Boat* (1942); *Wildcat* (1942); *A Letter from Bataan* (1942 short); *Wrecking Crew* (1942); *Aerial Gunner* (1943); *Alaska Highway* (1943); *Submarine Alert* (1943); *Minesweeper* (1943); *Timber Queen* (1944); *Speed to Spare* (1948); *The Blazing Forest* (1952)

Edward Earle

BORN: July 16, 1882, Toronto, Canada
DIED: December 15, 1972, Woodland Hills, California

Earle was acting in films almost as soon as there were films in which to act, making his screen debut in 1913. He became a popular leading man of the mid– to late 1910s, but by the time sound pictures came along, he was in his mid–40s and had transitioned to featured and character parts. Most of his assignments in Pine-Thomas films were minor supporting roles, often as authority figures, and he sometimes appeared unbilled. He drew a meatier featured assignment in *Alaska Highway.*

Earle was a frequent television player in the 1950s, playing guest roles in series including *The Bob Cummings Show* and *Death Valley Days,* and also took part in Los Angeles theater until his retirement from acting in the early 1960s. He described his typical character type as "playing doctors, lawyers and bankers. They always pick me for the refined gentleman type."[7]

Off-screen, Earle, a hobbyist painter, was co-owner of the Artist's Supply Shop at the Hollywood Farmers' Market. At the time of his death in 1972, the 90-year-old Earle was a resident at the Motion Picture Country Home.

PINE-THOMAS FILMOGRAPHY: *Power Dive* (1941); *Aerial Gunner* (1943); *Alaska Highway* (1943); *Submarine Alert* (1943); *Soldiers of the Soil* (1943 short); *Tornado* (1943); *The Navy Way* (1944); *Double Exposure* (1944); *They Made Me a Killer* (1946); *Swamp Fire* (1946); *Big Town Scandal* (1948); *The Blazing Forest* (1952)

Rhonda Fleming

BORN: August 10, 1923, Hollywood, California

Pine-Thomas' last important redheaded leading lady, Rhonda Fleming (born Marilyn Louis) began playing small parts in films while still a teenager attending Beverly Hills High School. Her mother, Effie Graham, had been a performer herself, working with Al Jolson in the 1914-15 Broadway musical *Dancing Around*.

Young Marilyn was discovered by well-known Hollywood agent Henry Willson. She signed a contract with producer David O. Selznick in 1943; her first important film role came in Alfred Hitchcock's *Spellbound* (1945). As Miss Fleming later recalled, Hitchcock "said I'd be portraying a nymphomaniac, and I ran home to tell my family. We looked the word up in the dictionary and were pretty shocked."[8] Though she'd originally aspired to be a singer, few of her movie roles took advantage of her musical ability.

Her association with Pine-Thomas began when the producers borrowed her services from Selznick to co-star in *Adventure Island*. Three years later, she returned to the fold with *The Eagle and the Hawk*. In November 1951, having successfully completed her starring assignments in *Crosswinds* and *Hong Kong*, she signed for three more films with Pine-Thomas. Most of her P-T films would be opposite either John Payne or Ronald Reagan.

Married to interior decorator Tom Lane while she was still a teenager, Miss Fleming was granted a divorce from him while *Adventure Island* was in release. She would go on to marry five more times, and was widowed from spouse Darol Carlson in 2017.

Frequently dubbed the "Queen of Technicolor," it was an accolade Miss Fleming didn't especially value, as she would have preferred to be acknowledged for her acting. According to Carol Thomas Pantages, even though Miss Fleming was a vision to behold on the motion picture screen, it fell short of capturing the way she looked in person: "She was breathtakingly beautiful."[9]

Her movie career slowing by the early 1960s, Miss Fleming continued to work in television guest appearances. Her final feature film appearance (to date) came in *The Nude Bomb* (1980), for which her then-husband Ted Mann served as executive producer. In later years, disturbed by the lack of resources she had found when supporting her sister's bout with cancer, Miss Fleming and Mann made substantial charitable gifts to UCLA. The result was the Rhonda Fleming Mann Resource Center for Women with Cancer, opened in 1994.

PINE-THOMAS FILMOGRAPHY: *Adventure Island* (1947); *The Eagle and the Hawk* (1950); *The Last Outpost* (1951); *Crosswinds* (1951); *Hong Kong* (1952); *Tropic Zone* (1953); *Those Redheads from Seattle* (1953); *Jivaro* (1954)

Robert Lowery

BORN: October 17, 1913, Kansas City, Missouri
DIED: December 26, 1971, Hollywood, California

Born Robert Larkin Hanks, he grew up in Kansas City, Missouri, where he regularly demonstrated his athletic prowess, playing baseball and football. A sports injury resulted in him considering other activities. Musically talented (his mother had been a concert pianist), he aspired to be a singer. Moving to Hollywood in the mid–1930s, he played uncredited bits in two 1936 films, *Come and Get It* and *Great Guy*, before being signed to a contract by 20th Century–Fox.

While he never attained the heights of stardom in A films, Lowery spent much of the 1940s playing leads in B films, establishing a reputation as reliable and professional. During that decade, he racked up credits in low-budget pictures at Columbia, Monogram, and PRC, among others. Making his Pine-Thomas debut in 1944, Lowery was kept busy with three assignments. By August, he'd signed for three more, with the first announced as "High Man" (ultimately released as *High Powered*). In October 1946, *Daily Variety* reported that the busy actor had eight movies awaiting release, including four for Pine-Thomas. He played reporter Pete Ryan in two of P-T's "Big Town" series.

According to his son, Bob Hanks, Lowery "didn't really take acting very seriously," adding that among his primary motivators for working so much were his alimony payments and "a taste for expensive cars." Lowery's approach to the work, his son noted, was down-to-earth and uncomplicated; a favorite piece of advice he gave about acting was, "Keep your feet in the marks and pick up your paycheck."[10]

On-screen and off, Lowery was a ladies' man. "Many women fell all over him," said his son. The actor was married three times, first in 1941 to Vivian Wilcox, described by *Daily Variety* (August 23, 1943) as a "former Earl Carroll showgirl." During their marriage, the new Mrs. Lowery played a featured role in *Criminal Investigator* (1942), which starred Lowery. The couple separated in the summer of 1943, and the marriage ended in divorce the following year. In 1947, Lowery married actress Barbara "Rusty" Farrell, an even shorter union; she filed for divorce a year later, charging him with cruelty. When he was unencumbered, Hanks said, his father would "always have a gorgeous new girlfriend."

Not all of Lowery's derring-do was confined to soundstages, according to a column item in *Daily Variety* (January 8, 1946): "Just like a Pine-Thomas leading man in action, Bob Lowery took a left hook swung by a quarrelsome character outside a Sunset Boulevard café the other night and laid his assailant low." After *Jungle Flight* (1947), Lowery temporarily ended his association with Pine-Thomas, going on to other roles including that of Batman in a 1949 Columbia serial. A few years later, a supporting character in *Crosswinds* (1951) was Lowery's final P-T assignment.

Eight years after they'd co-starred in Pine-Thomas' *The Navy Way*, Lowery married Jean Parker. According to *Variety* (July 2, 1952), Lowery and Parker's "secret marriage" took place in Miami, Florida on May 29, 1951. The pair teamed up for a Los Angeles production of *Born Yesterday*, with Lowery giving a performance the *Los Angeles Times'* Katherine Von Blon (May 21, 1952) called "terrific … his was a realistic, down-to-earth portrayal, spiked with humor."

He continued to star in B movies into the early 1950s, but as the decade wore on he increasingly turned his attention to television, which had become a more reliable source of work. In 1956, he was cast in a leading role as Big Tim Champion in the NBC series *Circus Boy*. The show moved to ABC for an abbreviated second season, ending its run after 49 episodes. Also active on stage during this period, Lowery won strong reviews in 1955 for his performance as Lt. Greenwald in a touring company of *The Caine Mutiny Court Martial*, co-starring William Bendix.

During the 1966-67 season, he had a recurring role in the CBS sitcom *Pistols 'n' Petticoats*. His final film performance came in the Doris Day comedy *The Ballad of Josie*, released in 1967. Although he played Day's husband, the part was short-lived, as his drunken lout of a character met his maker less than ten minutes into the film. In his later years, when not busy with acting assignments, Lowery operated a travel agency.

Lowery died on December 26, 1971, at his Los Angeles apartment, collapsing from an apparent heart attack while on the phone with his mother. Summoned by Lowery's mother, the police found the actor already dead upon their arrival. Though all of his marriages had ended in either divorce or separation, his two surviving ex-wives attended his funeral.

Noting Lowery's busy career, his Associated Press obituary quoted a friend as saying, "Hell, for a while there it seemed like he was in a picture every week."[11]

PINE-THOMAS FILMOGRAPHY: *The Navy Way* (1944); *Dark Mountain* (1944); *Dangerous Passage* (1944); *High Powered* (1945); *They Made Me a Killer* (1946); *I Cover Big Town* (1947); *Danger Street* (1947); *Jungle Flight* (1947); *Crosswinds* (1951)

Chester Morris

BORN: February 16, 1901, New York City, New York
DIED: September 11, 1970, New Hope, Pa.

Though Morris (born as John Chester Brooks Morris) was a native of New York City, the family subsequently relocated to Mount Vernon, New York. Show business was in his blood. His mother was a comedienne billed as Etta Hawkins; his father, William Morris, was a successful stage actor who often worked with impresario David Belasco. Morris studied at the New York School of Fine Arts.

He earned his first credited screen role, while still a teenager, in *An Amateur Orphan* (1917). Morris skipped classes so as to work (for $5 a week) in his first motion picture. According to a later profile, "The first his parents knew of it was when the picture was released … and the theatre manager billed him as a local boy who'd made good on the screen."[12] His first Broadway appearance came when he supported Lionel Barrymore in *The Copperhead* (1918).

In the late 1920s, Morris began acting steadily in films. He was nominated for an Academy Award as Best Actor for his performance as a gangster in *Alibi* (1929). He was soon established as a leading actor, his appearance in the prison drama *The Big House* (1930) being among his best-received.

In the 1940s, Morris would play his most recognizable role in a series of "Boston Blackie" films for Columbia. Interspersed with those assignments (the series ultimately continued through 14 installments), were eight films for Pine-Thomas. For P-T, Morris typically played seemingly carefree, flippant men who failed to take much seriously, but invariably rose to the occasion when danger or crisis demanded. Off-screen, Morris was an accomplished amateur magician who appeared in hundreds of USO shows during World War II.

Morris was married twice, first to actress Suzanne Kilbourne in 1926, with whom he had a son and a daughter. Fourteen years later, they were divorced. A few days later, he married second wife Lillian Kenton Barker; the couple had a son, Kenton, in 1944.

After making his last film for Pine-Thomas in 1944, Morris would appear primarily in the Boston Blackie series until it wound down in 1949. He also essayed the character in a short-lived 1944 radio series. Little seen in 1950s films (though he played an evil hypnotist in AIP's 1956 drive-in favorite *The She-Creature*), Morris was active on Broadway in the 1960s, appearing in *Advise and Consent* (1960–61) and *The Subject Was Roses* (1965–66). He co-starred with Patrick O'Neal and Phyllis Newman in *Diagnosis: Unknown*, a medical mystery drama seen on CBS-TV in the summer of 1960. Asked in the mid–1960s (his own as well as the century's) whether he planned to retire anytime soon, Morris said, "Lord, no. I have too many people to support."[13]

Morris played his last film part shortly before his death, in *The Great White Hope* (1970). By then, he had been diagnosed with stomach cancer, though he continued to work on stage as long as possible. At the time of his death in September 1970, he was appearing in a Pennsylvania production of *The Caine Mutiny Court Martial*. His death was attributed to an overdose of barbiturates.

PINE-THOMAS FILMOGRAPHY: *No Hands on the Clock* (1941); *I Live on Danger* (1942); *Wrecking Crew* (1942); *Aerial Gunner* (1943); *High Explosive* (1943); *Tornado* (1943); *Gambler's Choice* (1944); *Double Exposure* (1944)

Jean Parker

BORN: August 11, 1915, Deer Lodge, Montana
DIED: November 30, 2005, Woodland Hills, California

Pine-Thomas' favorite leading lady of the 1940s was born as Lois May Green, daughter of Andrew and Pearl Burch Green. As a teenager, with her parents both unemployed and struggling financially, she was adopted by a family living in Pasadena.

Miss Parker was brought to the attention of MGM executives by Louis B. Mayer's secretary, Ida Koverman, who spotted a newspaper picture of the pretty teenager after she won a poster design contest while still a high schooler. (Though she was said to have appeared atop a float in the Tournament of Roses Parade with her winning poster, the actress later told film historian Dan Van Neste, "That was made up by the studio publicity people.")[14]

Said syndicated columnist Robbin Coons (July 11, 1933), she was tested for MGM cameras with the instruction, "Just talk and walk around…. They gave her no lines; so she talked about her pets—her goldfish, her dog, her cat—for five minutes." The personality test impressed executives, who signed her to a contract so quickly that she had to complete her high-school education on the MGM lot.

On loanout to RKO, the up-and-coming young actress played one of her first important roles as Beth in *Little Women* (1933). After less than two years at MGM, the still-teenaged Parker received star billing for the first time in *Have a Heart* (1934), studio publicity telling audiences, "You made her a star!" But the studio was reportedly not pleased when their young contract player eloped with her first husband at the age of 20. Even in her 20s, Miss Parker was a plainspoken woman who, as her son Bob Hanks later said, "was honest with people," sometimes to her detriment. By the late 1930s, she was freelancing, and soon found her best employment offers came from Poverty Row studios.

During the 1940s, Miss Parker worked almost constantly in B movies, many of her assignments at Poverty Row studios like Monogram and PRC. She worked with a variety of interesting co-stars during this period, including Laurel and Hardy (The *Flying Deuces*), John Carradine (*Bluebeard*), and Lon Chaney (*Dead Man's Eyes*). At Monogram, she

Jean Parker, pictured with then-husband Doug Dawson (right), enjoys dinner with Bill Thomas.

played the title character in *Detective Kitty O'Day* (1944) and a sequel the following year, *Adventures of Kitty O'Day*.

Before Pine-Thomas Productions was formed, Miss Parker made an impression on Bill Thomas when she went on a publicity tour for *Santa Fe Trail* (1940). Seeing that only Errol Flynn received a more enthusiastic reaction from the public than Parker, he concluded that she still had more drawing power than other studios realized. Her work in P-T's first film, *Power Dive*, led to an ongoing association with the company. By one account, "Pine and Thomas customarily let Jean design and buy her own clothes and keep them after a picture is finished. The bills are split fifty-fifty, with the result that the producers get off cheap and Jean has one of the hugest wardrobes anywhere."[15]

Like her frequent co-star Richard Arlen, Jean Parker not only acted in Pine-Thomas films with an aviation theme, but had a real-life interest in the field. In the early 1940s, she and then-husband Doug Dawson owned and operated a flight service in Palm Springs. The Japanese attack on Pearl Harbor in December 1941 indirectly led to the demise of their business, as most of their planes were commandeered for use in the war effort. Aside from Arlen, Miss Parker's other most frequent co-star at Pine-Thomas was Chester Morris. "Everyone wondered which actor I had a crush on," she said years later, "Arlen or Morris. I liked them both but not in that way."[16]

Off-screen, Parker was married four times. Miss Parker separated from her first husband, newspaperman George MacDonald, in April 1939, and was granted an uncontested divorce from him in January 1940. In early 1941, Miss Parker announced her plans to marry H. Dawson Sanders, known professionally as radio commentator Douglas Dawson. They were wed in mid–February, but she filed for divorce in 1942. In 1944, she wed Dr. Curtis Grotter, described in Hedda Hopper's syndicated column (August 25, 1944) as "formerly [a] foreign newspaper correspondent and now in the insurance business in Hollywood."

Professionally, her time continued to be devoted mostly to B movies. When her initial contract with Pine-Thomas was completed, she signed on for more. Ultimately she made 11 films for the unit in a period spanning less than five years. Carol Thomas Pantages, who knew her then, recalled that, like Rhonda Fleming, she was a beautiful woman who, while photographing well, looked even better in person.

Though they had known each other for several years, it was in Pine-Thomas' *The Navy Way* (1944) that Miss Parker first co-starred with actor Robert Lowery, who would later become her fourth husband and the father of her son. While there was "a lot of flirtation" between the two on the set of *The Navy Way*, according to their son Bob Hanks, nothing came of it at the time; she was still married to Dr. Grotter.

After World War II, Miss Parker was burned out on B movies, and wished to work in the theater. In early 1949, she was back on the West Coast with a touring company of "Born Yesterday," playing the starring part of Billie Dawn. She had deviated from the typical pattern by delving into stage work after her motion picture success, noting, "What one gains in pictures shouldn't be underrated. Films will give an actor polish and finesse in his work."[17]

In the summer of 1949, she filed for divorce from Dr. Curt Grotter. "He had an attitude of extreme possessiveness," Miss Parker told a judge in December. "In New York he interfered with my rehearsals and my stage work to such an extent that producers became hesitant to work with me."[18] She and Robert Lowery married in 1951, and welcomed a son, Robert, the following year. By the mid–1950s, they were living apart, with Miss Parker raising their son on her own. In 1957, legal papers were filed for a formal separation, but a divorce was never finalized prior to his death in 1971.

She made her final film for the Dollar Bills when she was assigned a featured role in 1953's *Those Redheads from Seattle*. After being off movie screens for several years, she played her last film role for producer A.C. Lyles in his Western drama *Apache Uprising* (1965). In later years, Miss Parker appeared in a few TV commercials, and ran an informal acting school, where one of her pupils was a young Elaine Stritch.

Miss Parker became a resident at the Motion Picture Country Home in 1998, and died there in 2005, due to complications from a stroke. In the last years of her life, she was suffering from dementia. She was survived by her son, Robert Lowery Hanks, and by two granddaughters.

If her P-T films were not the most prestigious of her career, she enjoyed them nonetheless. According to Miss Parker's son, Bob Hanks, "There was always a smile on my mother's face when she talked about Pine and Thomas."

PINE-THOMAS FILMOGRAPHY: *Power Dive* (1941); *Flying Blind* (1941); *No Hands on the Clock* (1941); *Torpedo Boat* (1942); *I Live on Danger* (1942); *Wrecking Crew* (1942); *High Explosive* (1943); *Alaska Highway* (1943); *Minesweeper* (1943); *The Navy Way* (1944); *One Body Too Many* (1944); *Those Redheads from Seattle* (1953)

John Payne

BORN: May 28, 1912, Roanoke, Virginia
DIED: December 6, 1989, Malibu, California

John Howard Payne was born to a well-to-do family in Roanoke, Virginia, one of three sons of George Washington Payne and his wife Ida. After a privileged childhood,

John's future became more uncertain when his father died on the brink of the Great Depression. Over the next several years, he worked toward a college education whenever funds permitted, hoping to become a writer.

Instead, show business beckoned. His singing voice won him a regular radio spot as "The South Singer." Offered the chance to join a theatrical road company, he demonstrated his potential as an actor, leading him toward Hollywood. He played his first minor film roles in the mid–1930s, making his debut in *Dodsworth* (1936). Going under contract with Warner Brothers in 1938, he was unhappy with his assignments and asked for his release in 1940. Payne spent much of the 1940s at 20th Century–Fox (interrupted by his wartime service as a flight instructor). Acclaimed as a singer, he was seen by Fox as a lightweight leading man, often in musicals with studio stars Alice Faye and Betty Grable. Payne may be best-remembered today for co-starring in *Miracle on 34th Street*.

Payne finally broke his ties with Fox in 1947, tired of the sameness of his roles. As a freelancer, he sought scripts that would present a tougher screen image, starring in *films noir* like *The Saxon Charm* (1948) and *Kansas City Confidential* (1952). The male lead in the Pine-Thomas Western *El Paso* (1949) began his successful collaboration with the Dollar Bills.

"Ever since I came to Hollywood, I wanted to make adventure films," Payne said. "It seemed like a good, healthy way to make a living."[19] Not inclined to take himself or his work too seriously, Payne later commented, "It was a remunerative profession. I certainly couldn't have earned that much money any other way that I can think of."[20]

Pine-Thomas' busiest leading man of the 1950s (starring in ten films), John Payne had the sensibilities of a businessman to complement his acting talent. He shared his producers' views on the importance of public relations. "You can't just make a picture and retire to your swimming pool," Payne told columnist Hedda Hopper (September 14, 1952). "You've got to know your public…. I don't believe the majority of the top people in the industry know whom they're making pictures for … Citizens of Keokuk don't react to films in the same way as New York audiences do." He successfully negotiated profit participation in his later films and formed his own production company, Window Productions.

Physically fit throughout his career, Payne was adept at playing parts with action scenes. His association with Pine-Thomas Productions, spanning eight years, was mutually profitable and enjoyable. According to Bill Thomas, Payne wrote him a letter that said, "You're a real fine guy, Bill, and although words are sometimes feeble tools, I want you to know that you are one of the best friends I have ever had the good fortune to make in this business."[21]

When movie assignments slowed, Payne took the starring role in a television Western, *The Restless Gun*, which aired from 1957 to 1959. The actor was seriously injured in 1961, when he was struck by a car in New York City, leaving him with facial scars that he chose not to have corrected with plastic surgery. He continued to act occasionally, starring in and directing the low-budget crime drama *They Ran for Their Lives* (1968). Payne also appeared in the 1974 Broadway-bound revival of *Good News*, reuniting him with frequent Fox co-star Alice Faye. His last performance came in a 1975 episode of TV's *Columbo*.

Married three times, Payne's first two wives were actresses Anne Shirley, whom he married in 1937, and Gloria DeHaven, from whom he was divorced in 1948. His third and final wife was Alexandra Crowell Curtis (known as Sandy), the ex-wife of actor Alan

Curtis. Payne was the father of three children, including actress Julie Payne, whose mother was Miss Shirley.

Payne died at his Malibu home of heart failure.

PINE-THOMAS FILMOGRAPHY: *El Paso* (1949); *Captain China* (1950); *The Eagle and the Hawk* (1950); *Tripoli* (1950); *Passage West* (1951); *Crosswinds* (1951); *Caribbean* (1952); *The Blazing Forest* (1952); *The Vanquished* (1953); *Hell's Island* (1955); *Bailout at 43,000* (1957)

Philip Reed

BORN: March 25, 1908, New York, New York
DIED: December 7, 1996, Los Angeles, California

Smoothly handsome Philip Reed, who looked born to don a tuxedo, was originally named Milton Le Roy Treinis. Enrolled at Cornell University, he chose to forego completing his degree in favor of acting in vaudeville and stock companies. Billed as Milton LeRoy, the actor was seen in two Broadway shows of the 1932-33 season: *Ballyhoo of 1932*, and *Melody*. But he was soon in Hollywood, where he was renamed Phillip Reed. (In later years, Reed usually spelled the first name as "Philip.") Making his film debut in 1933, Reed played one of his first important roles a year later in Universal's *Glamour* (1934). He would appear in more than 25 films before interrupting his career for wartime service.

He served in the U.S. Navy from 1942 to 1945, and began his association with Pine-Thomas shortly after his discharge. He was assigned the starring role in Pine-Thomas' only continuing series, playing in four "Big Town" installments, though some critics thought him ill-suited to the part of a hardened newspaper editor. Later, he demonstrated his versatility, using his polished persona to good effect in villainous roles. In the 1950s, Reed performed frequently on television, including several guest appearances on *Alfred Hitchcock Presents*. His last motion picture credit came when he was featured in the 1965 Elvis film *Harum Scarum*.

Usually suave and charming on-screen, Reed could charm the ladies in real life as well. Syndicated columnist Harrison Carroll (May 24, 1948) joked that the actor "must go for the name Ann. He's been dating Ann Miller, Ann Rutherford, and Ann Sothern." He didn't marry until nearly the age of 50, wedding Audrey Gillin in 1957. He died in 1996, survived by his wife.

PINE-THOMAS FILMOGRAPHY: *People Are Funny* (1946); *Hot Cargo* (1946); *Big Town* (1947); *I Cover Big Town* (1946); *Big Town after Dark* (1947); *Big Town Scandal* (1948); *Manhandled* (1949); *Tripoli* (1950)

Walter Reed

BORN: February 10, 1916, Bainbridge Island, Washington
DIED: August 20, 2001, Santa Cruz, California

The man born as Walter Reed Smith was an unpretentious and utilitarian actor who largely took work where he found it, becoming a mainstay of low-budget films and serials. After acting in theatrical stock companies, he received his Hollywood break in Hollywood thanks to actor Joel McCrea. He became a contract player at RKO in the early 1940s, but his momentum as an up-and-coming player was interrupted by his service in World War II. Handsome and athletic enough to play leads in his early career, he later concentrated primarily on character roles. When television came along, he embraced the new medium as well, later explaining, "You're only an actor as long as you are working."[22]

Reed was a late addition to the Pine-Thomas group, making his debut in *Captain China*. Though he mostly played minor characters in their films, he was a useful man to take along on location shoots, as he could easily step up if there was a last-minute need for another speaking role. Reed continued acting in films and television into the early 1970s, his final motion picture performance a brief appearance in *Tora! Tora! Tora!* (1970). Beginning in the mid–1960s, he had a second career as a real estate broker and investor. Reed was the brother of singer turned television emcee Jack Smith, the longtime host of *You Asked for It*.

The widowed actor died of kidney failure in 2001 at his home in Santa Cruz, California. Three children and his brother survived him.

PINE-THOMAS FILMOGRAPHY: *Captain China* (1950); *The Eagle and the Hawk* (1950); *The Lawless* (1950); *Tripoli* (1950); *Caribbean* (1952); *The Blazing Forest* (1952); *Sangaree* (1953); *Those Redheads from Seattle* (1953); *Hell's Island* (1955); *The Far Horizons* (1955)

Ralph Sanford

BORN: May 21, 1899, Springfield, Mass.
DIED: June 20, 1963, Los Angeles, Calif.

The popular character actor was born Ralph Dayton Sanford; his father, Arthur, was a salesman. His initial entry into show business was in vaudeville, where he became a dancing partner in vaudeville for Ray Bolger, their act titled "A Pair of Nifties." After they went their separate ways, Sanford worked as a supporting actor and stage manager on Broadway in the late 1920s and early 1930s, though few of his shows were hits. While still based on the East Coast, he began playing roles in short films, but his career as a character actor picked up steam after he relocated to Hollywood in the mid–1930s.

Sanford worked often for Pine-Thomas in the 1940s, with *Alaska Highway* and *Shaggy* providing two of his most substantial roles. He typically played comedic supporting characters for the Dollar Bills, but other producers and directors often cast him as a tough guy. Though his parts were rarely sizable, he did appear in some genuine film classics, including *The Best Years*

Character actor Ralph Sanford played comedic roles in several P-T films, including *Alaska Highway*.

of our Lives (1946) and *Friendly Persuasion* (1956). In the 1950s and early 1960s, he was seen frequently in television appearances, including a recurring assignment on *The Life and Legend of Wyatt Earp*.

A longtime resident of Tarzana, Sanford died of a heart ailment in 1963, survived by his mother, wife Betty, and a sister. He was buried in his hometown of Springfield, Massachusetts.

PINE-THOMAS FILMOGRAPHY: *No Hands on the Clock* (1941); *Torpedo Boat* (1942); *I Live on Danger* (1942); *Wildcat* (1942); *High Explosive* (1943); *Alaska Highway* (1943); *Submarine Alert* (1943); *Minesweeper* (1943); *High Powered* (1945); *They Made Me a Killer* (1946); *Shaggy* (1948)

Will Wright

BORN: March 26, 1894, San Francisco, Calif.
DIED: June 19, 1962, Hollywood, Calif.

William Henry Wright was a former vaudevillian and ex–newspaper reporter who became a familiar face to moviegoers of the 1940s, from middle age onward supporting roles in more than 100 films. His features lent themselves to playing grouchy, crotchety men who worked as judges, politicians, or clerks.

Cast as minor characters in his early Pine-Thomas films, he was allotted more screen time in his final two appearances. Wright played a comically inept police chief in *Danger Street* (1947), and was fourth-billed in *Disaster* (1948), as the hero's boss (and heroine's father). Wright worked almost constantly up until shortly before his death from cancer in 1962, but by the 1950s was busy primarily in television. *I Love Lucy* fans will recognize him as both the sheriff who jails Lucy and Ricky in "Tennessee Bound," as well as the locksmith who frees them from the shackles of "The Handcuffs." In the 1960s, he made three appearances as crabby Mayberry resident Ben Weaver on *The Andy Griffith Show*. His final film role, as a doctor in *Cape Fear* (1962), was released just a few weeks prior to his passing.

He was survived by his wife Nell, to whom he had been married for more than 40 years, as well as a daughter, Bette, a grandson, and two sisters.

PINE-THOMAS FILMOGRAPHY: *Wildcat* (1942); *A Letter from Bataan* (1942 short); *Submarine Alert* (1942); *Minesweeper* (1943); *The Navy Way* (1944); *Take It Big* (1944); *Dangerous Passage* (1944); *High Powered* (1945); *They Made Me a Killer* (1946); *Hot Cargo* (1946); *Danger Street* (1947); *Disaster* (1948)

APPENDIX II:
PINE-THOMAS CREW

As producers, Bill Pine and Bill Thomas openly acknowledged the importance of their experienced and flexible crew members, several of whom remained on the company payroll full-time. Pine and Thomas frequently rewarded their most valued employees with profit participation in the company's projects, at a time when this was not commonplace. *Daily Variety* (January 31, 1944) reported that production manager Doc Merman and screenwriter Maxwell Shane, both with the company from its earliest days, would receive percentage deals on upcoming films.

Below are brief biographical sketches of nine crew members who worked on multiple Pine-Thomas projects, including their most prolific directors and screenwriters, their longtime publicity man, and the cinematographer who shot dozens of their films.

William Berke

Born: October 3, 1903, Milwaukee, Wisconsin
Died: February 15, 1958, Los Angeles, California

The action-oriented Pine-Thomas director was born in Milwaukee to Hungarian immigrants, whose family name was originally Berkowitz. Arriving in Hollywood in the late 1910s, William Lester Berke, still a teenager, first obtained work as an actor in silent films. Billed as "William Lester," he appeared in several Westerns shot by Vitagraph at the company's West Coast facility. Over the next ten years, he learned the motion picture business from the ground up, working as a cameraman and sometimes screenwriter.

In the early 1930s, Berke established his own production company to make independent films. From early in his career, he was noted for his ability to do a lot with a little. As *Variety* (April 19, 1933) said of his feature *City Hall*, "The fact that William Berke … operated on a restricted budget didn't seem to keep a goodly portion of brains from getting into the production." However, as Berke said in a later interview, that acclaim didn't produce the results he expected. "So I thought I was a great man," he explained. "I sat back in my chair to wait for the Hollywood big shots to plead with me to work for them. And I sat and sat and nothing happened."

Disillusioned, he decided that "nobody wanted good pictures," just action films turned out quickly. "And I said if that's what they wanted I'd give it to 'em."[1] A prolific director with substantial experience in B films, Berke directed more than 75 feature films over a 15-year period. Among his output were multiple entries in Sam Katzman's "Jungle Jim" series, starring Johnny Weissmuller, and numerous B Westerns.

He worked often with Gene Autry, and, according to *Film Bulletin* (September 6, 1941), "revived the boxoffice [*sic*] importance of ... Autry." Berke's grandson, Bill, recalled riding in the car with his father past the Gene Autry Museum, and being told, "Your grandfather and Gene Autry were really good friends."[2] Indeed, the grateful star once autographed a photo to Berke, writing, "To my pal Bill, the man who made all of my pictures #1 box office."

Berke was associated (non-exclusively) with Pine-Thomas for much of the 1940s, beginning with *Tornado* (1943). Reviewing that picture, *Film Daily* (August 11, 1943) wrote, "The direction of William Berke is punchy and swift. His staging of a number of fight sequences will get quite a rise out of the fans." Ultimately, Berke directed ten fast-paced action films for the company.

In the 1950s, while continuing to produce and direct feature films, Berke also busied himself with television assignments, directing multiple episodes of modestly budgeted Western and crime dramas. He produced the filmed version of *The Goldbergs* that was done for first-run syndication after the demise of the original live program.

Berke's last film, *The Lost Missile*, made for his own production company, became something of a family affair, due in part to an unexpected tragedy. On February 15, 1958, while the film was in production, Berke died at his North Hollywood home, suffering a heart attack at the age of 54. Berke's son Lester, then a student at UCLA, dropped out of school in order to help complete his father's film, stepping into the director's chair. Even grandson Bill, still a baby, can be glimpsed in the finished film; he's one of the extras in the scene depicting an underground shelter.

In addition to his son and grandson, the late William Berke was survived by wife Gertrude, and daughter Gale. Lester (1934–2004), after taking his father's place on *The Lost Missile*, went on to a successful career of his own, including a stint as producer of the television series *Airwolf*.

Lewis R. Foster

BORN: August 5, 1898, Brookfield, Missouri
DIED: June 10, 1974, Tehachapi, California

Lewis Ransom Foster was born to parents Joseph and Florence. His father was a traveling salesman, an occupation that Lewis also pursued as a young man.

A former newspaperman, Foster's early work in the motion picture industry came in the mid–1920s at the Hal Roach Studio, where he served as assistant to director F. Richard Jones. He earned his first screenwriting credits when producer Roach assigned him to be a gag man. He developed material for comedians including Laurel and Hardy, and was promoted to the director's chair in 1929 with their comedy short *Unaccustomed as We Are*.

Foster's collaborations with Bill Thomas began in 1938, when the writer was hired to punch up the jokes in *Campus Confessions*, the first film for which Thomas earned an Associate Producer credit. Thomas recalled Foster, who "became a life-long friend," as "a tall, husky man, outwardly sober, only his eyes betrayed the warmth and humor that electrified his work."[3] Thomas was taken aback on their first encounter, when Foster refused his request to attend a meeting in the producer's office. Visiting Foster in the Paramount Writers' Building, Thomas "learned Lew had been suffering from temporary blackouts and couldn't make it from one office to another."[4]

After the two men had collaborated on several projects, Thomas was asked by other producers what Foster had earned at Paramount. He did his pal a good turn by intentionally quoting an inflated price. The amount Thomas named became Foster's standard for later projects. Years later, Thomas joked, "It never dawned on me that someday, I'd have to match that figure!"[5] As his career flourished, Foster received an Academy Award for Best Original Story with his contribution to *Mr. Smith Goes to Washington*, and was nominated again as co-author of the screenplay of *The More the Merrier* (1943).

After working on two early Pine-Thomas projects (*I Live on Danger* and *Alaska Highway*), Foster returned to the Pine-Thomas fold in 1949, directing and co-authoring the screenplay of *Manhandled*. He would write and direct several of Pine-Thomas' biggest hits of the 1950s.

In 1936, Foster married actress Dorothy Wilson, who had been a WAMPAS Baby Star in 1932. They welcomed a son, Kendall, in 1938. Mr. and Mrs. Lewis Foster remained together until his death.

Fred Jackman, Jr.

BORN: January 8, 1913, Los Angeles, California
DIED: December 9, 1982, Los Angeles, California

Born Frederick Hammond Jackman, Pine and Thomas' most frequently employed cinematographer was introduced to the motion picture business in the late 1920s by his father Fred. (Although the younger man would use the name Fred Jackman, Jr., professionally, he was technically not a junior, as his father's full name was Frederick Woodward Jackman.) The elder Mr. Jackman was a cameraman who served as supervising cinematographer for producer Mack Sennett from 1918 to 1922, and directed a number of his shorts. It was the family trade; the younger Fred's uncle, Floyd, worked in the same field. As a teenager, Fred Jackman, Jr., lived with his family on North Hillcrest Avenue, and graduated from Beverly Hills High School.

In the late 1930s, Fred, Jr., and his brother George were working for their father, "a specialist in producing miniatures and special effects for moving pictures," at the Fred Jackman Process Corporation.[6] It was a skill set that would come in handy a few years later, when Jackman, Jr., shot Pine-Thomas films such as *Tornado*, with its simulated scenes of weather damage.

Kept on the Pine-Thomas payroll year-round in the 1940s, Jackman was a valued member of the unit. His expertise was put to good use not only during filming but during the pre-production period, when the work of planning camera angles and blocking scenes helped shorten the number of days actually needed to shoot film with actors.

In the 1950s Jackman began directing in television, concentrating primarily on action-oriented shows like *Manhunt* and *Death Valley Days*. In 1959, he was an Emmy nominee for his cinematography on TV's *Alcoa Theatre*. Later realizing that he enjoyed his post behind the camera more than being in the director's chair, he returned to that

Cast and crew of *Wrecking Crew,* including a smiling Chester Morris (upper middle, dark necktie). Peeking over Morris's shoulders are director Frank McDonald (at left, with mustache) and co-star Richard Arlen (slightly above and to the right). Standing tall alongside Morris (with hat and folded arms) is production manager Doc Merman. At the right end of the row below Morris is Bill Pine. Third from left in that same row is cinematographer Fred Jackman, Jr. Note that some wisenheimer has changed his name on the clapper to "Jerkman" (Frank McDonald Papers, Box 13, American Heritage Center, University of Wyoming).

field, overseeing the filming of *The Partridge Family*. Jackman continued to work at his craft until shortly before his death, one of his later credits being Director of Photography on TV's *Quincy*.

He was married three times. After his divorce from first wife Margaret, Jackman met and married actress Nancy Kelly while both were employed by Pine-Thomas. That marriage, which took place in 1946, ended in divorce as well. Testifying to the Superior Court of Los Angeles in 1951, Miss Kelly complained "that they were continually harassed by creditors even though he earned between $20,000 and $25,000 a year."[7]

After marrying third wife Dorothy Jane, Jackman helped his stepson, Nick McLean, Sr., begin a career in the film industry. A director of photography in film (*The Goonies*) and television, where his credits include *Evening Shade* and *Friends*, McLean recalled, "My stepfather told me the whole trick in cinematography is balance—color, light, composition, camera moves, etc.—and through the years I find it's the Number One answer to a good picture."[8]

Jackman passed away from emphysema at the age of 69, survived by his wife, four sons, and a daughter.

A.C. Lyles

BORN: May 17, 1918, Jacksonville, Florida
DIED: September 27, 2013, Los Angeles, California

Born Andrew Craddock Lyles, Jr., he loved movies from his childhood, when a screening of Paramount's *Wings* (1927), starring Richard Arlen, prompted him to ask for a job. Ten years old, he was hired to hand out flyers at the movie theater, his earliest association with Paramount. "When I was 14," he said, "I talked the local paper into letting me interview visiting stars."[9] According to syndicated columnist Hedda Hopper (October 30, 1941), Lyles was still in his teens when he met Bill Pine on a publicity tour, who gave him a picture autographed, "To a young man who'll go far."

Though his name was nowhere to be found in the credits of Pine-Thomas movies, Lyles was one of the most valued and steadily employed of the company's staff. Lyles, "an impoverished kid from Florida," according to Carol Thomas Pantages, arrived in Hollywood determined to break into the film industry. She described him as "very personable," and noted that, starting with a temporary mailroom job, "he ingratiated himself"[10] with nearly everyone he met. Skilled at networking long before the term even came into use, Lyles made a favorable impression wherever he went.

In the early 1940s, Lyles became the publicist for the Pine-Thomas unit. Though his bosses were themselves no slouches when it came to the art of managing public relations, Lyles managed to impress them with his ability to publicize Pine-Thomas films.

Lyles clearly paid close attention to the working methods of the Pine-Thomas unit, and the experience served him well. In the 1960s, with Pine-Thomas temporarily defunct, Lyles began producing a series of low-budget Westerns for Paramount release. Like his mentors' films, he favored titles that promised action—*Apache Uprising* (1965), *Hostile Guns* (1967). Knowing he was serving a predominantly middle-aged or older audience, Lyles stocked his films with actors who were largely past their prime in the motion picture industry—*Town Tamer* (1965) alone offered, aside from top-billed star Dana Andrews, appearances by Bruce Cabot, Pat O'Brien, Sonny Tufts, Coleen Gray, and more. True to his Pine-Thomas background, Lyles boasted to syndicated columnist Bob Thomas (September 13, 1966), "I can get more on the screen for less money than any producer in town."

Off-screen, Lyles had a brief early marriage to actress Martha Vickers, and Carol Thomas Pantages recalled that he was "brokenhearted" when it ended. However, he went on to marry Martha French, who was not involved in the motion picture industry, in 1955, and that union lasted until his death in 2013. Aside from his wife, Lyles was survived by a niece.

"His history in the movie business is certainly unique," said Sherry Lansing, then chairwoman of Paramount's motion picture division, in 1998. "There's nobody I met who doesn't love him, and there are very few people I've met who don't know him."[11]

Daniel Mainwaring

BORN: February 27, 1902, Oakland, California
DIED: January 31, 1977, Los Angeles, California

The man who wrote both detective novels and screenplays under the pseudonym Geoffrey Homes was in actuality Daniel Mainwaring, born to parents Edward and Constance Mainwaring. His father, a Britisher by birth, was employed by the U.S. Forest Service. Daniel was one of eight Mainwaring children; they later adopted another son.

Mainwaring attended Fresno State College, receiving a degree in 1924. After graduation, he worked as a teacher, and as a reporter for newspapers including the *San Francisco Chronicle*. Like many of Pine and Thomas' associates, Mainwaring first toiled in Hollywood as a publicist, originally for Warner Brothers. He published his first novel, *One Against the Earth*, in 1933, the only book he would publish under his real name. With the release of *The Man Who Murdered Himself* in 1936, Mainwaring launched a successful career as a mystery writer, calling himself Geoffrey Homes. His first association with Pine and Thomas came when they adapted his book *No Hands on the Clock* as a feature film. He later went on to write screenplays for the unit.

Bill Thomas reported one of Mainwaring's personal idiosyncrasies: "It was a fact that when Mainwaring pounded the typewriter, he dug his right heel into the carpet. It was rumored Mainwaring's progress in Hollywood could be traced from carpet hole to carpet hole."[12] Always mindful of saving money, Thomas had the carpet taken up in Mainwaring's office, and a throw rug placed to give his employee's anxious foot something less expensive to grind.

Moving on from Pine-Thomas, Mainwaring adapted his own 1946 mystery novel *Build My Gallows High* into *Out of the Past* (1947), one of the acknowledged classics of *film noir*. He later wrote the screenplay, based on Jack Finney's novel "The Body Snatchers," for the highly successful and influential film *Invasion of the Body Snatchers* (1956). In later years, Mainwaring contributed scripts to television series such as *Adventures in Paradise* and *Mannix*.

He died of cancer shortly before his 75th birthday, survived by wife Sally, daughters Dannie and Deborah, and a grandchild.

Frank McDonald

BORN: November 9, 1899, Baltimore, Maryland
DIED: March 8, 1980, Oxnard, California

Frank Burgess McDonald worked steadily in the motion picture industry for nearly 30 years, helming around 100 films. Born in Baltimore, he was the son of Florence and Samuel McDonald; his middle name was his mother's maiden name. After finishing high school, he attended Baltimore City College.

Initially, McDonald considered following in the footsteps of his father, employed with the B&O Railroad. But he was intrigued with show business from his first forays into amateur theatricals. According to a journalist doing a profile of Baltimore's native son, McDonald "skipped college to go on the stage in 1917 ... his first professional job was as a burglar in a vaudeville act."[13]

In the early 1920s, McDonald worked often with producer-director Melville Burke. Over the next several years, he amassed several credits as an actor in Broadway shows, although he never landed in a hit. He was cast as a drug addict in *Puppets* (1925), and a gangster in Burke's *Just to Remind You* (1931). He also spent five years as a stage manager and director at the renowned Elitch Gardens Theatre in Denver, Colorado.

He entered the motion picture industry in 1933, initially employed as a dialogue director at Warner Brothers. According to a 1937 studio biography, his debut film as director was "From This Dark Stairway" (subsequently retitled *The Murder of Dr. Harrigan*), but the first to see release was *Broadway Hostess* in late 1935. He quickly developed a reputation for doing yeoman's work on modestly budgeted films. Said Hollywood journalist Joe Pearson, whose column appeared in *Hollywood Motion Picture Review*, "Noted as a thoroughly competent director who can turn a weak story into sound entertainment and develop a poor cast into a well integrated unit by his ingenuity, McDonald has none of the so-called artistic temperament.... He is a kind, patient, soft spoken, tolerant, extremely alert and likable gentleman."[14]

In 1934, McDonald married Goodee Montgomery (whose given name was Virginia). Previously a Broadway and vaudeville performer noted particularly for her dancing skills, Miss Montgomery had signed as a Fox contract player in 1930. Active in motion pictures through the mid–1930s, her credits included *Charlie Chan Carries On* (1931) and *Stolen Harmony* (1935). Early in their married lives, the couple claimed to have made a pact designed to keep their careers in perspective: "All talk pertaining to motion picture work is banned at the evening meal with a penalty of a $50 fine, such conversation being limited to the breakfast period.... Each is permitted three dinner guests a week but movie chatter is prohibited."[15] In 1940, newspapers reported that Mrs. McDonald, who had suffered a spinal injury as well as a fall at home, "has been in a plaster cast from waist to neck for the last six months."[16] Her acting career cut short, she went on to become a successful watercolor artist.

McDonald kept busy in the 1950s directing Western dramas for both films and television, having a long association with *The Life and Legend of Wyatt Earp*. His final directorial credits came with the film *Mara of the Wilderness* (1965), and the television sitcom *Get Smart*.

He died in 1980, two years after being widowed.

Lewis B. "Doc" Merman

BORN: September 7, 1900, New York, New York
DIED: September 7, 1979, Los Angeles, California

Like his boss Bill Pine, "Doc" Merman was born in New York City to parents who were immigrants from Russia. He was the son of Benjamin and Frances Emmerman, and his given name was Louis. He would use a modified version of his birth name in Hollywood, but would be known to friends and co-workers as "Doc."

As Pine-Thomas' longtime production manager Merman was tasked with keeping a film on schedule and within budget. Bill Thomas later commented, "Doc was the ramrod. It was his responsibility to get things moving and keep them that way. He got rough, but the crew loved him.... He was worth his weight in gold!"[17] The responsibility sometimes put him into conflict with directors, who almost invariably wanted more time and more money to make the picture better.

On the job, according to his bosses, Merman's techniques were anything but subtle. Aside from the whistle he habitually wore around his neck, columnist Erskine Johnson (July 11, 1943) reported another Merman technique, involving a needle some ten inches long. "When Doc decides that work is lagging through some individual taking too much time at the job, he produces the needle, brandishes it menacingly before the face of his victim and then makes a terrific jab at his victim's posterior." Luckily for Pine and Thomas' hapless crew members, the needle was made of rubber.

Carol Thomas Pantages, describing him many years later as "a great big guy," formed an impression of a man with a tough exterior but "a heart of gold." As a child visiting her father's movie sets, she recalled of Merman, "He used to order these huge deli sandwiches with onions," which didn't seem appealing to a young girl at all. In the 1940s, Merman was involved with the Hollywood U.S.O; as reported in *Daily Variety* (September 11, 1946), he organized a fundraising show for the organization, securing the participation of numerous Pine-Thomas players, including Jack Haley, Robert Lowery, Jean Parker, and Chester Morris.

An unceasingly hard worker, who demanded as much of himself as the crew he supervised, Merman was hospitalized during the production of the film *Mr. Reckless* (1948), after suffering a collapse due to exhaustion. While recuperating, he sent a jovial note to his colleagues, saying, "All of you (deleted) who thought you were going to knock me off, sorry to disappoint you. I'll be around for a good many years." True to the company's philosophy of the-show-must-go-on, Merman wrote that he expected to be released from the hospital shortly, "at which time I shall come directly to the studio and beat the holy hell out of you.... Work never killed anybody, so when I get back, we will *really* start to work."[18]

Over the course of his career, Merman made several attempts to establish a production company he could call his own, but with no more than limited success. According to *Daily Variety* (September 11, 1946), he formed Merman-David Pictures, Inc. with partner William B. David. A few years later, Merman teamed with actress Maureen O'Hara's then-husband, Will Price, in Price-Merman Productions. Merman filed for bankruptcy in 1960; a *Los Angeles Times* story (October 6, 1960) noted that he incurred nearly $250,000 of debt while operating an unsuccessful television production company, Crest Productions. However, he continued to be steadily employed in his later years. He was an asso-

Three bad hombres on the set of *The Last Outpost*: (left to right) Bill Thomas, Bill Pine, and production manager Doc Merman.

ciate producer on the unsuccessful CBS sitcom *The Betty Hutton Show* (1959–60), and in 1960 joined the staff of 20th Century–Fox as executive production manager.

Merman died on his 79th birthday at Cedars-Sinai Hospital in Los Angeles, after suffering a heart attack. Survivors were his wife Rose, daughter Phyllis, and two grandchildren.

Maxwell Shane

BORN: August 26, 1905, Paterson, New Jersey
DIED: October 25, 1983, Los Angeles, California

Before establishing himself in the motion picture field, Shane studied law, and worked as a journalist and publicist. In the summer of 1926, Shane was hired to handle publicity for the Harry Langdon unit at First National Pictures. He later served as president of the Hillman-Shane advertising agency, which had numerous clients from the motion picture industry. He married Evelyn Finkenstein in December 1926, and fathered two children—son Arnold, born in 1930, and daughter Sondra, four years later.

While working as a publicist, Shane began to pursue his interest in screenwriting. According to the *Los Angeles Times* (September 21, 1925), he sold scenarios titled "Jazz Train" and "Married Men's Morals." Even before Pine-Thomas Productions was formed,

Shane was collaborating with Bill Thomas on screenplays, beginning with *This Way Please* (1937). When the new production company was formed in 1940, Shane was recruited to script the first three films.

He was by far the most prolific screenwriter associated with the company; not until 1944's *Take It Big*, a musical comedy, was there a P-T film to which Shane didn't contribute. Frequently assigned to adapt original stories the producers bought from freelance writers, Shane ultimately penned more than 30 screenplays for the company. Said William Thomas of Shane, "Max was a perfect associate, gifted with an easygoing temperament, good judgment, and a philosophical bent."[19]

He made his directorial debut with *Fear in the Night* (1947). That fall, Shane ended his association with Pine-Thomas. Shane, partnered with magazine publisher Maxwell Geffin, formed an independent production company, Geffin-Shane Productions, Inc. Away from Pine-Thomas, Shane directed *City across the River* (1949) and *The Glass Wall* (1953). After Bill Pine's death in 1955, Shane returned to the Pine-Thomas fold as a partner, writing and directing *Nightmare* (1956), a remake of his earlier *Fear in the Night*.

In the early 1960s, Shane was hired as a writer-producer for television's *Thriller*, hosted by Boris Karloff. Under Shane's guidance, the anthology series primarily focused on suspense melodramas, not unlike those seen weekly on CBS' *Alfred Hitchcock Presents*. Shane left the show during its first season after it was revamped to incorporate more elements of horror. His final work came when he contributed scripts to the NBC adventure series *Maya* (1967–68).

On October 25, 1983, Shane died at the Motion Picture Country Home at the age of 78. He was survived by his children, and five grandchildren.

F. Paul Sylos

BORN: October 12, 1900, Brooklyn, New York
DIED: April 20, 1976, Los Angeles, California

Art director Frank Paul Sylos was a vital member of the Pine-Thomas production team from the company's earliest days, beginning on *Power Dive* (1941), and continuing through the unit's last film of the 1950s, *Bailout at 43,000* (1957).

He was born in Brooklyn to Joseph and Rose Sylos, who had emigrated to the U.S. from Italy. The Sylos family, including Frank's younger brother and two younger sisters, subsequently relocated to New Haven, Connecticut. Sylos earned a bachelor's degree in Fine Arts from Yale University. Prior to his arrival in Hollywood in the mid–1930s, he worked as an art director for advertising agencies on the East Coast, and was a published magazine illustrator, affiliated for some years with *Liberty*. After a brief first marriage that ended in divorce, Sylos married Kathryn Pumilia in 1941.

Sylos was applauded for making the most of limited movie budgets. As one trade publication tactfully put it, Sylos "did some unusually effective work in designing sets for the Pine-Thomas productions which permitted the Director of Photography to suggest expansive scenes with a minimum of actual set-construction."[20] Aside from his work in Pine-Thomas films of the 1940s, Sylos' art direction enhanced the visuals of *noir* films like *Dillinger* (1945) and the low-budget sleeper *When Strangers Marry* (1944). He spent much of the 1950s as art director on television's *The Loretta Young Show*, with his work receiving an Emmy nomination in 1959.

Sylos retired a few years prior to his death in 1976, which was due to a lung tumor. He was survived by his wife Kathryn, son Paul and daughter Kathleen, his siblings, and four grandchildren. His son (usually credited onscreen as Paul Sylos, Jr.) followed in his footsteps, entering the industry in the early 1960s and going on to have a long association with Aaron Spelling, for whom he served as art director on popular series like *The Love Boat* and *Dynasty*.

Chapter Notes

In the 1970s, Bill Thomas collaborated with Thelma Kling on a memoir, tentatively titled "Hollywood's Fabulous Dollar Bills; or, How to Make Money Making Movies," a copy of which was obtained by the author. This source is cited in notes as "memoir." The author also obtained from a private dealer Thomas' personal scrapbook, an oversized volume containing press clippings, correspondence, and photographs documenting his career. This source is cited in notes as "scrapbook."

Preface

1. Memoir, p. 422.
2. Bob Herzberg, *Shooting Scripts: From Pulp Westerns to Film* (Jefferson, NC: McFarland, 2005), p. 36.
3. Memoir, foreword.
4. Leonard Maltin, foreword to *B Movies: An Informal Survey of the American Low-Budget Film* by Don Miller (New York: Curtis, 1973), p. 7.

The Dollar Bills

1. Bill Pine and Bill Thomas, "Thanks for the Use of the Hall," *Hollywood Reporter*, October 31, 1949.
2. Robbin Coons, "Movieland's Mass Producers Have Lots Fun," *Bluefield* (WV) *Daily Telegraph*, May 19, 1943.
3. Hedda Hopper, "Two Dollar Bills," *Chicago Tribune*, April 13, 1947.
4. Kirsten Fermaglich, "Jewish Americans Changed Their Names, But Not at Ellis Island," https://the-conversation.com/jewish-americans-changed-their-names-but-not-at-ellis-island-96152, accessed October 4, 2018.
5. Richard English, "Gaudiest Producers in Hollywood," *Saturday Evening Post*, January 3, 1953.
6. "They Cash in on Low-Cost Film Output," *La Crosse* (WI) *Tribune*, February 3, 1949.
7. Memoir, p. 359.
8. William C. Thomas, "Producer Recalls the Good Old Days," *Detroit News*, undated clipping, scrapbook.
9. Carol Thomas Pantages, personal interview. All other quotes from Pantages in this section are from this interview.

10. Memoir, p. 19.
11. Memoir, p. 24.
12. Memoir, p. 148.
13. Bill Thomas, "Bill Pine," *Hollywood Reporter*, September 23, 1946.
14. James Bacon, "An Old Time Press Agent's Parrot Tale," *Mt. Vernon* (IL) *Register-News*, July 24, 1963.
15. Elizabeth Wilson, "They Wish Upon a Star—and Win!" *Liberty*, June 1945.
16. Florabel Muir, "'Tokyo Rose' Gets Pine-Thomas Goat," unsourced clipping, ca. 1946, scrapbook.
17. Wilson, "They Wish."
18. "Fact Diggers Are Being Kept Busy in Movies," *Lima* (OH) *News*, April 7, 1938.
19. "Hollywood Roundup," *Brainerd* (MN) *Daily Dispatch*, December 2, 1939.
20. English, "Gaudiest Producers."
21. Memoir, p. 111.
22. Edwin Schallert, "Deanna Again Shunning Romance; Marshall Latest Leading Man," *Los Angeles Times*, November 8, 1937.
23. Undated clipping, ca. 1939, scrapbook.
24. Memoir, p. 148.
25. Memoir, p. 160.
26. David N. Bruskin, *The White Brothers: Jack, Jules & Sam White* (Metuchen, NJ: Scarecrow, 1990), p. 345.
27. Bruskin, *The White Brothers*, p. 346.
28. Bruskin, *The White Brothers*, p. 348.
29. Memoir, p. 177.
30. W.E. Oliver, "Ad Writers Make Their Job Easy," unsourced clipping, ca. 1942, scrapbook.
31. Red Kahn, "Who Says It Must be Millions or Nothing?" *Motion Picture Herald*, January 24, 1948.
32. "Not Bad, Just Normal, Assert Pine-Thomas

of Business," *Showmen's Trade Review*, January 29, 1949.

33. Victor Gunson, "Filmdom's Shirt-Sleeved Producers," Uniontown (PA) *Morning Herald*, October 23, 1945.

34. *Ibid.*

35. Bob Hanks, personal interview.

36. Arlene Dahl, personal interview. All other quotes from Arlene Dahl in this section are from this interview.

37. Thomas, "Bill Pine."

38. Wilson, "They Wish."

39. Brian Taves, "The B Film: Hollywood's Other Half," in Tino Balio, *Grand Design: Hollywood as a Modern Business Enterprise*. (Berkeley: University of California Press, 1995), p. 314.

40. Gene Hundsaker, "Excitement is Success Key for Pair Who Have Made Many Profitable Movies," Long Beach (CA) *Press-Telegram*, July 25, 1950.

41. John Reddy, "Hollywood's Dollar Bills," *Esquire*, June 1945.

42. Bill Pine and Bill Thomas, "Merchants of Mayhem," *Hollywood Reporter*, October 23, 1944.

43. Memoir, p. 184.

44. Marjory Adams, "Sterling Hayden in 'Heavy' Role in Million-Dollar Film 'El Paso,'" *Boston Globe*, February 25, 1949.

45. Hedda Hopper, "Hedda Hopper Looks at Hollywood," *Filmland*, October 1947.

46. Bob Thomas, "Pine-Thomas Routine Like Kaiser," Big Spring (TX) *Daily Herald*, May 24, 1945.

47. Frederick C. Othmann, "Movie Making According to Blueprint," *Los Angeles Citizen-News*, January 19, 1944.

48. Thomas, "Bill Pine."

49. Thomas Wood, "Ante Upped for Pine and Thomas," unsourced clipping, scrapbook.

50. "Filmland Folk Air Pet Peeves," *Indianapolis Times*, May 16, 1950.

51. "Films Not Doomed, Say Producers," *Seattle Times*, October 11, 1951.

52. Memoir, p. 311.

53. Gene Hundsaker, "'Dollar Bills' Swap Action for Ideas in Film Thrillers," *Houston Chronicle*, July 30, 1950.

54. W. Henry Cooke, Los Angeles County Conference on Community Relations, letter to Pine and Thomas, October 20, 1950, scrapbook.

55. Memoir, p. 329.

56. English, "Gaudiest Producers."

57. Ethel Rosen, "Hollywood-Vine Yard," *Film Daily*, undated clipping, ca. 1953, scrapbook.

58. Bill Pine and Bill Thomas, "Thanks for the Use of the Hall," *Hollywood Reporter*, October 31, 1949.

59. Dorothy Roe, "Teen-Agers 'Boss' Markets," Middletown (OH) *Journal*, September 4, 1953.

60. English, "Gaudiest Producers."

61. "Pine, Thomas Visit the Grass-Roots—Get Ideas," *Canadian Moving Picture Digest*, December 17, 1949.

62. Memoir, p. 368.

63. "'Dollar Bills' Tire of Being 'Nickel-and-Dimed to Death'; Lift Ceiling Off Budgets," *Daily Variety*, February 24, 1954.

64. English, "Gaudiest Producers."

65. Edwin Schallert, "'Dollar Bills' Grow into Millions Class; Oscar Surprises Buoy Event," *Los Angeles Times*, March 30, 1952.

66. "William Pine Dies of Heart Attack," *Film Daily*, May 2, 1955.

67. Memoir, p. 417.

68. Memoir, p. 226.

69. Bill Jeffries, email to author, April 8, 2018.

70. *Ibid.*

71. "Sunless Morning Becomes Electric," *New Orleans Item*, November 6, 1955.

72. Angel Pine, personal interview. All other quotes from Angel Pine in this section are from this interview.

73. "PT, Near 75-Picture Mark, Hews to Rule That There Are No Rules," *Variety*, February 11, 1953.

The Films

1. "Hollywood Roundup," Corona (CA) *Daily Independent*, March 18, 1941.

2. Unsourced clipping, ca. 1941, scrapbook.

3. "Production Notes," Press preview program, *Forced Landing*, ca. 1941, scrapbook.

4. Edwin Schallert, "Epic Grecian Struggle Inspires Battle Drama," *Los Angeles Times*, May 19, 1941.

5. David N. Bruskin, *The White Brothers: Jack, Jules & Sam White* (Metuchen, NJ: Scarecrow, 1990), p. 350.

6. Bruskin, *The White Brothers*, p. 348.

7. May Mann, "Arline Judge Makes Triple-Play to Be Movie Glamour Queen," Ogden (UT) *Standard-Examiner*, April 12, 1942.

8. Unsourced clipping, ca. 1943, scrapbook.

9. "Story of 'Aerial Gunner' Goes Back to Old Friendship Between Captain Dailey and Producer Pine of Hollywood," *Valley Morning Star* (Harlingen, TX), May 7, 1943.

10. Red Kahn, "Who Says It Must Be Millions or Nothing?" *Motion Picture Herald*, January 24, 1948.

11. Unsourced clipping, ca. 1943, scrapbook.

12. Memoir, p. 211.

13. Memoir, p. 224.

14. William Gargan, *Why Me? An Autobiography* (New York: Doubleday, 1969), p. 156.

15. Maxwell Shane, "Follow That Woman" [screenplay]. Undated. Box 5, Maxwell Shane Papers, 1936–1967. American Heritage Center, University of Wyoming, Laramie, Wyoming.

16. Bruskin, *The White Brothers*, p. 379.

17. "Yanks Capture Mystery Woman 'Tokyo Rose,'" Cameron (TX) *Herald*, June 27, 1946.

18. Maxine Garrison, "Maxine Lunches with Tokyo Rose," *Pittsburgh Press*, October 2, 1945.

19. Johnny Weissmuller, Jr., *Tarzan, My Father* (Toronto: ECW Press, 2002), p. 109.

20. Virginia MacPherson, "Jane Dreams of Love—Gets Laugh!" *Salt Lake Tribune*, March 6, 1946.

21. Alan Napier, *Not Just Batman's Butler: The Autobiography of Alan Napier* (Jefferson, NC: McFarland, 2015), p. 262.

22. Brunell, Christopher, *Zuzu's Wonderful Life in the Movies: The Story of Karolyn Grimes* (Seattle, WA: Artful Dragon, 2000), p. 71.

23. Briggs, Colin. "Barbara Britton: 'All Things Bright and Beautiful,'" *Classic Images*, July 2004.

24. Milton M. Raison, "Writing for Pine and Thomas a Hazardous Occupation," *Variety*, January 7, 1948.

25. "Small Budgets Turn Out Fine B Movies," *Salt Lake Tribune*, April 20, 1947.

26. Maxwell Shane, "Waterfront at Midnight" [screenplay]. June 17, 1947. Box 7, Shane papers.

27. "Not Bad, Just Normal, Assert Pine-Thomas of Business," *Showmen's Trade Review*, January 29, 1949.

28. Richard English, "Gaudiest Producers in Hollywood," *Saturday Evening Post*, January 3, 1953.

29. Emery Wister, "Pulse-Feeler's Latest: Sea-Going Horse Opera," *Charlotte* (NC) *News*, undated, ca. 1949.

30. Gene Freese, *Classic Movie Fight Scenes: 75 Years of Bare Knuckle Brawls, 1914–1989* (Jefferson, NC: McFarland, 2017), p. 76.

31. Unsourced clipping, ca. 1950, scrapbook.

32. E.K. O'Shea, Paramount Film Distributing Corporation, "To All Division and Branch Managers U.S. and Canada," May 26, 1950, scrapbook.

33. Memoir, p. 311.

34. Geoffrey Homes, "New Study of Migratory Workers in California," *New York Times*, March 5, 1950.

35. Michael Ciment and Joseph Losey, *Conversations with Losey* (London: Methuen, 1985), p. 92.

36. Memoir, p. 328.

37. Memoir, p. 343.

38. Herbert Larson, "Movie Producers on 'Listening Tour,' Want Name for Picture," *Oregonian* (Portland, OR), October 11, 1951.

39. Ronald Reagan and Richard G. Hubler. *Where's the Rest of Me?* (New York: Dell, 1981), p. 248.

40. "Dollar Bills Hit Top Production Peak in Filmland," *Denton* (TX) *Record-Chronicle*, August 10, 1952.

41. Arlene Dahl, personal interview. All other quotes from Miss Dahl in this section are from this interview.

42. Tom Gill, *Gentleman of the Jungle* (New York: Dell, 1940), p. 23.

43. Memoir, p. 363.

44. Reagan and Hubler, *Where's the Rest of Me?*, p. 284.

45. Paul Phaneuf, "Rhonda Fleming: That Natural Gift," *Films of the Golden Age* #52, Spring 2008.

46. "Producer to Tell Denver Parley About His 3-D Experiences," *Rocky Mountain News* (Denver, CO), May 26, 1953.

47. *Ibid.*

48. Hannsberry, *Femme Noir: Bad Girls of Film* (Jefferson, NC: McFarland, 1998), p. 135.

49. Rex Strother, email to author, October 9, 2018.

50. David J. Hogan, *Film Noir FAQ: All That's Left to Know About Hollywood's Golden Age of Dames, Detectives, and Danger* (Milwaukee, WI: Applause, 2013), p. 299.

51. McCabe, *Cagney* (New York: Knopf, 1997), p. 279.

52. Ronald L. Davis, *Words into Images: Screenwriters on the Studio System* (Jackson: University Press of Mississippi, 2007), p. 205.

53. Jay Fultz, *In Search of Donna Reed* (Iowa City: University of Iowa Press, 1998), pp. 105–106.

54. George Weltner, interoffice memorandum to Barney Balaban, Paramount Pictures, February 14, 1955, scrapbook.

55. Memoir, p. 22.

56. Charlton Heston, *In the Arena: An Autobiography* (New York: Simon and Schuster, 1995), pp. 128–29.

57. Paul Hochuli, "Gov. Shivers Gets Raves as Actor in Upcoming Pine-Thomas Picture," *Houston Press*, November 2, 1954.

58. Memoir, p. 413.

59. David Kyle Foster, *Love Hunger: A Harrowing Journey from Sexual Addiction to True Fulfillment* (Minneapolis, MN: Chosen, 2014), p. 138.

60. Shonda Holm Croly, personal interview.

61. Frank Freeman, letter to Pine and Thomas, August 29, 1942, scrapbook.

62. Maxwell Shane, "We Refuse to Die" [screenplay], July 1, 1942. Box 4, Maxwell Shane Papers, 1936–1967. American Heritage Center, University of Wyoming, Laramie, Wyoming.

63. Maxwell Shane, "Soldiers of the Soil" [screenplay], August 1942. Box 4, Maxwell Shane Papers, 1936–1967. American Heritage Center, University of Wyoming, Laramie, Wyoming.

64. *Ibid.*

Appendix I: Pine-Thomas Players

1. Memoir, p. 198.

2. Jim Sprinkle, "Texas Is Always Lucky for Richard Arlen, Star Claims," *Valley Morning Star* (Harlingen, TX), October 24, 1942.

3. English, "Gaudiest Producers."

4. Robbin Coons, "He-Man Market One That Never Wanes in Films: Richard Arlen No. 1 Example of Two-Fisted Stars' Invincibility," *Port Arthur* (TX) *News*, September 19, 1943.

5. Frederick Othman, "A's or Else, Arlen Tells Producers," unsourced clipping, ca. 1944, scrapbook.

6. Philip K. Scheuer, "Westerns Nobody But Public Likes," *Los Angeles Times*, July 25, 1965.

7. Dick Kidson, "Farmers Market Today," *Los Angeles Times*, March 19, 1960.

8. Karen Burroughs Hansberry, *Femme Noir:*

Bad Girls of Film (Jefferson, NC: McFarland, 1998), p. 132.

9. Carol Thomas Pantages, personal interview.

10. Robert Lowery Hanks, personal interview. All other quotes from Hanks in this section are from this interview.

11. "Robert Lowery, Actor, Dies at 57," *Wisconsin State Journal*, September 27, 1971.

12. "Chester Morris' Career Interesting," *Valley Morning Star* (Harlingen, TX), May 7, 1943.

13. Margaret Harford, "Chester Morris: An Actor Who Plays Hard at Work," *Los Angeles Times*, November 4, 1966.

14. Dan Van Neste, "An Interview with Jean Parker," *Films of the Golden Age*, Summer 1997.

15. Bob Hall, "Buy-Buy-Blues," *Hollywood*, July 1942.

16. Van Neste, "An Interview."

17. Edwin Schallert, "Jean Parker, Home at Last, Seeks 'Born Yesterday' Role for Screen," *Los Angeles Times*, January 16, 1949.

18. "Actress Jean Parker Divorces Third Mate," *Los Angeles Times*, December 30, 1949.

19. Karen Burroughs Hansberry, *Femme Noir: Bad Girls of Film* (Jefferson, NC: McFarland, 1998), p. 519.

20. Burt A. Folkart, "John Payne, 77, Star of Movie Musicals, Remembered for 'Miracle on 34th Street,'" *Los Angeles Times*, December 7, 1989.

21. Memoir, p. 360.

22. Tom Goldrup and Jim Goldrup, *The Encyclopedia of Feature Players of Hollywood*, v. 3 (Duncan, OK: BearManor Media, 2012), p. 34.

Appendix II:
Pine-Thomas Crew

1. Frederick C. Othman, "Horse Opera Minus Gunplay, Startles Republic Studios," *Xenia* (OH) *Gazette*, November 13, 1939.

2. Bill Berke, personal interview.

3. Memoir, p. 119.

4. *Ibid.*

5. Memoir, p. 143.

6. "Disaster Maker at Burbank Perfects Miniature Scenes," *Los Angeles Times*, September 18, 1938.

7. "Nancy Kelly Obtains Final Divorce Decree," *Los Angeles Times*, February 2, 1951.

8. Nick McLean, Sr., personal interview.

9. Alene Mosby, "Publicity Man's Career Reads Like Alger Story," *El Paso* (TX) *Times*, July 29, 1951.

10. Carol Thomas Pantages, personal interview. All other quotes in this section from Carol Thomas Pantages are from this interview.

11. Dennis McLellan, "Producer Was Paramount Institution," *Los Angeles Times*, October 1, 2013.

12. Memoir, p. 233.

13. Norman Clark, "Frank McDonald, Picture Director, Is Ex-Baltimorean," unsourced clipping, ca. 1937. Frank McDonald Papers, American Heritage Center, Laramie, Wyoming.

14. Joe Pearson, "Frank McDonald," undated clipping, *Hollywood Motion Picture Review*, ca. 1938. McDonald Papers.

15. Read Kendall, "Around and About in Hollywood," *Los Angeles Times*, October 24, 1935.

16. "Actress, Injured, Launches Career as Artist from Hobby," *Los Angeles Times*, July 22, 1940.

17. Memoir, p. 219.

18. Doc Merman memorandum, "My dear dear Crew," October 27, 1947. McDonald Papers.

19. Memoir, p. 96.

20. "Technical Progress in 1941," *American Cinematographer*, January 1942.

BIBLIOGRAPHY

Books

Balaban, David. *The Chicago Movie Palaces of Bala-ban and Katz.* Charleston, SC: Arcadia, 2006.

Brunell, Christopher. *Zuzu's Wonderful Life in the Movies: The Story of Karolyn Grimes.* Seattle, WA: Artful Dragon, 2000.

Bruskin, David N. *The White Brothers: Jack, Jules and Sam White.* Metuchen, NJ: Scarecrow, 1990.

Ciment, Michel, and Joseph Losey. *Conversations with Losey.* London: Methuen, 1985.

Davis, Ronald L. *Words into Images: Screenwriters on the Studio System.* Jackson: University Press of Mississippi, 2007.

Dixon, Wheeler W. *The "B" Directors: A Biographical Directory.* Metuchen, NJ: Scarecrow, 1985.

Foster, David Kyle. *Love Hunger: A Harrowing Journey from Sexual Addiction to True Fulfillment.* Minneapolis, MN: Chosen, 2014.

Freese, Gene. *Classic Movie Fight Scenes: 75 Years of Bare Knuckle Brawls, 1914–1989.* Jefferson, NC: McFarland, 2017.

Fultz, Jay. *In Search of Donna Reed.* Iowa City: University of Iowa Press, 1998.

Galbraith, Stuart, IV. *The Toho Studios Story: A History and Complete Filmography.* Lanham, MD: Scarecrow, 2008.

Gargan, William. *Why Me? An Autobiography.* New York: Doubleday, 1969.

Gill, Tom. *Gentleman of the Jungle.* New York: Dell, 1940.

Goldrup, Tom, and Jim Goldrup. *The Encyclopedia of Feature Players of Hollywood,* vol. 3. Duncan, OK: BearManor Media, 2012.

Hannsberry, Karen Burroughs. *Bad Boys: The Actors of Film Noir.* Jefferson, NC: McFarland, 2008.

_____. *Femme Noir: Bad Girls of Film.* Jefferson, NC: McFarland, 2010.

Herzberg, Bob. *Shooting Scripts: From Pulp Westerns to Film.* Jefferson, NC: McFarland, 2005.

Heston, Charlton. *In the Arena: An Autobiography.* New York: Simon & Schuster, 1995.

Homes, Geoffrey. *No Hands on the Clock.* New York: Bantam, 1946.

Maltin, Leonard, ed. *Leonard Maltin's Movie Encyclopedia.* New York: Plume, 1995.

McCabe, John. *Cagney.* New York: Knopf, 1997.

Miller, Don. *B Movies.* New York: Ballantine, 1988.

Murphy, Bruce F. *The Encyclopedia of Murder and Mystery.* New York: Palgrave, 2001.

Napier, Alan. *Not Just Batman's Butler: The Autobiography of Alan Napier.* Jefferson, NC: McFarland, 2015.

Parish, James Robert, and William T. Leonard. *Hollywood Players: The Thirties.* New Rochelle, NY: Arlington House, 1976.

Reagan, Ronald, and Richard G. Hubler. *Where's the Rest of Me?* New York: Dell, 1981.

Slaughter, Frank G. *Sangaree.* New York: Popular Library, 1964.

Walker, Brent E. *Mack Sennett's Fun Factory: A History and Filmography of His Studio and His Keystone and Mack Sennett Comedies, with Biographies of Players and Personnel.* Jefferson, NC: McFarland, 2010.

White, Lionel. *The Big Caper.* New York: Fawcett Crest, 1955.

Articles

Briggs, Colin. "Barbara Britton: 'All Things Bright and Beautiful.'" *Classic Images,* July 2004.

Dibbern, Doug. "The Violent Poetry of the Times: The Politics of History in Daniel Mainwaring and Joseph Losey's The Lawless." In Frank Krutnick et al., eds., *"Un-American" Hollywood: Politics and Film in the Blacklist Era.* New Brunswick, NJ: Rutgers University Press, 2007.

English, Richard. "Gaudiest Producers in Hollywood." *Saturday Evening Post,* January 3, 1953.

Ingram, Frances. "John Payne: Living Out the Dream." *Classic Images* #233, November 1994.

Phaneuf, Paul. "Rhonda Fleming: That Natural Gift." *Films of the Golden Age* #52, Spring 2008.

Reddy, John. "Hollywood's Dollar Bills," *Esquire,* June 1945.

Taves, Brian. "The B Film: Hollywood's Other Half."

In Tino Balio, *Grand Design: Hollywood as a Modern Business Enterprise*. Berkeley: University of California Press, 1995.

Van Neste, Dan. "Jean Parker: Cinderella Girl." *Films of the Golden Age* #9, Summer 1997.

Wilson, Elizabeth. "They Wish Upon a Star—and Win!" *Liberty*, June 1945.

Interviews

Berke, Bill. Telephone and email, September 12, 2018.

Croly, Shonda Holm. Telephone and email, August 21–23, 2018.

Dahl, Arlene. Telephone. September 13, 2018.

Hanks, Robert Lowery. Telephone and email, January 6, 2018.

Jeffries, William. Email, April 6, 2018.

Marks, Dennie. Telephone and email, October–November 2018.

McLean, Nick, Sr. Email, April 25, 2018.

Pantages, Carol Thomas. Telephone and email. April–December 2018.

Pine, Angel. Telephone and email, August–November 2018.

Archival Materials

McDonald, Frank. Papers, 1935–1976. American Heritage Center, University of Wyoming, Laramie, Wyoming.

Shane, Maxwell. Papers, 1936–1967. American Heritage Center, University of Wyoming, Laramie, Wyoming.

Thomas, William C., [as told to] Thelma Kling. "Hollywood's Fabulous Dollar Bills; or, How to Make Money Making Movies." Typescript. Author's collection.

Vital Records

Kagen, Ida, petition for citizenship, District Court of the U.S. at Los Angeles, California, August 3, 1932. Digital image available at www.ancestry.com.

"List or Manifest of Alien Passengers for the U.S. Immigration Officer at Port of Arrival," *S.S. Island*, July 23, 1904. Digital image available at www.ancestry.com.

Pinchasic, Esther, naturalization record, #48604, April 27, 1928. Digital image available at www.ancestry.com.

Pine, William H., and Anna Baum, certificate and record of marriage, #15351, June 14, 1916. Department of Health, City of New York.

Pine, William Howard, draft registration card, Los Angeles, California, April 25, 1942. Digital image available at www.ancestry.com.

United States Federal Census (1910, 1920, 1930, 1940). Digital images available at www.ancestry.com.

Websites

AFI Catalog of Feature Films, https://catalog.afi.com

Media History Digital Library, www.mediahistoryproject.org

YouTube, www.youtube.com

INDEX

Numbers in **bold italics** indicate pages with illustrations